YOTSUBA&!

3

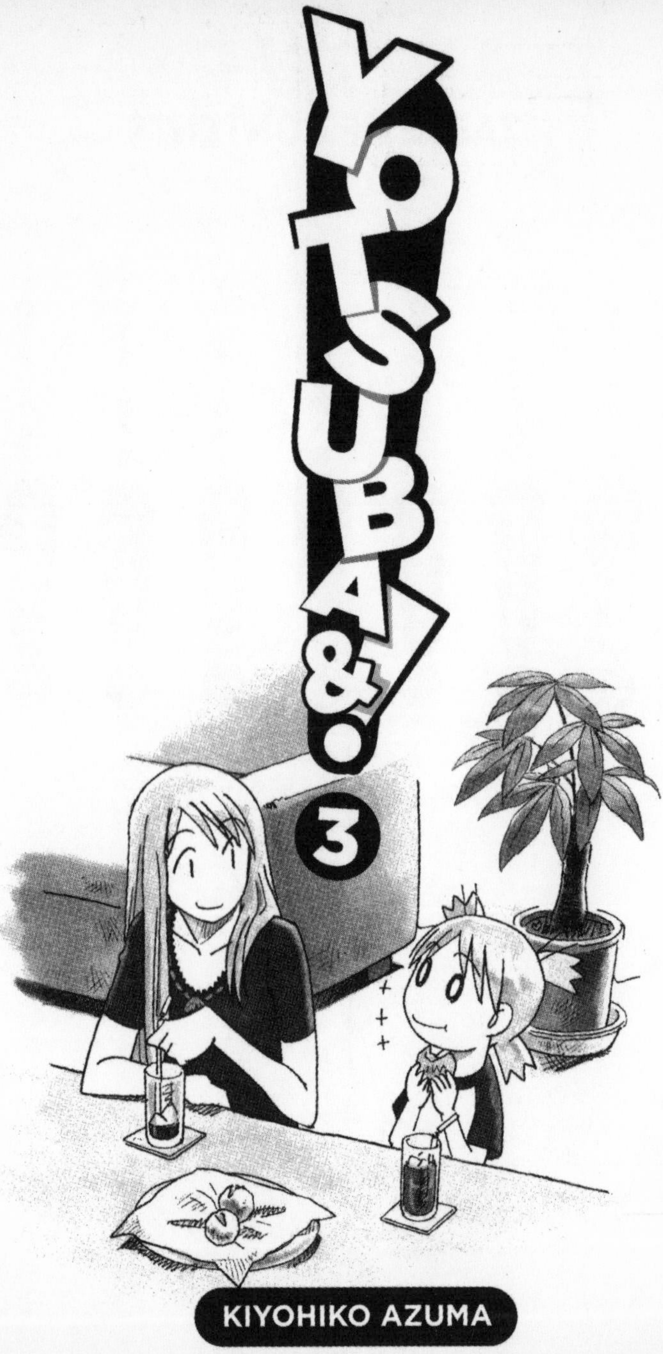

KIYOHIKO AZUMA

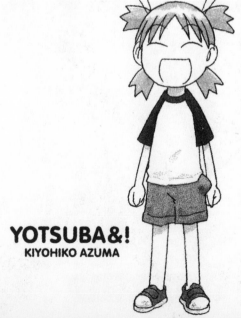

TABLE OF CONTENTS

YOTSUBA&!
KIYOHIKO AZUMA

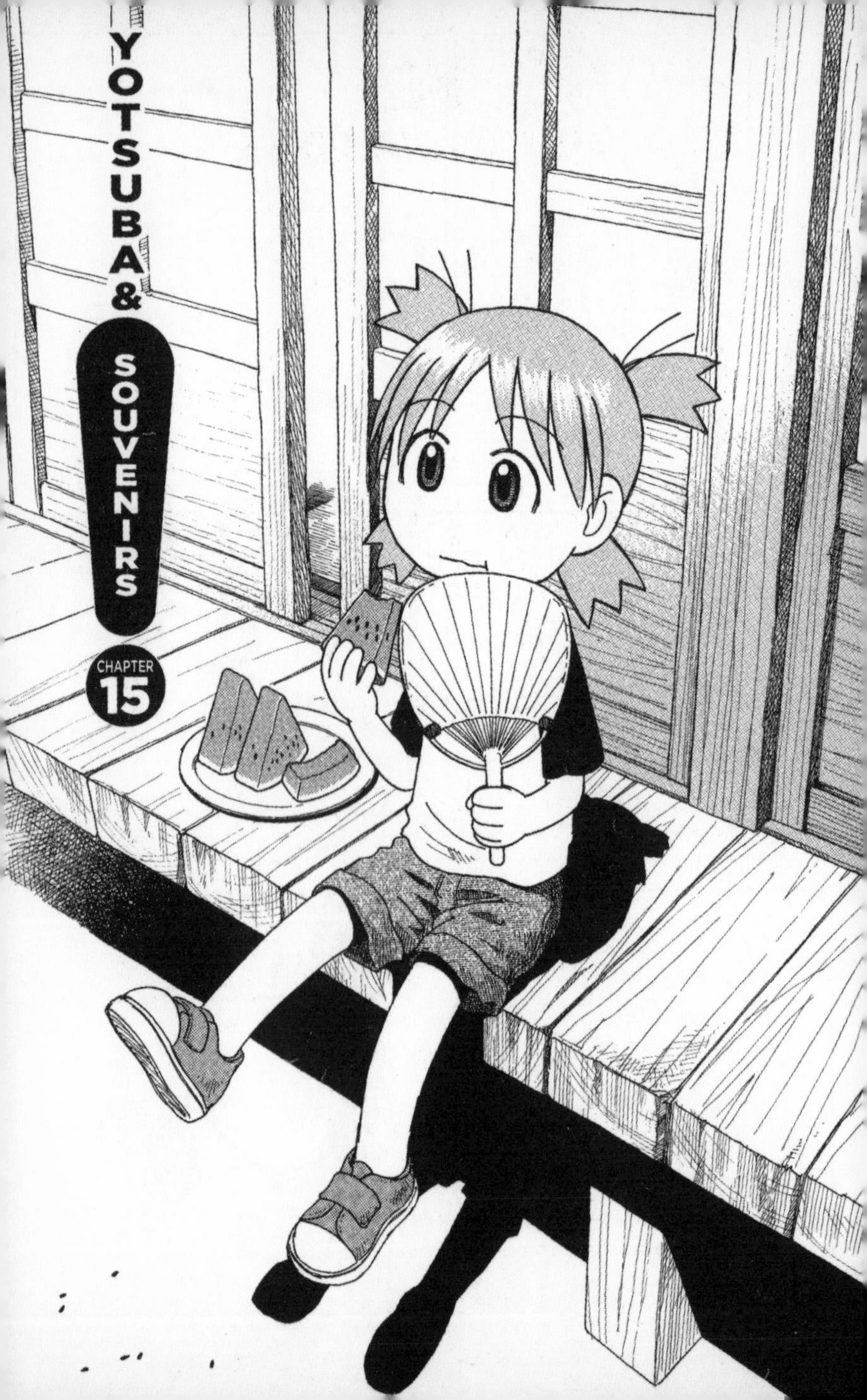
YOTSUBA&
SOUVENIRS
CHAPTER 15

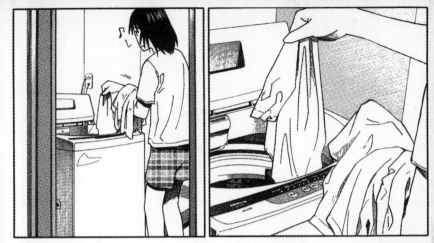

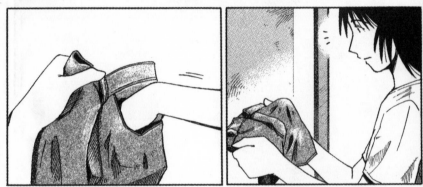

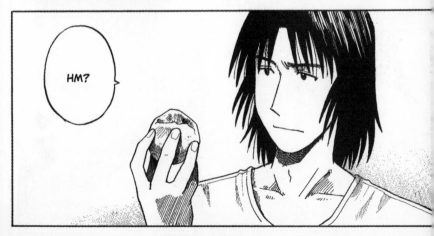

HM?

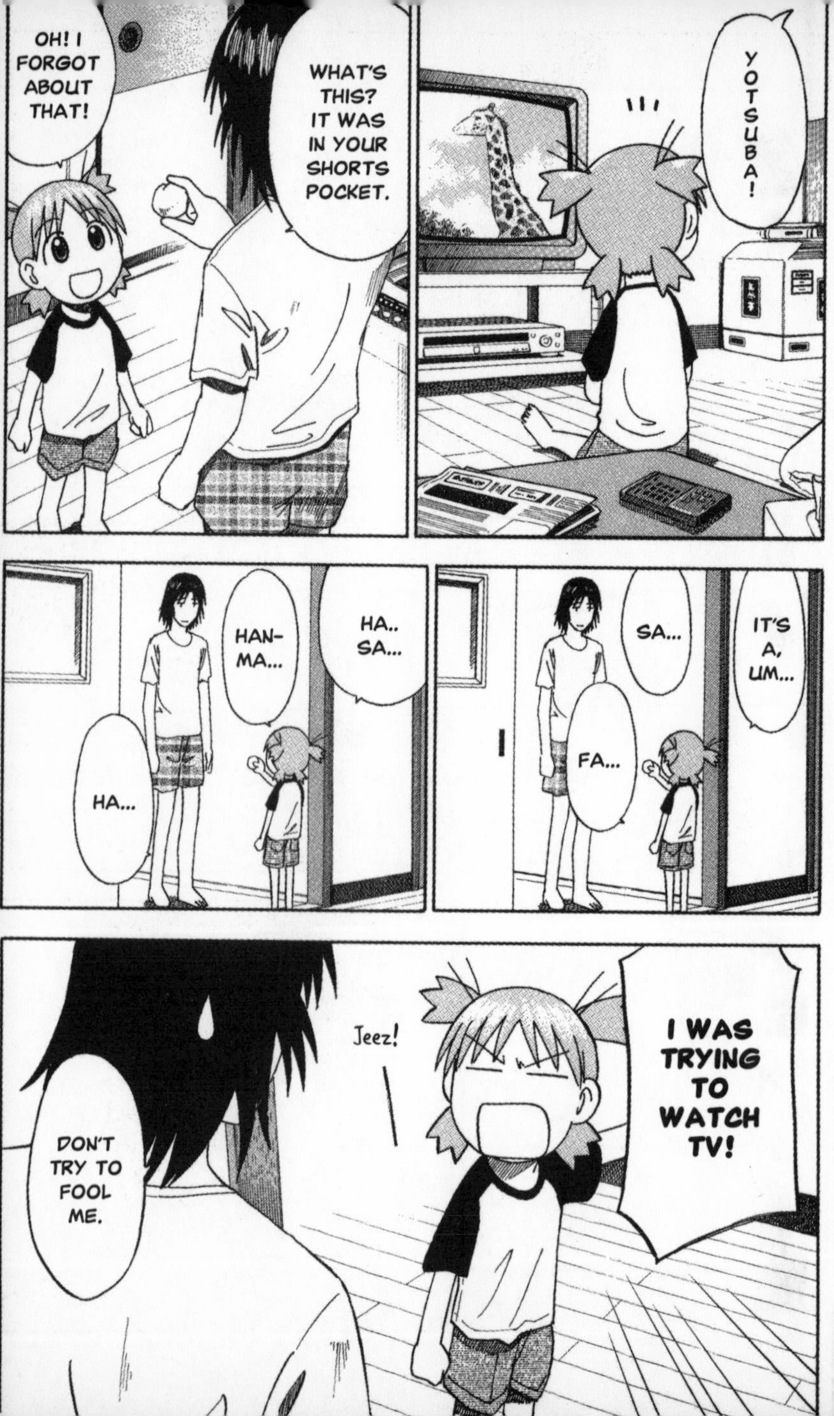
YOTSUBA!
WHAT'S THIS? IT WAS IN YOUR SHORTS POCKET.
OH! I FORGOT ABOUT THAT!
IT'S A, UM...
SA...
FA...
HA.. SA...
HAN-MA...
HA...
I WAS TRYING TO WATCH TV!
Jeez!
DON'T TRY TO FOOL ME.

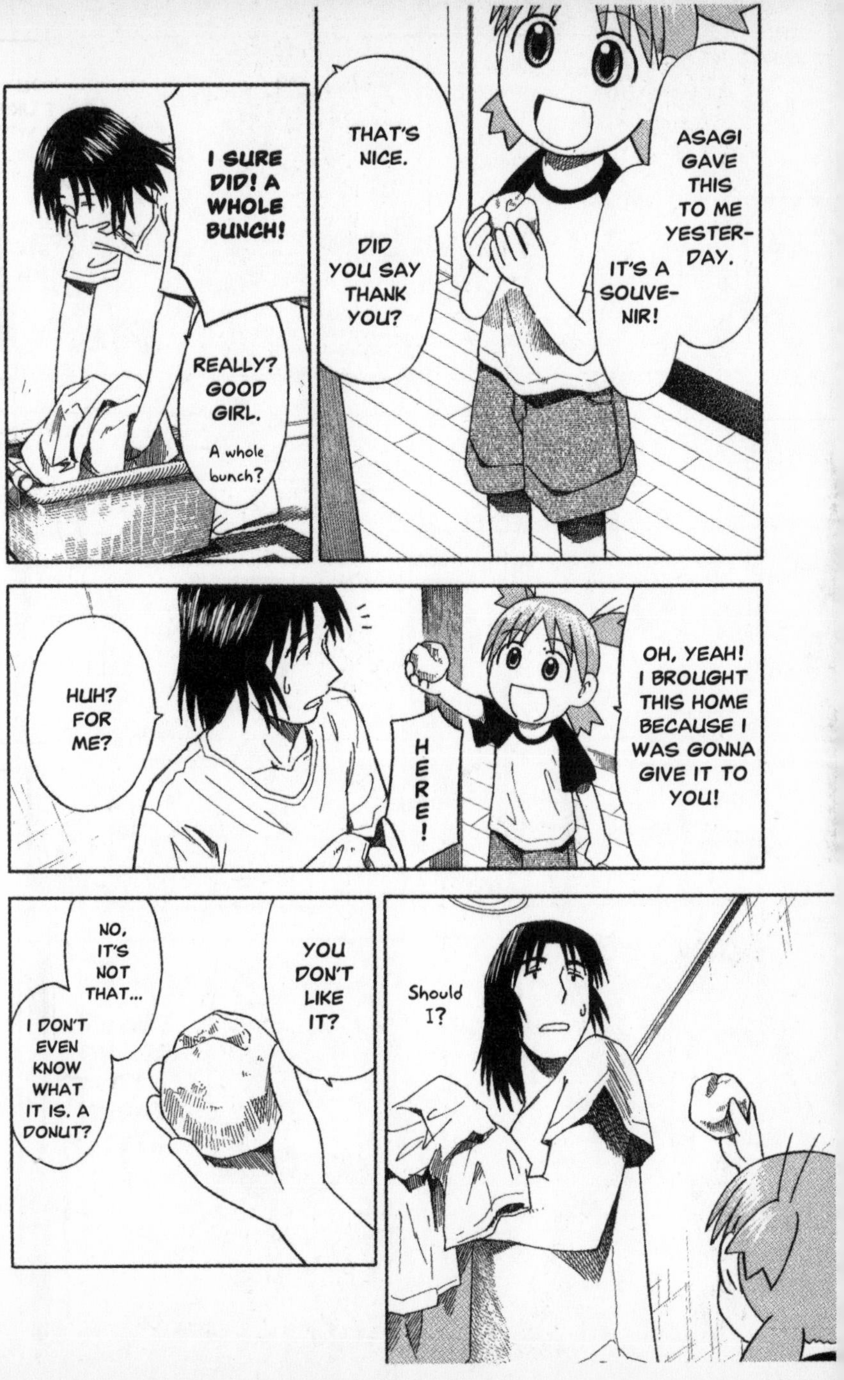

ASAGI GAVE THIS TO ME YESTERDAY.
IT'S A SOUVENIR!
THAT'S NICE.
DID YOU SAY THANK YOU?
I SURE DID! A WHOLE BUNCH!
REALLY? GOOD GIRL.
A whole bunch?
OH, YEAH! I BROUGHT THIS HOME BECAUSE I WAS GONNA GIVE IT TO YOU!
HERE!
HUH? FOR ME?
Should I?
YOU DON'T LIKE IT?
NO, IT'S NOT THAT...
I DON'T EVEN KNOW WHAT IT IS. A DONUT?

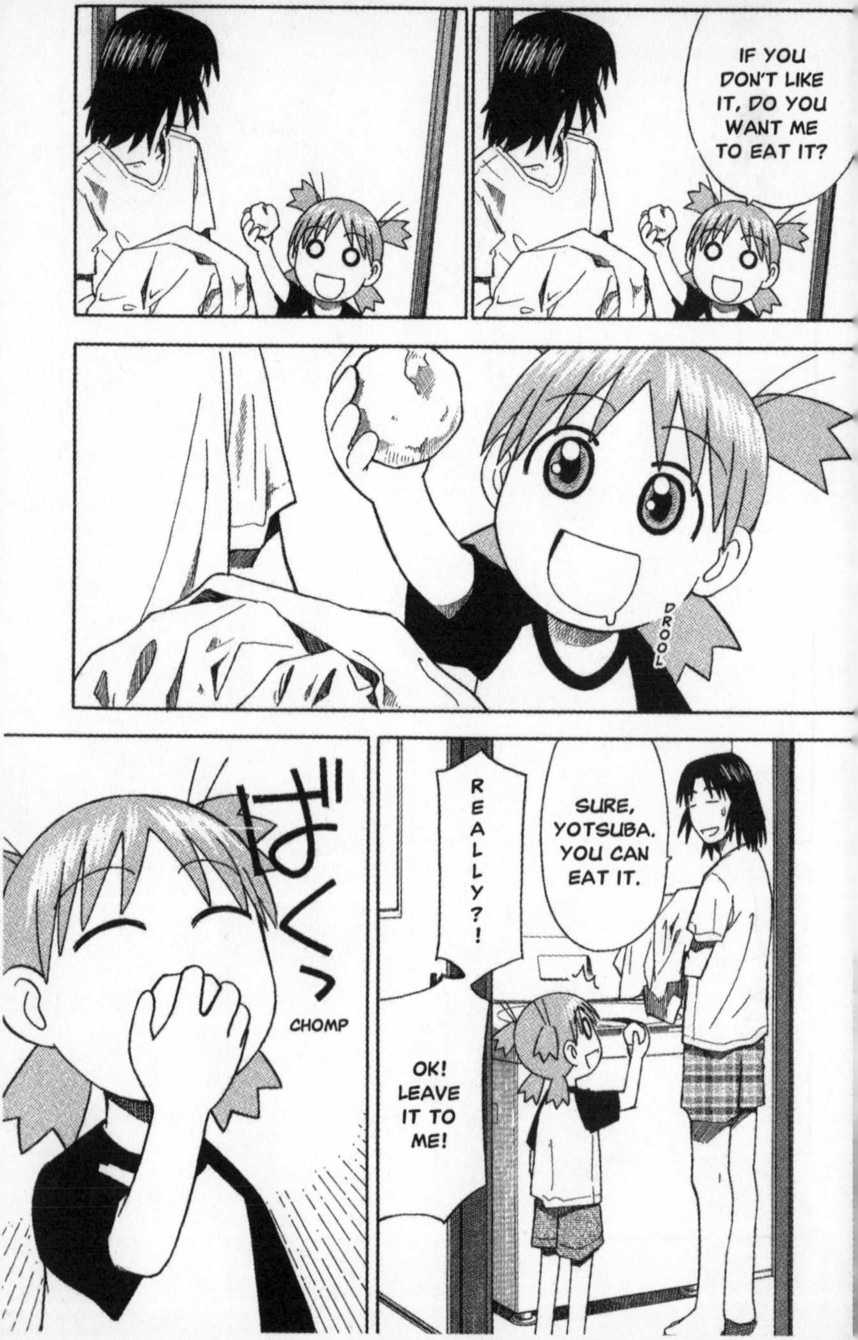
IF YOU DON'T LIKE IT, DO YOU WANT ME TO EAT IT?
DROOL
SURE, YOTSUBA. YOU CAN EAT IT.
REALLY?!
OK! LEAVE IT TO ME!
ぱくっ
CHOMP

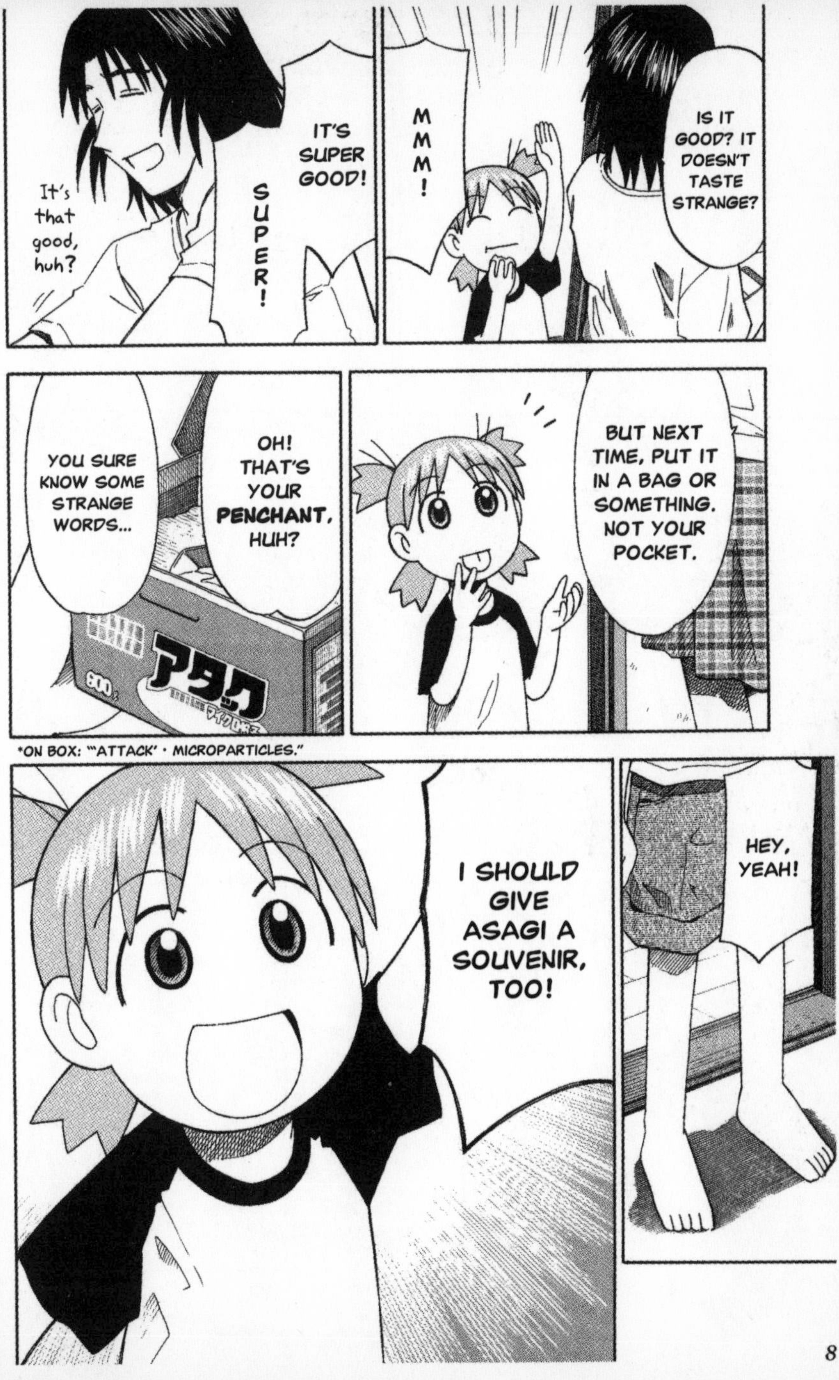
IS IT GOOD? IT DOESN'T TASTE STRANGE?
MMM!
IT'S SUPER GOOD!
SUPER!
It's that good, huh?
BUT NEXT TIME, PUT IT IN A BAG OR SOMETHING. NOT YOUR POCKET.
OH! THAT'S YOUR PENCHANT, HUH?
YOU SURE KNOW SOME STRANGE WORDS...
アタック
HEY, YEAH!
I SHOULD GIVE ASAGI A SOUVENIR, TOO!

*ON BOX: "'ATTACK' · MICROPARTICLES."

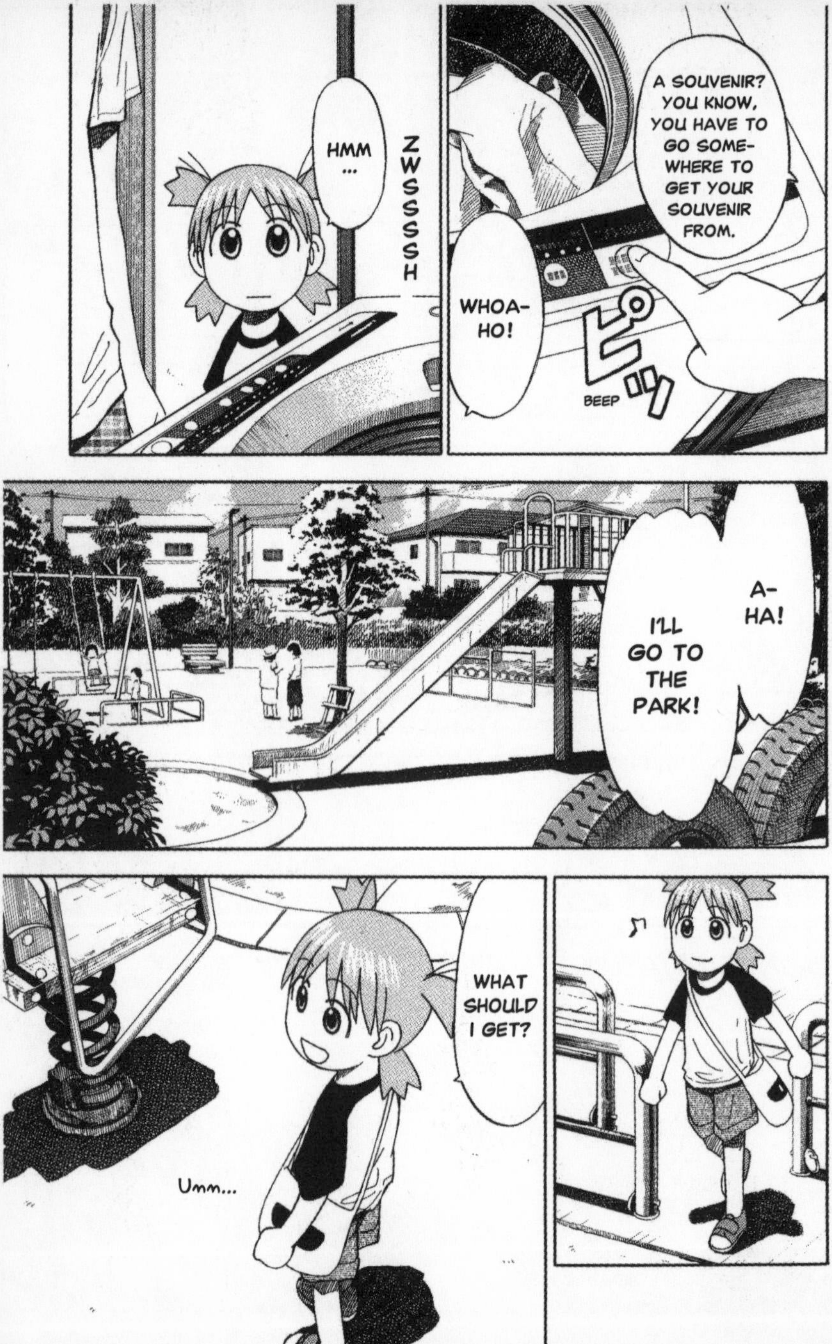
A SOUVENIR? YOU KNOW, YOU HAVE TO GO SOME-WHERE TO GET YOUR SOUVENIR FROM.
WHOA-HO!
BEEP
ZWSSSSH
HMM ...
A-HA!
I'LL GO TO THE PARK!
WHAT SHOULD I GET?
Umm...

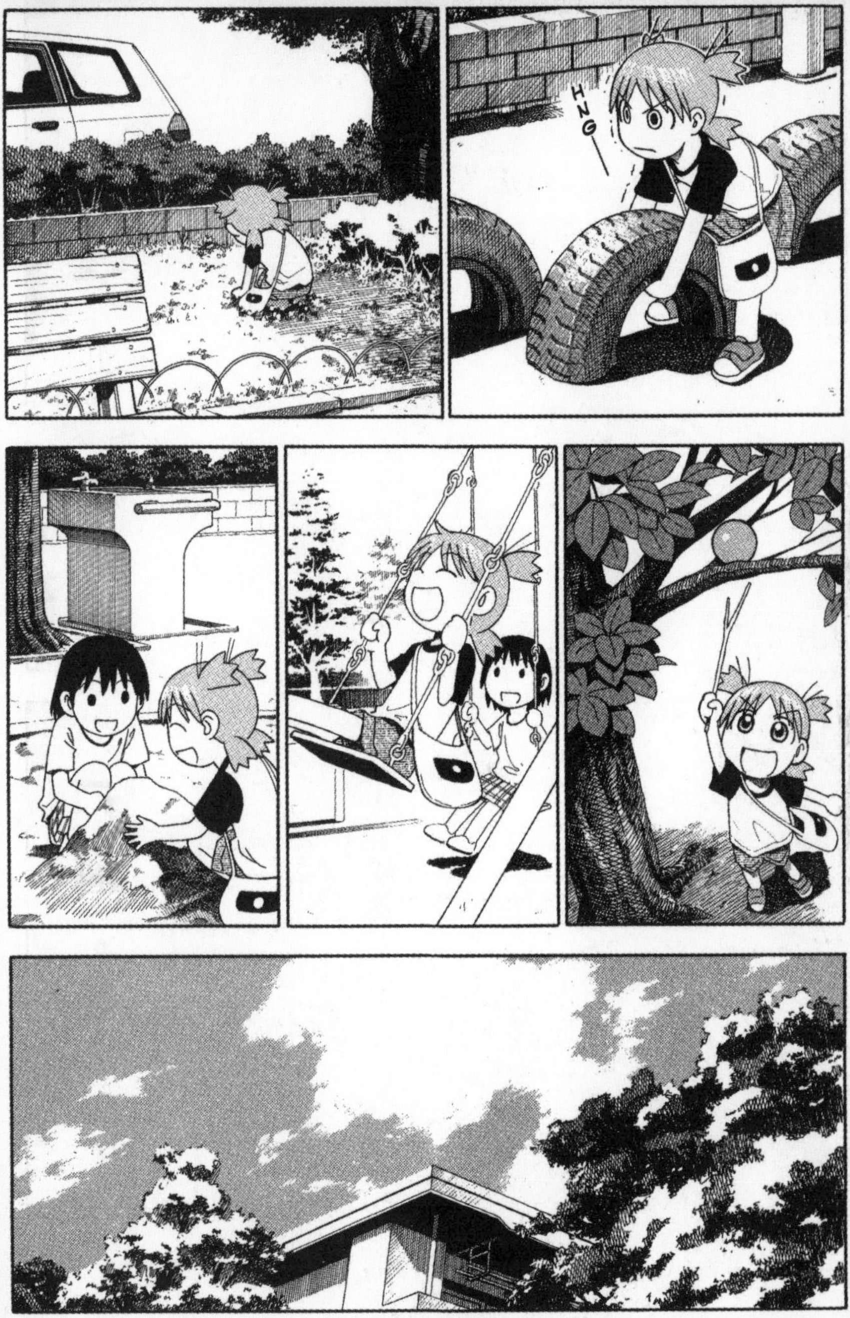
HNG—

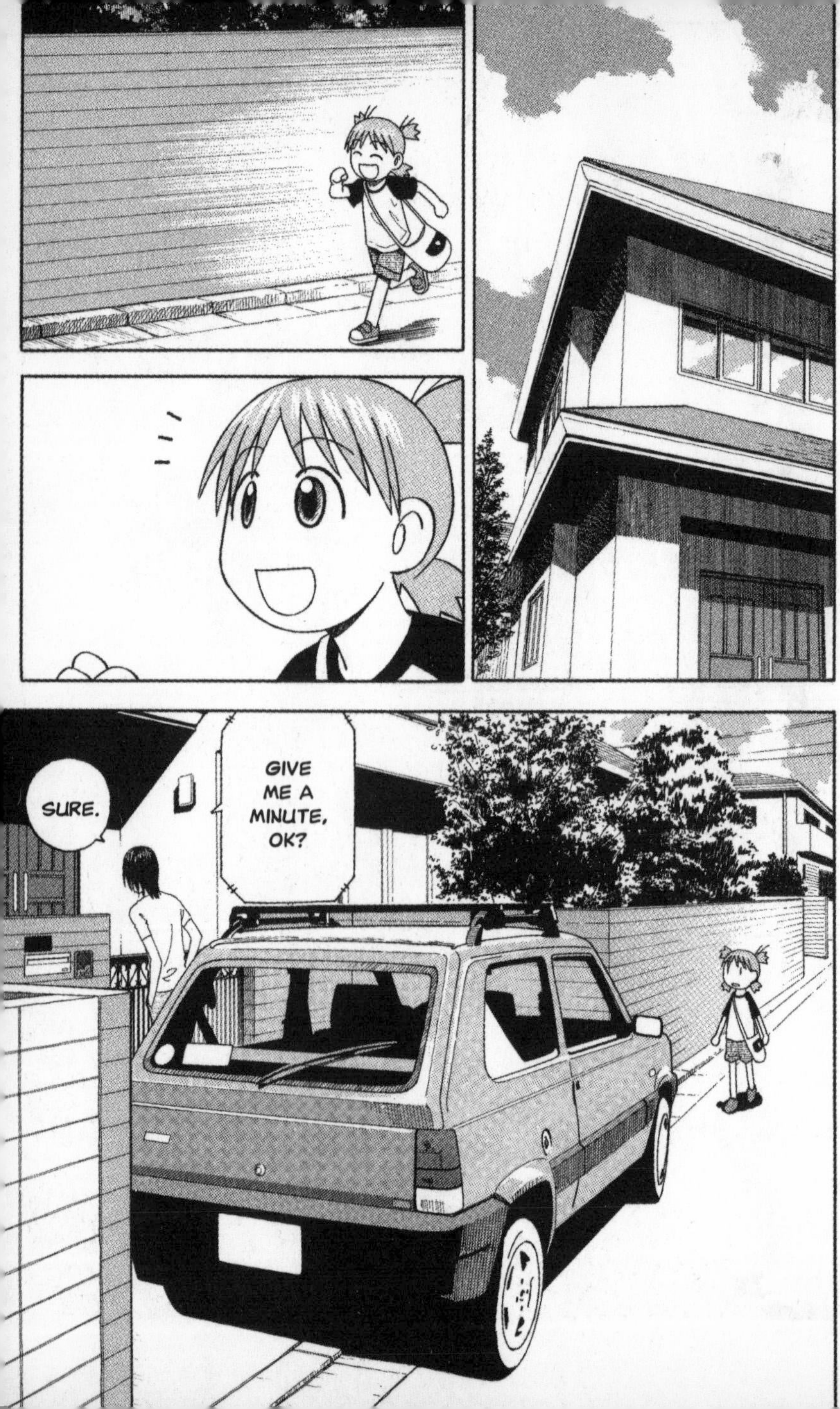
GIVE ME A MINUTE, OK?
SURE.

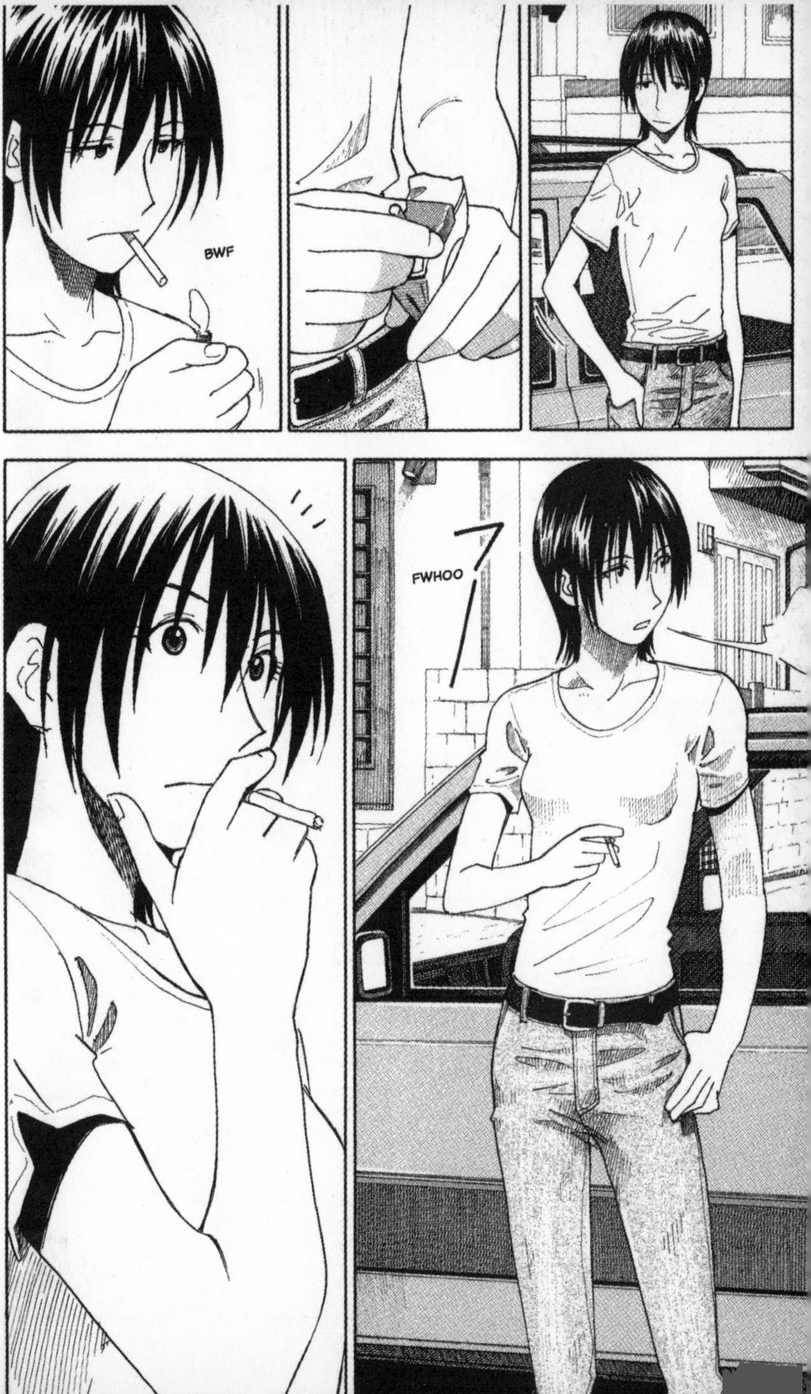
BWF
FWHOO

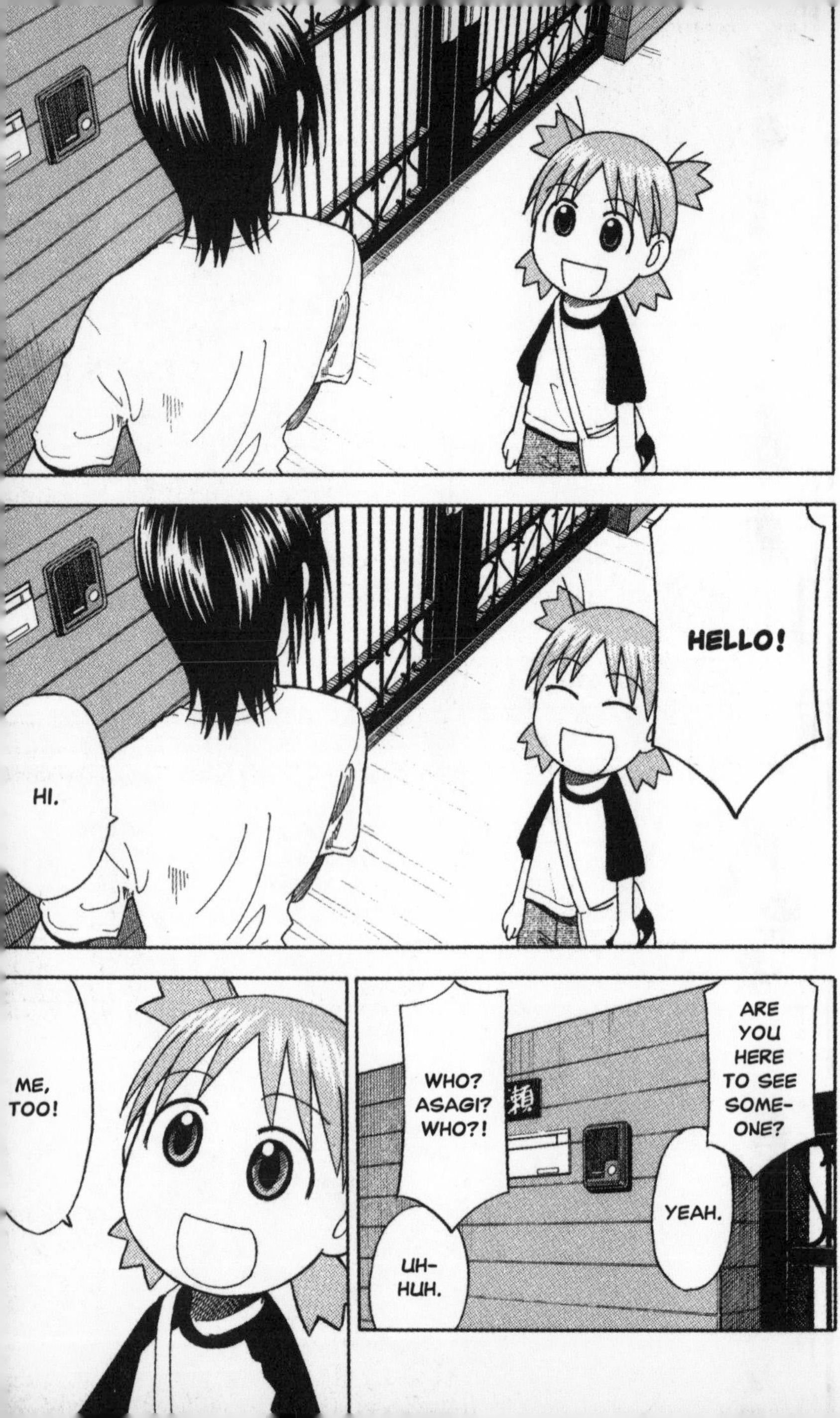
HELLO!
HI.
ARE YOU HERE TO SEE SOME-ONE?
YEAH.
WHO? ASAGI? WHO?!
瀬
UH-HUH.
ME, TOO!

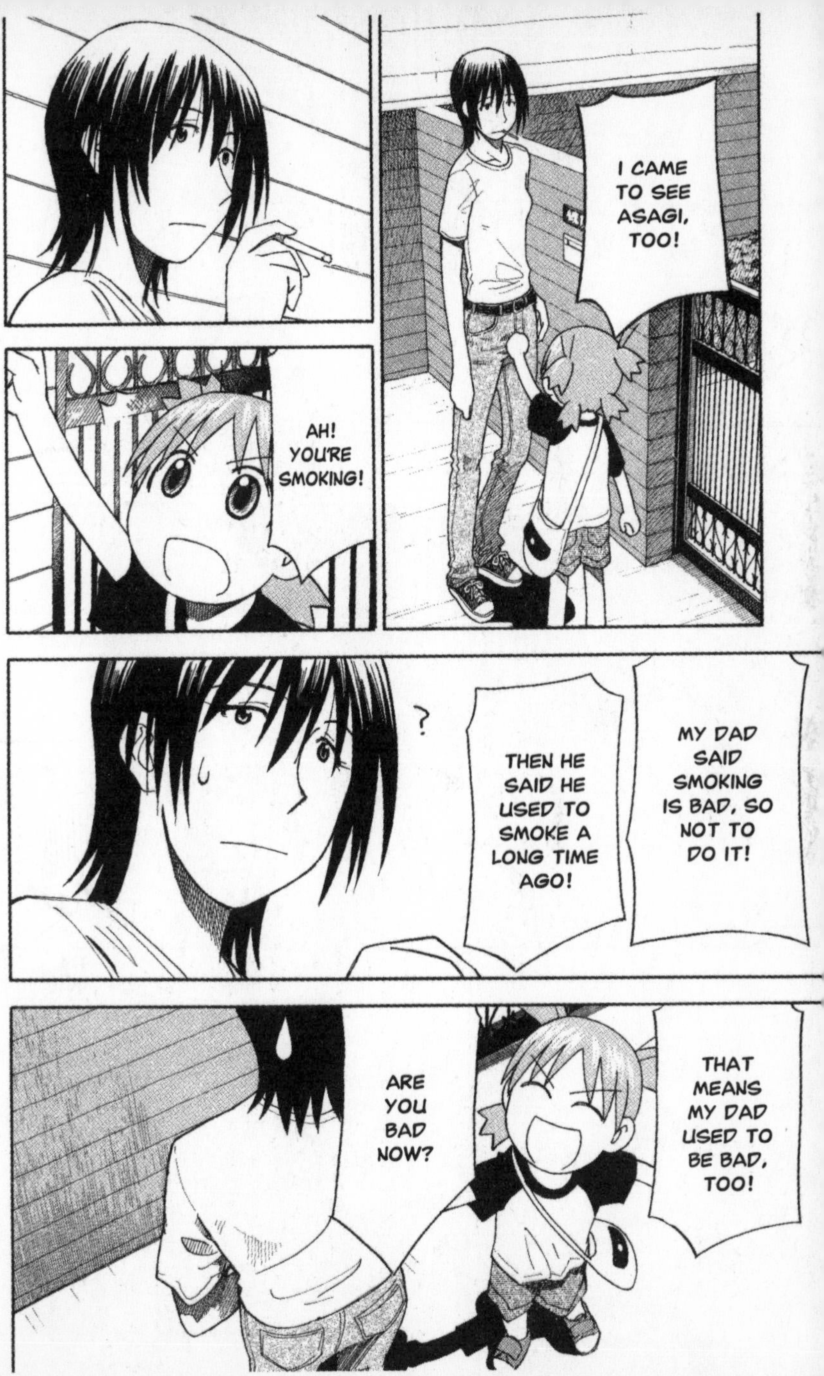
I CAME TO SEE ASAGI, TOO!
AH! YOU'RE SMOKING!
MY DAD SAID SMOKING IS BAD, SO NOT TO DO IT!
THEN HE SAID HE USED TO SMOKE A LONG TIME AGO!
?
THAT MEANS MY DAD USED TO BE BAD, TOO!
ARE YOU BAD NOW?

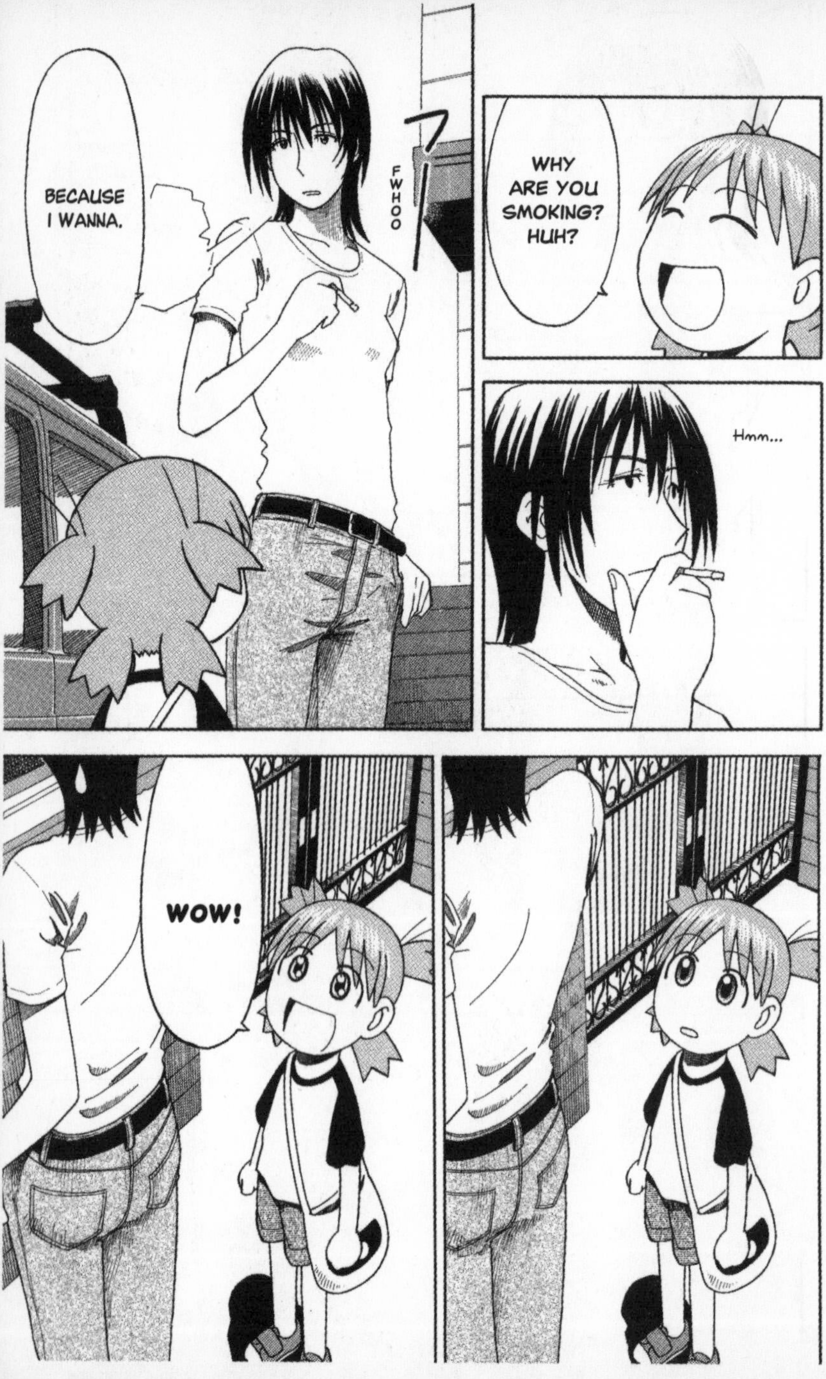
WHY ARE YOU SMOKING? HUH?
Hmm...
FWHOO
BECAUSE I WANNA.
WOW!

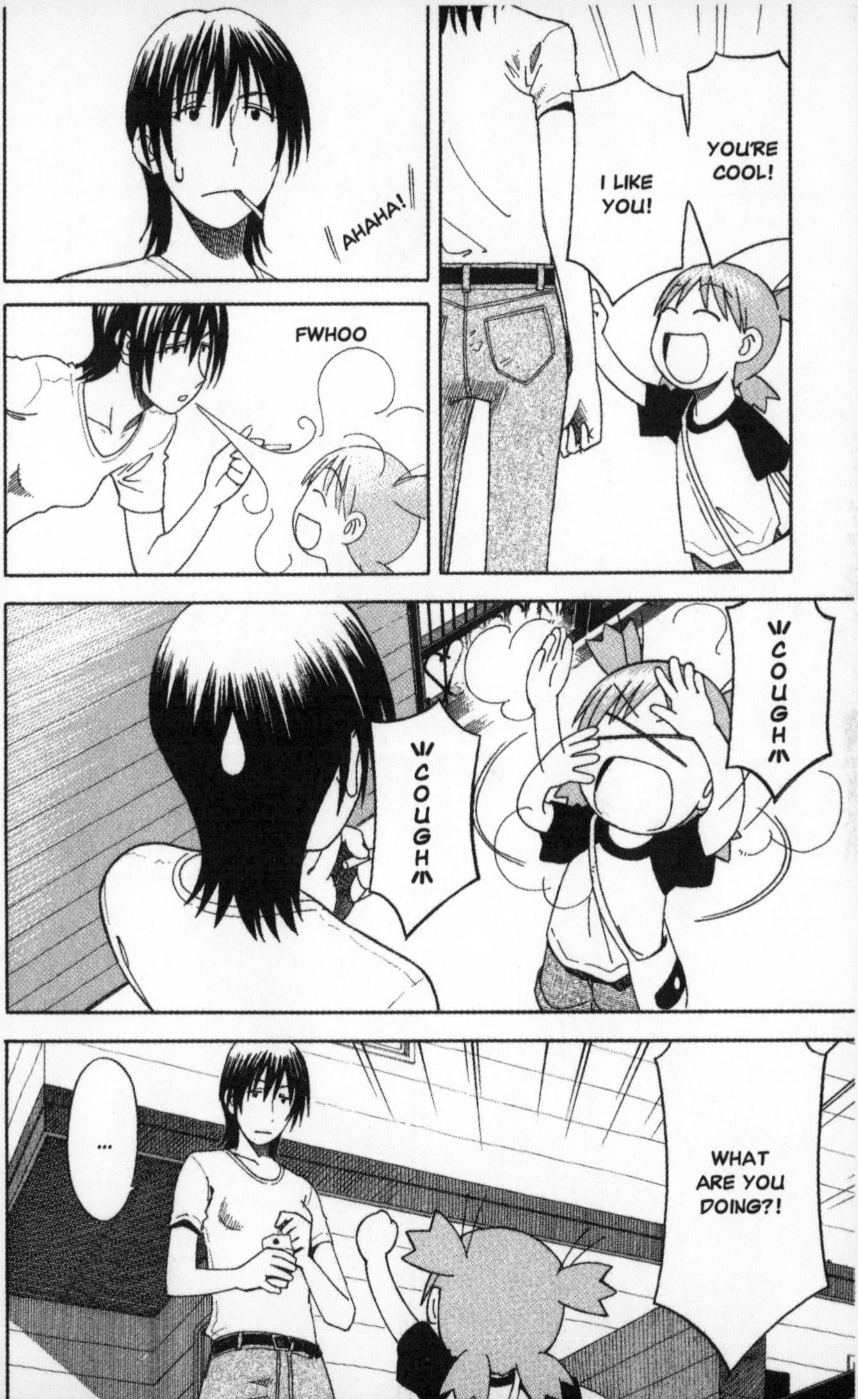
YOU'RE COOL!
I LIKE YOU!
AHAHA!
FWHOO
COUGH
COUGH
WHAT ARE YOU DOING?!
...

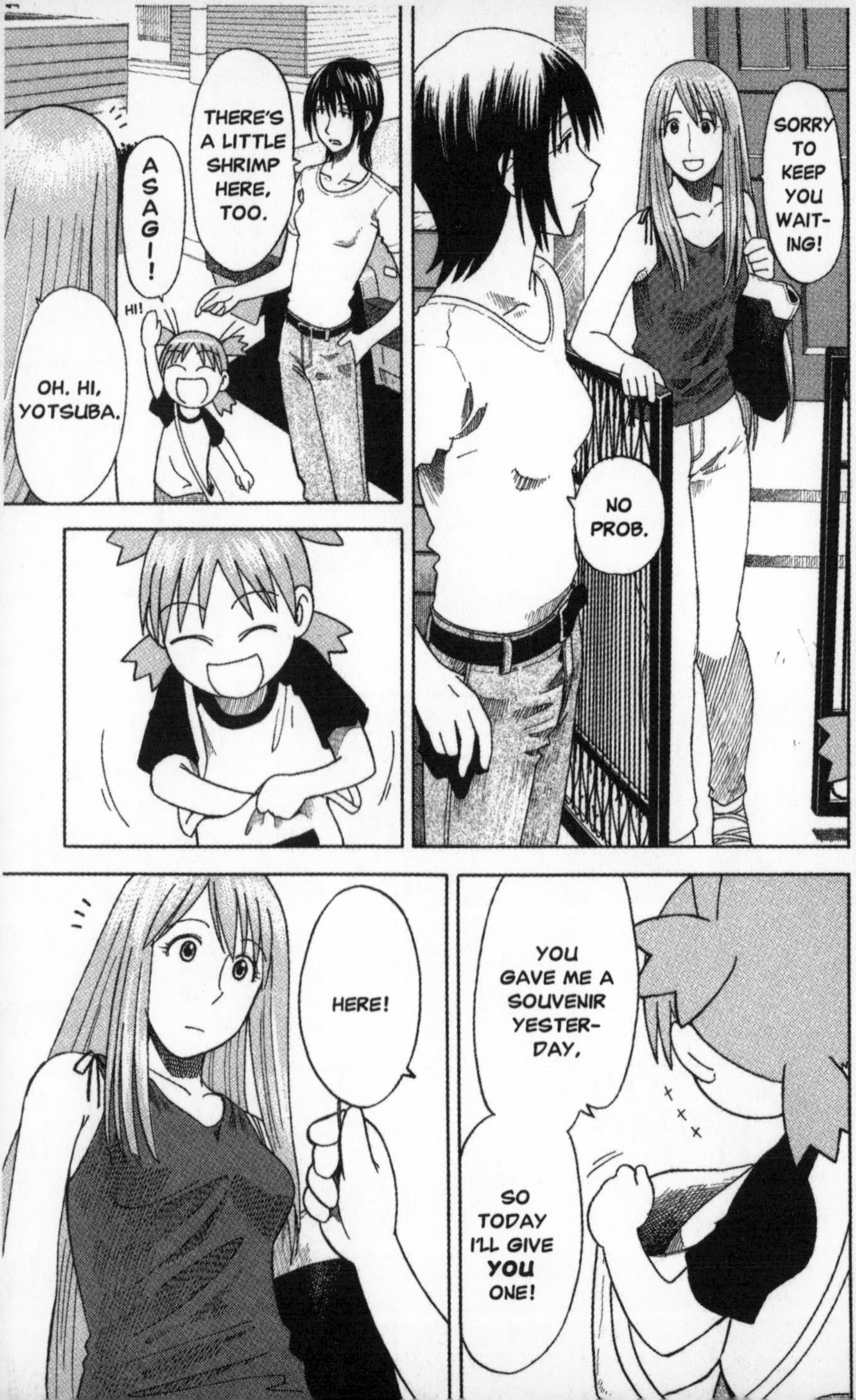
SORRY TO KEEP YOU WAITING!
NO PROB.
THERE'S A LITTLE SHRIMP HERE, TOO.
ASAGI!!
HI!
OH. HI, YOTSUBA.
YOU GAVE ME A SOUVENIR YESTERDAY,
SO TODAY I'LL GIVE **YOU** ONE!
HERE!

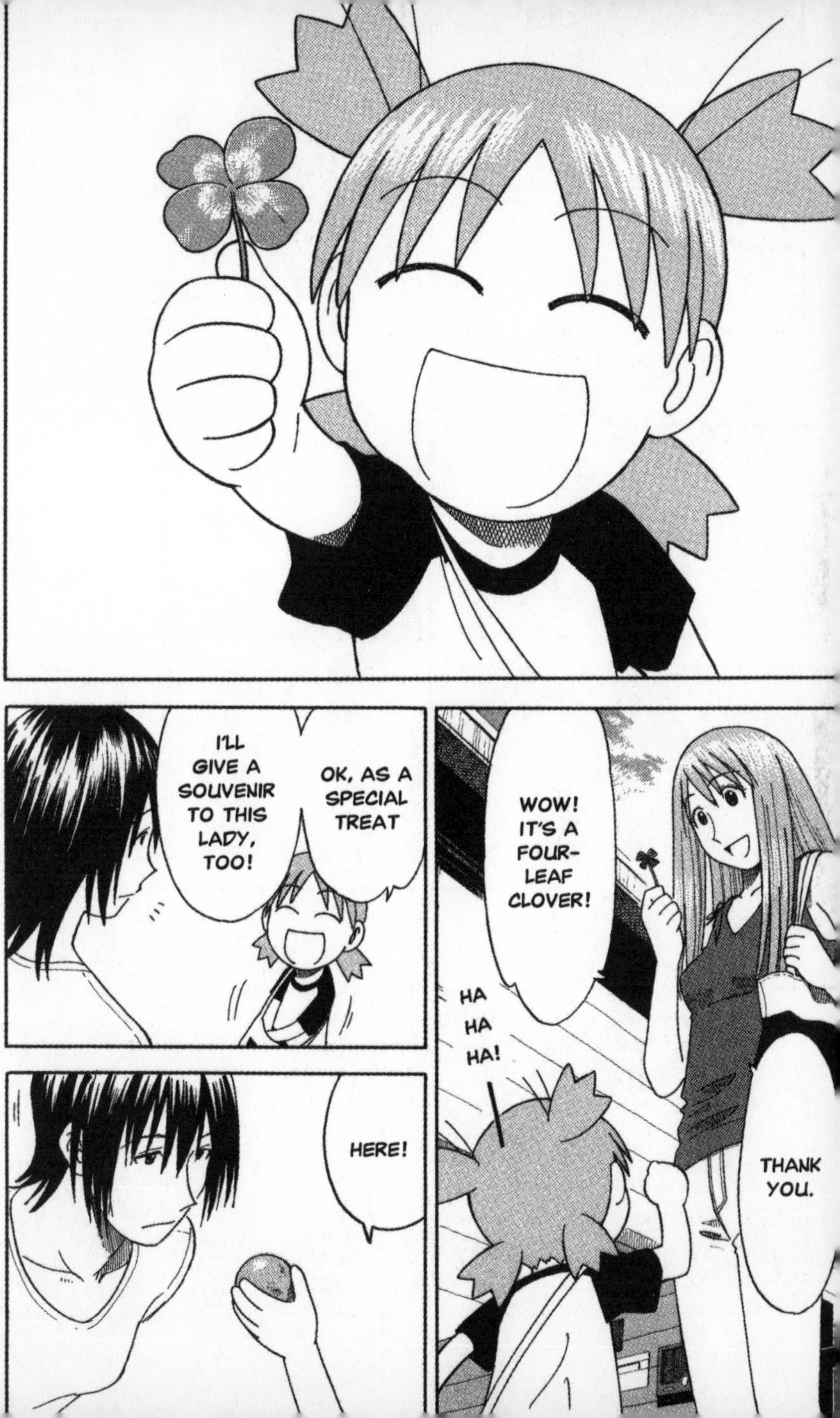
WOW! IT'S A FOUR-LEAF CLOVER!
HA HA HA!
THANK YOU.
OK, AS A SPECIAL TREAT
I'LL GIVE A SOUVENIR TO THIS LADY, TOO!
HERE!

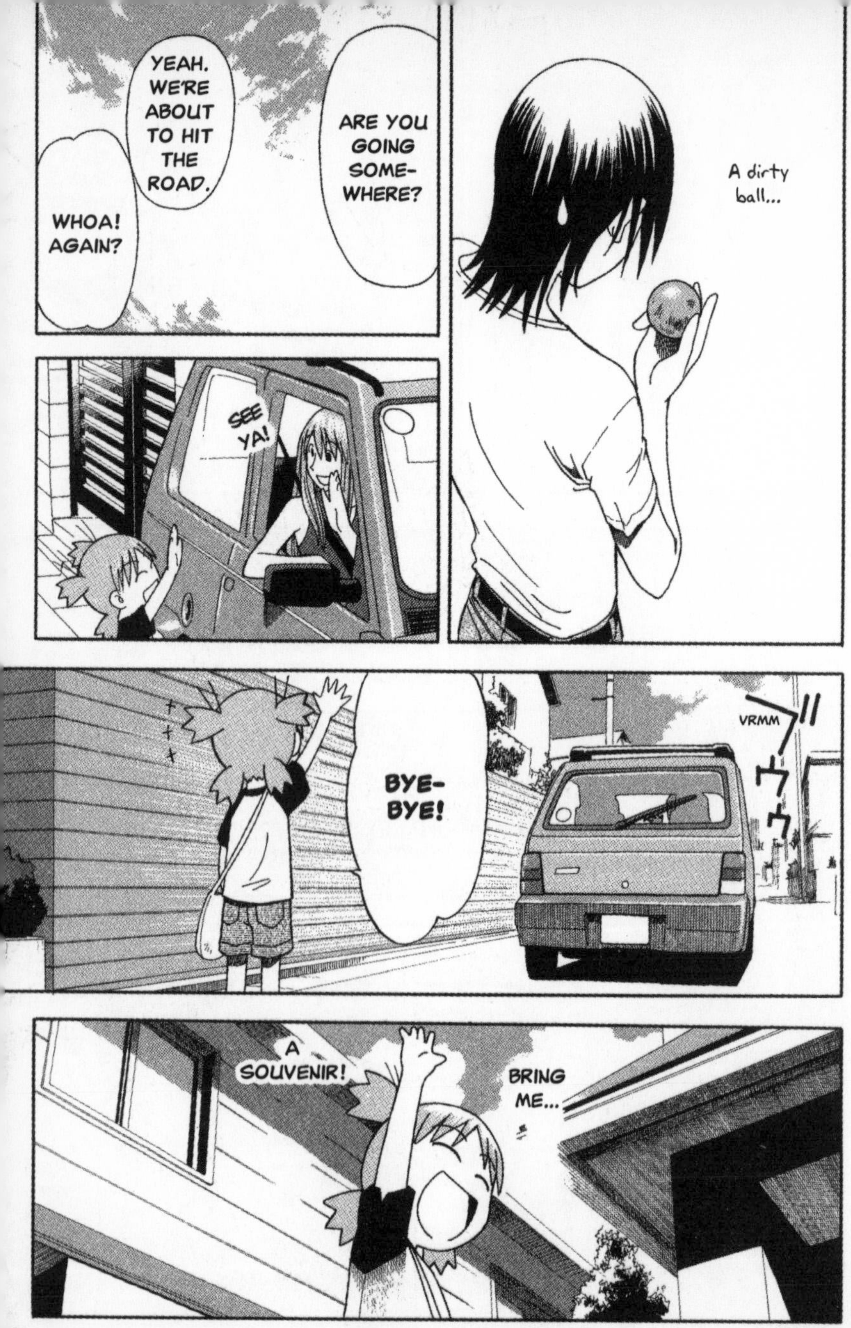
A dirty ball...
ARE YOU GOING SOME-WHERE?
YEAH. WE'RE ABOUT TO HIT THE ROAD.
WHOA! AGAIN?
SEE YA!
VRMM
BYE-BYE!
BRING ME...
A SOUVENIR!

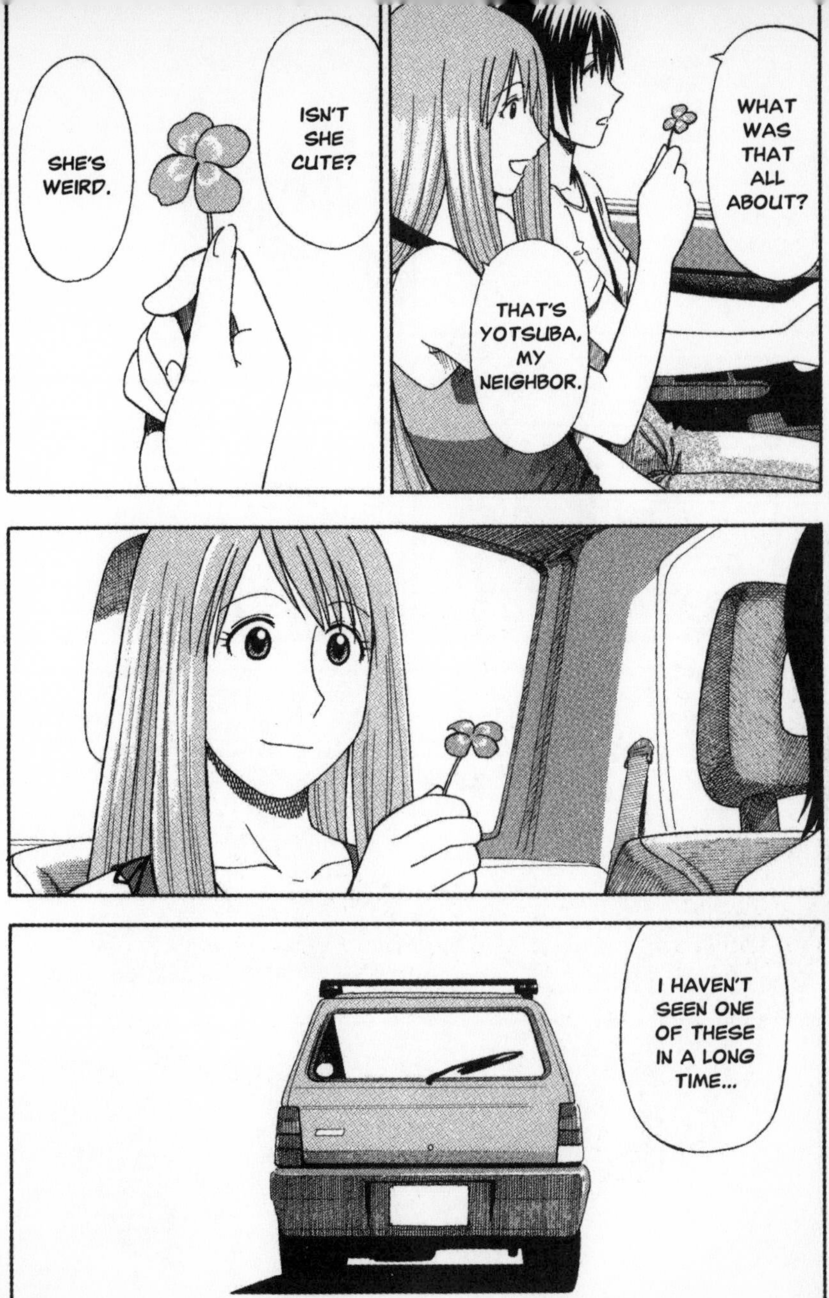
WHAT WAS THAT ALL ABOUT?
THAT'S YOTSUBA, MY NEIGHBOR.
ISN'T SHE CUTE?
SHE'S WEIRD.
I HAVEN'T SEEN ONE OF THESE IN A LONG TIME...

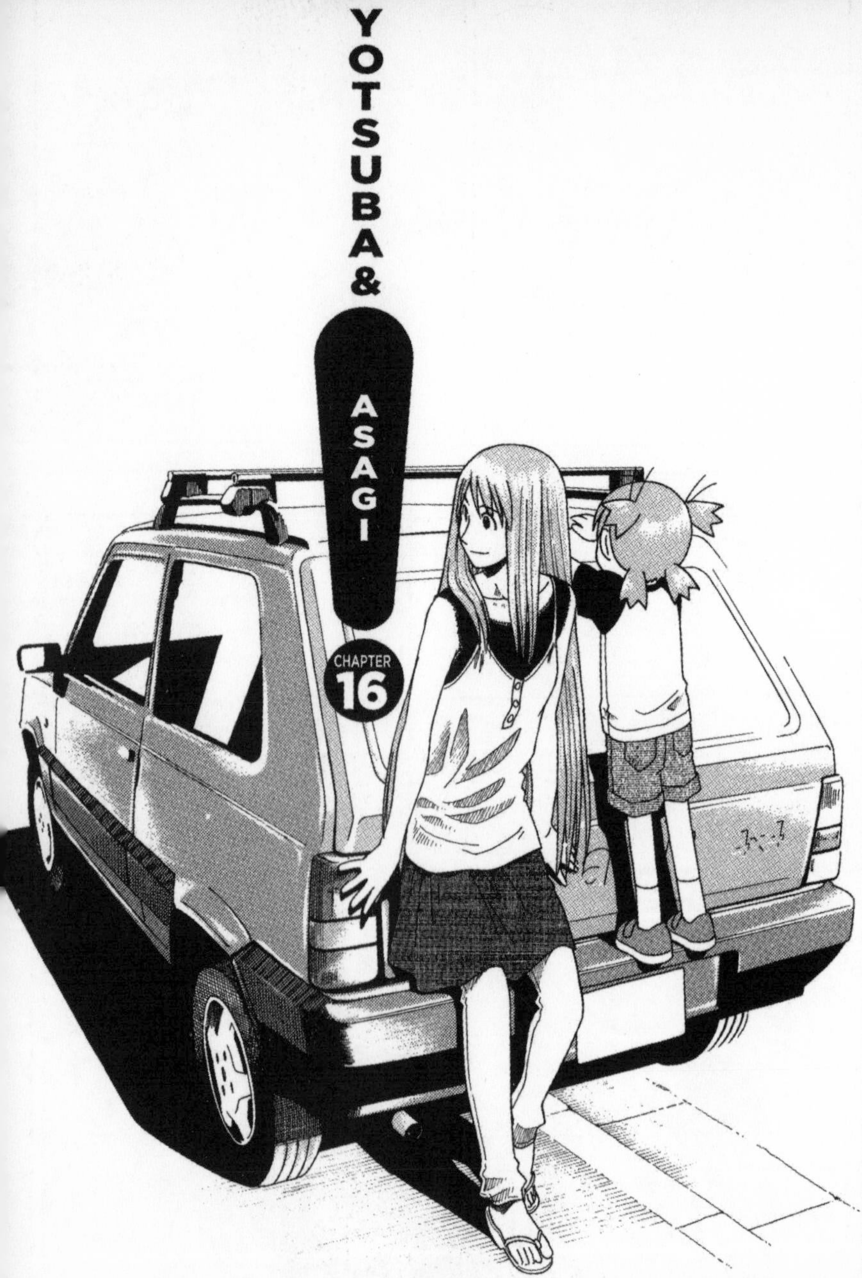
YOTSUBA&!
ASAGI
CHAPTER 16

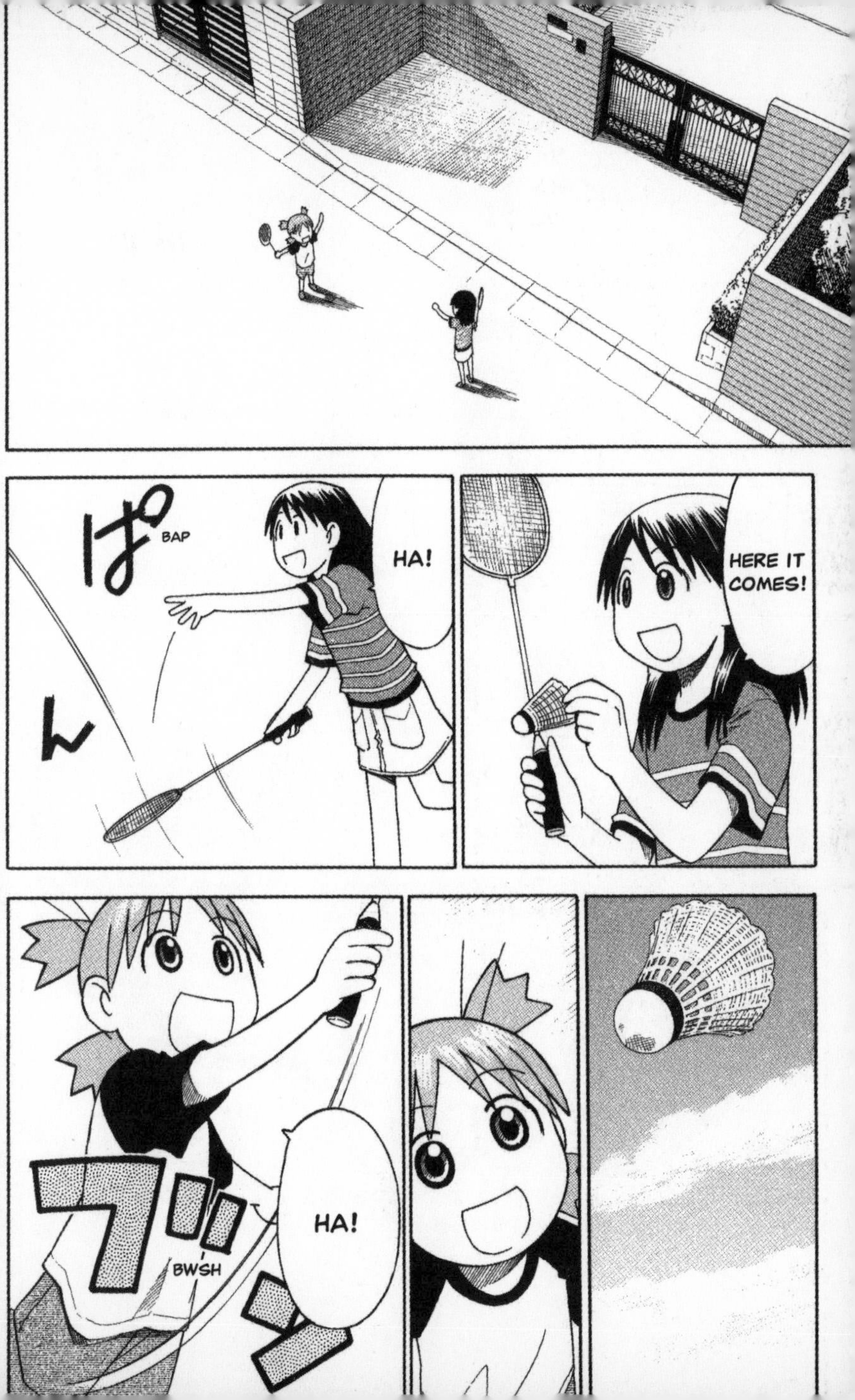
HERE IT COMES!
HA!
ぱん
BAP
HA!
BWSH

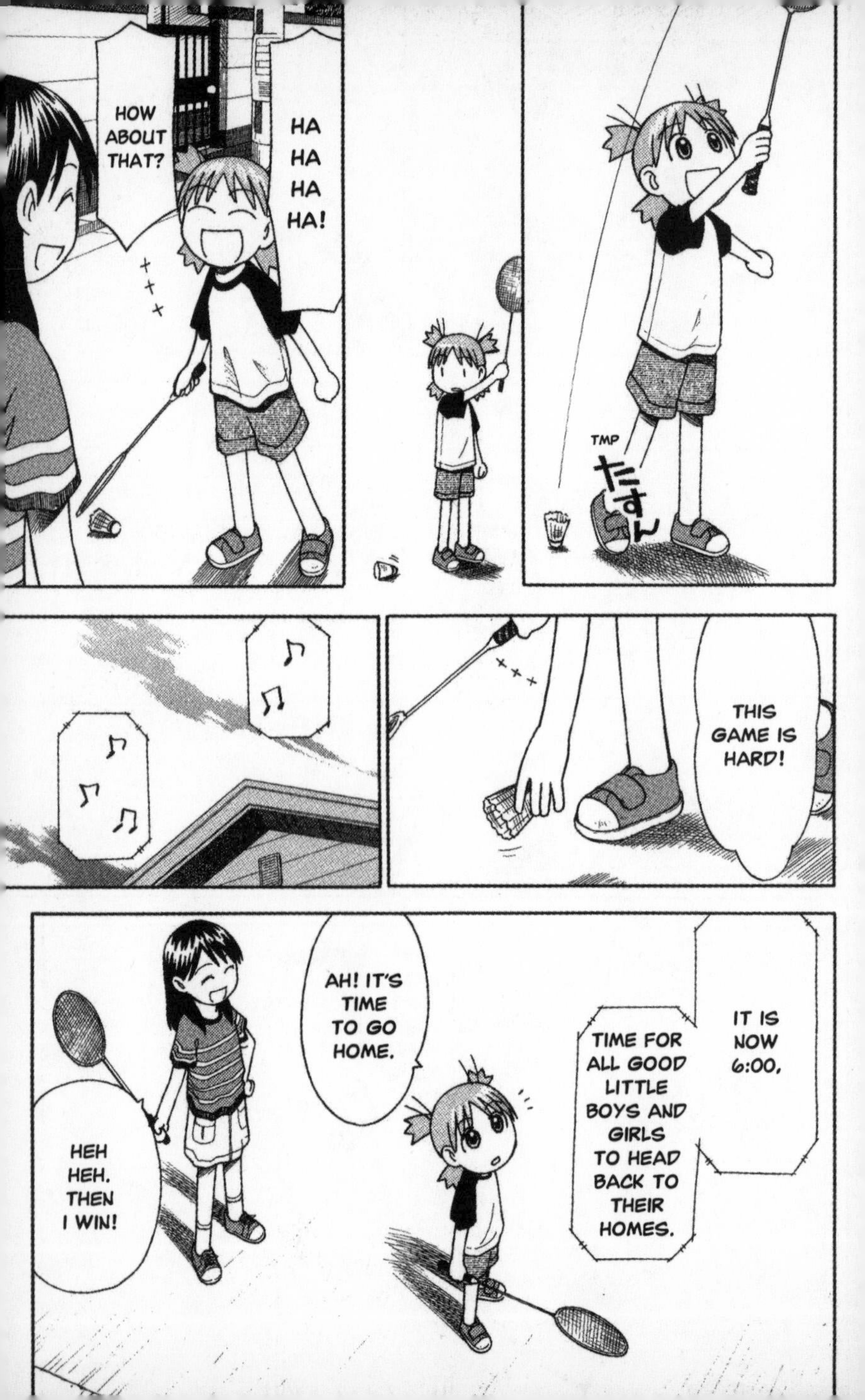
TMP
たすん
HA HA HA HA!
HOW ABOUT THAT?
THIS GAME IS HARD!
IT IS NOW 6:00,
TIME FOR ALL GOOD LITTLE BOYS AND GIRLS TO HEAD BACK TO THEIR HOMES.
AH! IT'S TIME TO GO HOME.
HEH HEH. THEN I WIN!

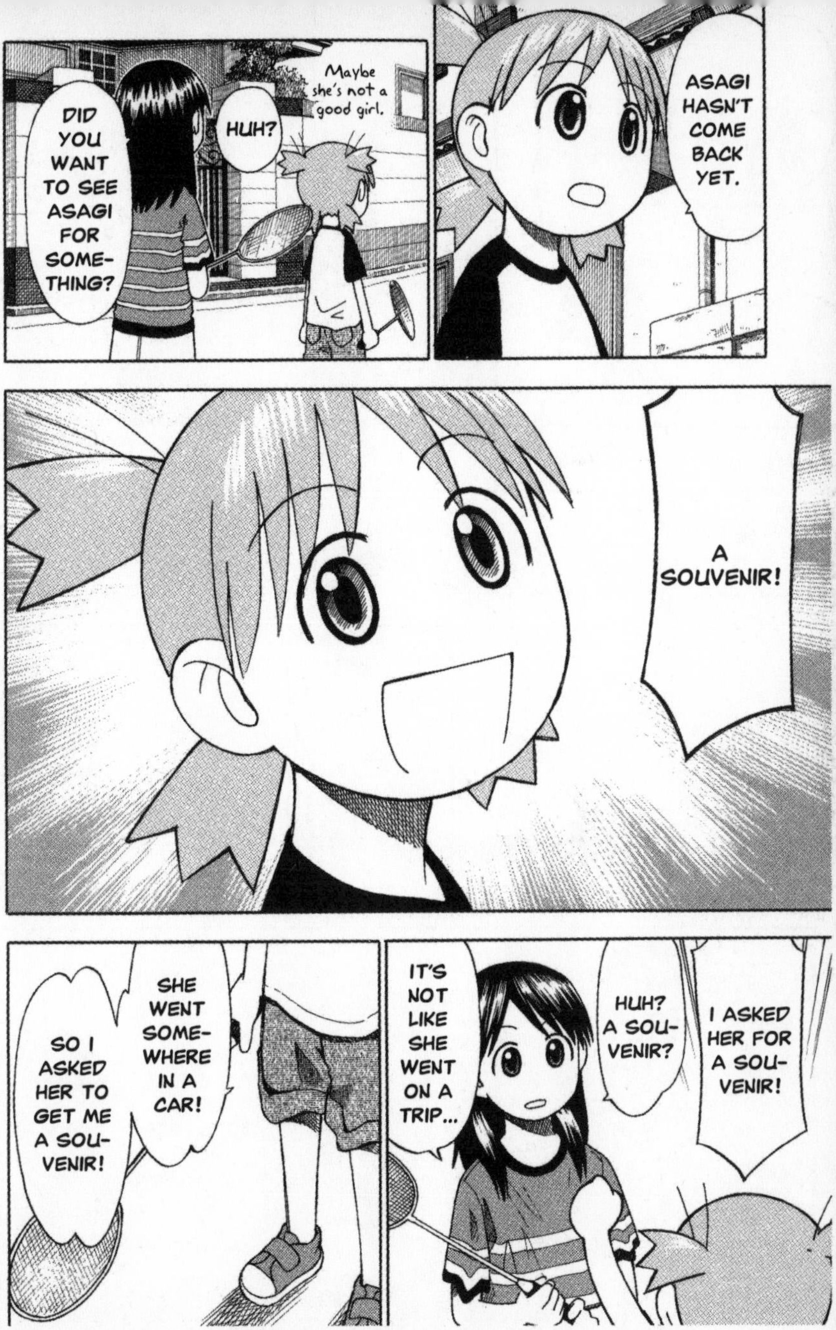
ASAGI HASN'T COME BACK YET.
Maybe she's not a good girl.
HUH?
DID YOU WANT TO SEE ASAGI FOR SOMETHING?
A SOUVENIR!
I ASKED HER FOR A SOUVENIR!
HUH? A SOUVENIR?
IT'S NOT LIKE SHE WENT ON A TRIP...
SHE WENT SOMEWHERE IN A CAR!
SO I ASKED HER TO GET ME A SOUVENIR!

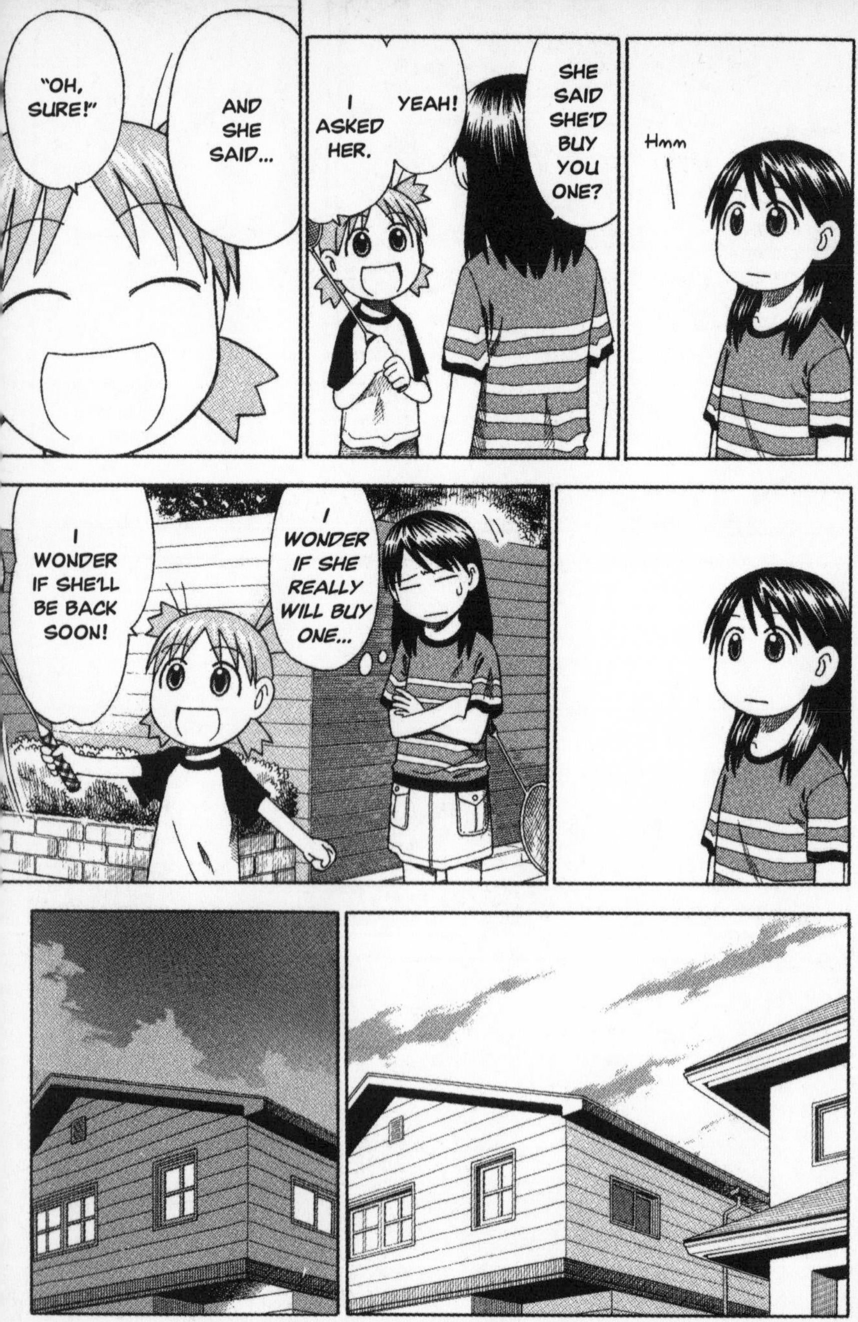
Hmm
SHE SAID SHE'D BUY YOU ONE?
YEAH! I ASKED HER.
AND SHE SAID...
"OH, SURE!"
I WONDER IF SHE REALLY WILL BUY ONE...
I WONDER IF SHE'LL BE BACK SOON!

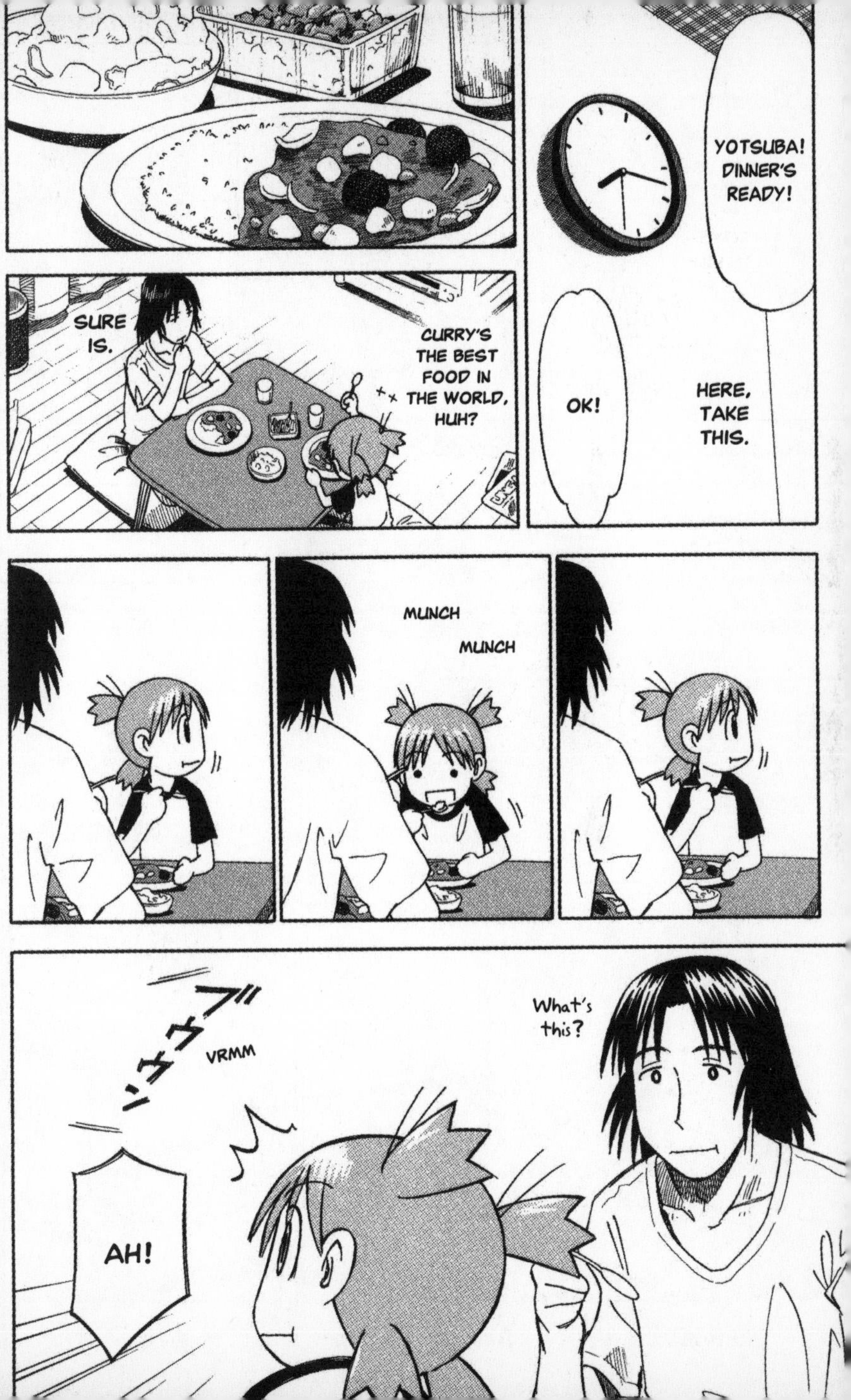
YOTSUBA! DINNER'S READY!
HERE, TAKE THIS.
OK!
CURRY'S THE BEST FOOD IN THE WORLD, HUH?
SURE IS.
MUNCH
MUNCH
What's this?
ブウゥン
VRMM
AH!

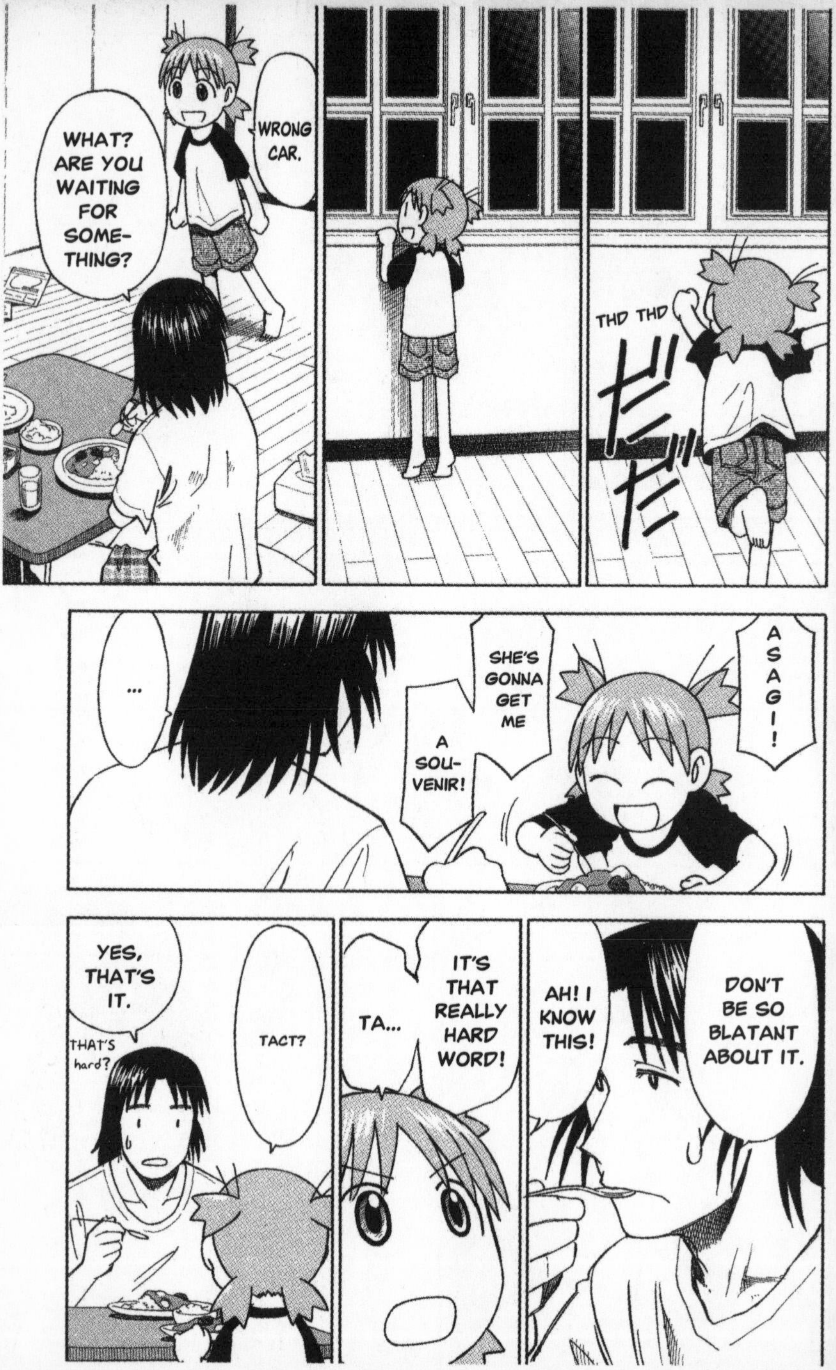
THD THD
WRONG CAR.
WHAT? ARE YOU WAITING FOR SOME-THING?
ASAGI!
SHE'S GONNA GET ME
A SOU-VENIR!
...
DON'T BE SO BLATANT ABOUT IT.
AH! I KNOW THIS!
IT'S THAT REALLY HARD WORD!
TA...
TACT?
YES, THAT'S IT.
THAT'S hard?

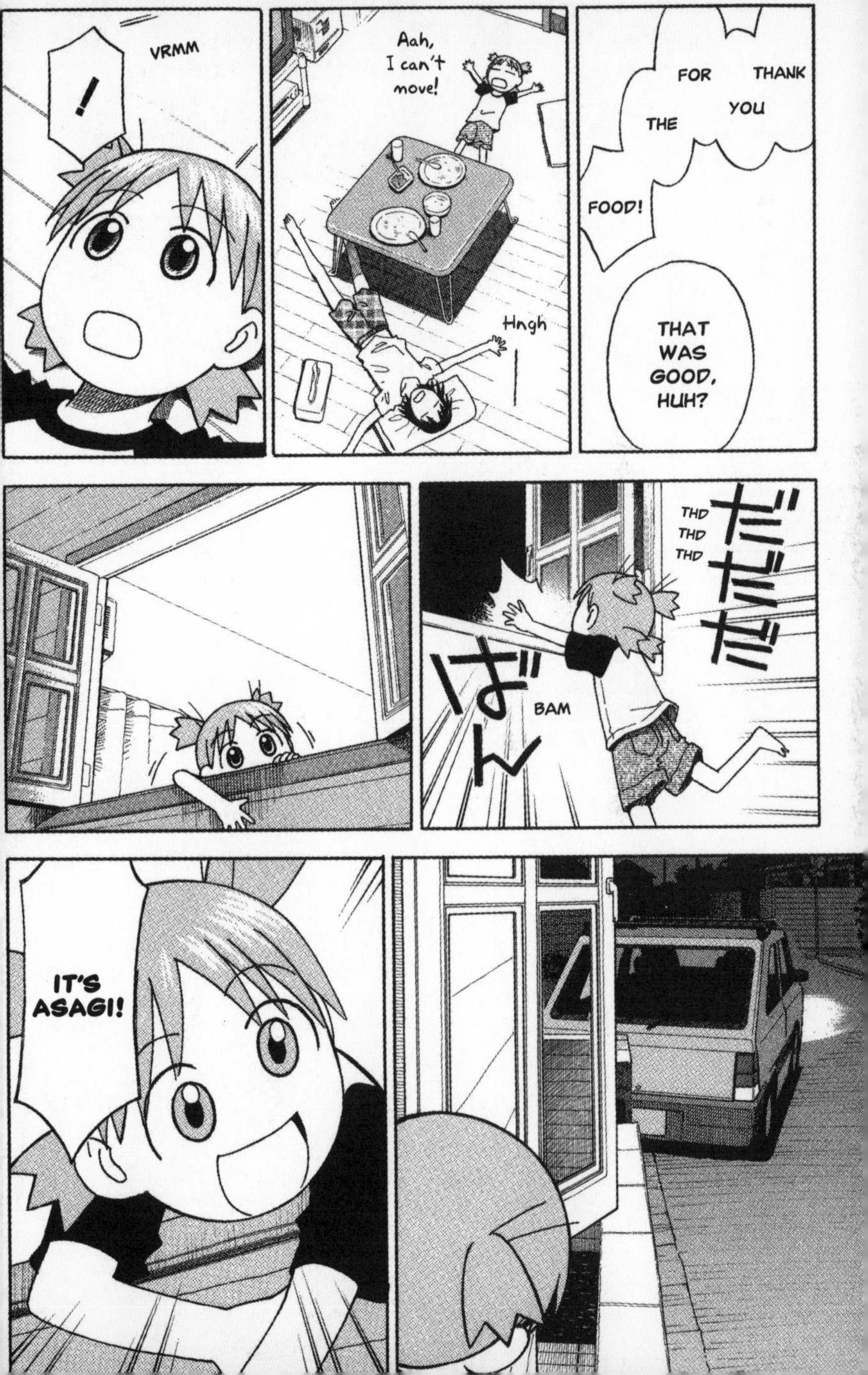
THANK YOU FOR THE FOOD!
THAT WAS GOOD, HUH?
Aah, I can't move!
Hngh
!
VRMM
THD THD THD
だだだ
ばん
BAM
IT'S ASAGI!

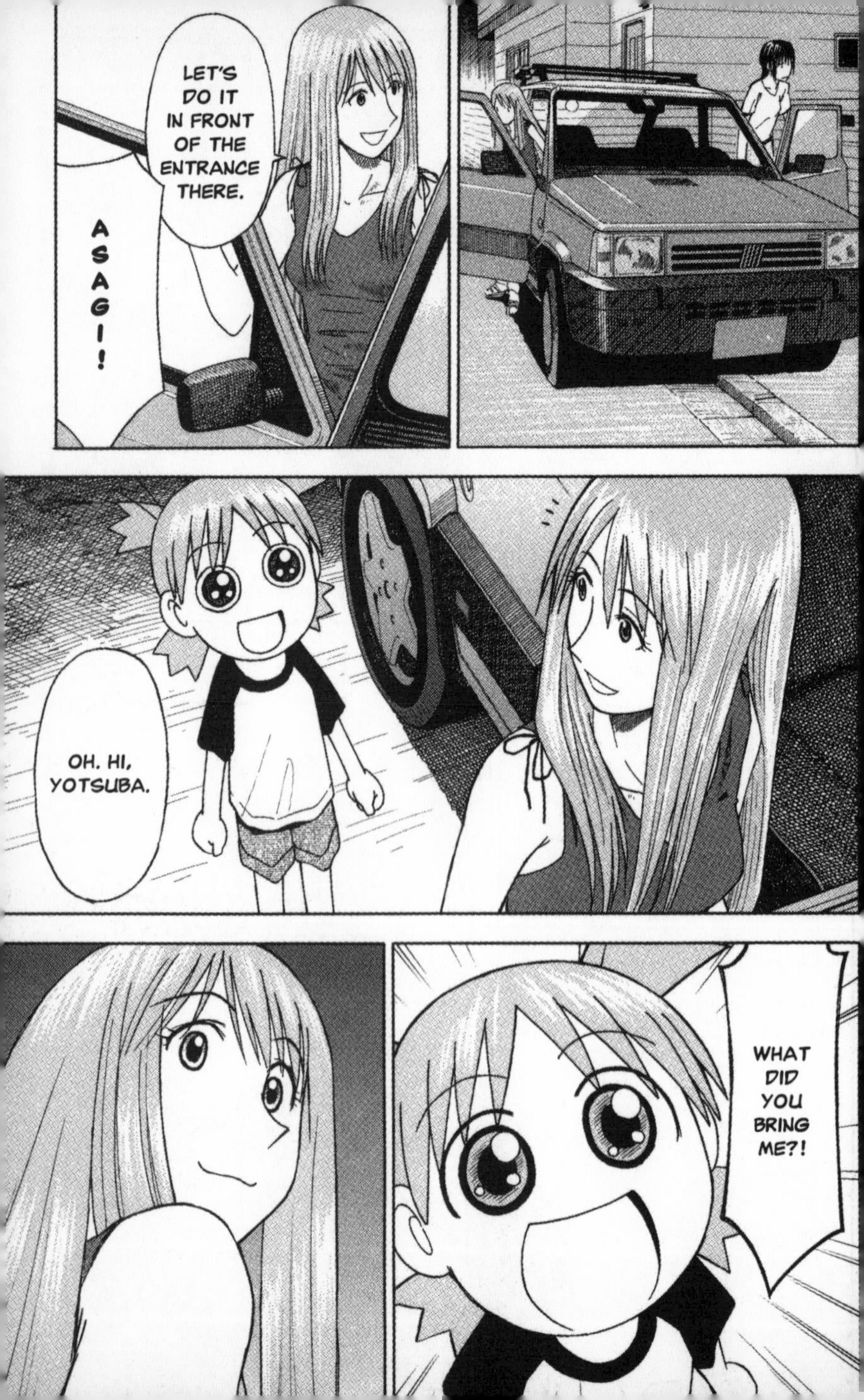

LET'S DO IT IN FRONT OF THE ENTRANCE THERE.
ASAGI!
OH. HI, YOTSUBA.
WHAT DID YOU BRING ME?!

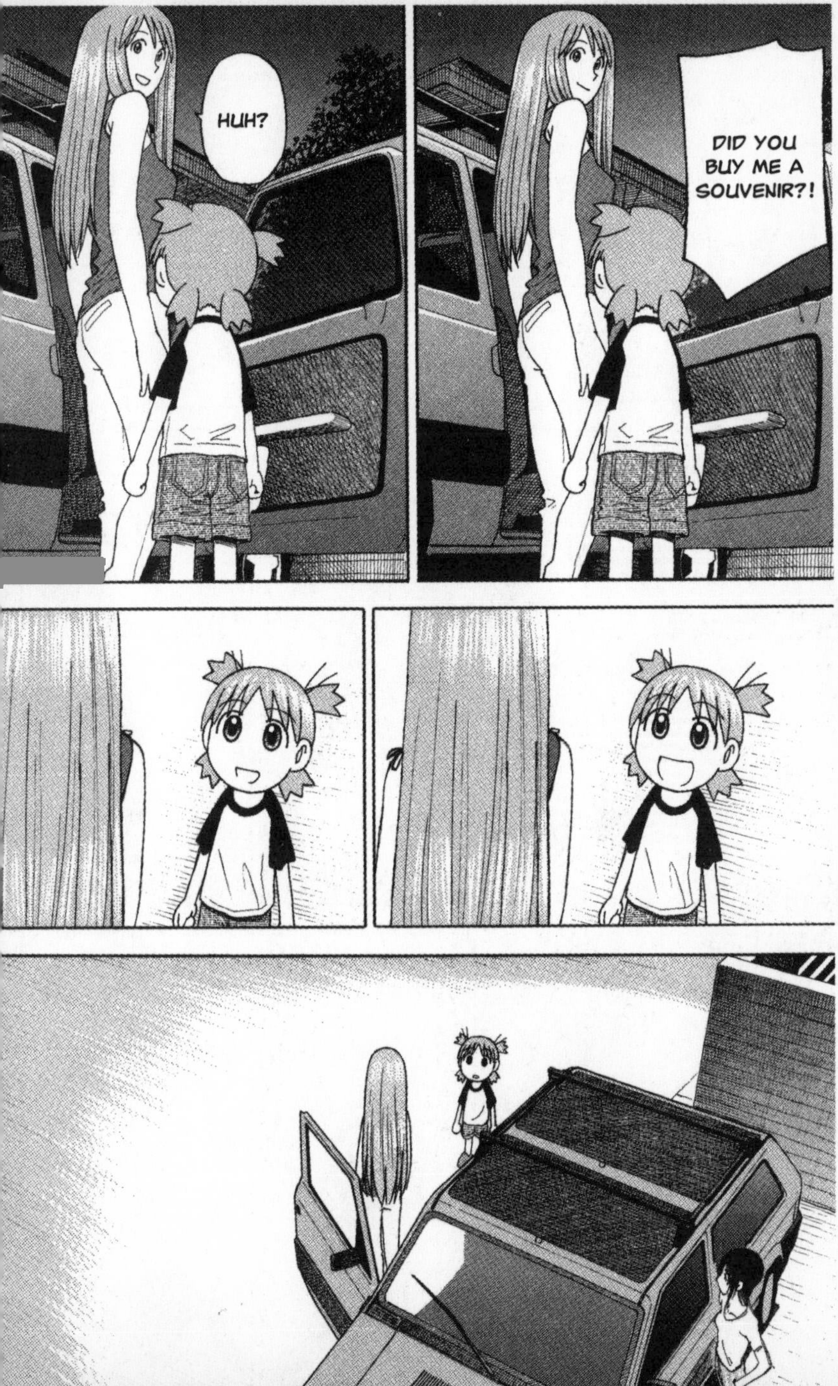
DID YOU BUY ME A SOUVENIR?!
HUH?

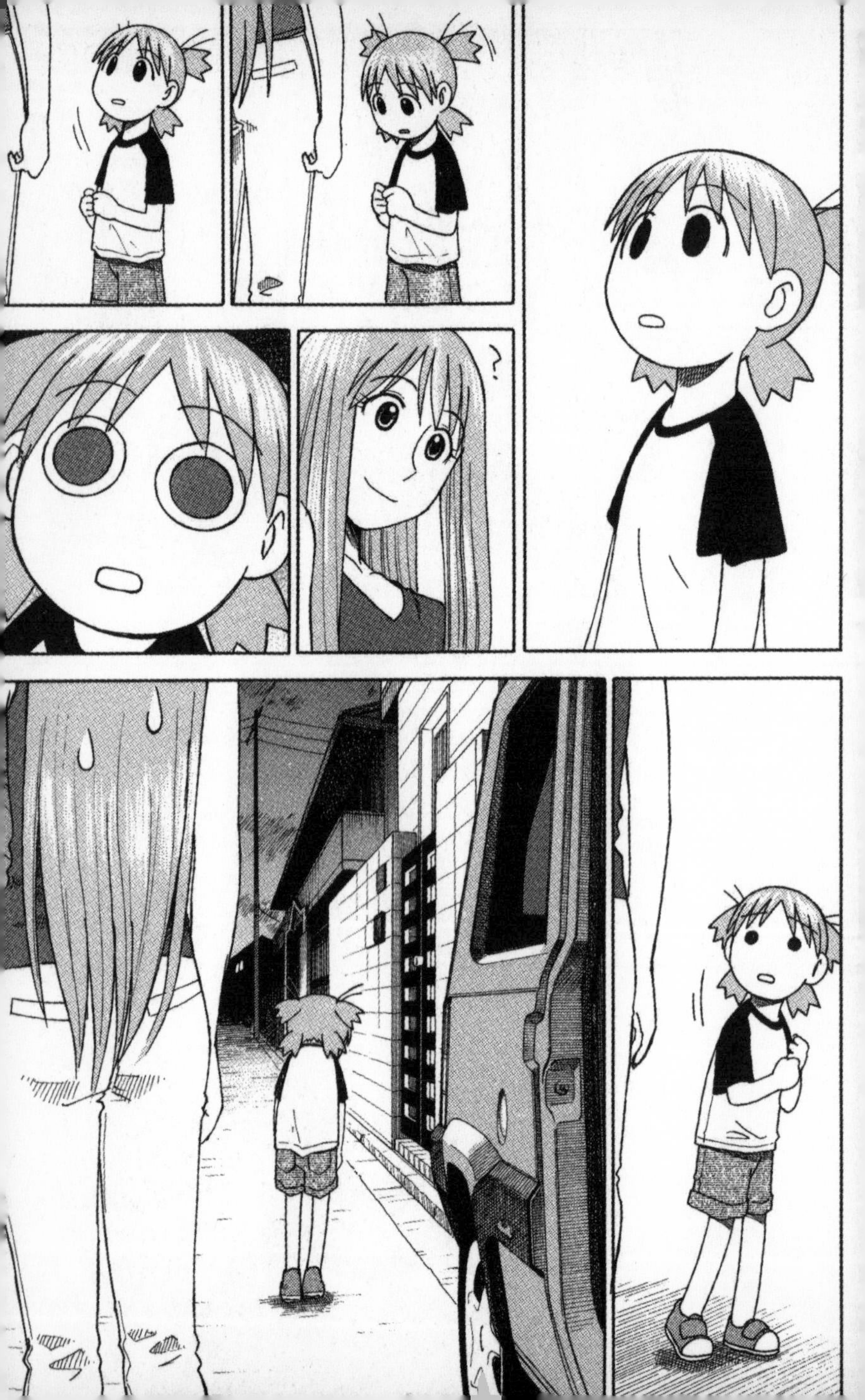
?

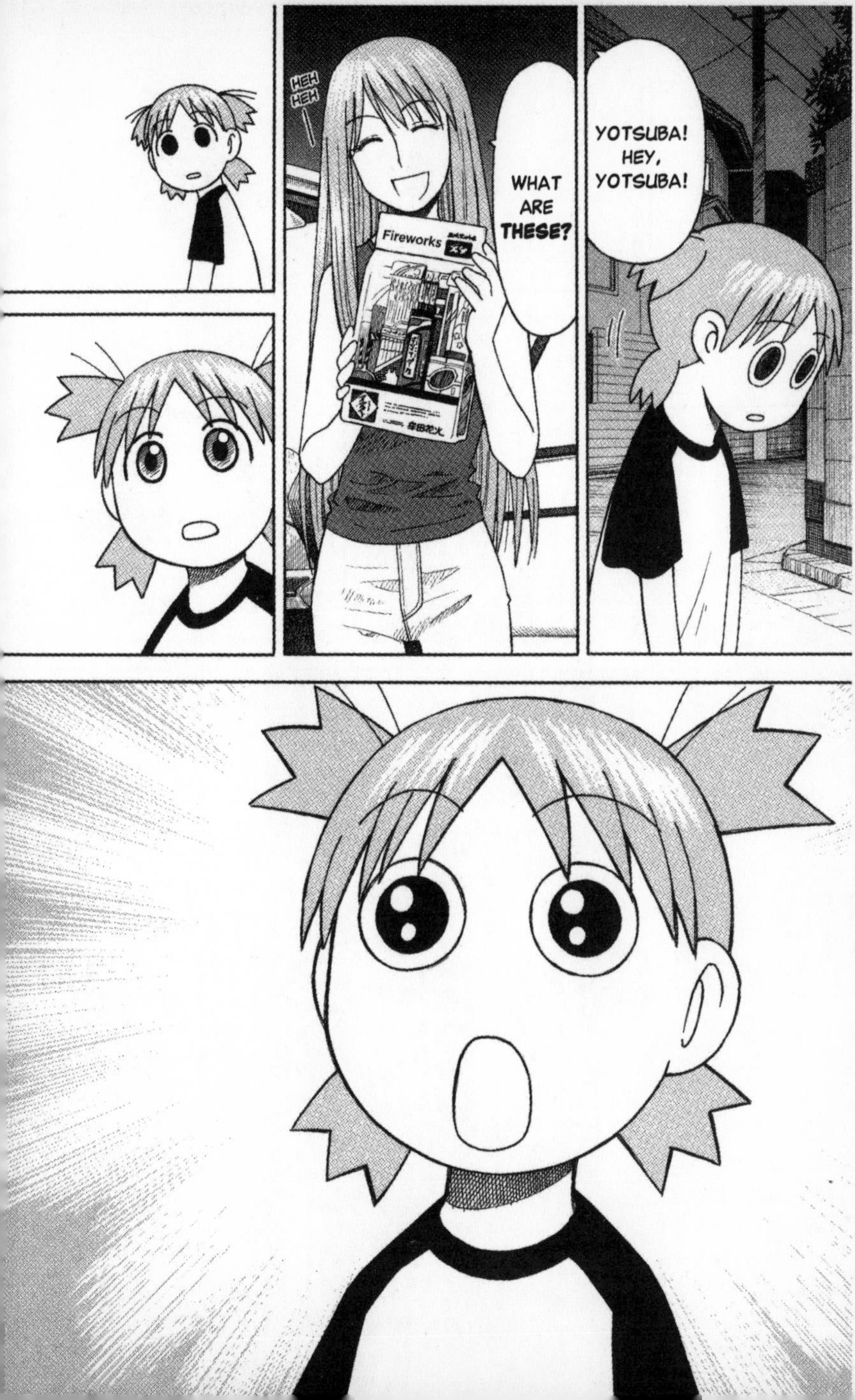
YOTSUBA! HEY, YOTSUBA!
WHAT ARE THESE?
HEH HEH
Fireworks

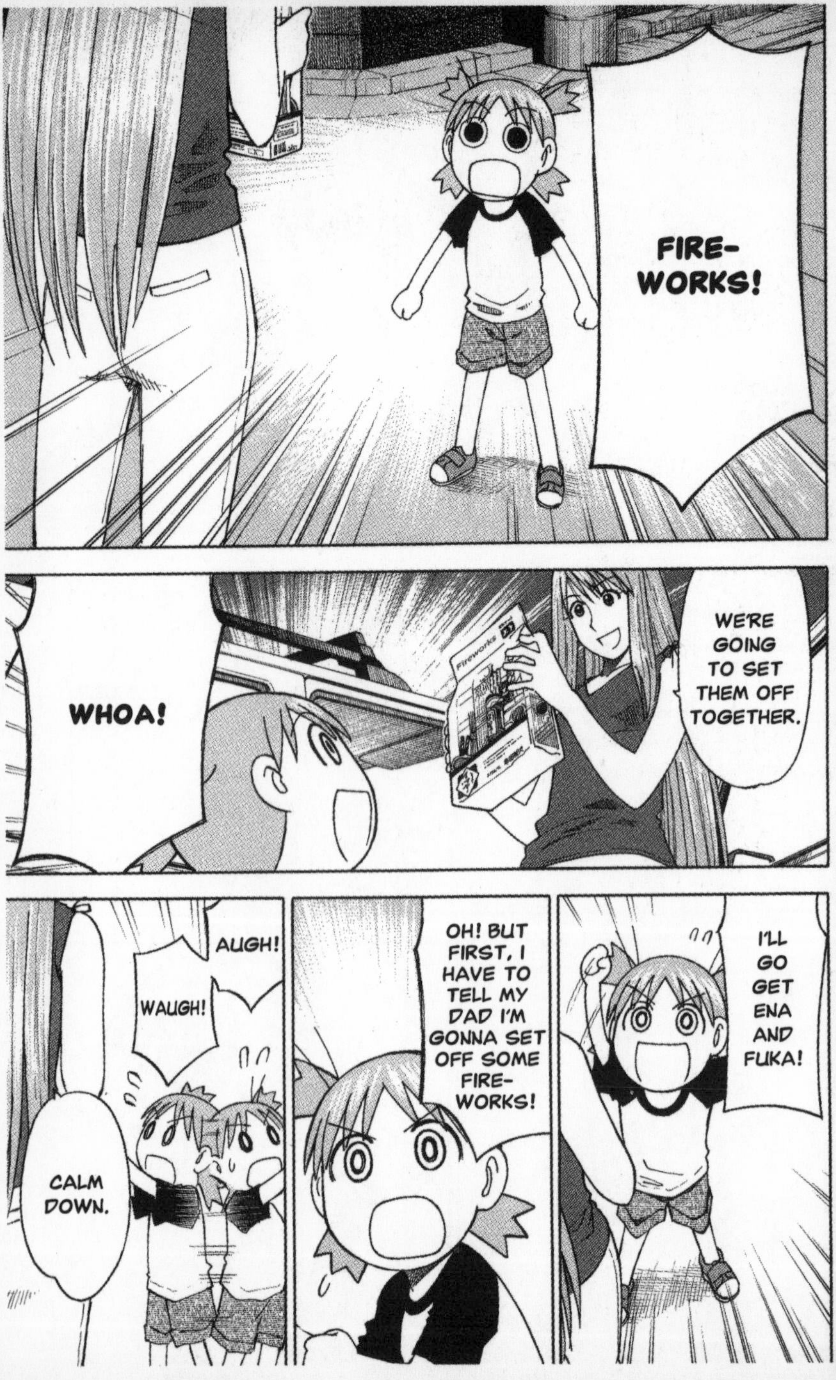
FIRE-WORKS!
WE'RE GOING TO SET THEM OFF TOGETHER.
Fireworks
WHOA!
I'LL GO GET ENA AND FUKA!
OH! BUT FIRST, I HAVE TO TELL MY DAD I'M GONNA SET OFF SOME FIRE-WORKS!
AUGH!
WAUGH!
CALM DOWN.

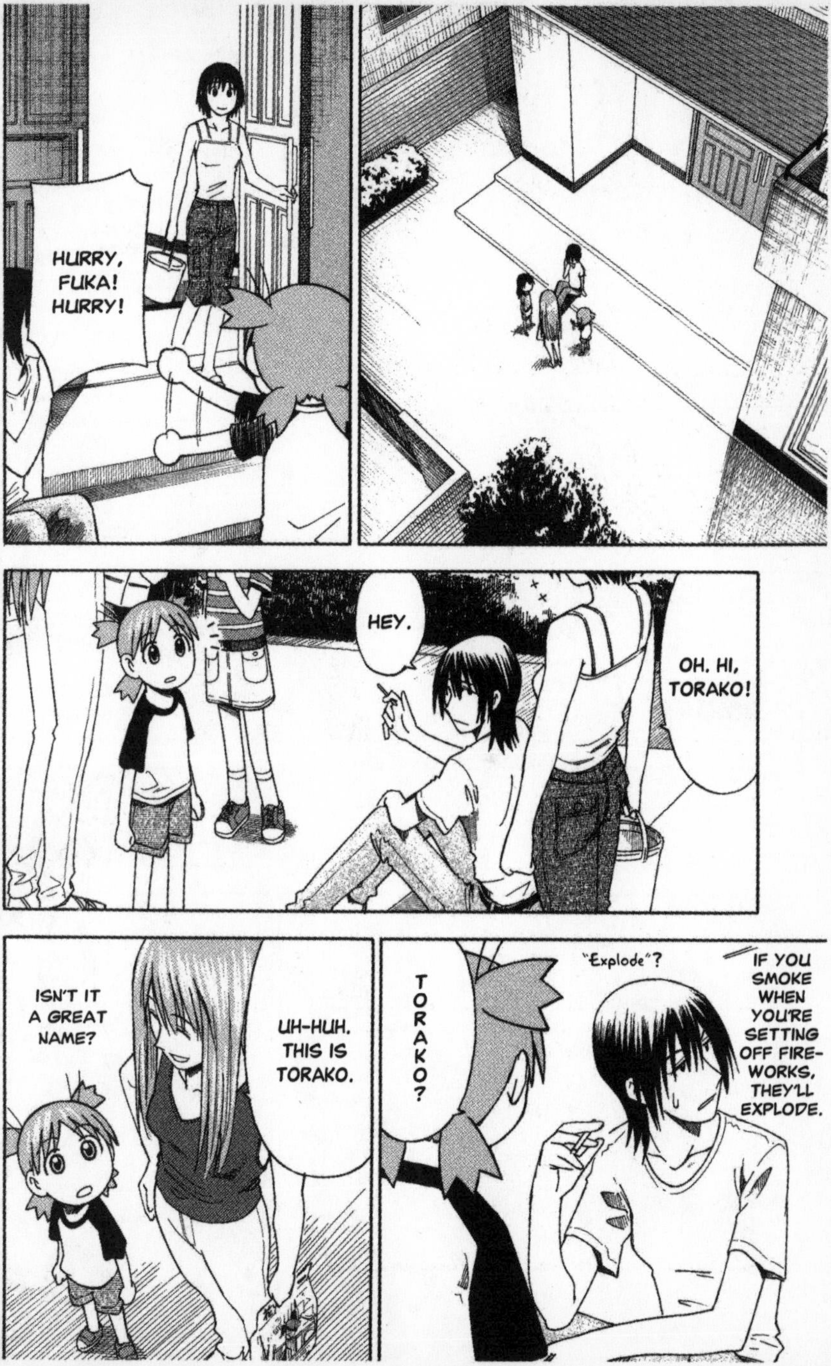
HURRY, FUKA! HURRY!
OH. HI, TORAKO!
HEY.
IF YOU SMOKE WHEN YOU'RE SETTING OFF FIRE-WORKS, THEY'LL EXPLODE.
"Explode"?
TORAKO?
UH-HUH. THIS IS TORAKO.
ISN'T IT A GREAT NAME?

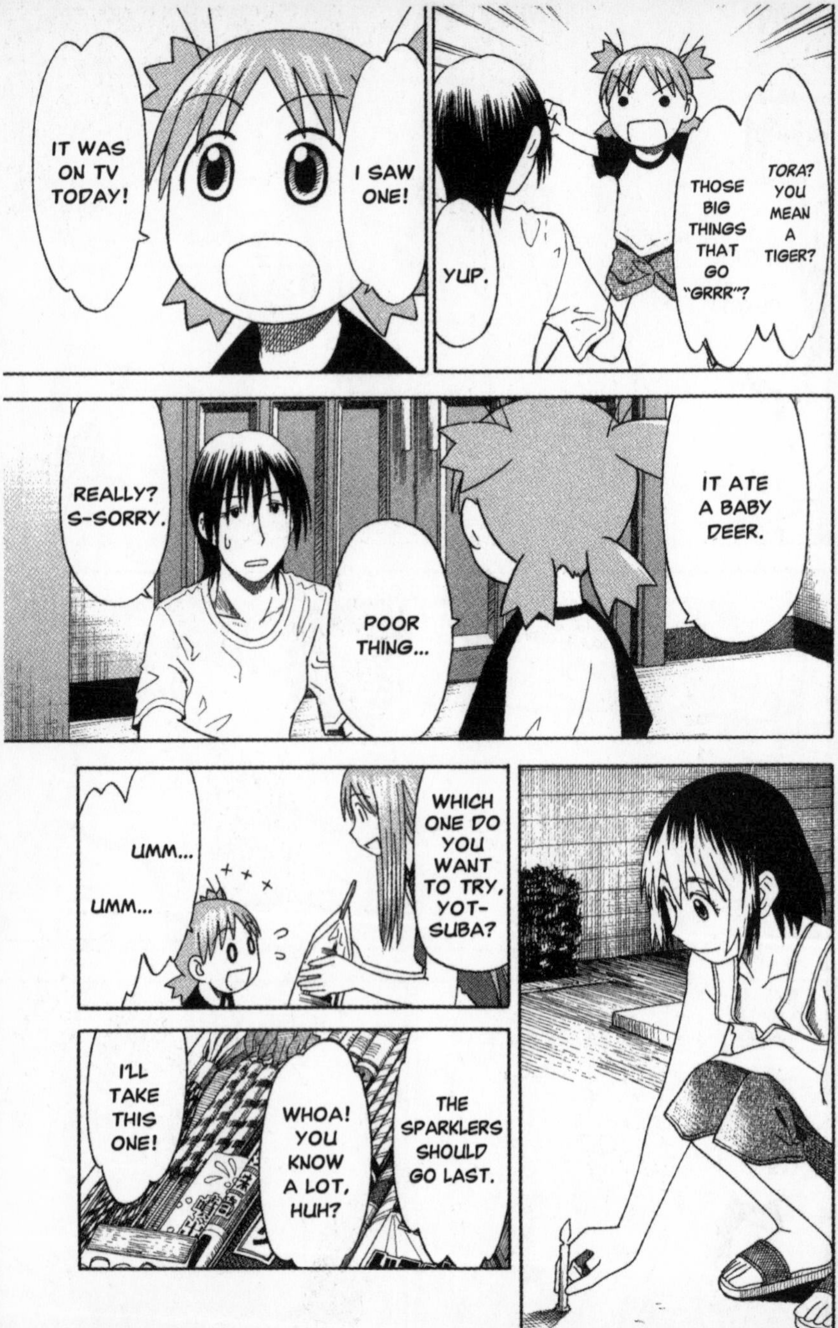
TORA? YOU MEAN A TIGER?
THOSE BIG THINGS THAT GO "GRRR"?
YUP.
I SAW ONE!
IT WAS ON TV TODAY!
IT ATE A BABY DEER.
POOR THING...
REALLY? S-SORRY.
WHICH ONE DO YOU WANT TO TRY, YOT-SUBA?
UMM...
UMM...
THE SPARKLERS SHOULD GO LAST.
WHOA! YOU KNOW A LOT, HUH?
I'LL TAKE THIS ONE!

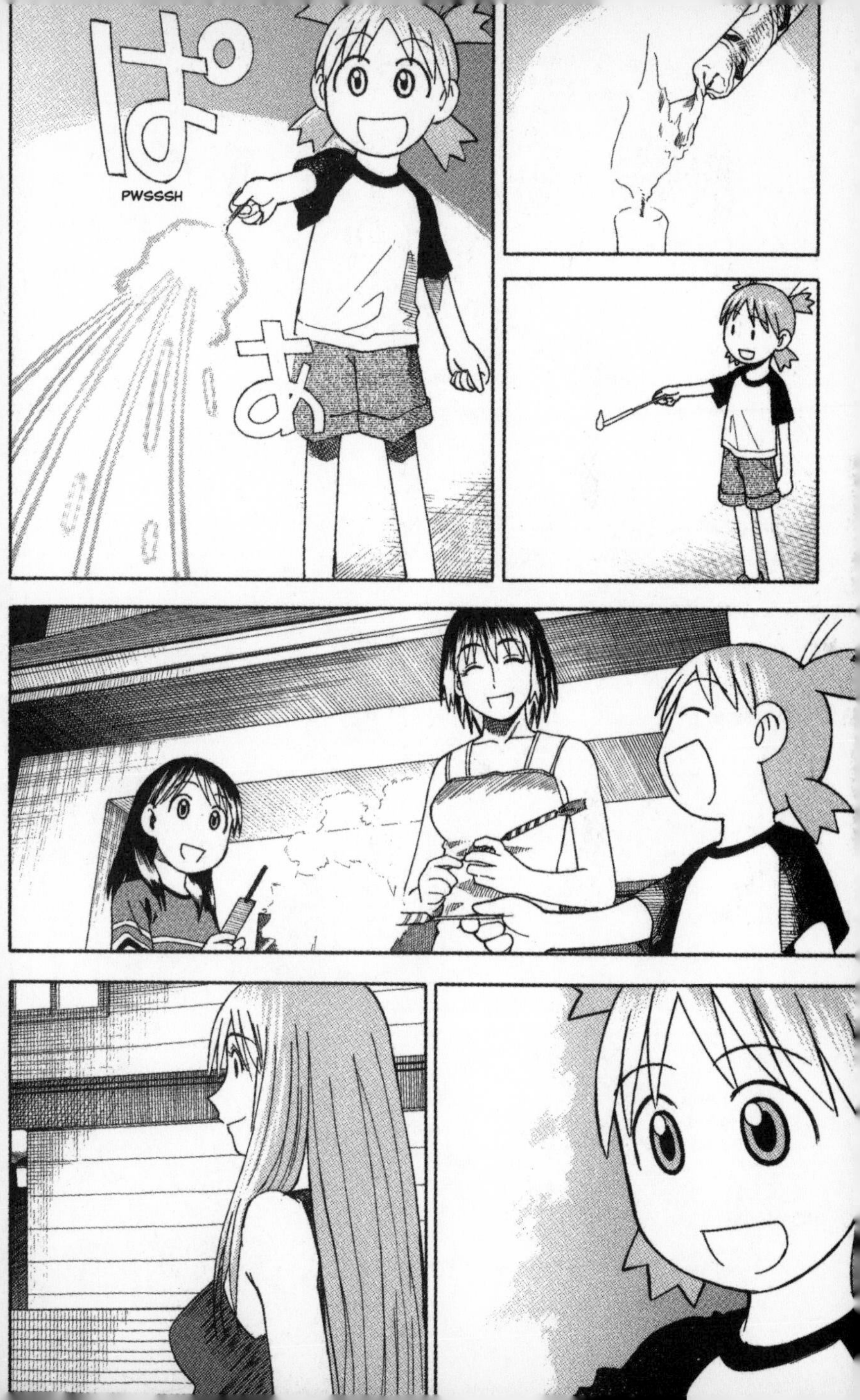
ぱぁ
PWSSSH

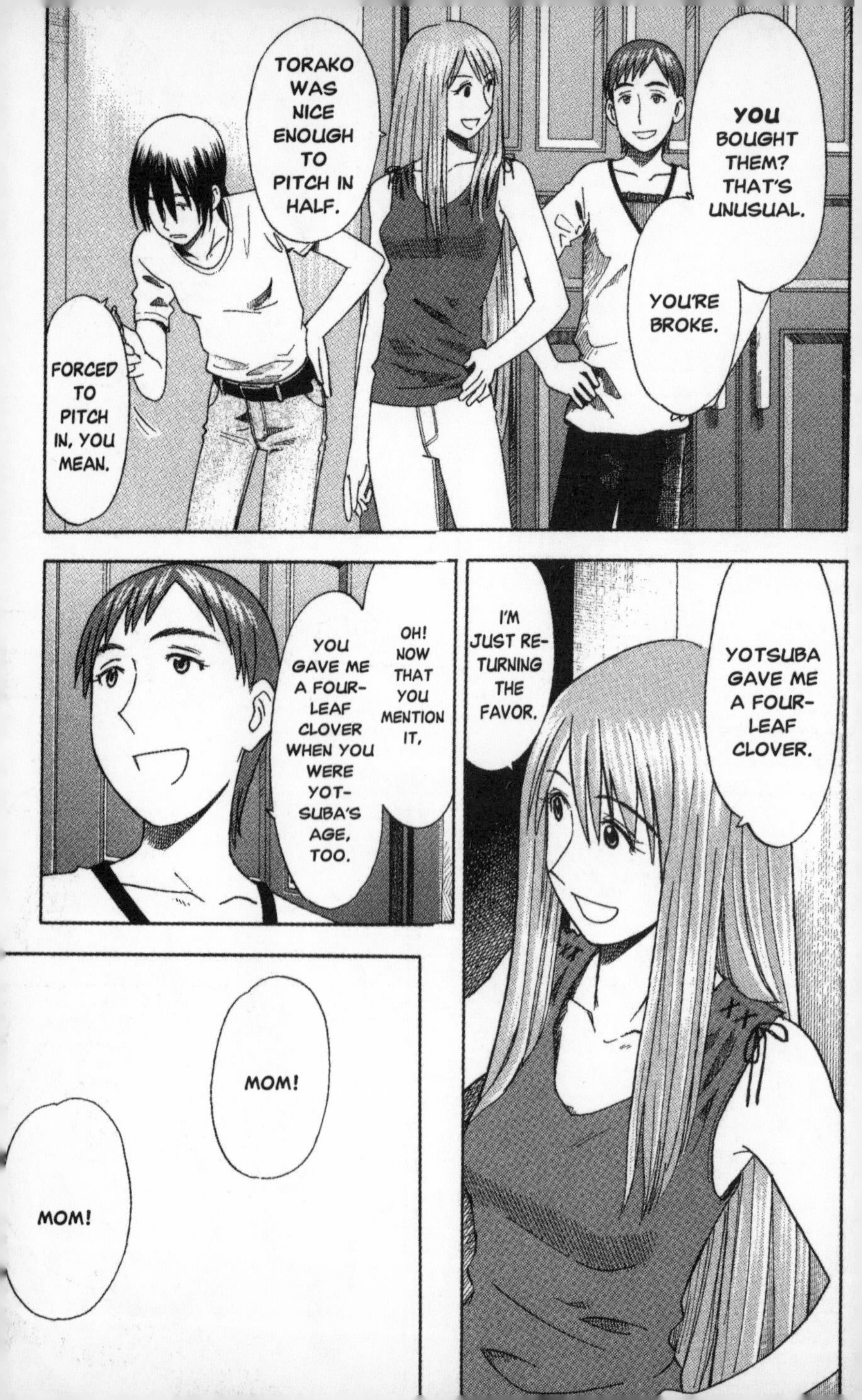
YOU BOUGHT THEM? THAT'S UNUSUAL.
YOU'RE BROKE.
TORAKO WAS NICE ENOUGH TO PITCH IN HALF.
FORCED TO PITCH IN, YOU MEAN.
YOTSUBA GAVE ME A FOUR-LEAF CLOVER.
I'M JUST RE-TURNING THE FAVOR.
OH! NOW THAT YOU MENTION IT,
YOU GAVE ME A FOUR-LEAF CLOVER WHEN YOU WERE YOT-SUBA'S AGE, TOO.
MOM!
MOM!

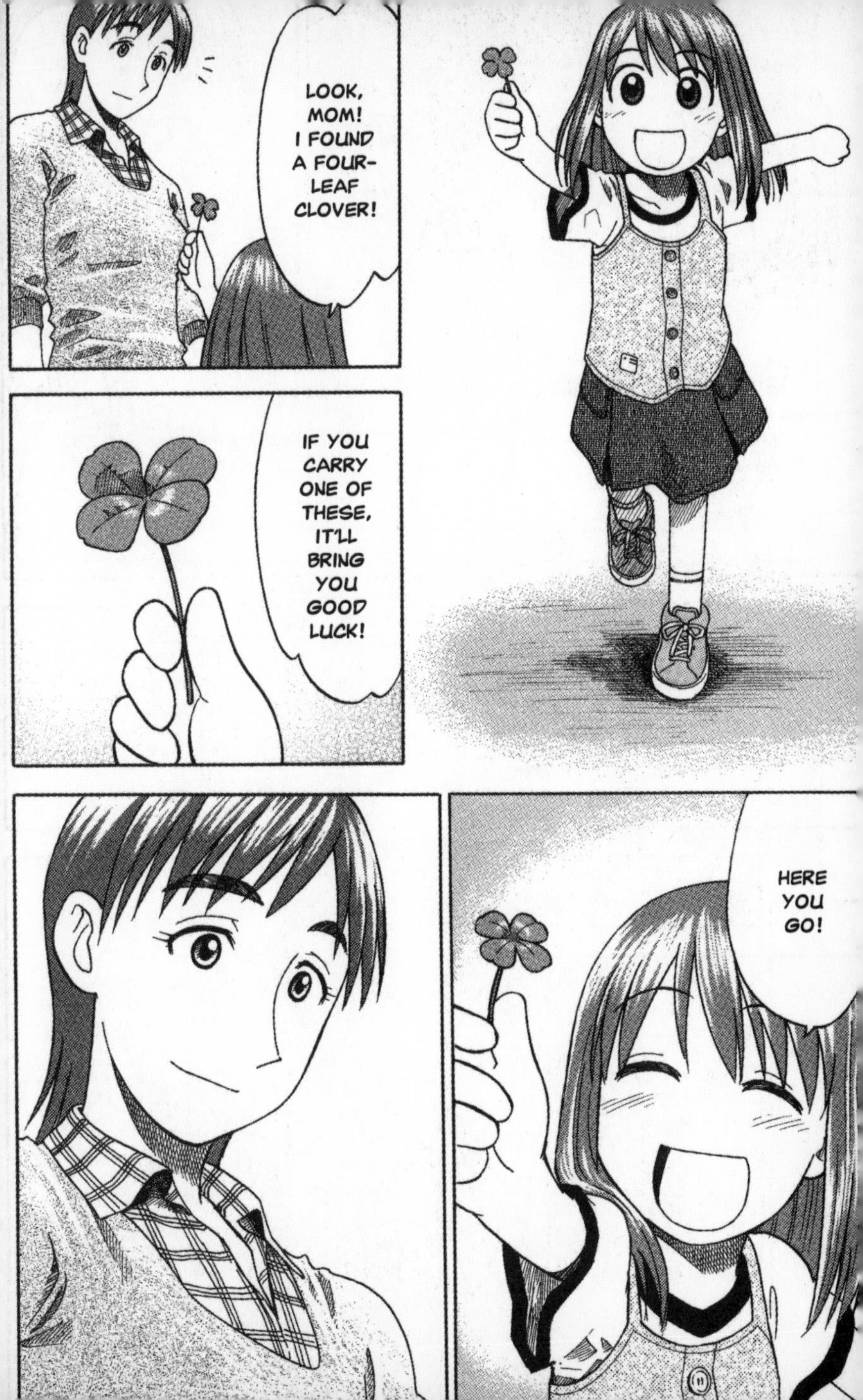
LOOK, MOM! I FOUND A FOUR-LEAF CLOVER!
IF YOU CARRY ONE OF THESE, IT'LL BRING YOU GOOD LUCK!
HERE YOU GO!

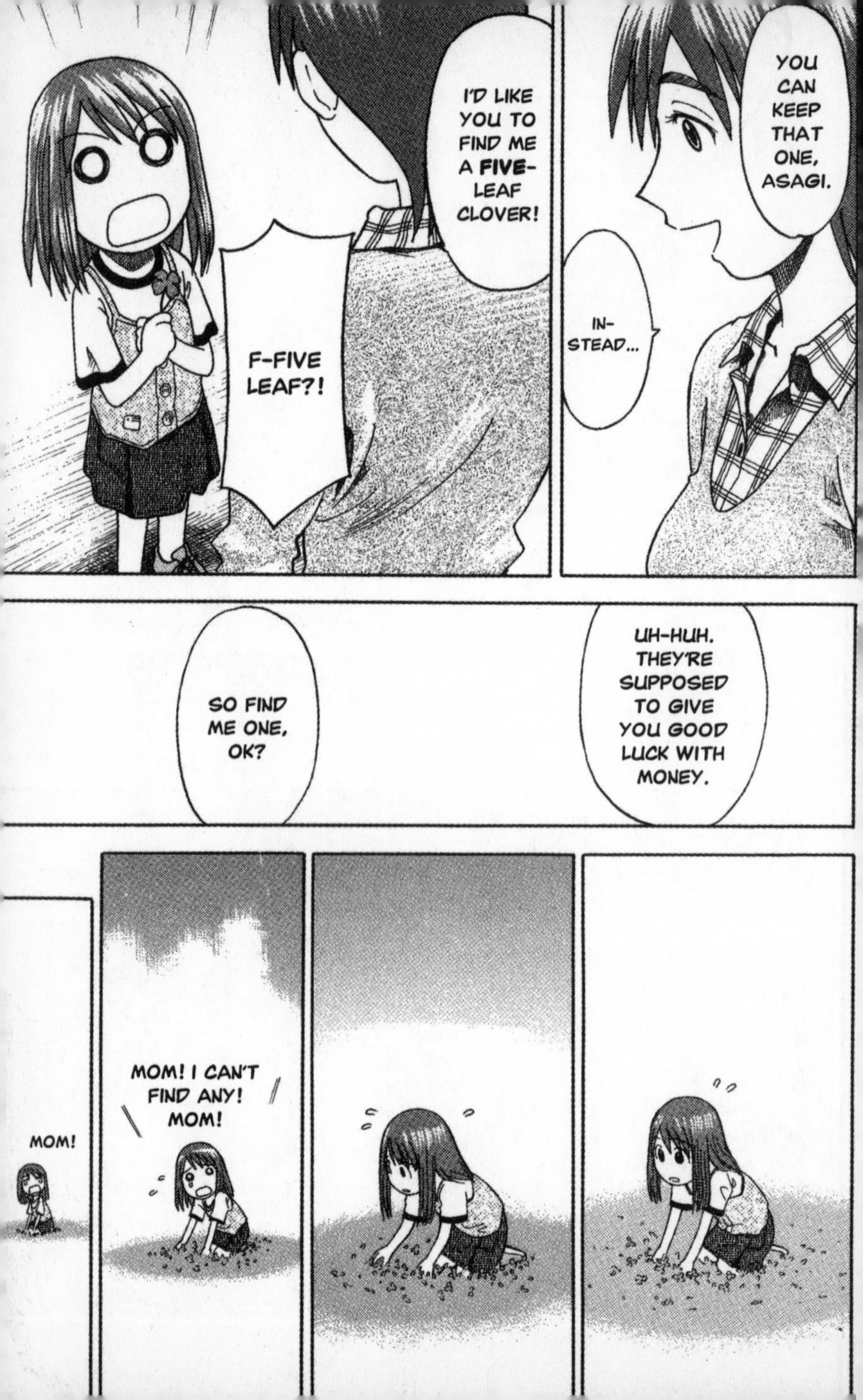
YOU CAN KEEP THAT ONE, ASAGI.
IN-STEAD...
I'D LIKE YOU TO FIND ME A **FIVE**-LEAF CLOVER!
F-FIVE LEAF?!
UH-HUH. THEY'RE SUPPOSED TO GIVE YOU GOOD LUCK WITH MONEY.
SO FIND ME ONE, OK?
MOM! I CAN'T FIND ANY! MOM!
MOM!

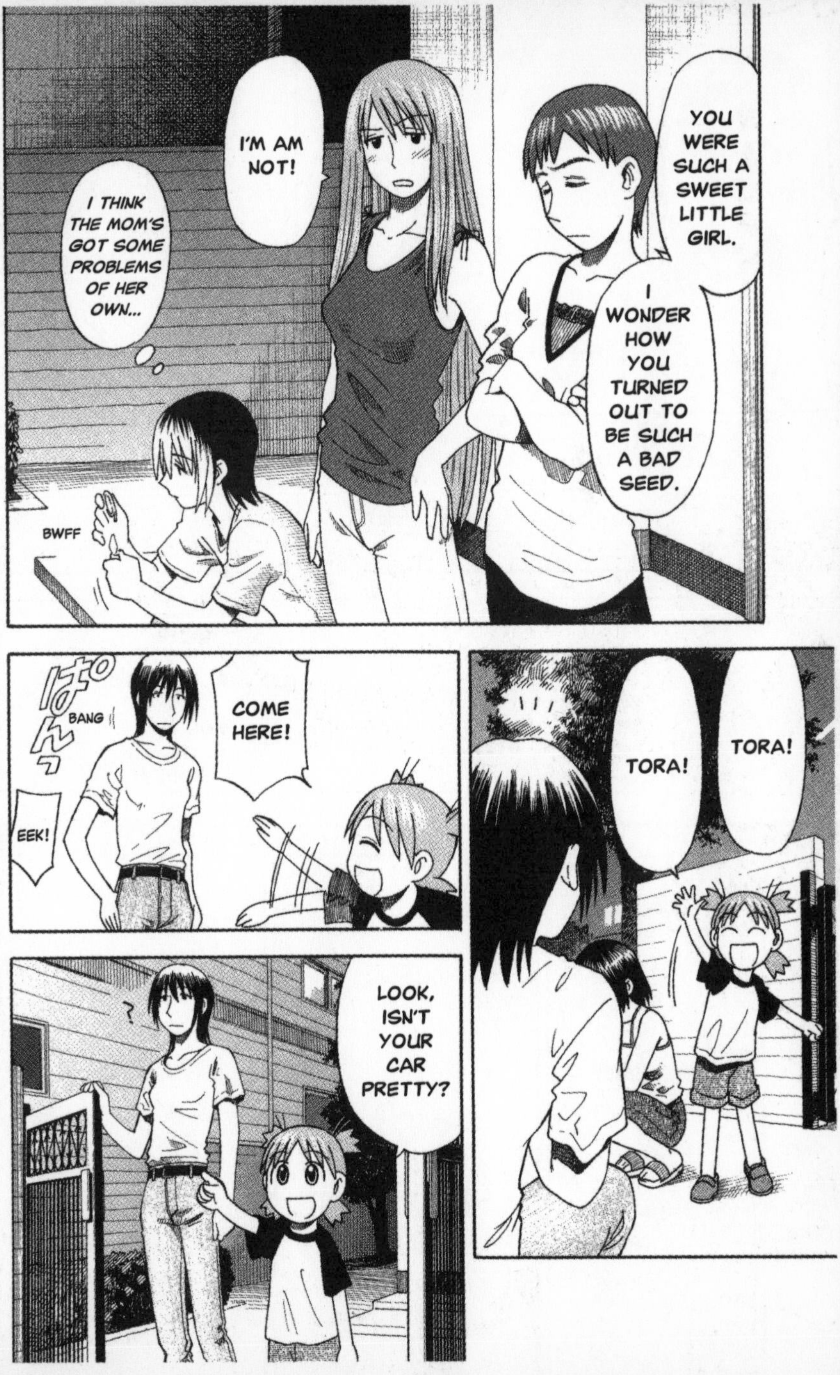
YOU WERE SUCH A SWEET LITTLE GIRL.
I WONDER HOW YOU TURNED OUT TO BE SUCH A BAD SEED.
I'M AM NOT!
I THINK THE MOM'S GOT SOME PROBLEMS OF HER OWN...
BWFF
TORA!
TORA!
COME HERE!
ぱんっ
BANG
EEK!
?
LOOK, ISN'T YOUR CAR PRETTY?

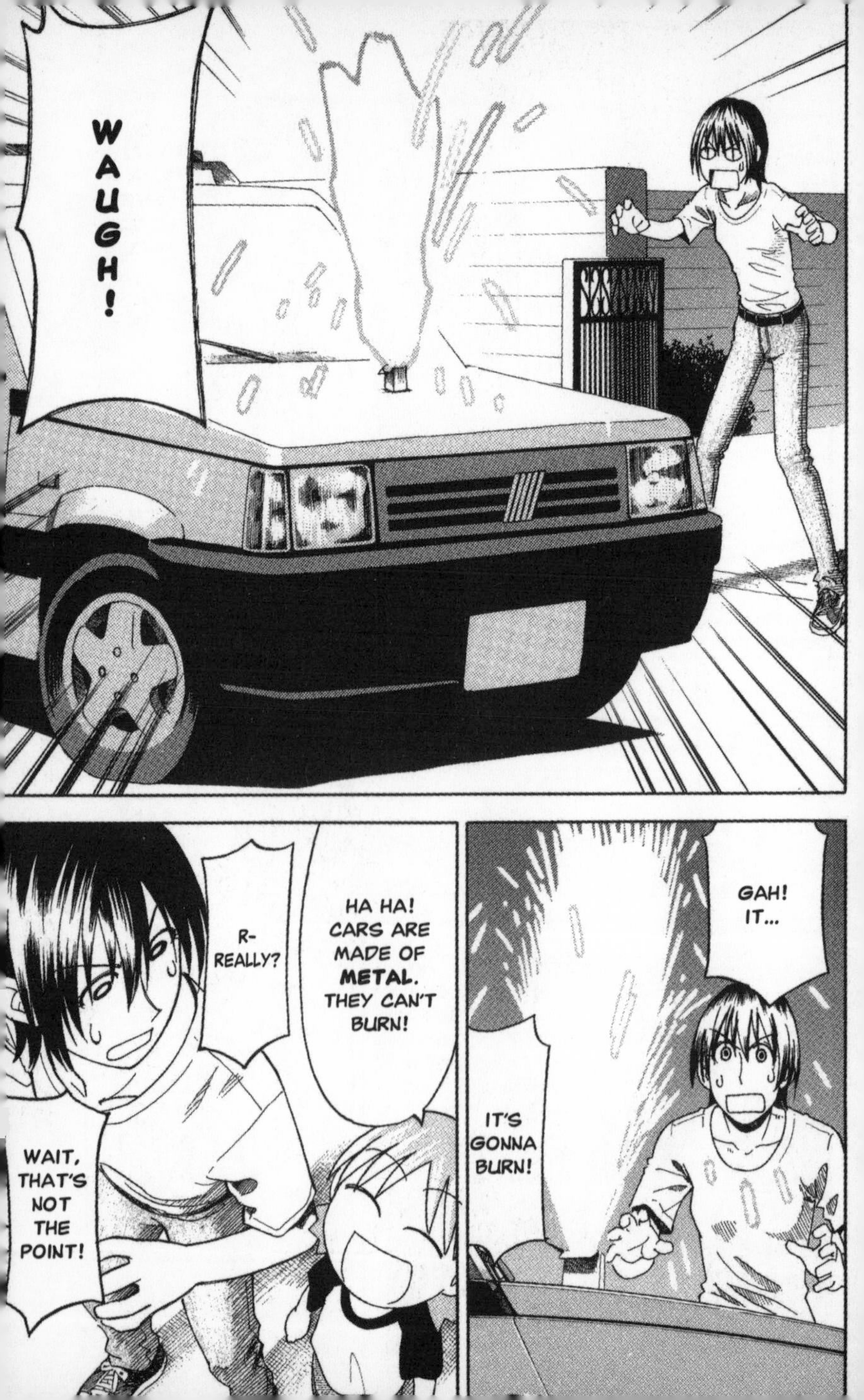
WAUGH!
GAH! IT...
IT'S GONNA BURN!
HA HA! CARS ARE MADE OF METAL. THEY CAN'T BURN!
R- REALLY?
WAIT, THAT'S NOT THE POINT!

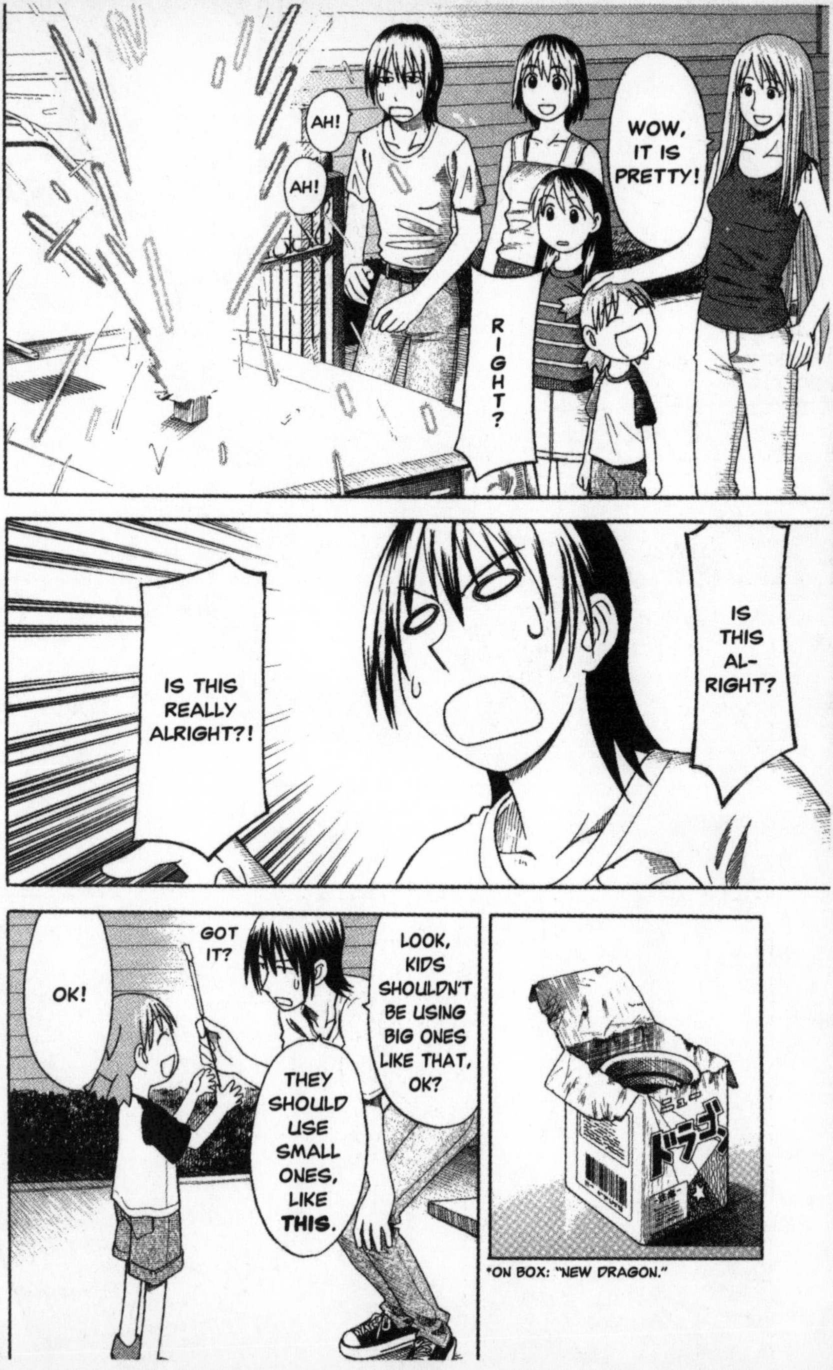
WOW, IT IS PRETTY!
RIGHT?
AH!
AH!
IS THIS AL-RIGHT?
IS THIS REALLY ALRIGHT?!
LOOK, KIDS SHOULDN'T BE USING BIG ONES LIKE THAT, OK?
THEY SHOULD USE SMALL ONES, LIKE **THIS**.
GOT IT?
OK!

*ON BOX: "NEW DRAGON."

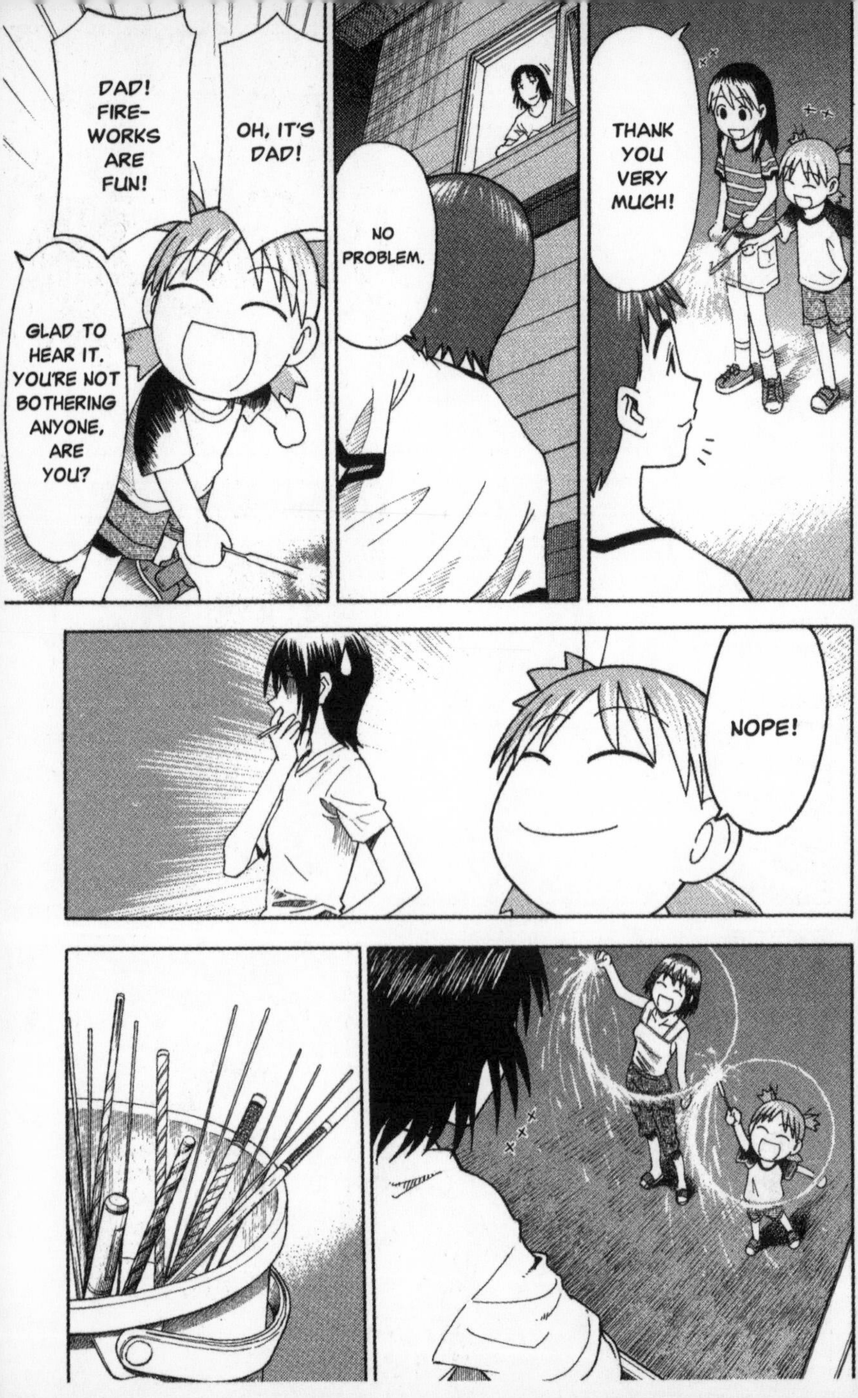
THANK YOU VERY MUCH!
NO PROBLEM.
OH, IT'S DAD!
DAD! FIRE-WORKS ARE FUN!
GLAD TO HEAR IT. YOU'RE NOT BOTHERING ANYONE, ARE YOU?
NOPE!

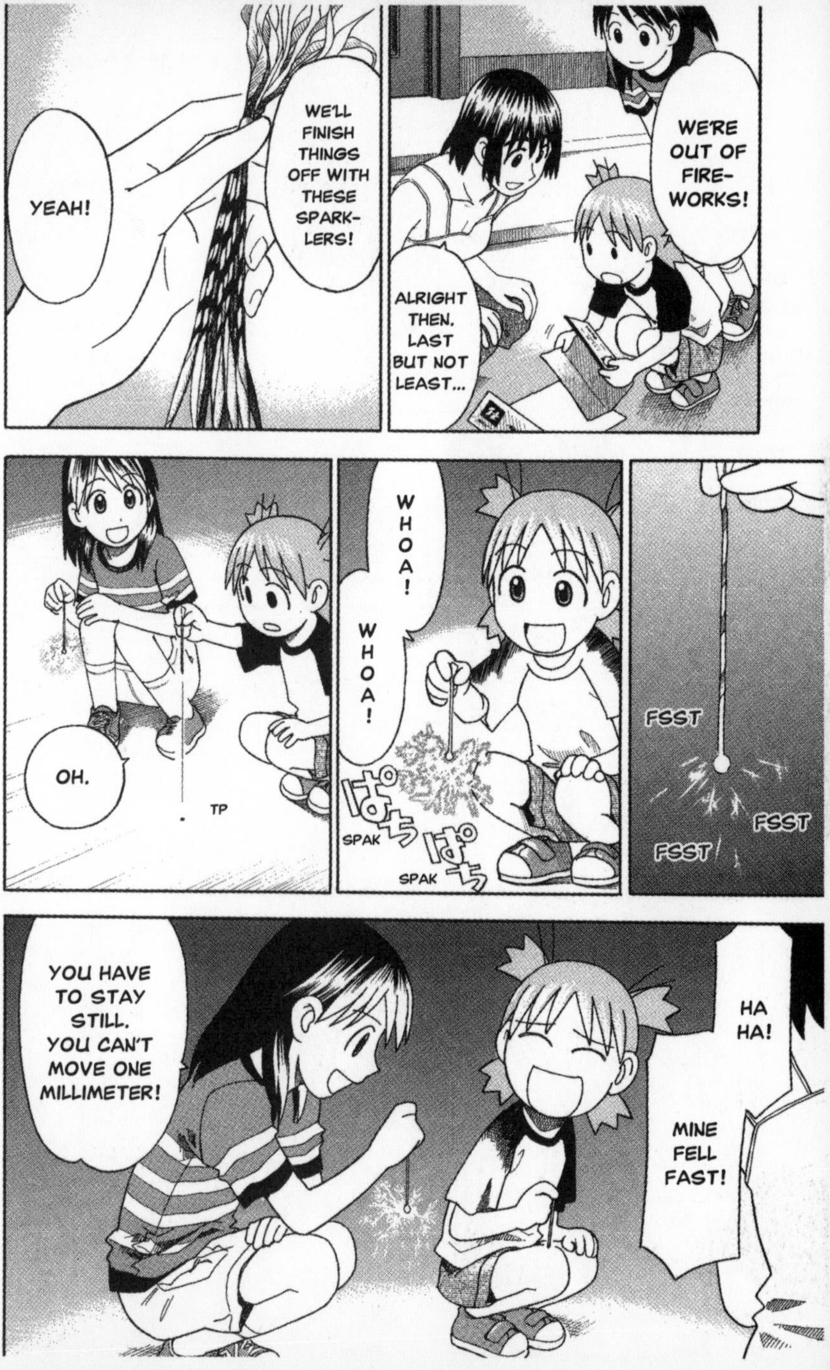
WE'RE OUT OF FIRE-WORKS!
ALRIGHT THEN. LAST BUT NOT LEAST...
WE'LL FINISH THINGS OFF WITH THESE SPARK-LERS!
YEAH!
FSST
FSST
FSST
WHOA!
WHOA!
ぱち SPAK
ぱち SPAK
OH.
TP
HA HA!
MINE FELL FAST!
YOU HAVE TO STAY STILL. YOU CAN'T MOVE ONE MILLIMETER!

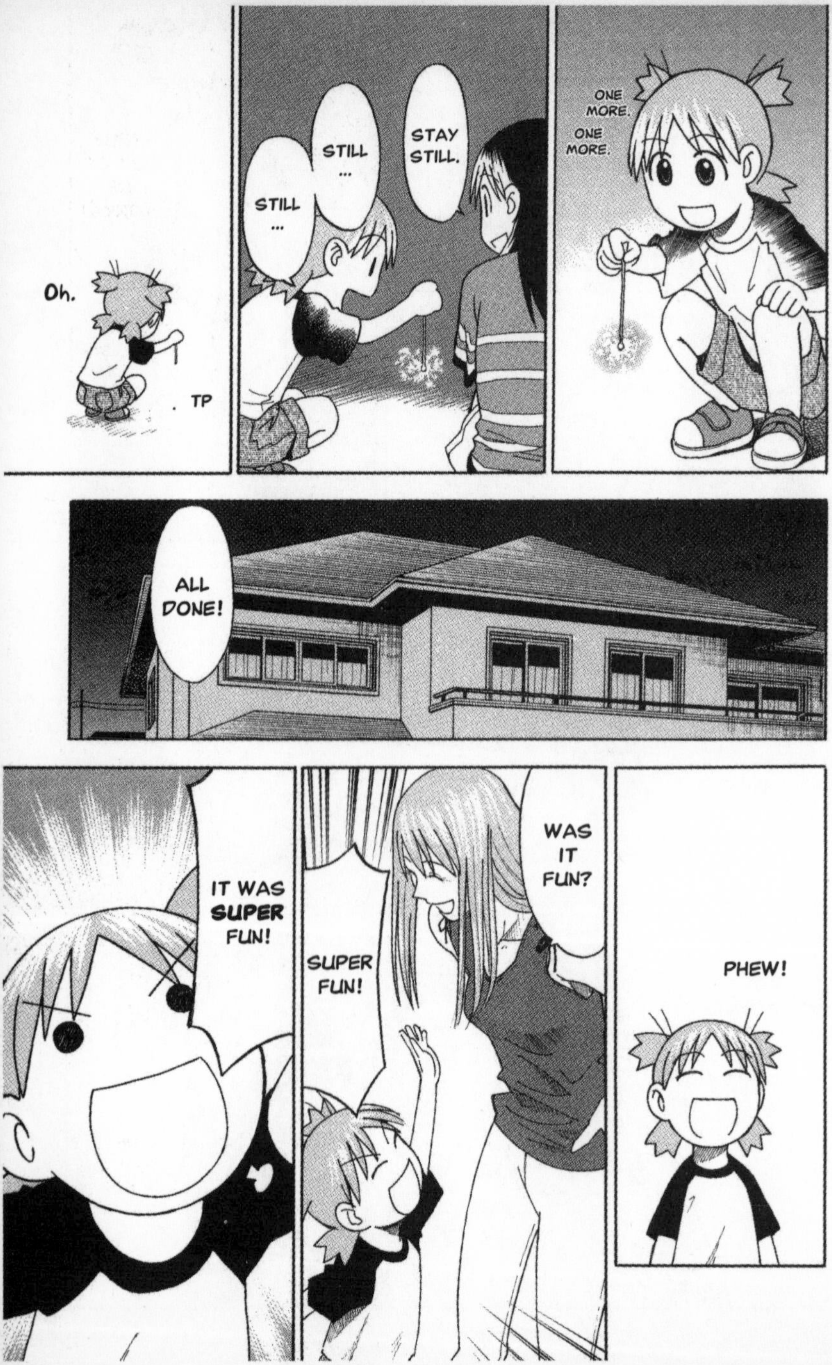
ONE MORE.
ONE MORE.
STAY STILL.
STILL ...
STILL ...
Oh.
TP
ALL DONE!
PHEW!
WAS IT FUN?
SUPER FUN!
IT WAS **SUPER** FUN!

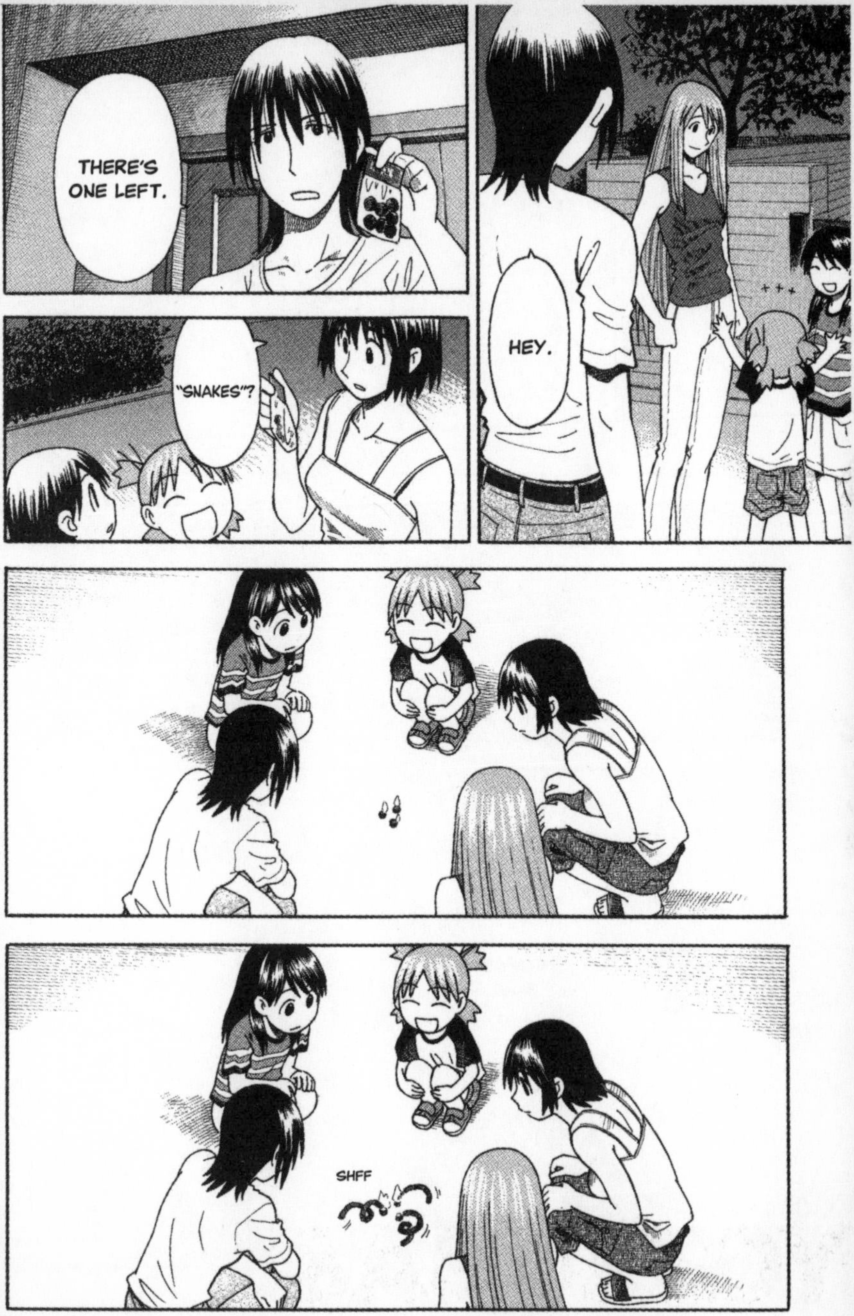
HEY.
THERE'S ONE LEFT.
"SNAKES"?
SHFF

YOTSUBA&!

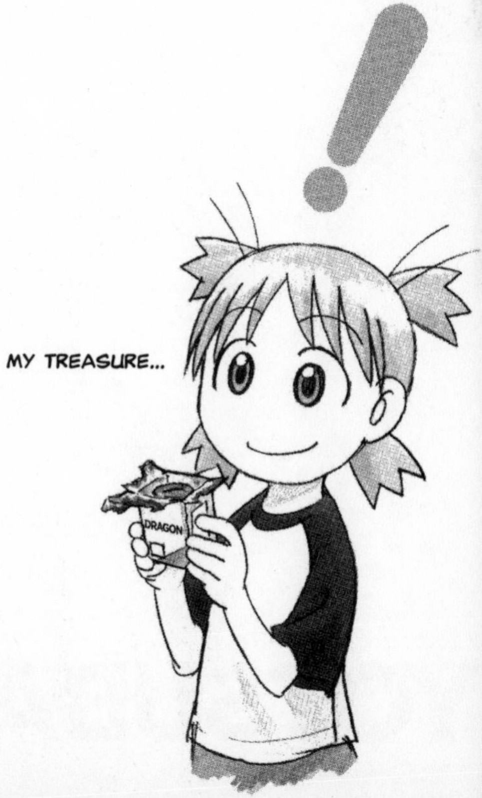
MY TREASURE...
DRAGON

YOTSUBA&
FLOWERS

CHAPTER 17

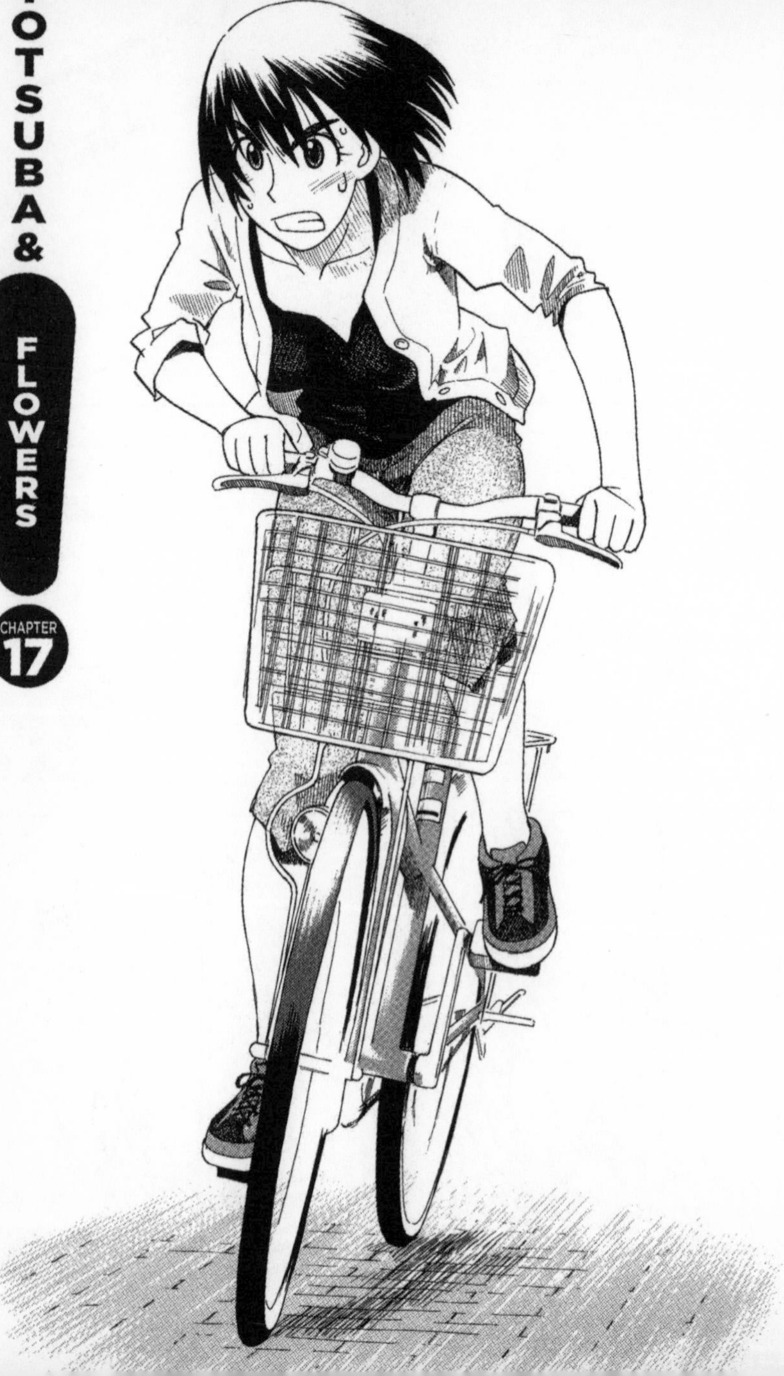

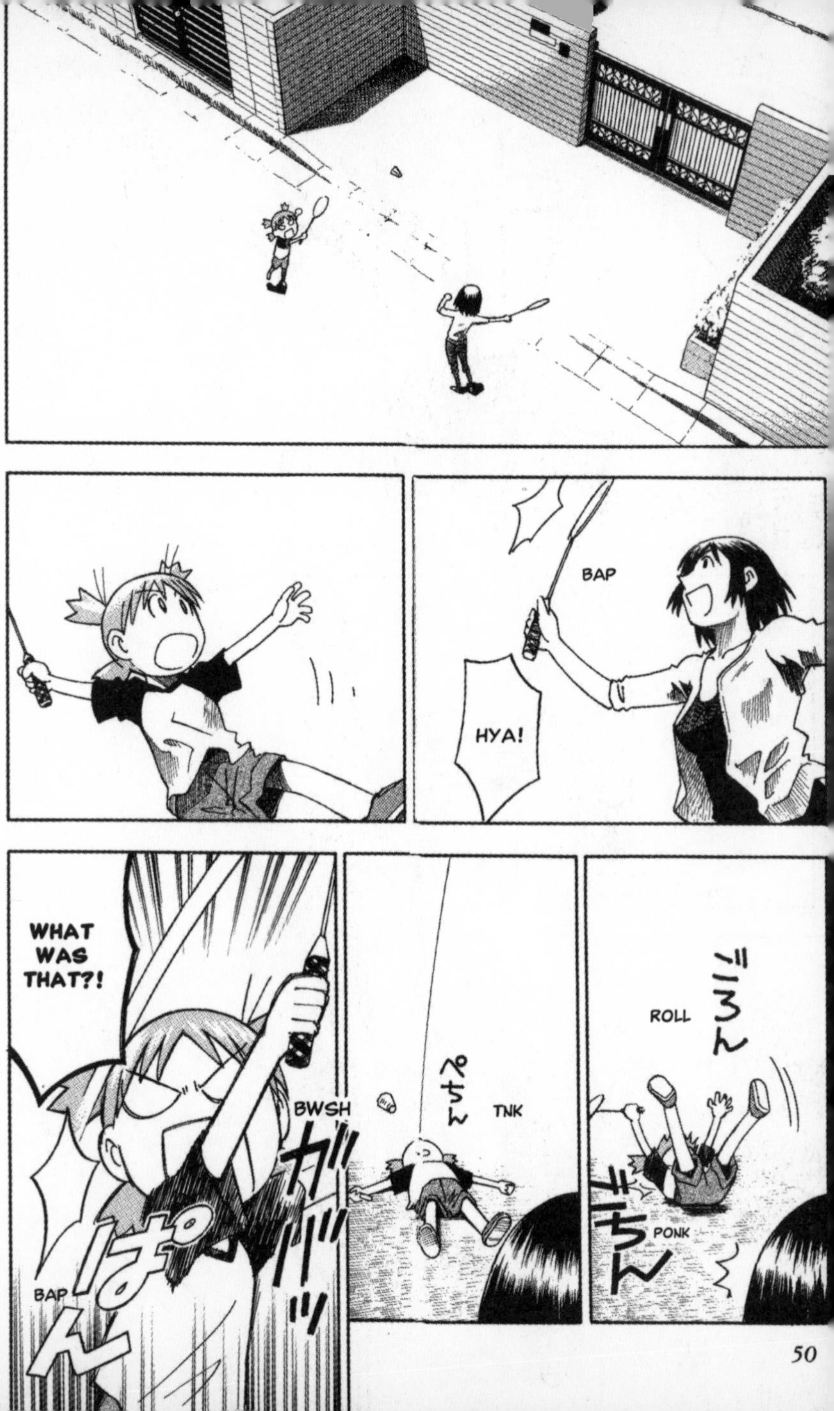
BAP
HYA!
ごろん
ROLL
ごちん
PONK
ぺちん
TNK
WHAT WAS THAT?!
BWSH
ガバッ
ぱん
BAP

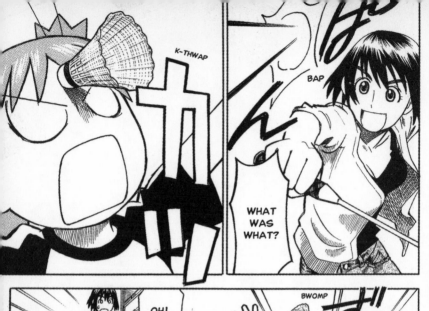

K-THWAP

BAP

WHAT WAS WHAT?

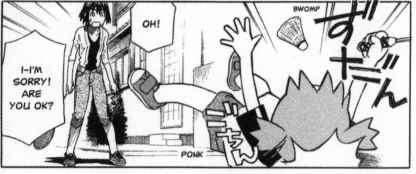

OH!

I-I'M SORRY! ARE YOU OK?

BWOMP

PONK

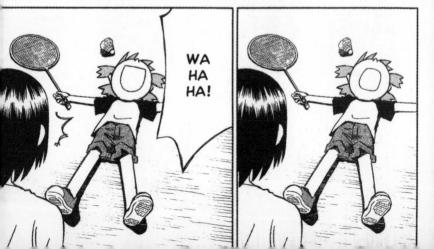

WA HA HA!

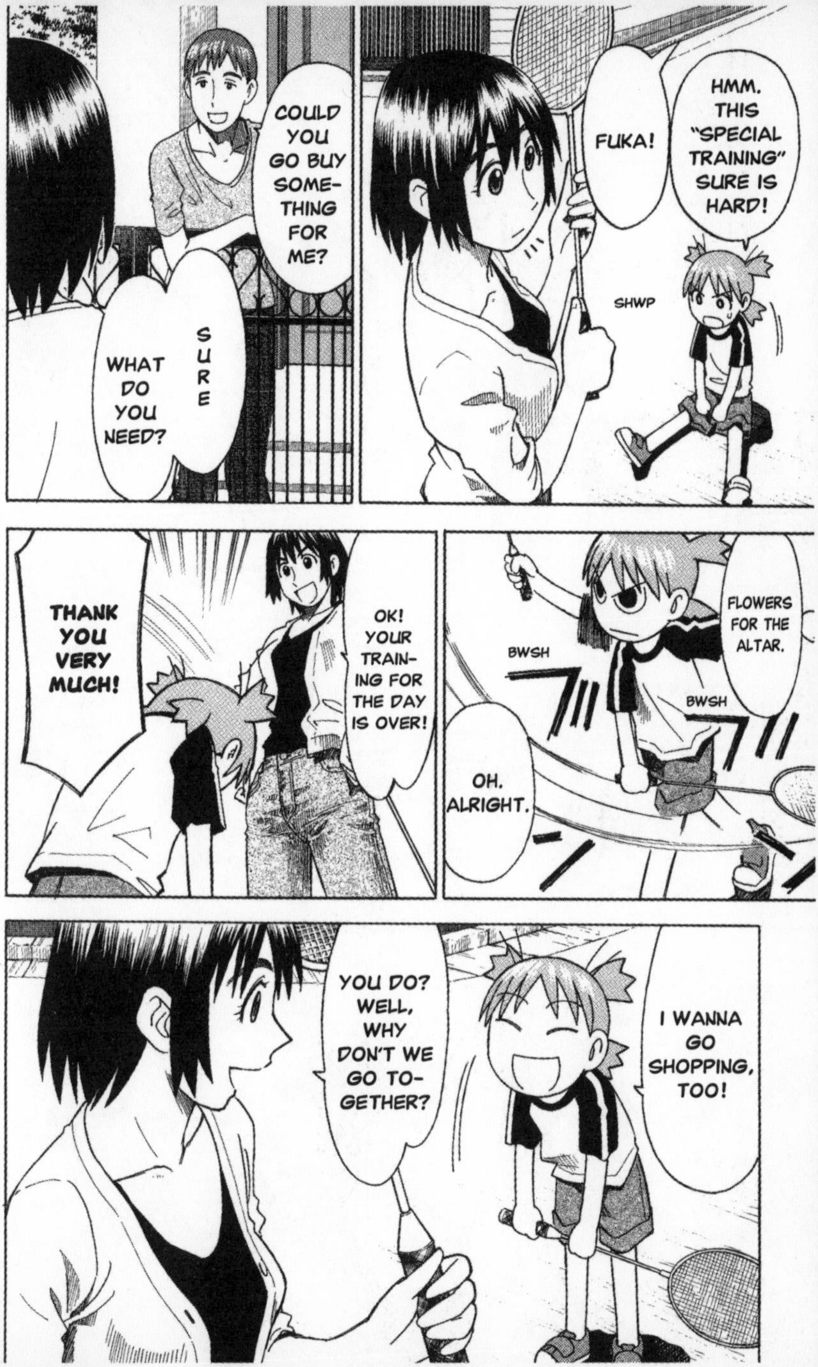
HMM. THIS "SPECIAL TRAINING" SURE IS HARD!
FUKA!
SHWP
COULD YOU GO BUY SOME-THING FOR ME?
SURE
WHAT DO YOU NEED?
FLOWERS FOR THE ALTAR.
BWSH
BWSH
OH. ALRIGHT.
OK! YOUR TRAIN-ING FOR THE DAY IS OVER!
THANK YOU VERY MUCH!
I WANNA GO SHOPPING, TOO!
YOU DO? WELL, WHY DON'T WE GO TO-GETHER?

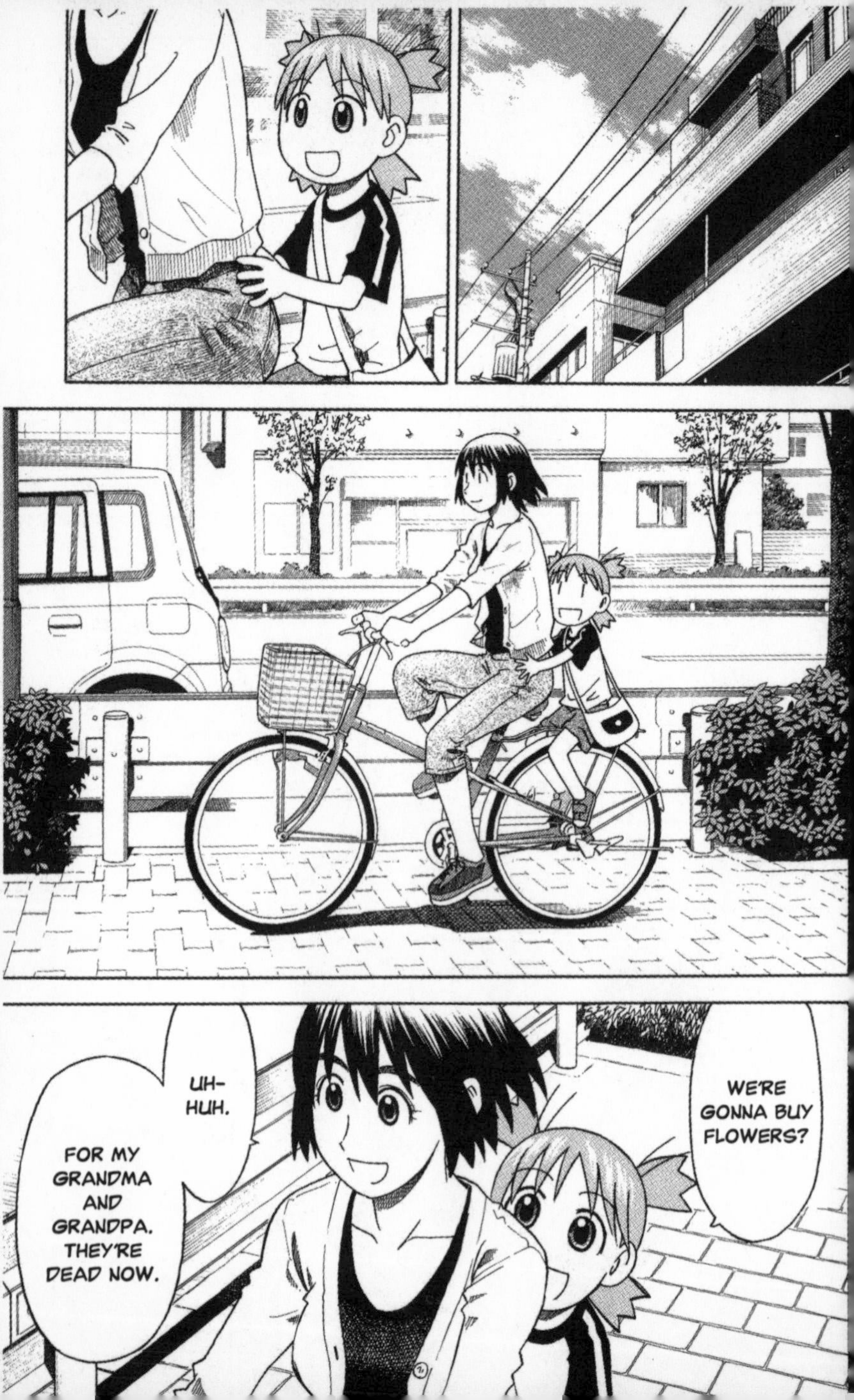
WE'RE GONNA BUY FLOWERS?
UH-HUH.
FOR MY GRANDMA AND GRANDPA. THEY'RE DEAD NOW.

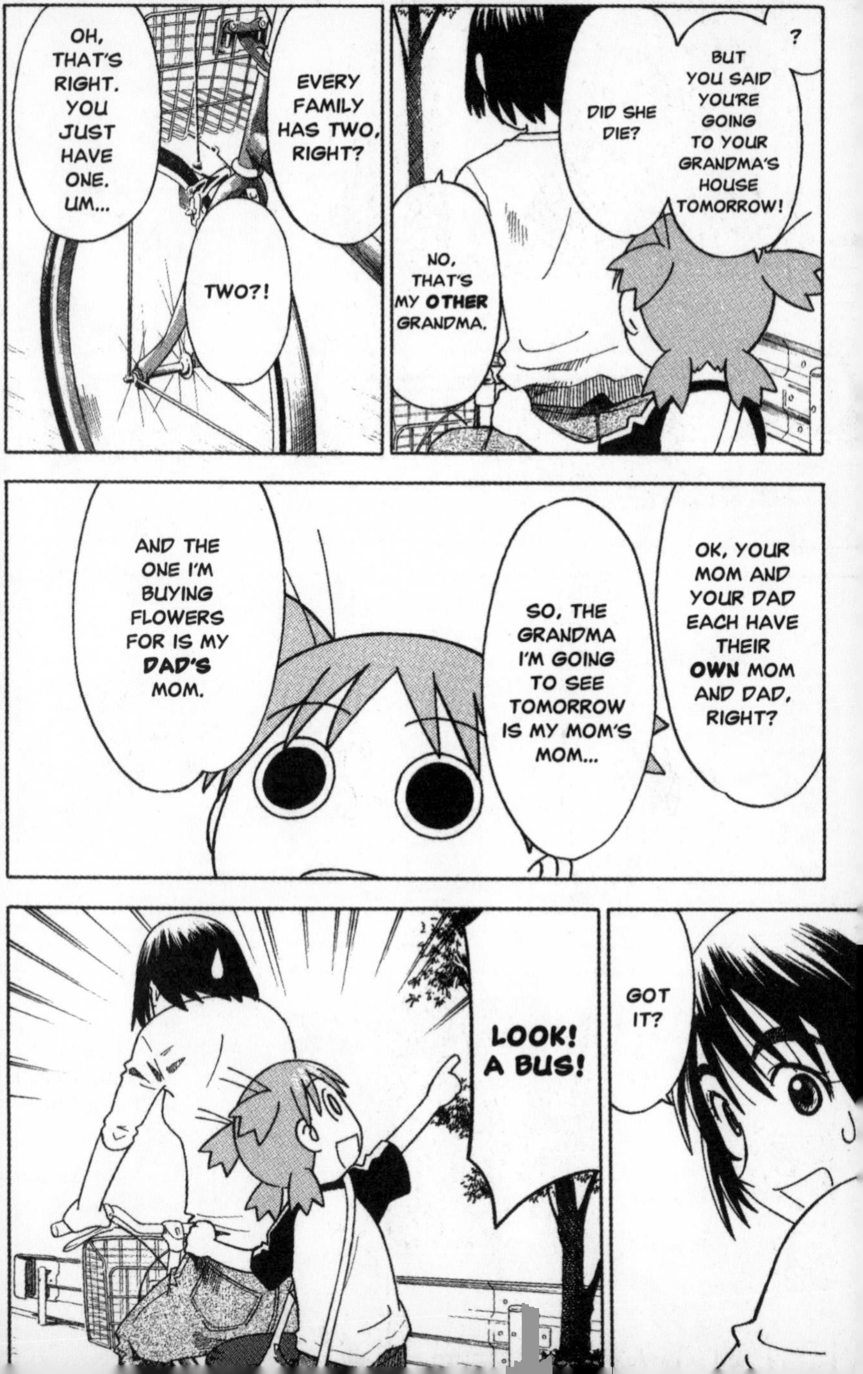
?
BUT YOU SAID YOU'RE GOING TO YOUR GRANDMA'S HOUSE TOMORROW!
DID SHE DIE?
NO, THAT'S MY **OTHER** GRANDMA.
EVERY FAMILY HAS TWO, RIGHT?
TWO?!
OH, THAT'S RIGHT. YOU JUST HAVE ONE. UM...
OK, YOUR MOM AND YOUR DAD EACH HAVE THEIR **OWN** MOM AND DAD, RIGHT?
SO, THE GRANDMA I'M GOING TO SEE TOMORROW IS MY MOM'S MOM...
AND THE ONE I'M BUYING FLOWERS FOR IS MY **DAD'S** MOM.
GOT IT?
LOOK! A BUS!

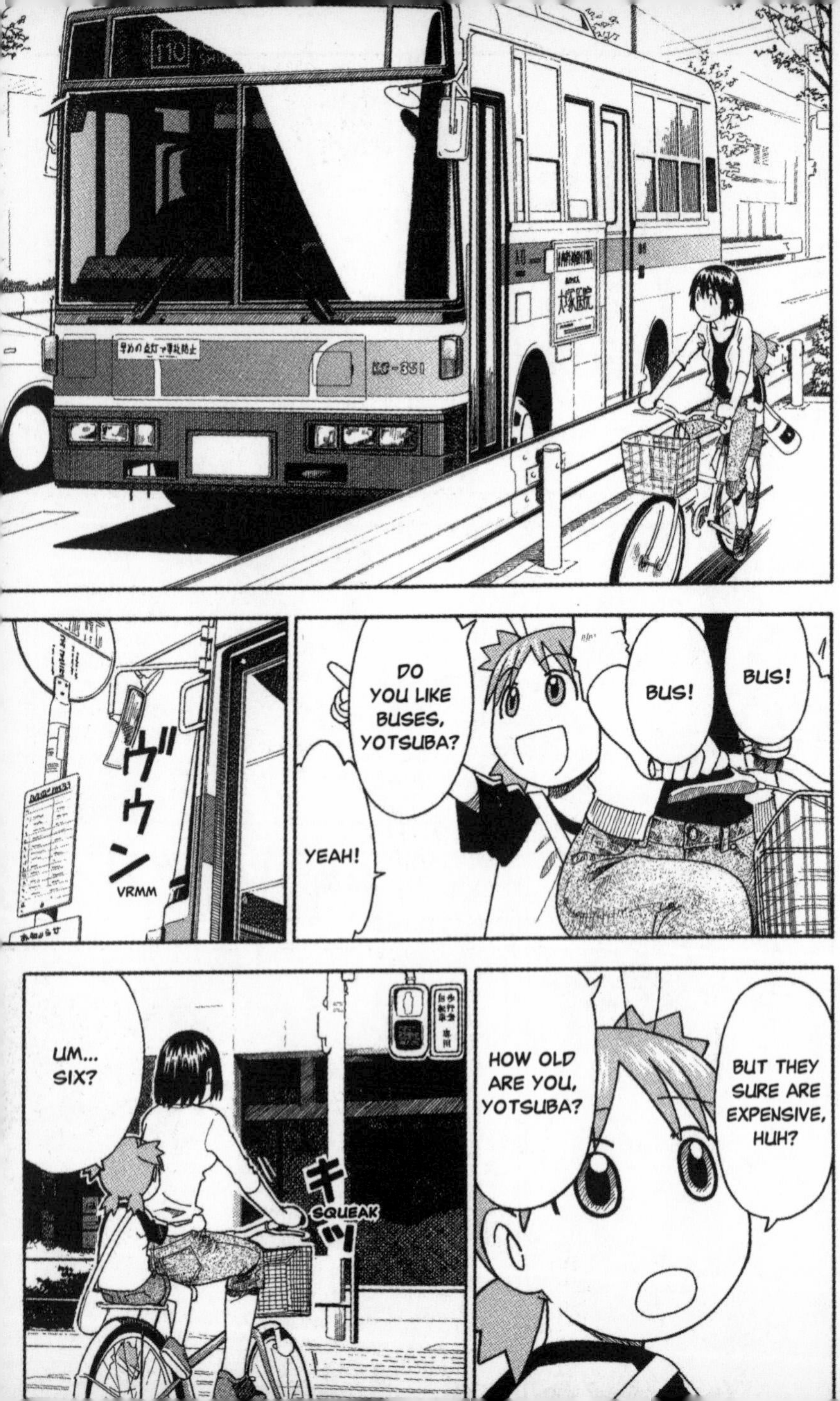
BUS!
BUS!
DO YOU LIKE BUSES, YOTSUBA?
YEAH!
ヴウン
VRMM
BUT THEY SURE ARE EXPENSIVE, HUH?
HOW OLD ARE YOU, YOTSUBA?
UM... SIX?
キッ
SQUEAK

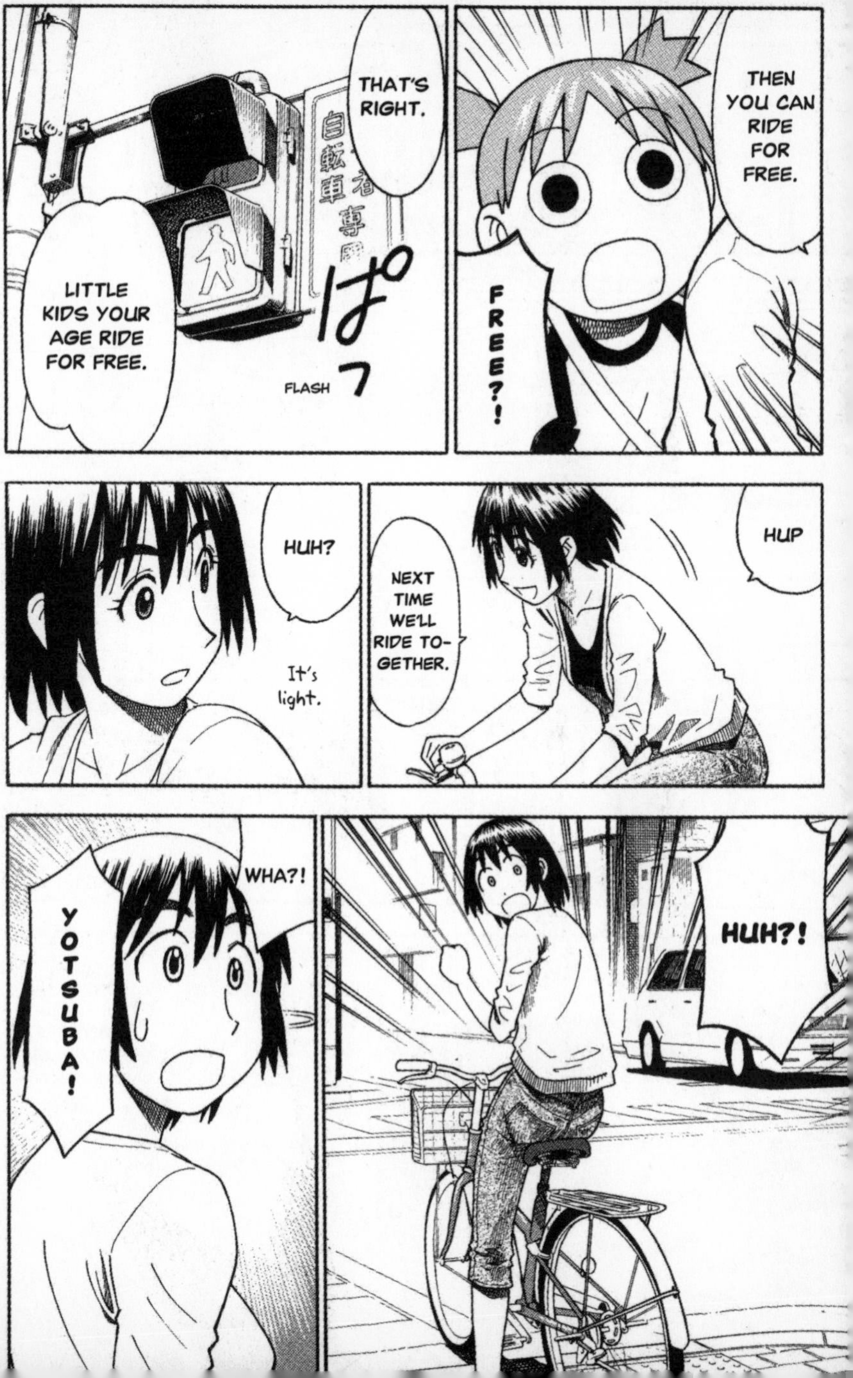
THEN YOU CAN RIDE FOR FREE.
FREE?!
THAT'S RIGHT.
FLASH
LITTLE KIDS YOUR AGE RIDE FOR FREE.
HUP
NEXT TIME WE'LL RIDE TO-GETHER.
HUH?
It's light.
HUH?!
WHA?!
YOTSUBA!

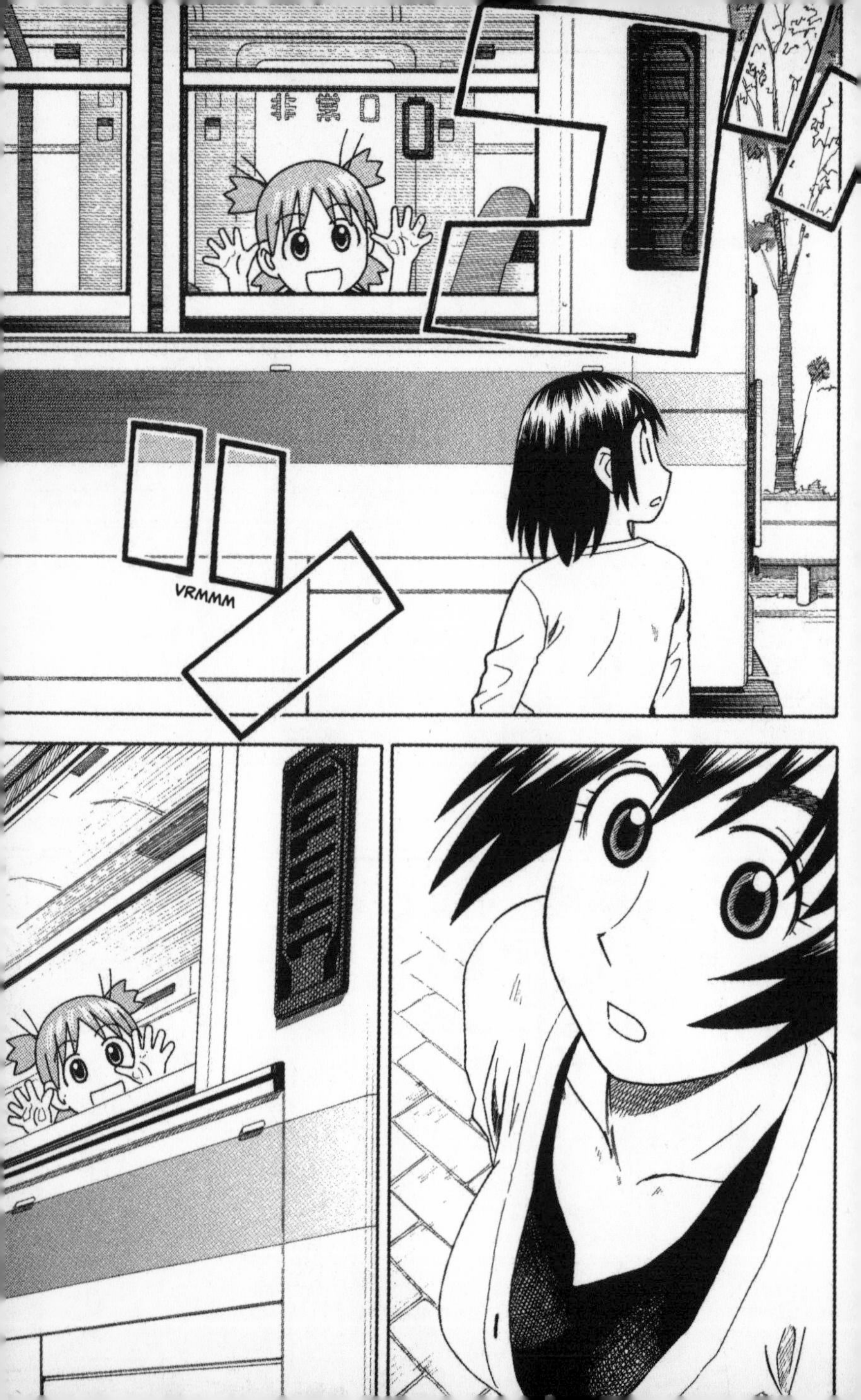
非常口
VRMMM

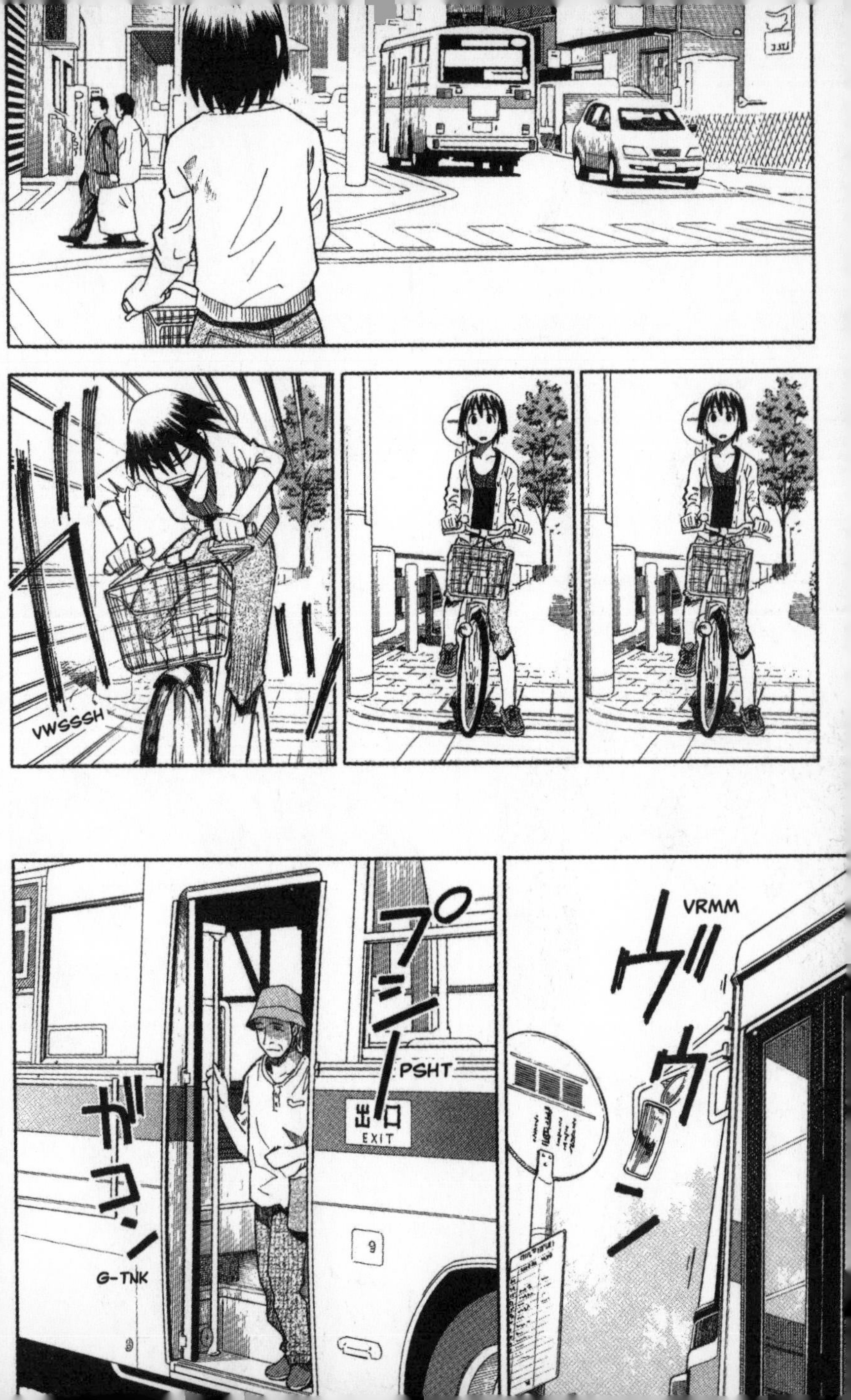
VWSSSH
VRMM
ヴゥーー
プシーー
PSHT
出口
EXIT
ガコーー
G-TNK

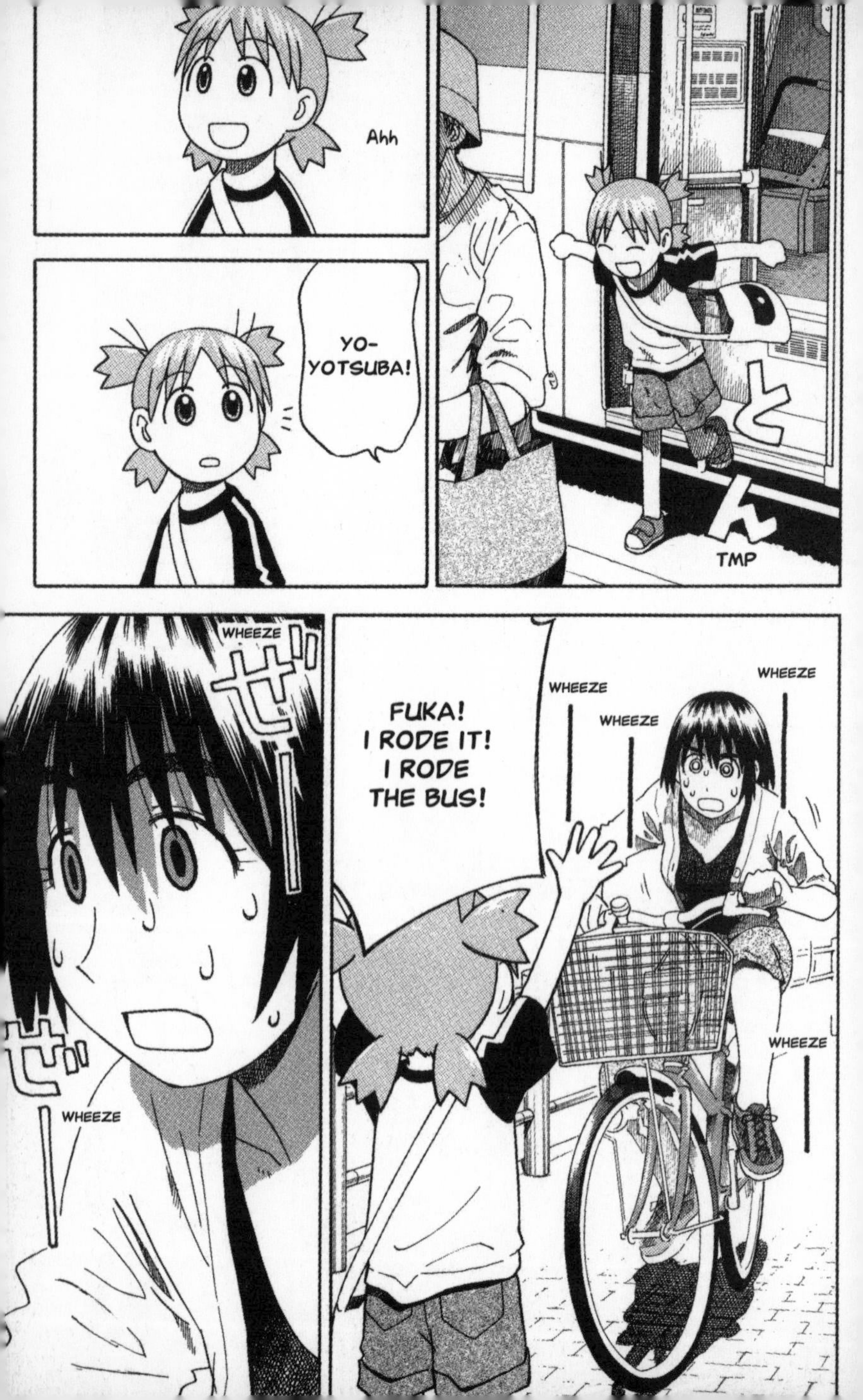

とん
TMP
Ahh
YO-
YOTSUBA!
FUKA!
I RODE IT!
I RODE
THE BUS!
WHEEZE
WHEEZE
WHEEZE
WHEEZE
WHEEZE
WHEEZE

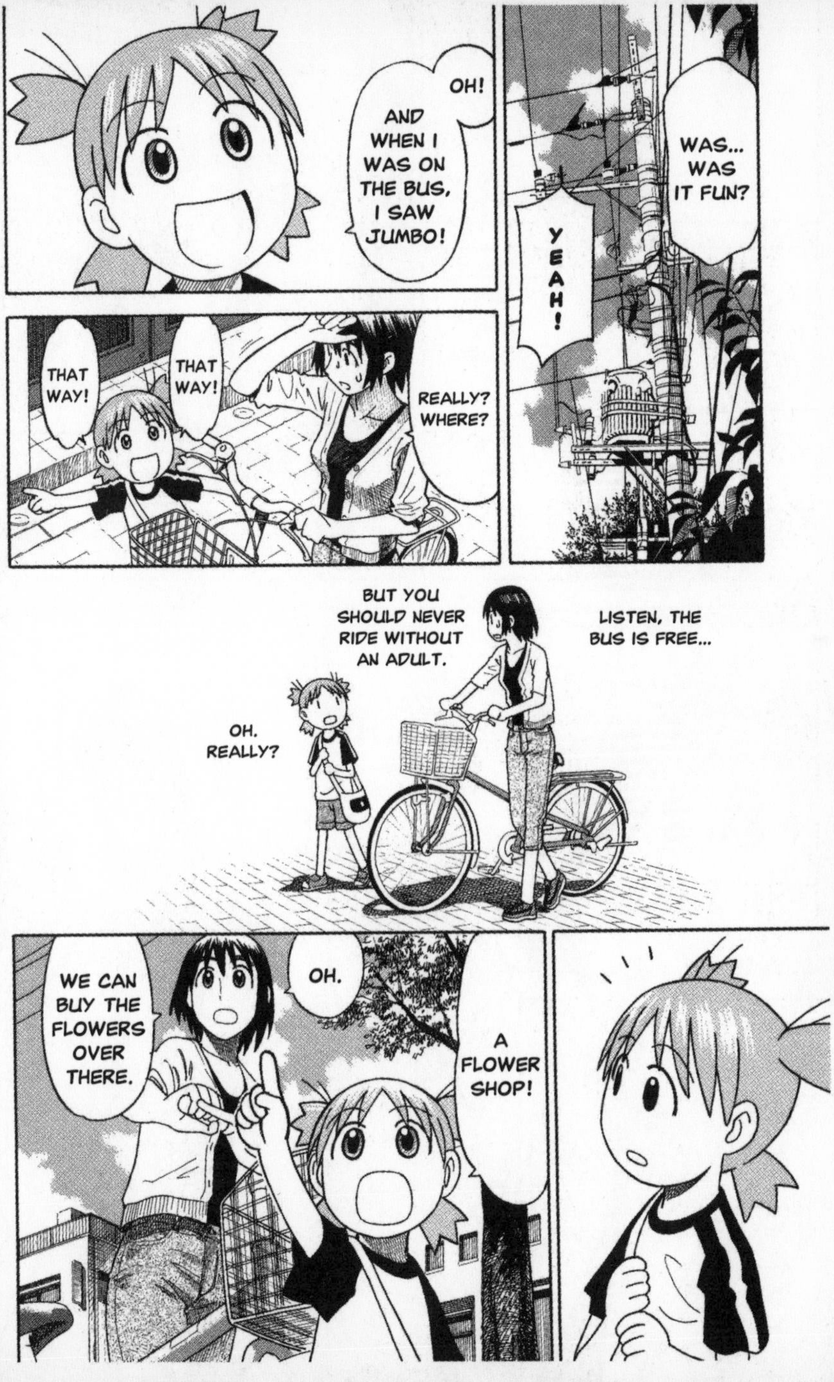

WAS... WAS IT FUN?
YEAH!
OH!
AND WHEN I WAS ON THE BUS, I SAW JUMBO!
REALLY? WHERE?
THAT WAY!
THAT WAY!
LISTEN, THE BUS IS FREE...
BUT YOU SHOULD NEVER RIDE WITHOUT AN ADULT.
OH. REALLY?
A FLOWER SHOP!
OH.
WE CAN BUY THE FLOWERS OVER THERE.

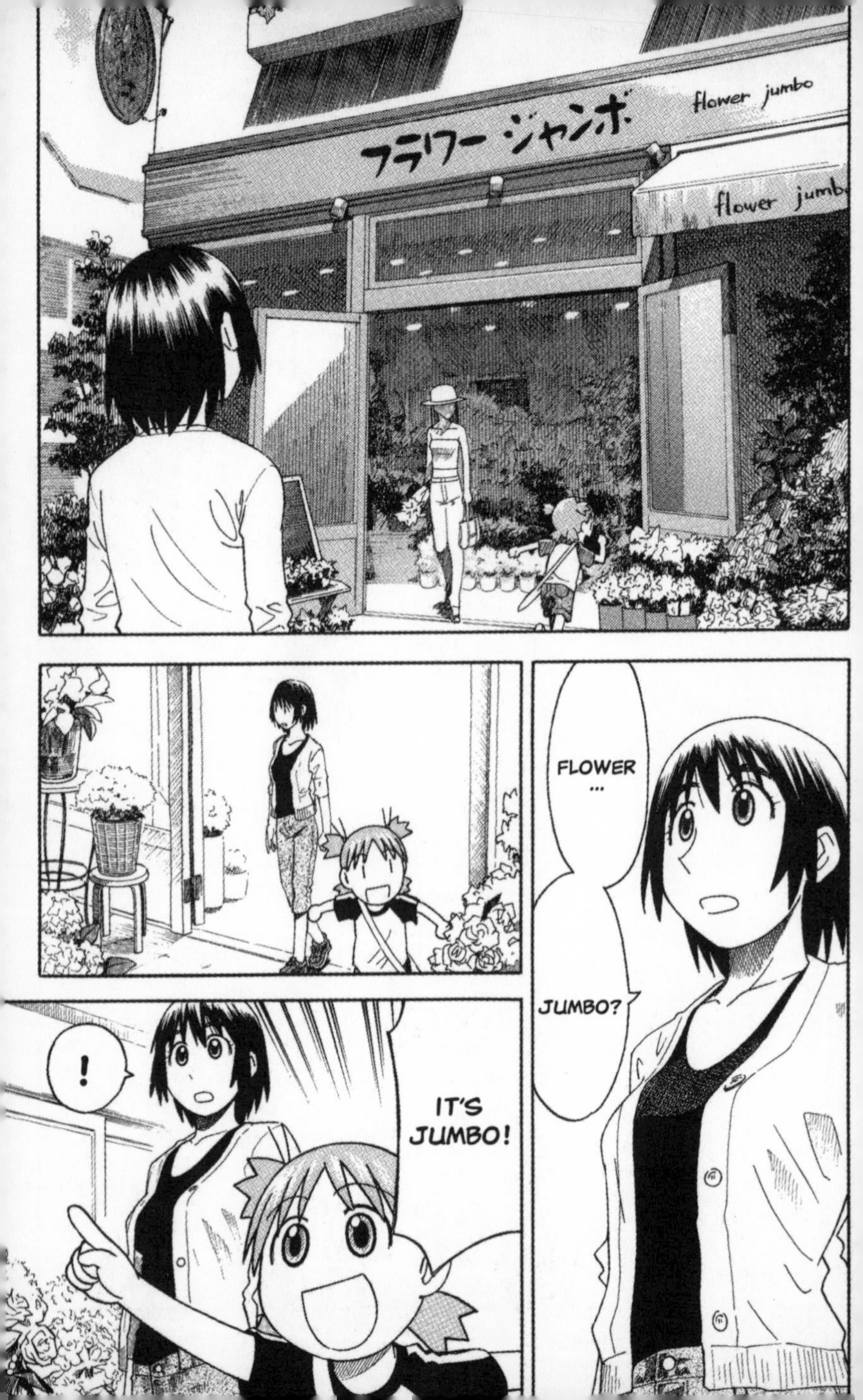
flower jumbo
フラワー ジャンボ
flower jumb
FLOWER ...
JUMBO?
!
IT'S JUMBO!

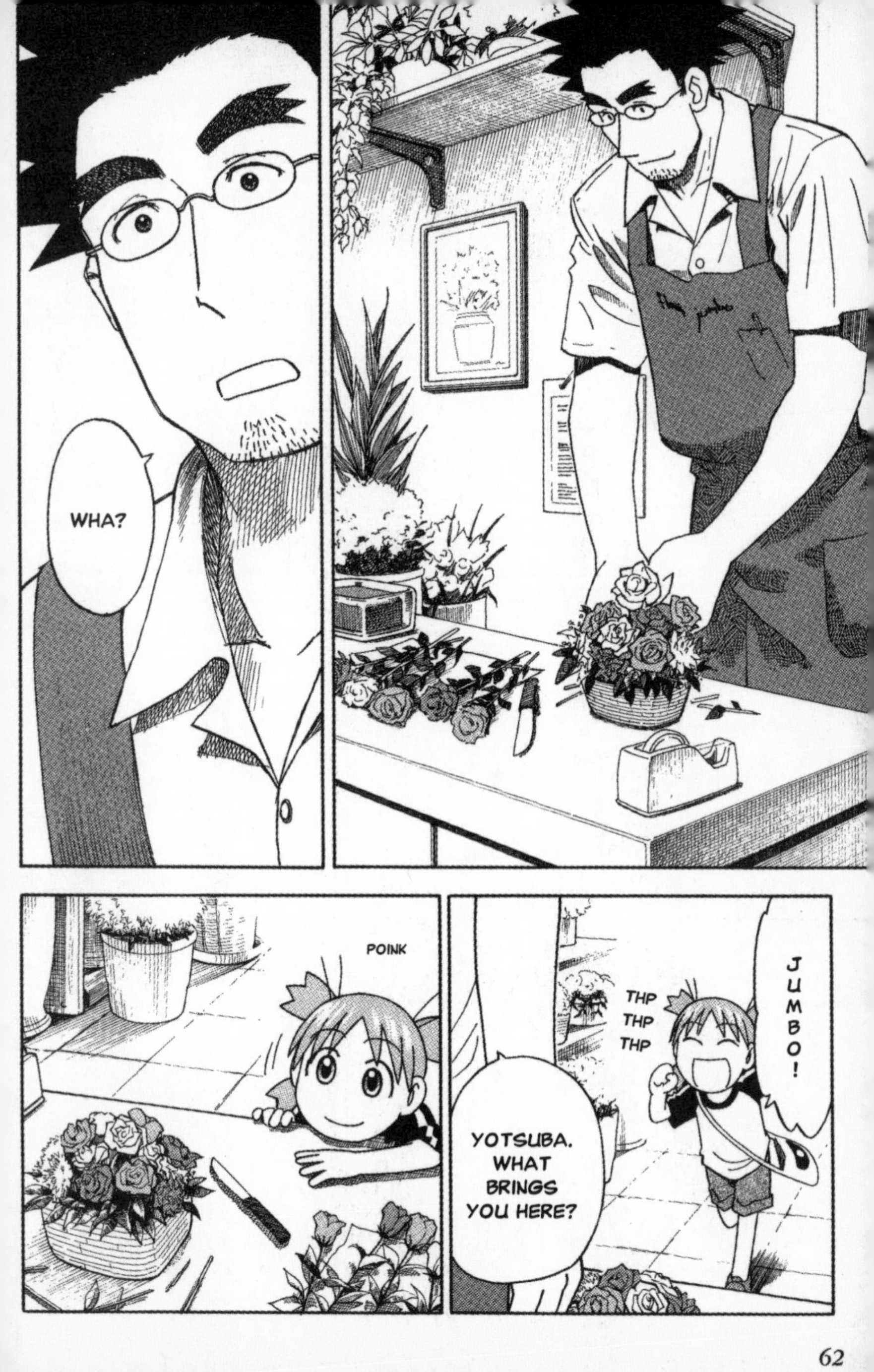
WHA?
JUMBO!
THP THP THP
YOTSUBA. WHAT BRINGS YOU HERE?
POINK

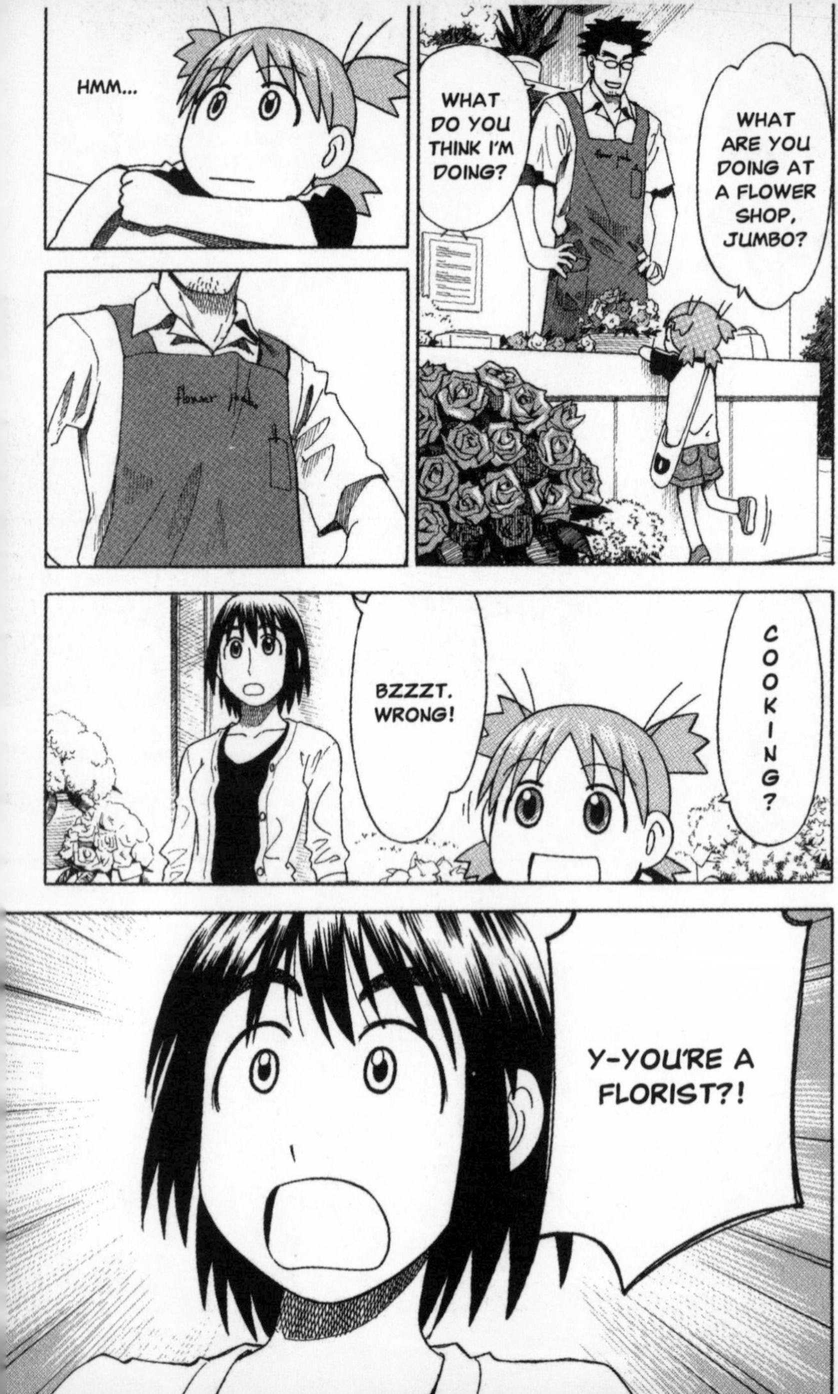
WHAT ARE YOU DOING AT A FLOWER SHOP, JUMBO?
WHAT DO YOU THINK I'M DOING?
HMM...
COOKING?
BZZZT. WRONG!
Y-YOU'RE A FLORIST?!

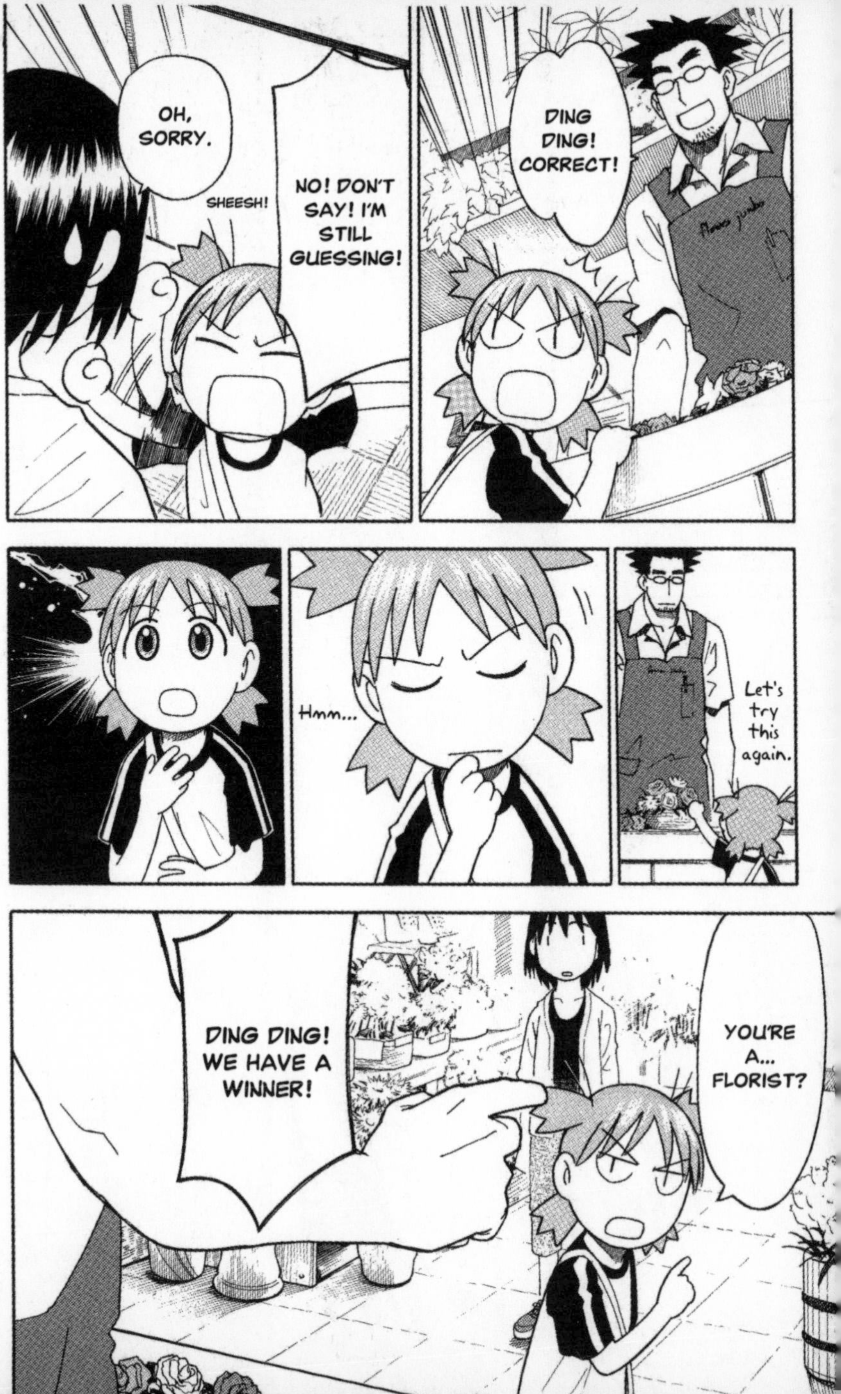
DING DING! CORRECT!
NO! DON'T SAY! I'M STILL GUESSING!
OH, SORRY.
SHEESH!
Let's try this again.
Hmm...
YOU'RE A... FLORIST?
DING DING! WE HAVE A WINNER!

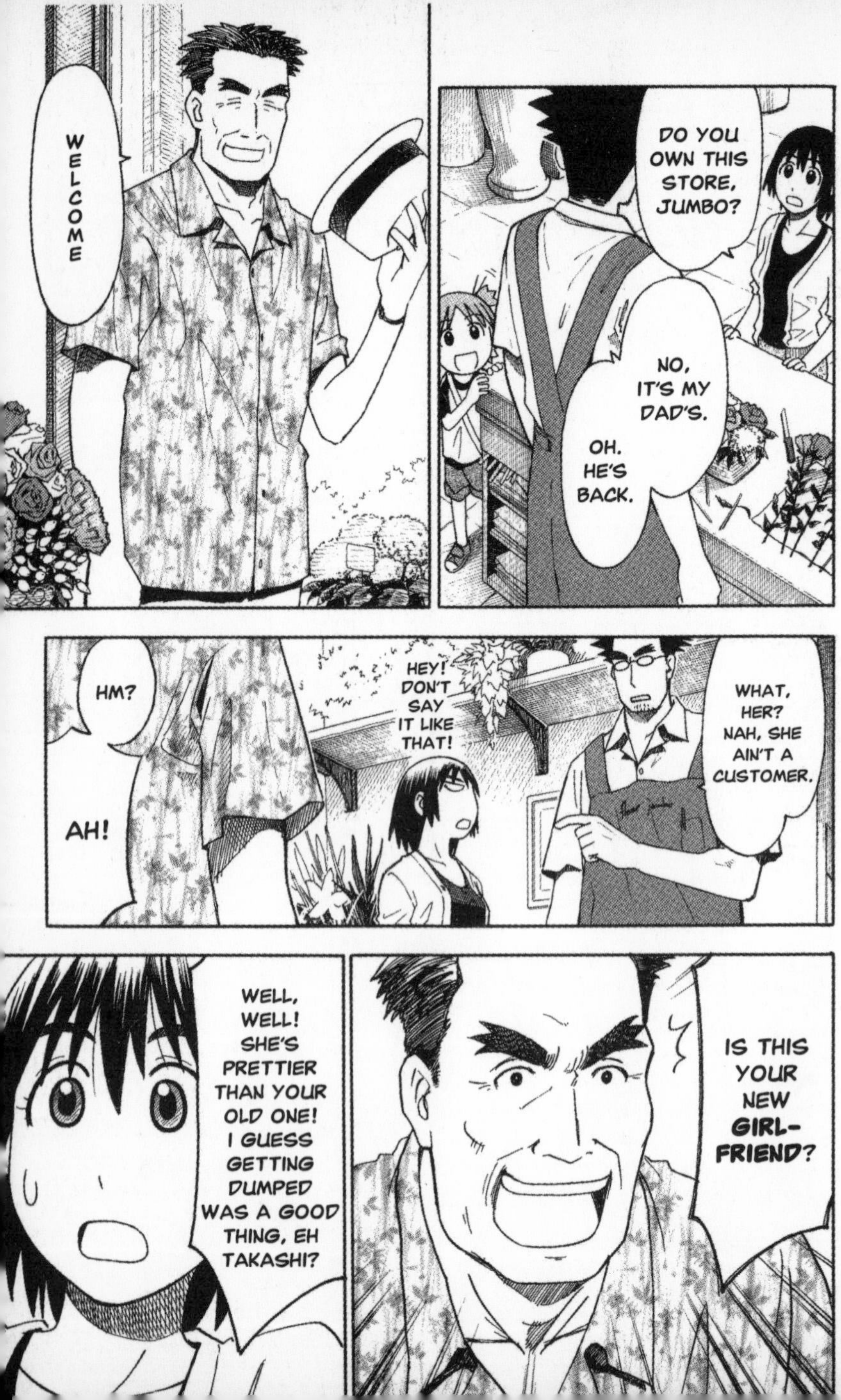
DO YOU OWN THIS STORE, JUMBO?
NO, IT'S MY DAD'S.
OH. HE'S BACK.
WELCOME
WHAT, HER? NAH, SHE AIN'T A CUSTOMER.
HEY! DON'T SAY IT LIKE THAT!
HM?
AH!
IS THIS YOUR NEW GIRL-FRIEND?
WELL, WELL! SHE'S PRETTIER THAN YOUR OLD ONE! I GUESS GETTING DUMPED WAS A GOOD THING, EH TAKASHI?

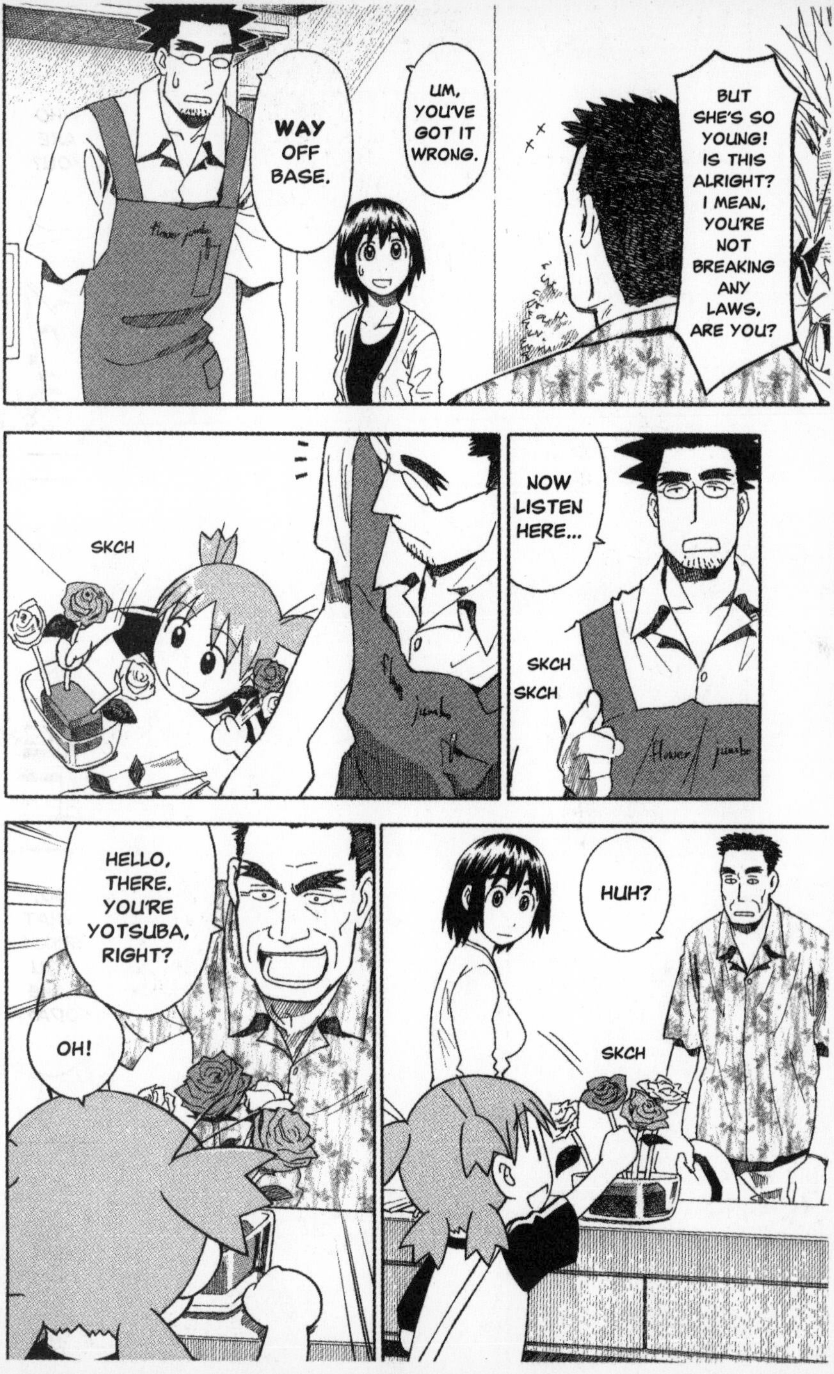
BUT SHE'S SO YOUNG! IS THIS ALRIGHT? I MEAN, YOU'RE NOT BREAKING ANY LAWS, ARE YOU?
UM, YOU'VE GOT IT WRONG.
WAY OFF BASE.
NOW LISTEN HERE...
SKCH
SKCH
SKCH
HUH?
SKCH
HELLO, THERE. YOU'RE YOTSUBA, RIGHT?
OH!

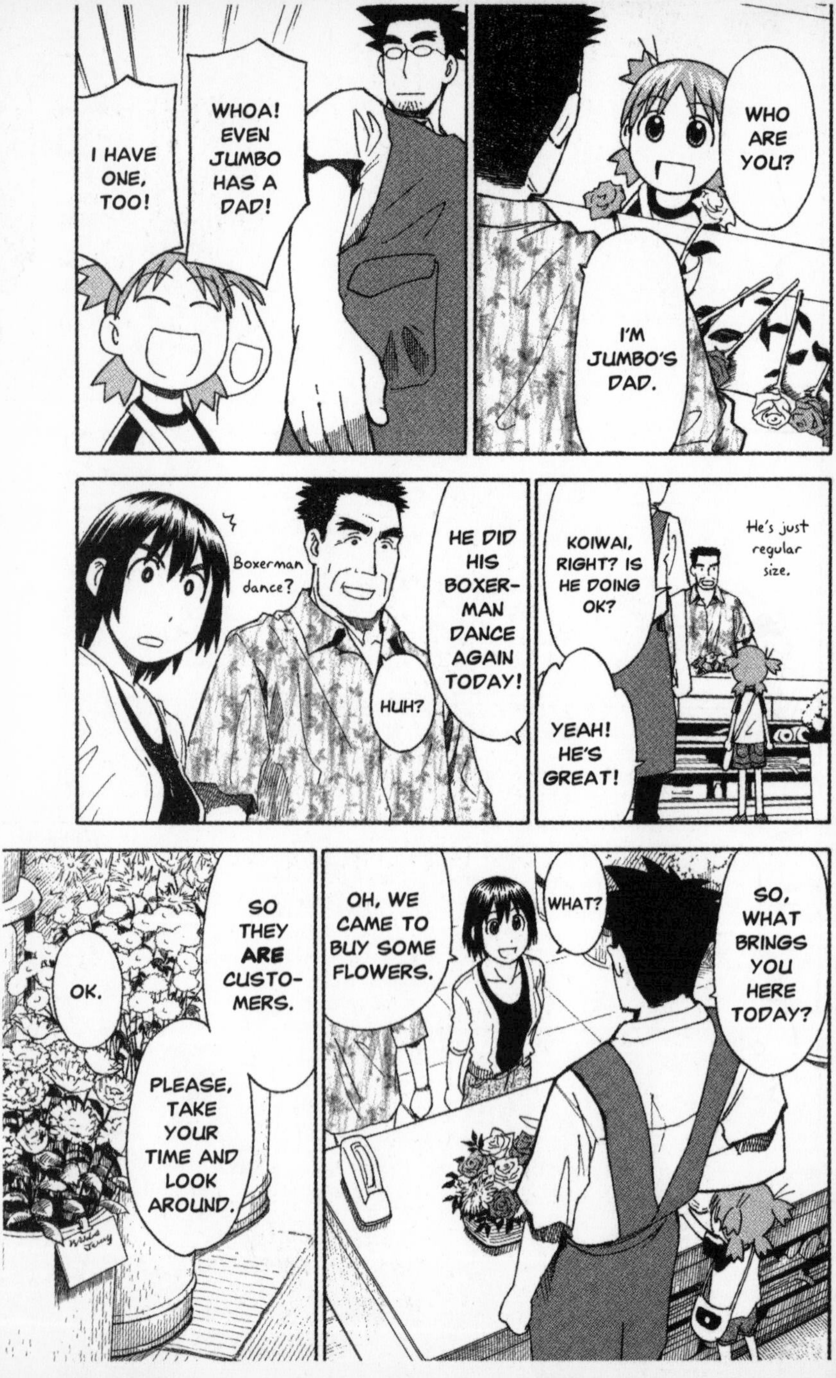
WHO ARE YOU?
I'M JUMBO'S DAD.
WHOA! EVEN JUMBO HAS A DAD!
I HAVE ONE, TOO!
KOIWAI, RIGHT? IS HE DOING OK?
YEAH! HE'S GREAT!
He's just regular size.
HE DID HIS BOXER-MAN DANCE AGAIN TODAY!
HUH?
Boxerman dance?
SO, WHAT BRINGS YOU HERE TODAY?
WHAT?
OH, WE CAME TO BUY SOME FLOWERS.
SO THEY **ARE** CUSTOMERS.
OK.
PLEASE, TAKE YOUR TIME AND LOOK AROUND.

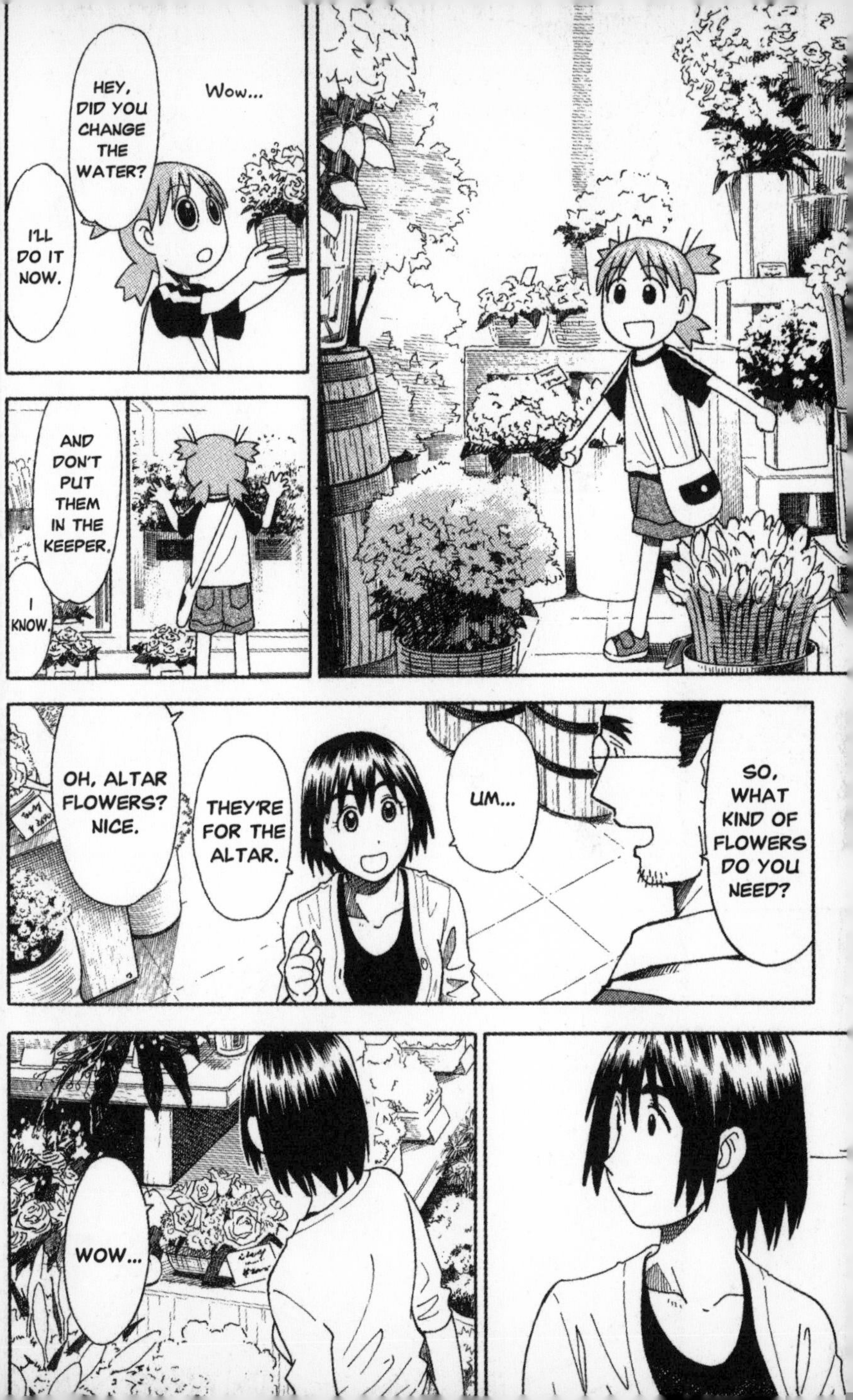
Wow...
HEY, DID YOU CHANGE THE WATER?
I'LL DO IT NOW.
AND DON'T PUT THEM IN THE KEEPER.
I KNOW.
SO, WHAT KIND OF FLOWERS DO YOU NEED?
UM...
THEY'RE FOR THE ALTAR.
OH, ALTAR FLOWERS? NICE.
WOW...

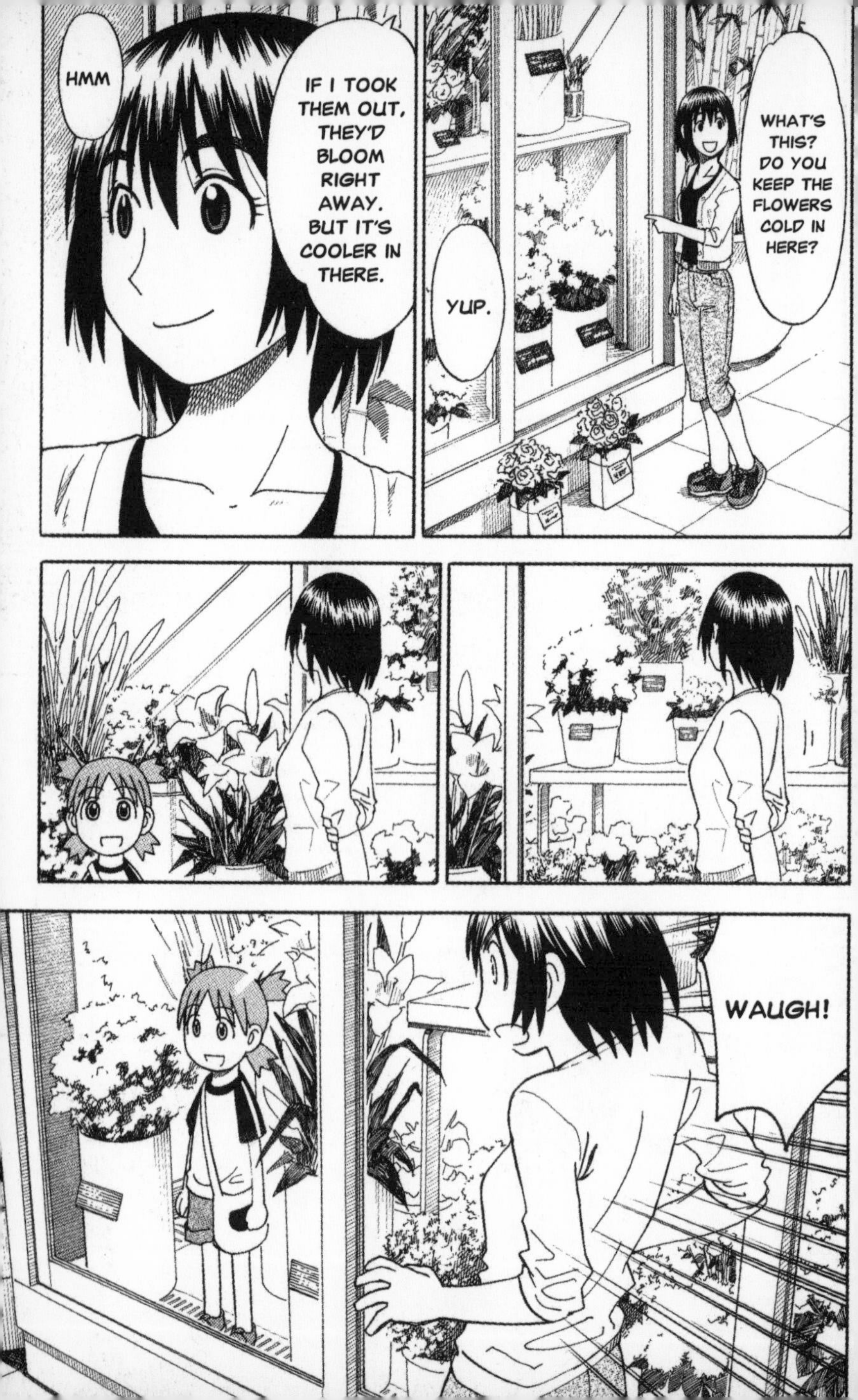
WHAT'S THIS? DO YOU KEEP THE FLOWERS COLD IN HERE?
YUP.
IF I TOOK THEM OUT, THEY'D BLOOM RIGHT AWAY. BUT IT'S COOLER IN THERE.
HMM
WAUGH!

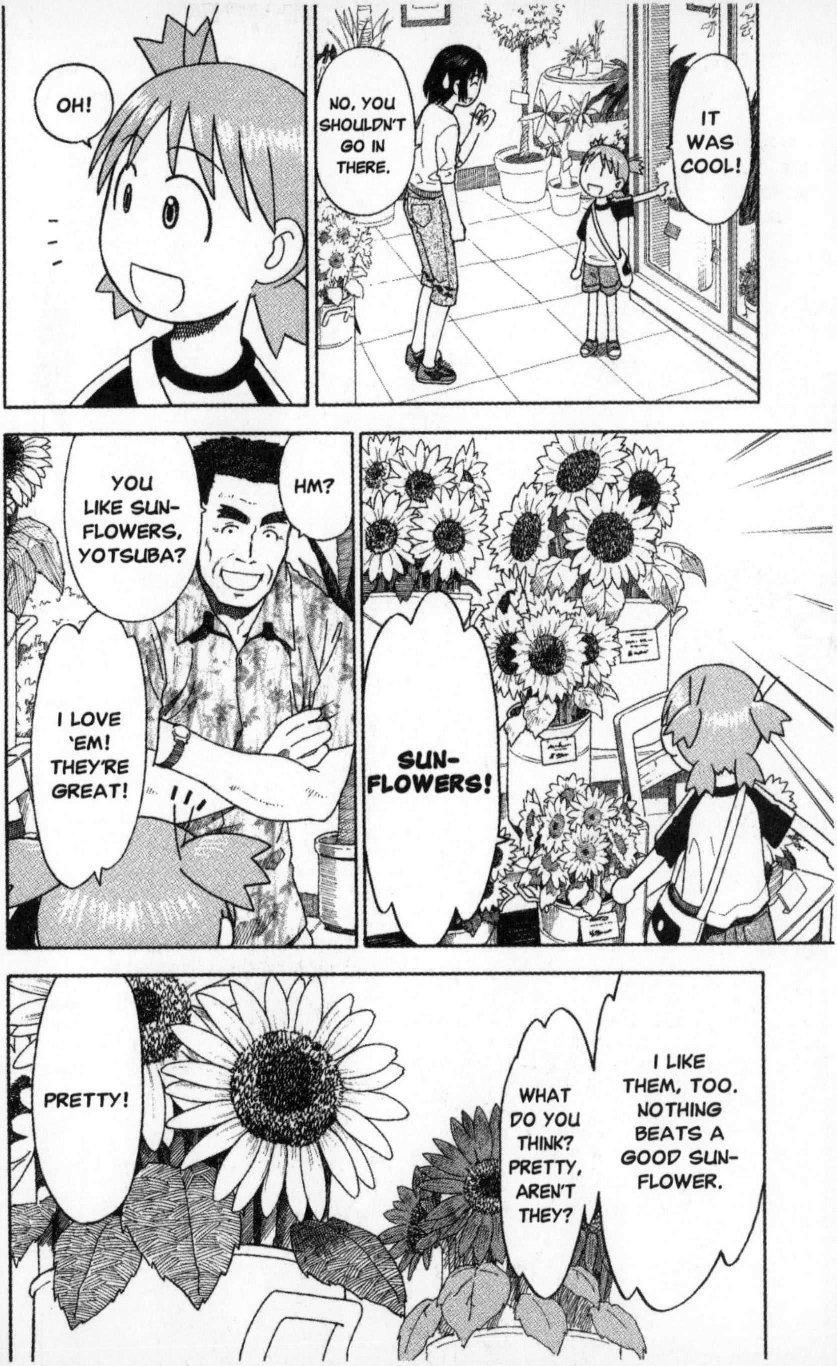
IT WAS COOL!
NO, YOU SHOULDN'T GO IN THERE.
OH!
SUN-FLOWERS!
HM?
YOU LIKE SUN-FLOWERS, YOTSUBA?
I LOVE 'EM! THEY'RE GREAT!
I LIKE THEM, TOO. NOTHING BEATS A GOOD SUN-FLOWER.
WHAT DO YOU THINK? PRETTY, AREN'T THEY?
PRETTY!

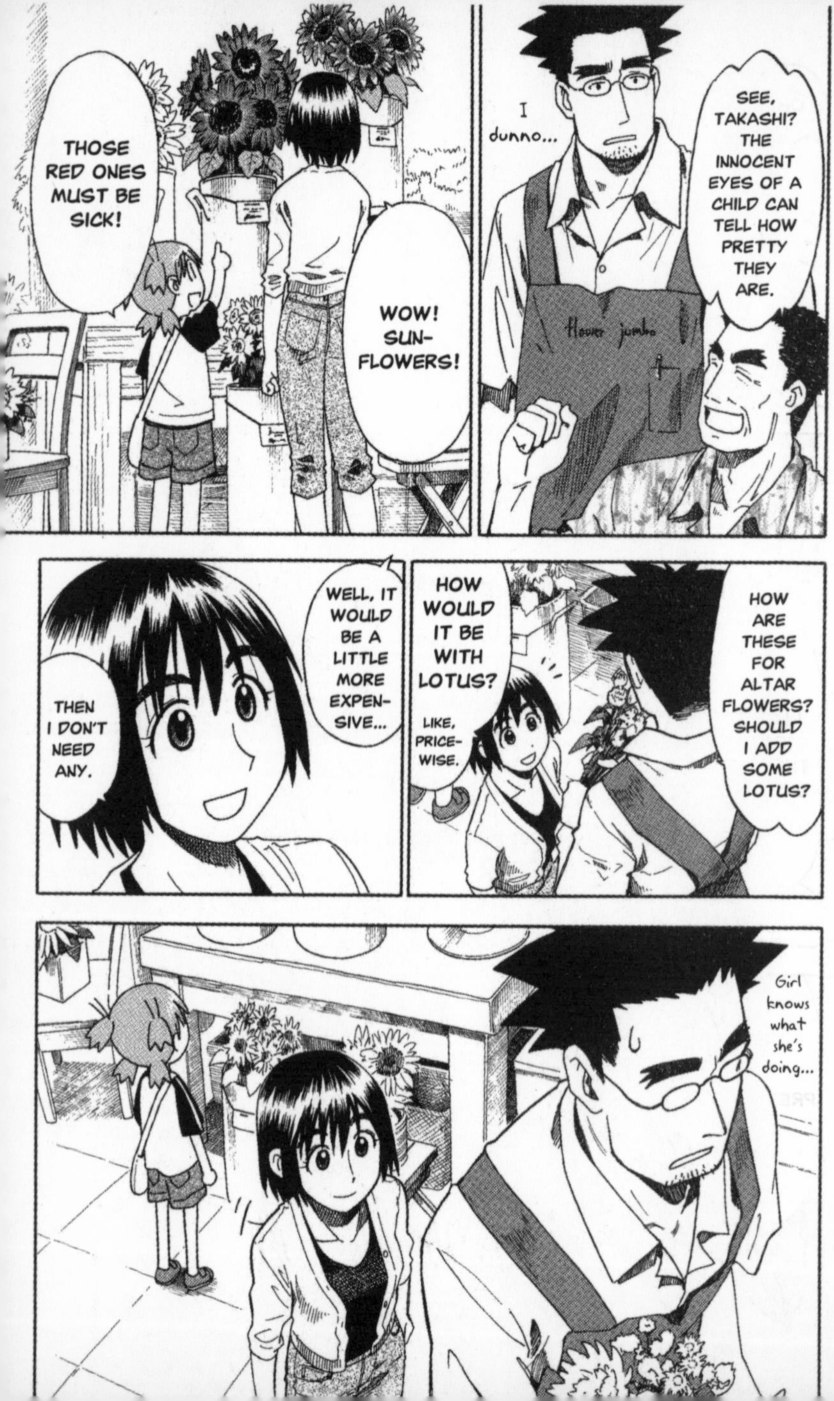
SEE, TAKASHI? THE INNOCENT EYES OF A CHILD CAN TELL HOW PRETTY THEY ARE.
I dunno...
flower jumbo
WOW! SUN-FLOWERS!
THOSE RED ONES MUST BE SICK!
HOW ARE THESE FOR ALTAR FLOWERS? SHOULD I ADD SOME LOTUS?
HOW WOULD IT BE WITH LOTUS?
LIKE, PRICE-WISE.
WELL, IT WOULD BE A LITTLE MORE EXPEN-SIVE...
THEN I DON'T NEED ANY.
Girl knows what she's doing...

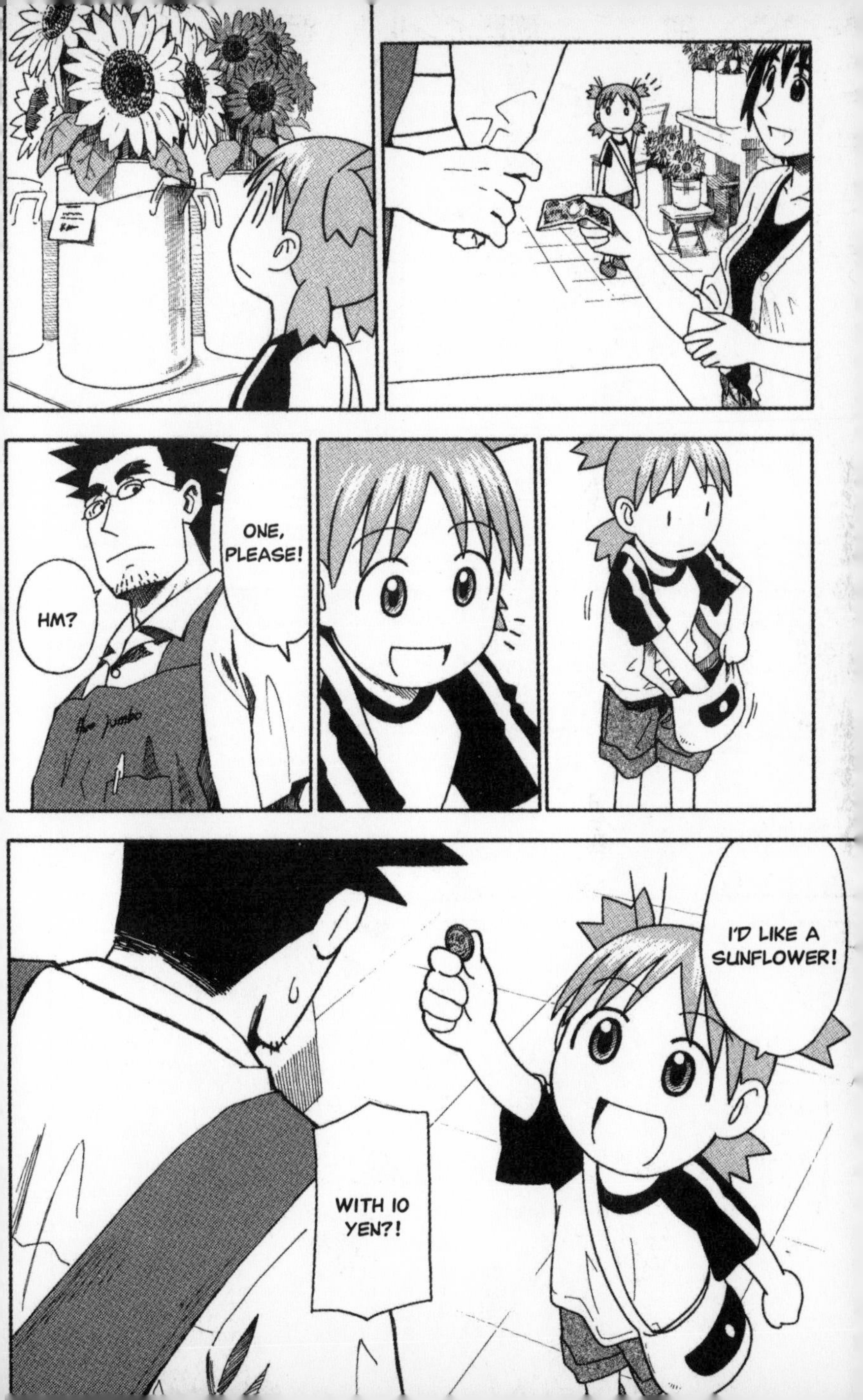
ONE, PLEASE!
HM?
I'D LIKE A SUNFLOWER!
WITH 10 YEN?!

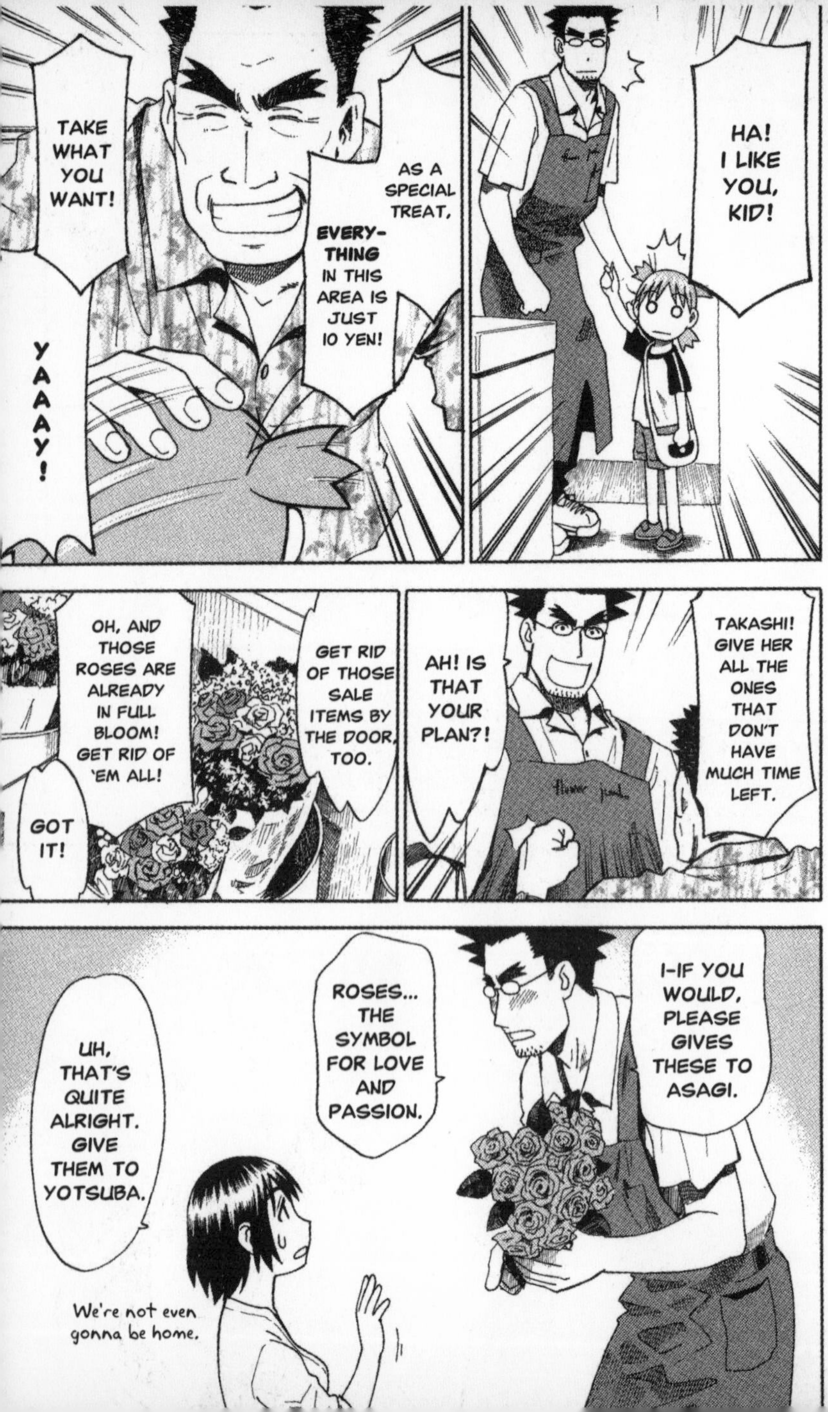
HA! I LIKE YOU, KID!
AS A SPECIAL TREAT, EVERY-THING IN THIS AREA IS JUST 10 YEN!
TAKE WHAT YOU WANT!
YAAAAY!
TAKASHI! GIVE HER ALL THE ONES THAT DON'T HAVE MUCH TIME LEFT.
AH! IS THAT YOUR PLAN?!
GET RID OF THOSE SALE ITEMS BY THE DOOR, TOO.
OH, AND THOSE ROSES ARE ALREADY IN FULL BLOOM! GET RID OF 'EM ALL!
GOT IT!
I-IF YOU WOULD, PLEASE GIVES THESE TO ASAGI.
ROSES... THE SYMBOL FOR LOVE AND PASSION.
UH, THAT'S QUITE ALRIGHT. GIVE THEM TO YOTSUBA.
We're not even gonna be home.

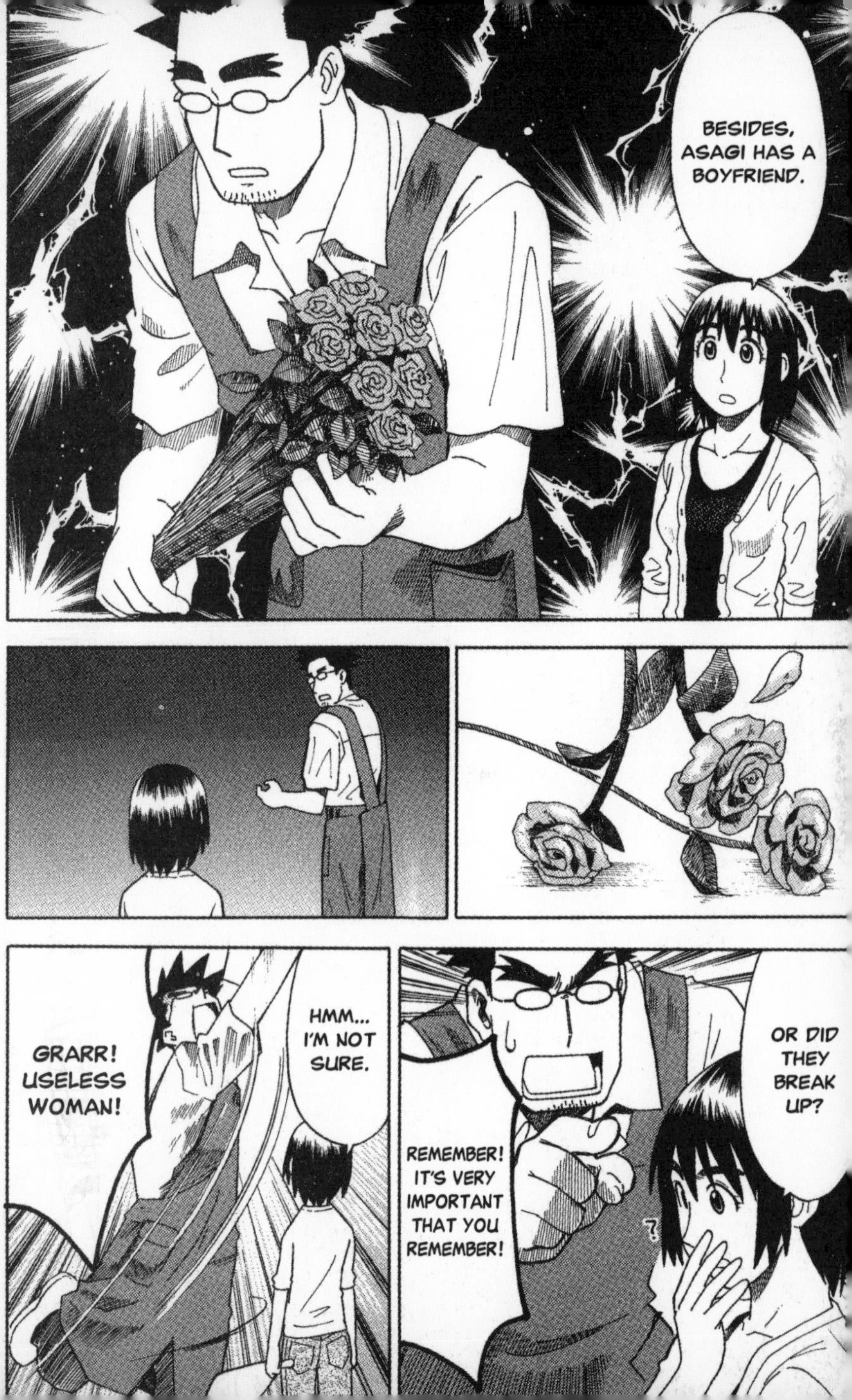
BESIDES, ASAGI HAS A BOYFRIEND.
OR DID THEY BREAK UP?
REMEMBER! IT'S VERY IMPORTANT THAT YOU REMEMBER!
HMM... I'M NOT SURE.
GRARR! USELESS WOMAN!

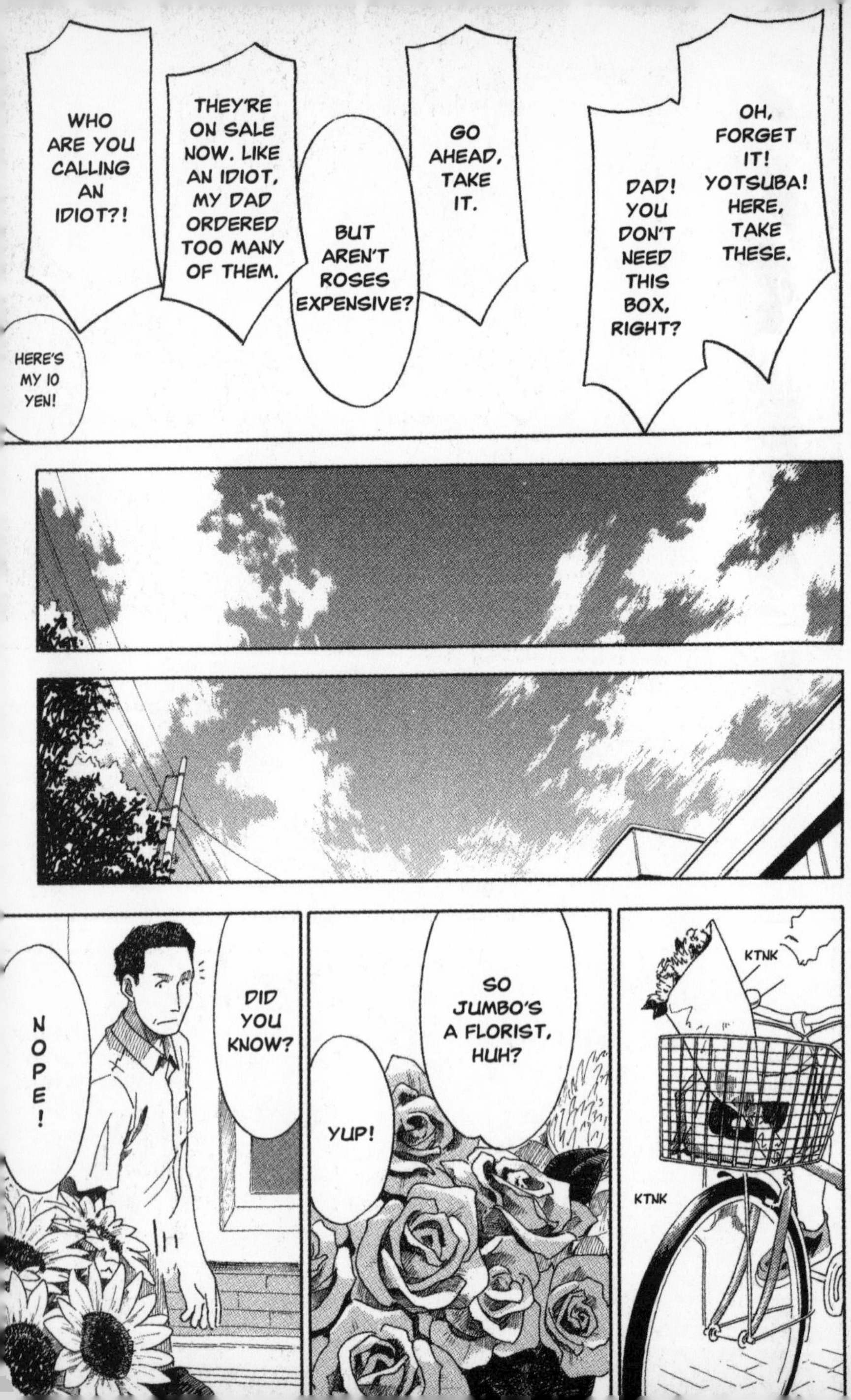
OH, FORGET IT! YOTSUBA! HERE, TAKE THESE.
DAD! YOU DON'T NEED THIS BOX, RIGHT?
GO AHEAD, TAKE IT.
BUT AREN'T ROSES EXPENSIVE?
THEY'RE ON SALE NOW. LIKE AN IDIOT, MY DAD ORDERED TOO MANY OF THEM.
WHO ARE YOU CALLING AN IDIOT?!
HERE'S MY 10 YEN!
KTNK
KTNK
SO JUMBO'S A FLORIST, HUH?
YUP!
DID YOU KNOW?
NOPE!

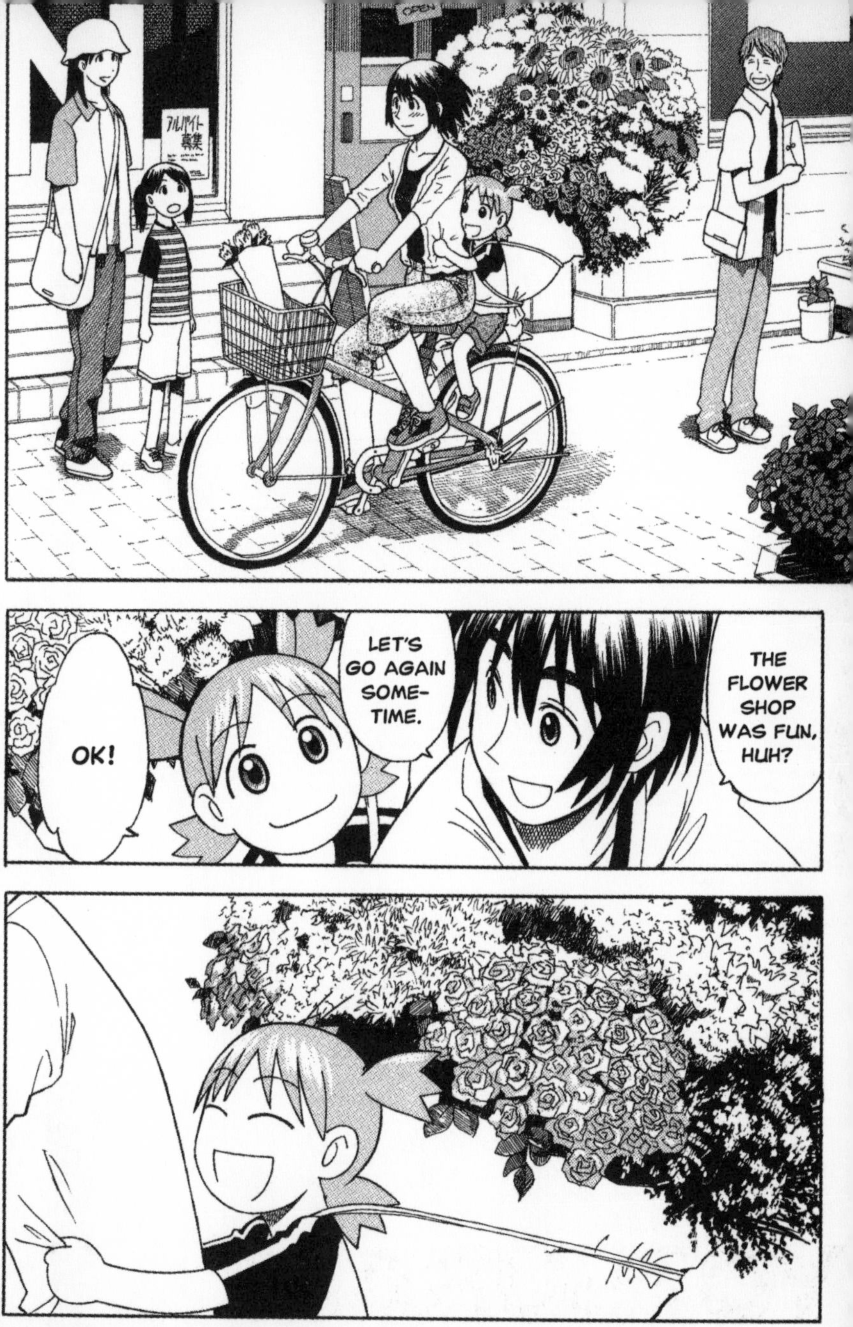
OPEN
アルバイト募集
THE FLOWER SHOP WAS FUN, HUH?
LET'S GO AGAIN SOME-TIME.
OK!

YOTSUBA&!

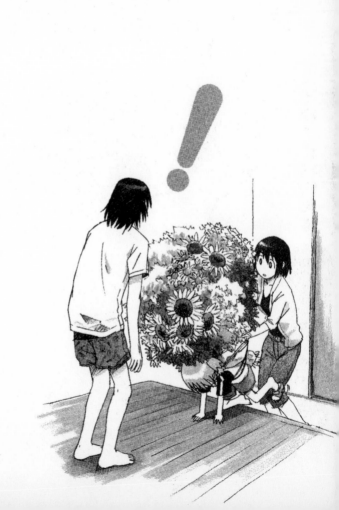

YOTSUBA & THE BON FESTIVAL

CHAPTER 18

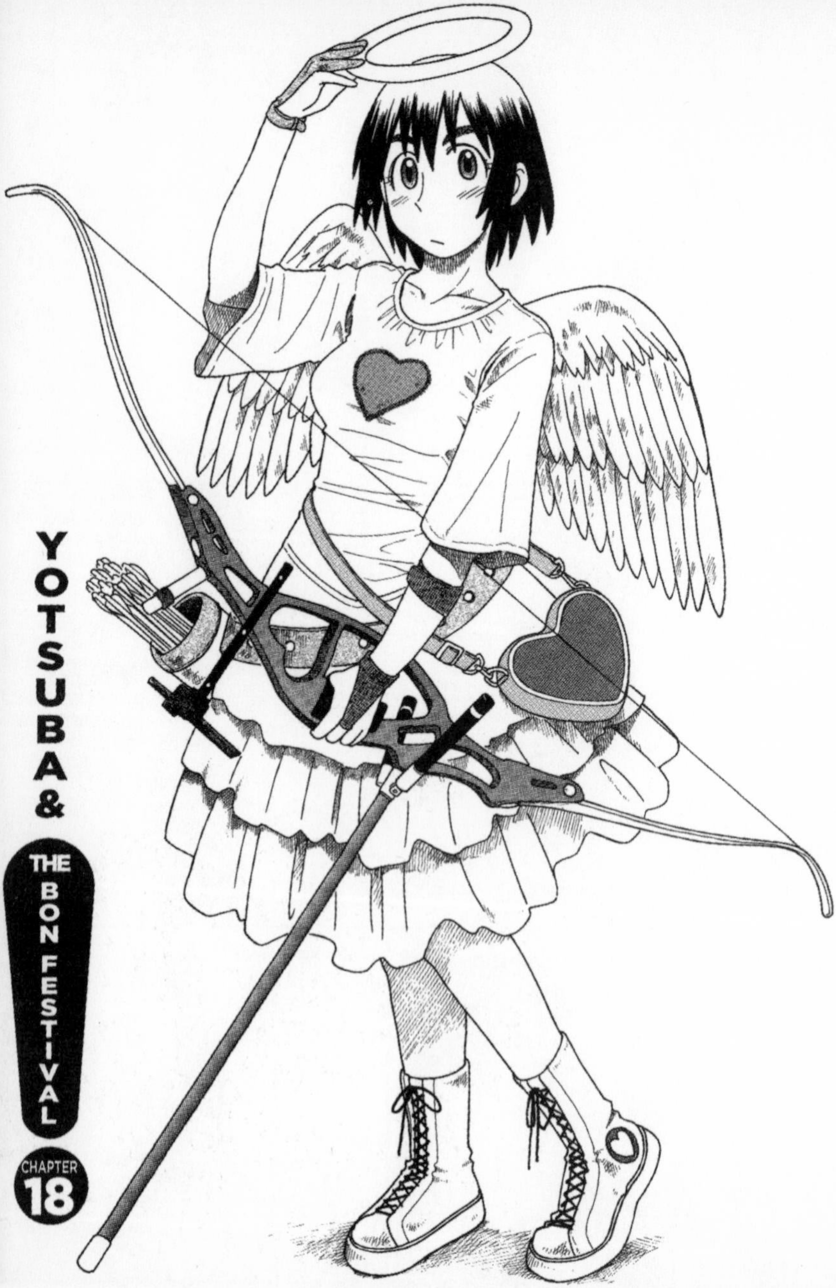

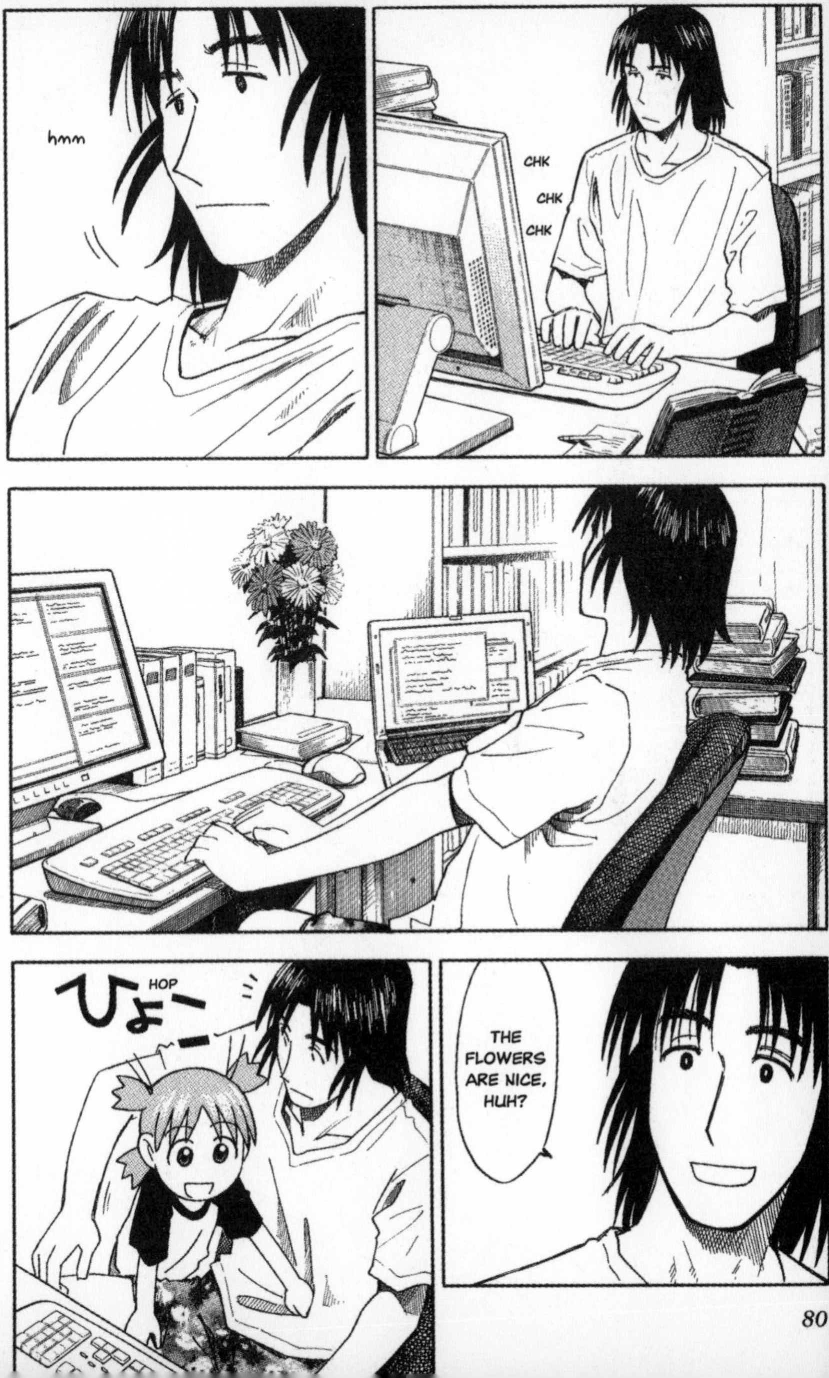
CHK
CHK
CHK
hmm
THE FLOWERS ARE NICE, HUH?
ひょーー
HOP

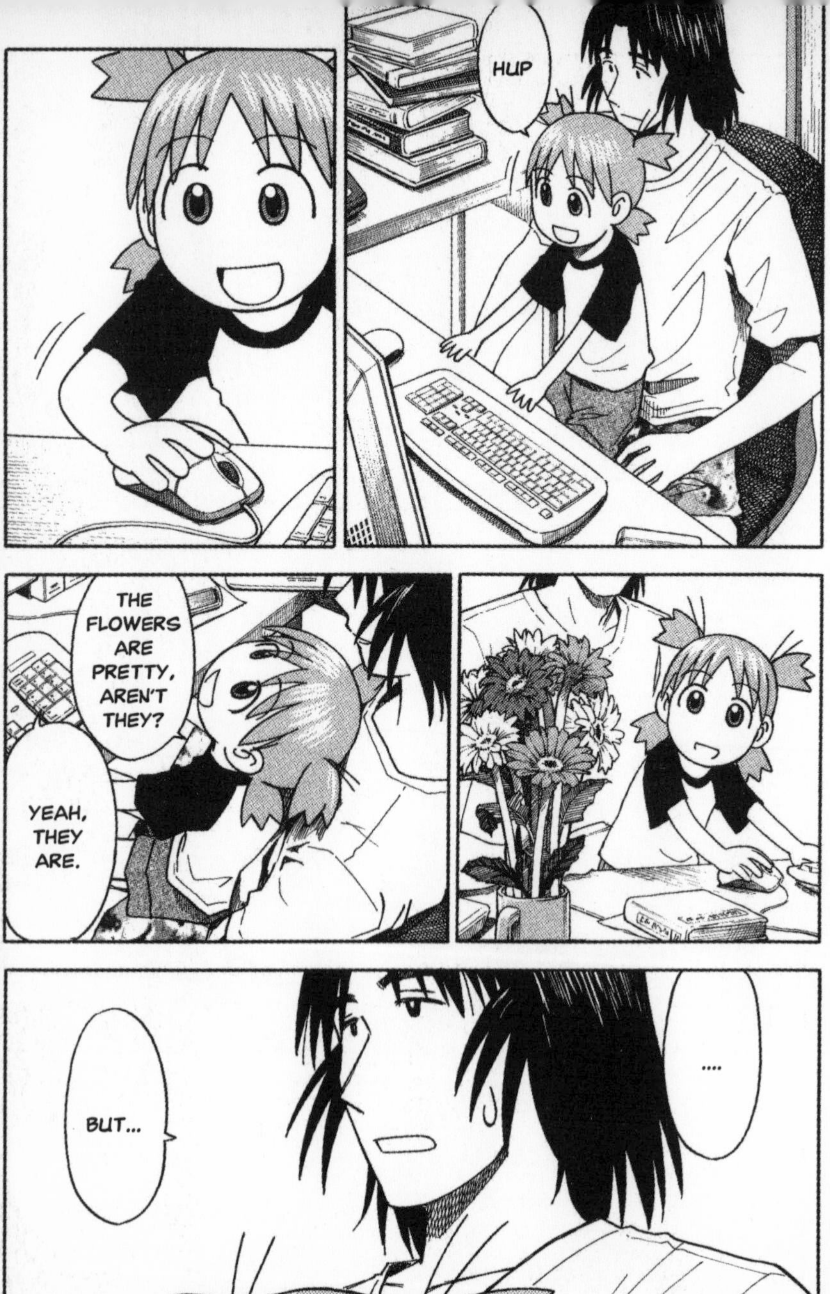
HUP
THE FLOWERS ARE PRETTY, AREN'T THEY?
YEAH, THEY ARE.
....
BUT...

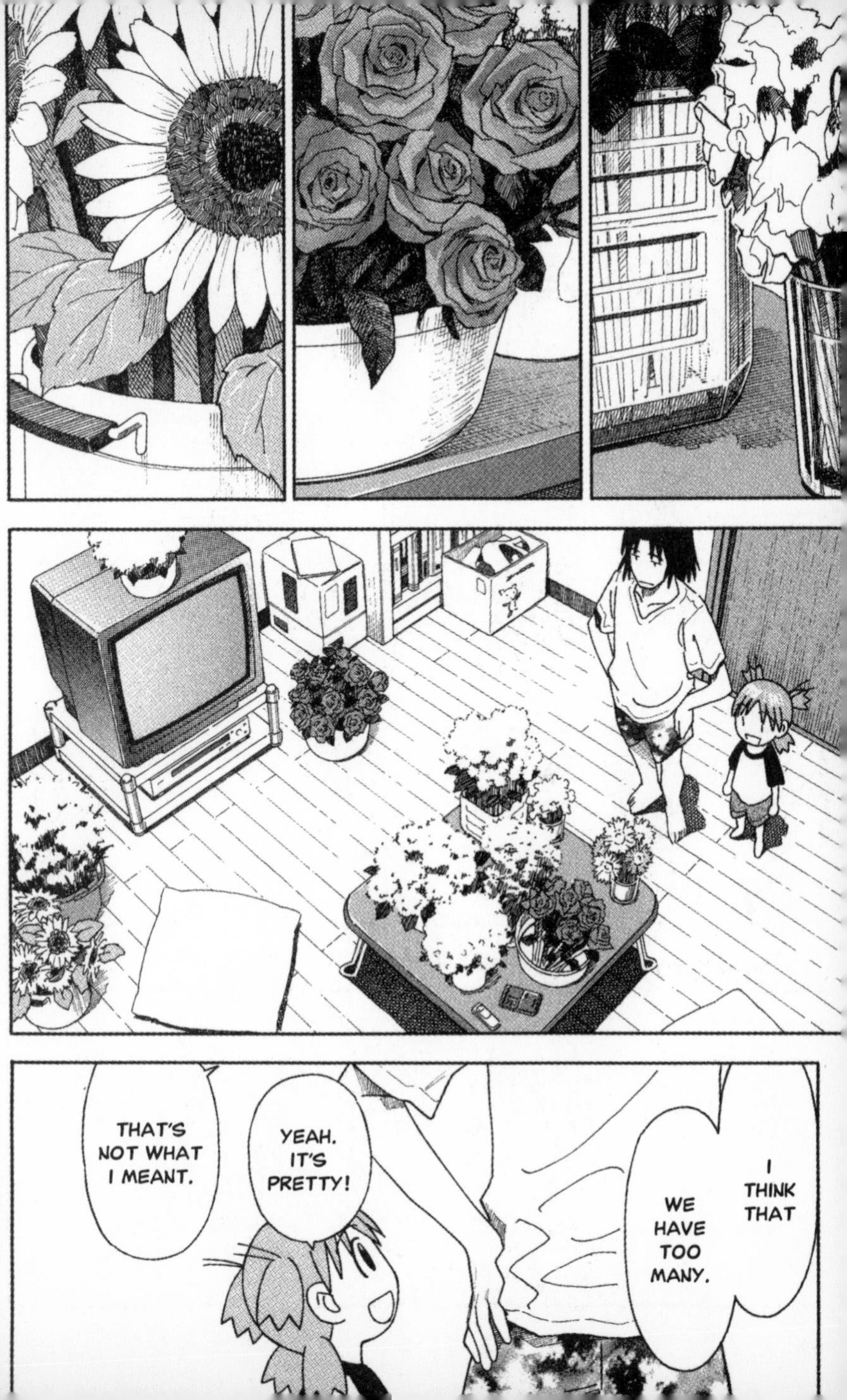
I THINK THAT WE HAVE TOO MANY.
YEAH. IT'S PRETTY!
THAT'S NOT WHAT I MEANT.

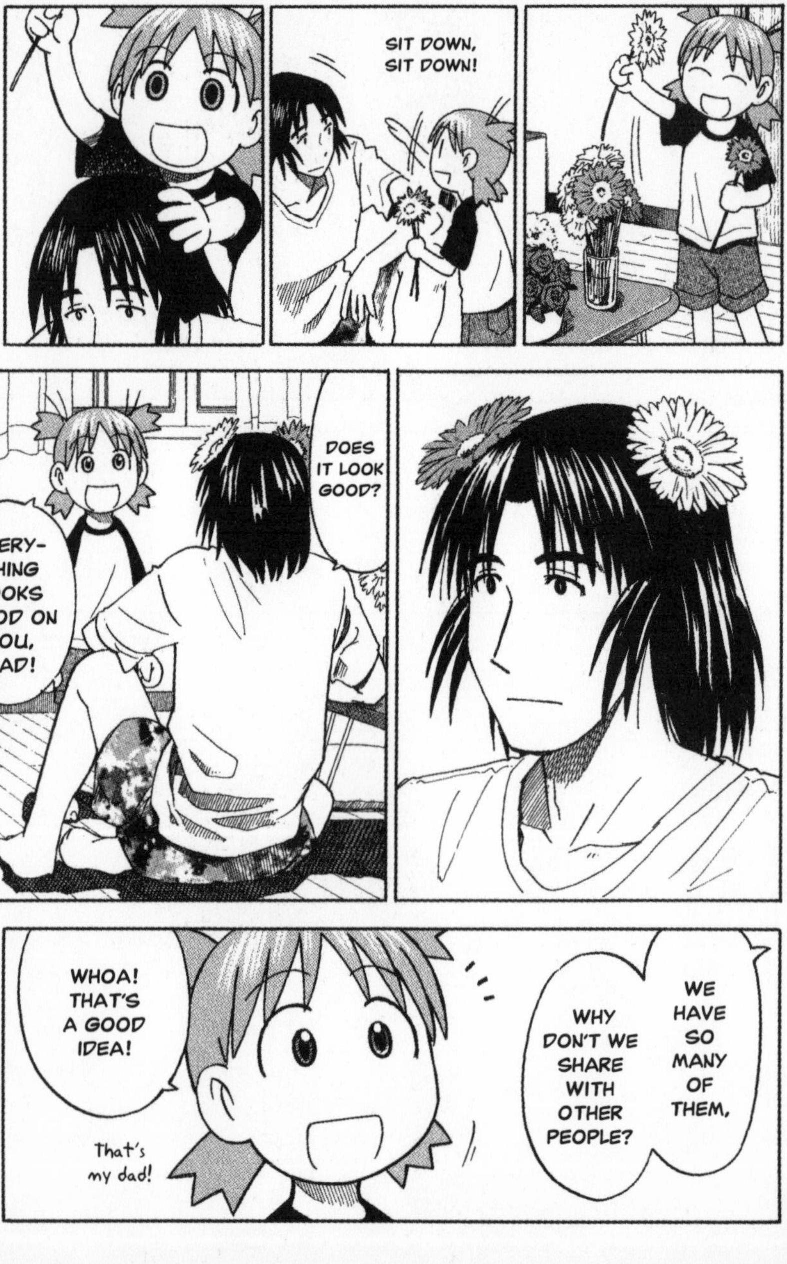
SIT DOWN, SIT DOWN!
DOES IT LOOK GOOD?
EVERY-THING LOOKS GOOD ON YOU, DAD!
WE HAVE SO MANY OF THEM,
WHY DON'T WE SHARE WITH OTHER PEOPLE?
WHOA! THAT'S A GOOD IDEA!
That's my dad!

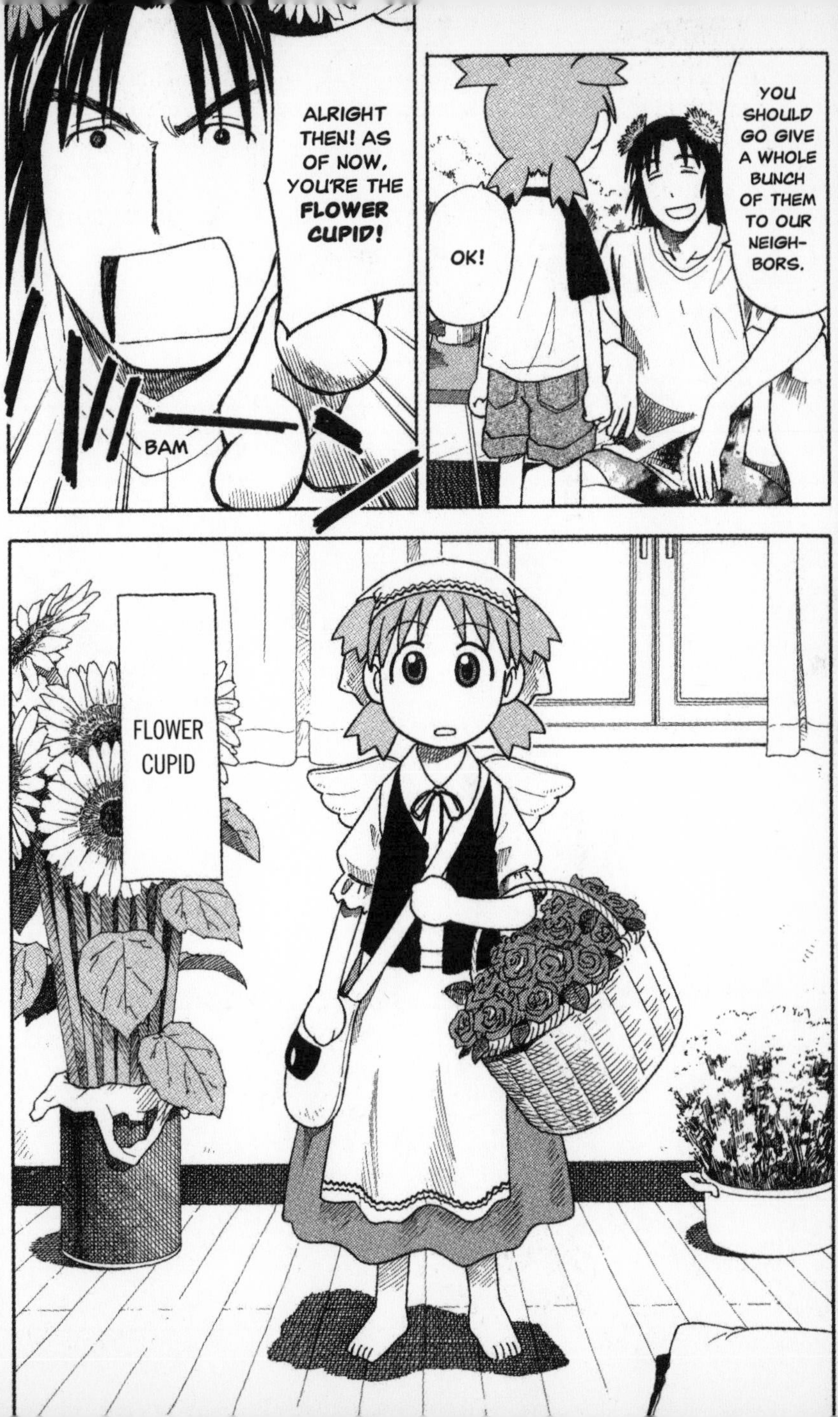
YOU SHOULD GO GIVE A WHOLE BUNCH OF THEM TO OUR NEIGH-BORS.
OK!
ALRIGHT THEN! AS OF NOW, YOU'RE THE **FLOWER CUPID!**
BAM
FLOWER CUPID

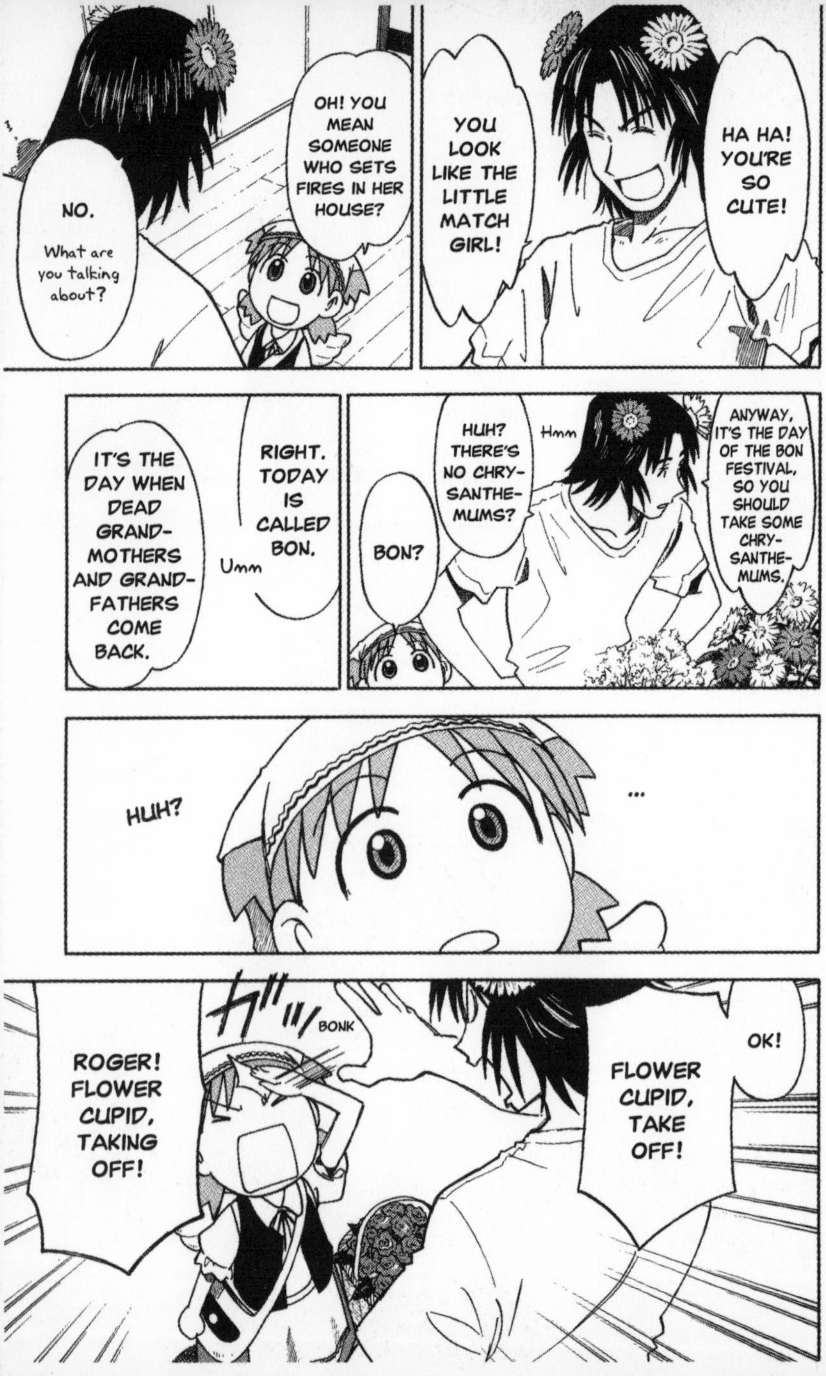
HA HA! YOU'RE SO CUTE!
YOU LOOK LIKE THE LITTLE MATCH GIRL!
OH! YOU MEAN SOMEONE WHO SETS FIRES IN HER HOUSE?
NO.
What are you talking about?
ANYWAY, IT'S THE DAY OF THE BON FESTIVAL, SO YOU SHOULD TAKE SOME CHRY-SANTHE-MUMS.
Hmm
HUH? THERE'S NO CHRY-SANTHE-MUMS?
BON?
RIGHT. TODAY IS CALLED BON.
Umm
IT'S THE DAY WHEN DEAD GRAND-MOTHERS AND GRAND-FATHERS COME BACK.
...
HUH?
OK!
FLOWER CUPID, TAKE OFF!
BONK
ROGER! FLOWER CUPID, TAKING OFF!

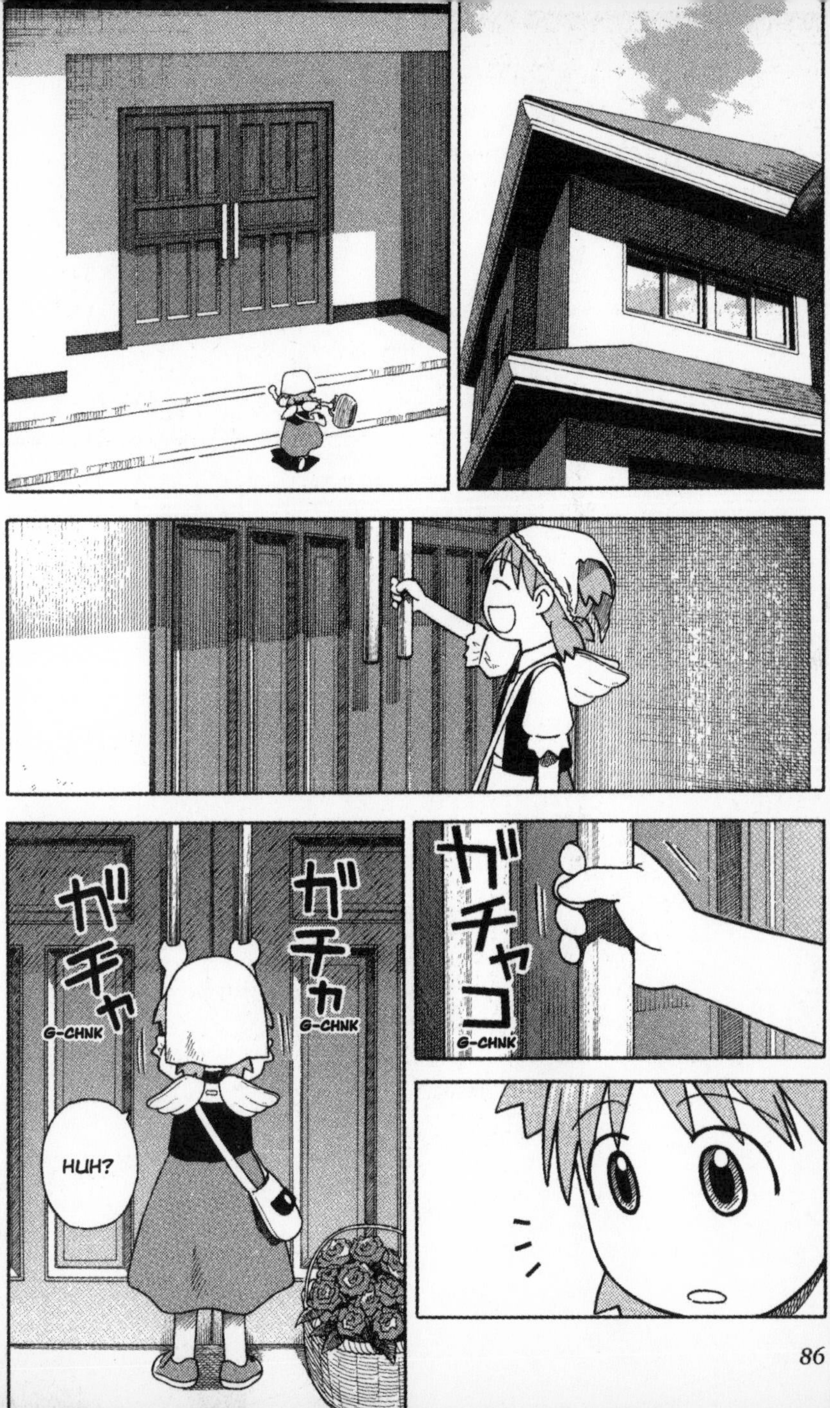
ガチャコ
G-CHNK
ガチャ
G-CHNK
ガチャ
G-CHNK
HUH?

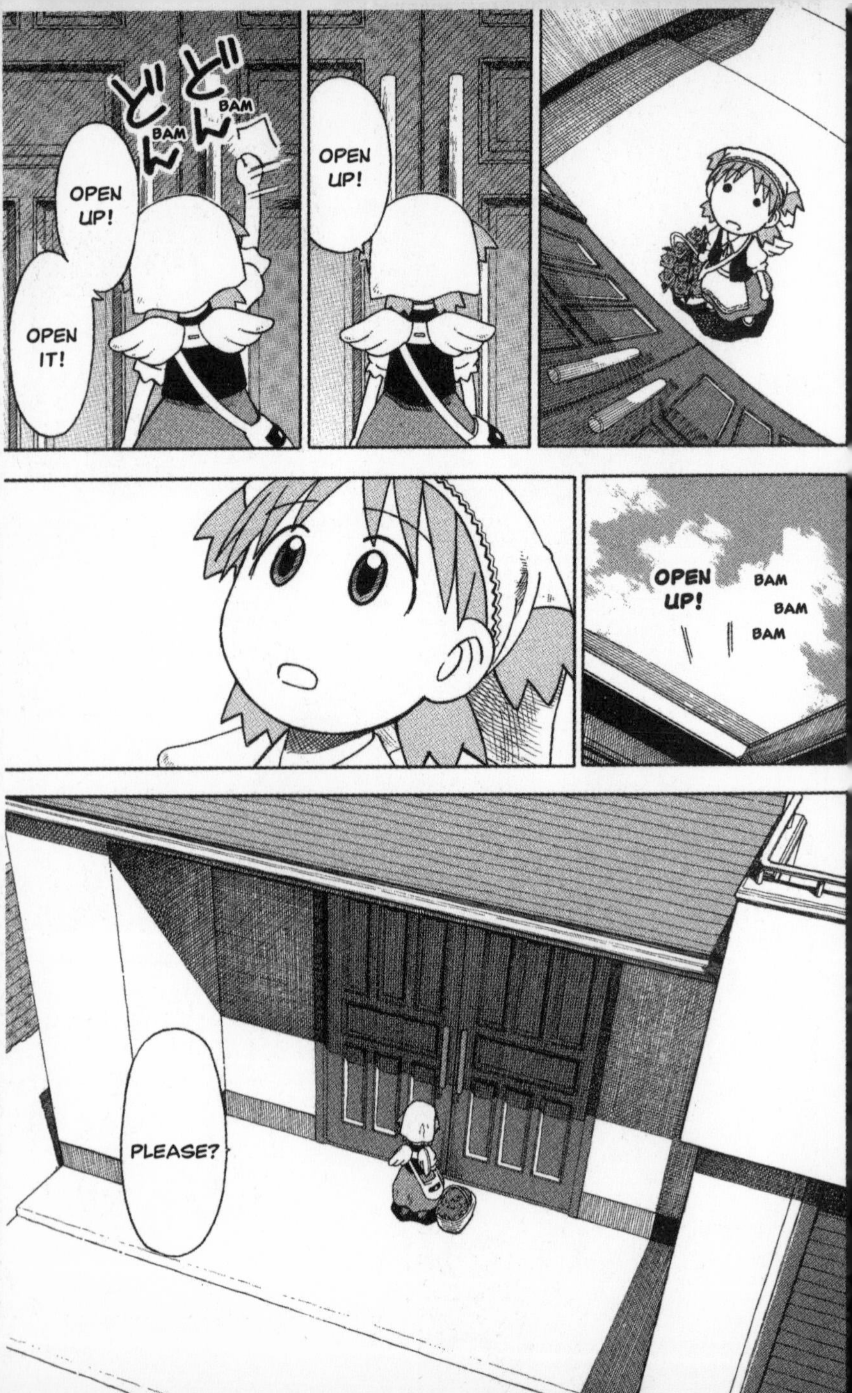
OPEN UP!
どん どん
BAM BAM
OPEN UP!
OPEN IT!
OPEN UP!
BAM BAM BAM
PLEASE?

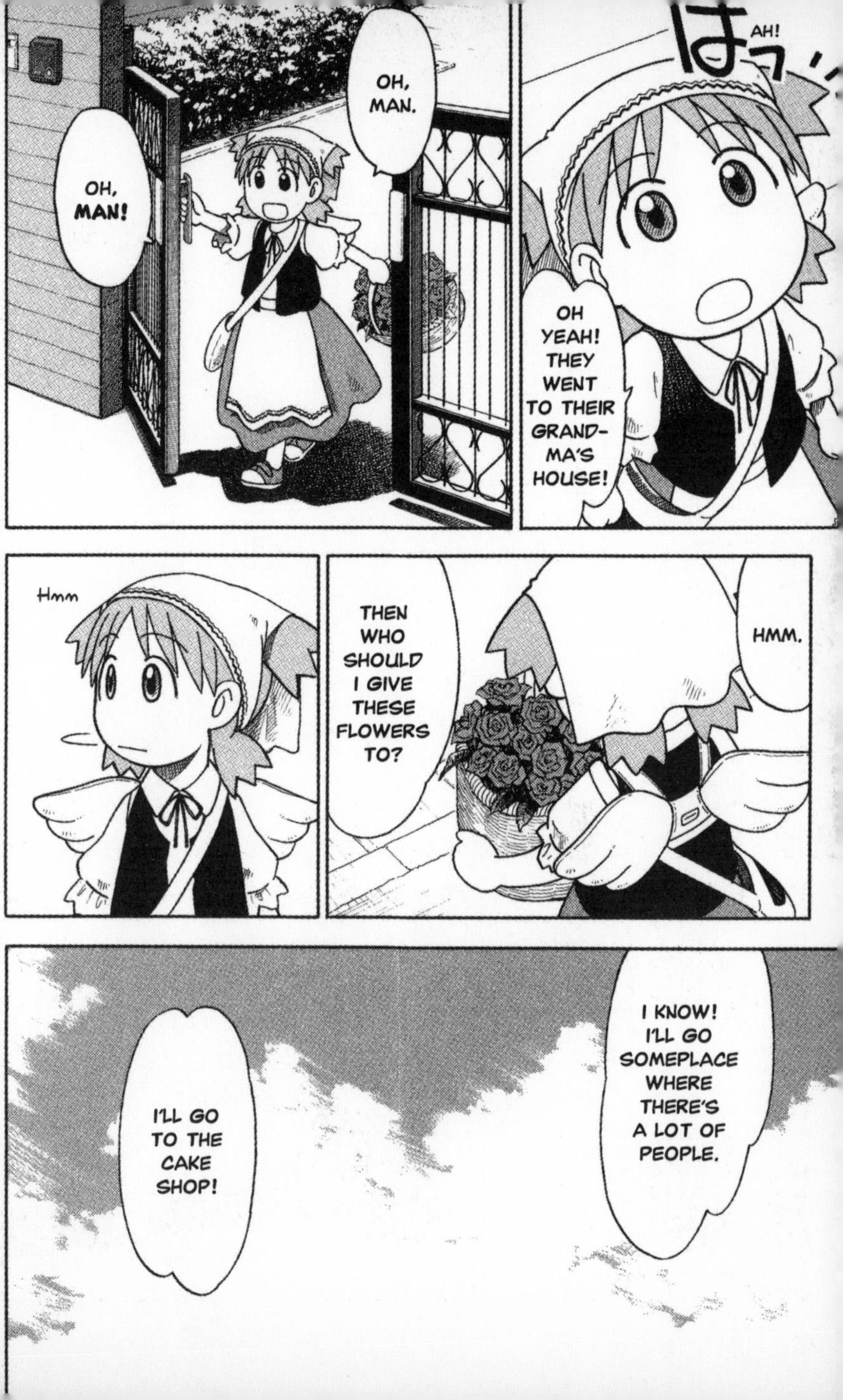
はっ
AH!
OH YEAH! THEY WENT TO THEIR GRAND-MA'S HOUSE!
OH, MAN.
OH, MAN!
HMM.
THEN WHO SHOULD I GIVE THESE FLOWERS TO?
Hmm
I KNOW! I'LL GO SOMEPLACE WHERE THERE'S A LOT OF PEOPLE.
I'LL GO TO THE CAKE SHOP!

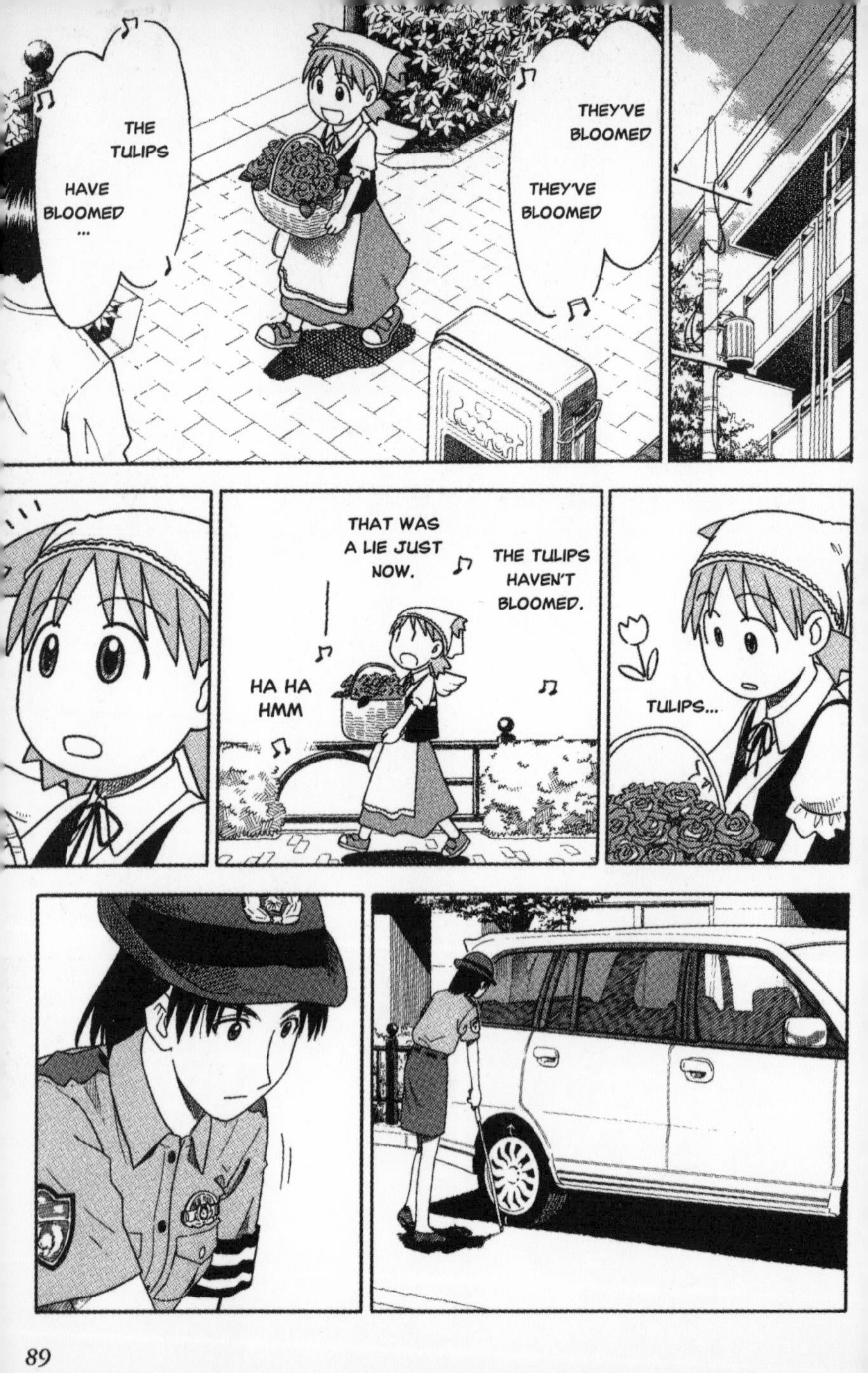
THEY'VE BLOOMED
THEY'VE BLOOMED
THE TULIPS
HAVE BLOOMED ...
TULIPS...
THE TULIPS HAVEN'T BLOOMED.
THAT WAS A LIE JUST NOW.
HA HA HMM

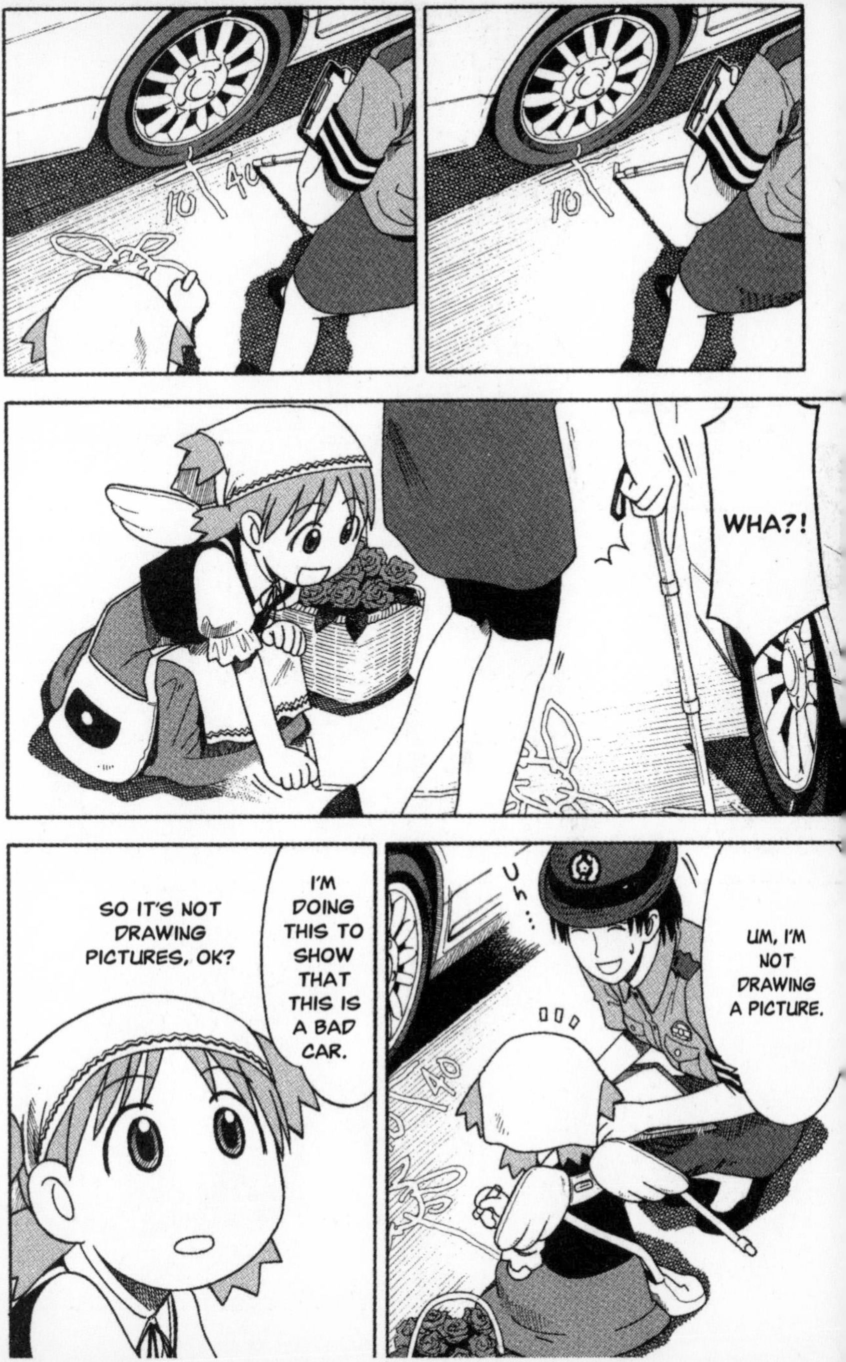
WHA?!
Uh...
UM, I'M NOT DRAWING A PICTURE.
I'M DOING THIS TO SHOW THAT THIS IS A BAD CAR.
SO IT'S NOT DRAWING PICTURES, OK?

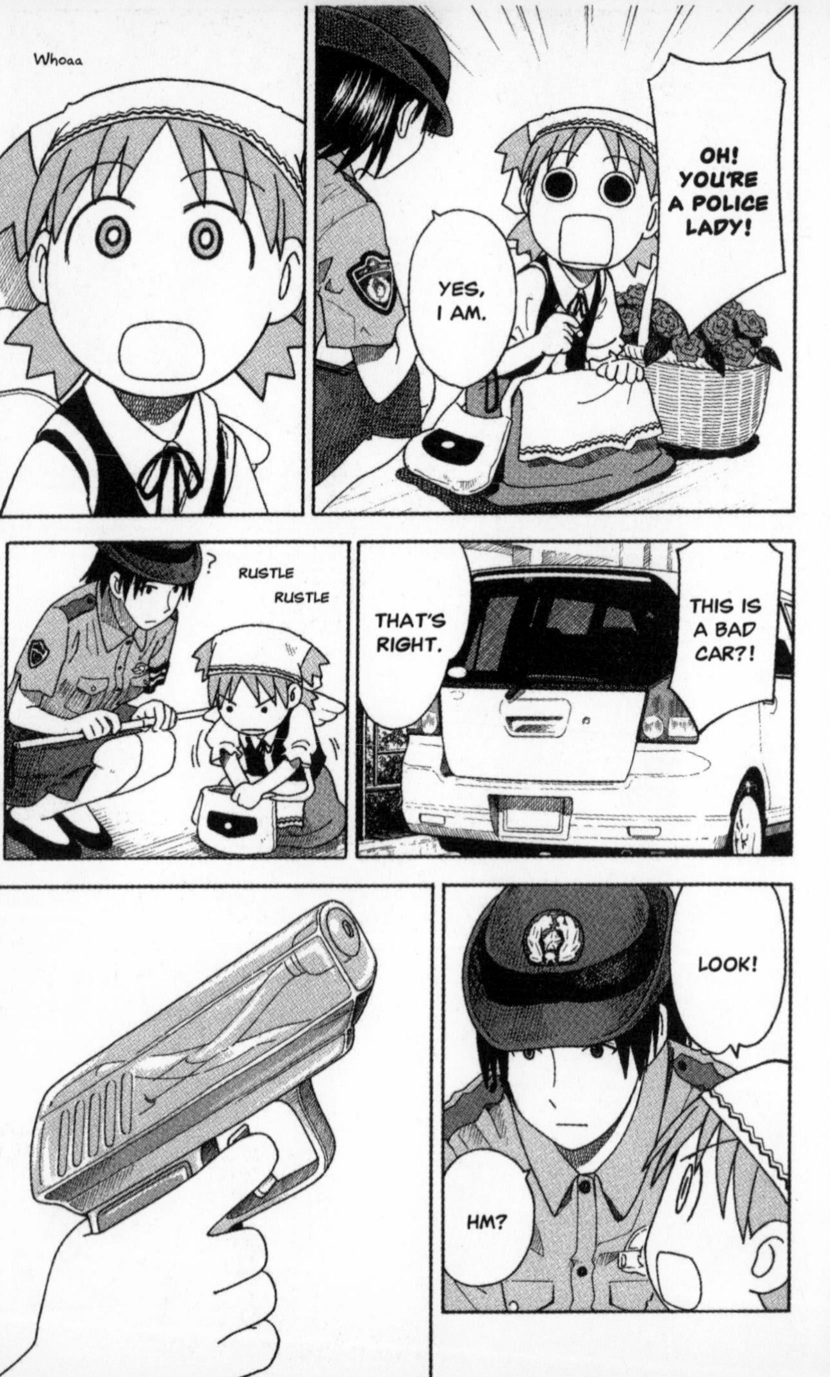

OH! YOU'RE A POLICE LADY!
YES, I AM.
Whoaa
THIS IS A BAD CAR?!
THAT'S RIGHT.
?
RUSTLE
RUSTLE
LOOK!
HM?

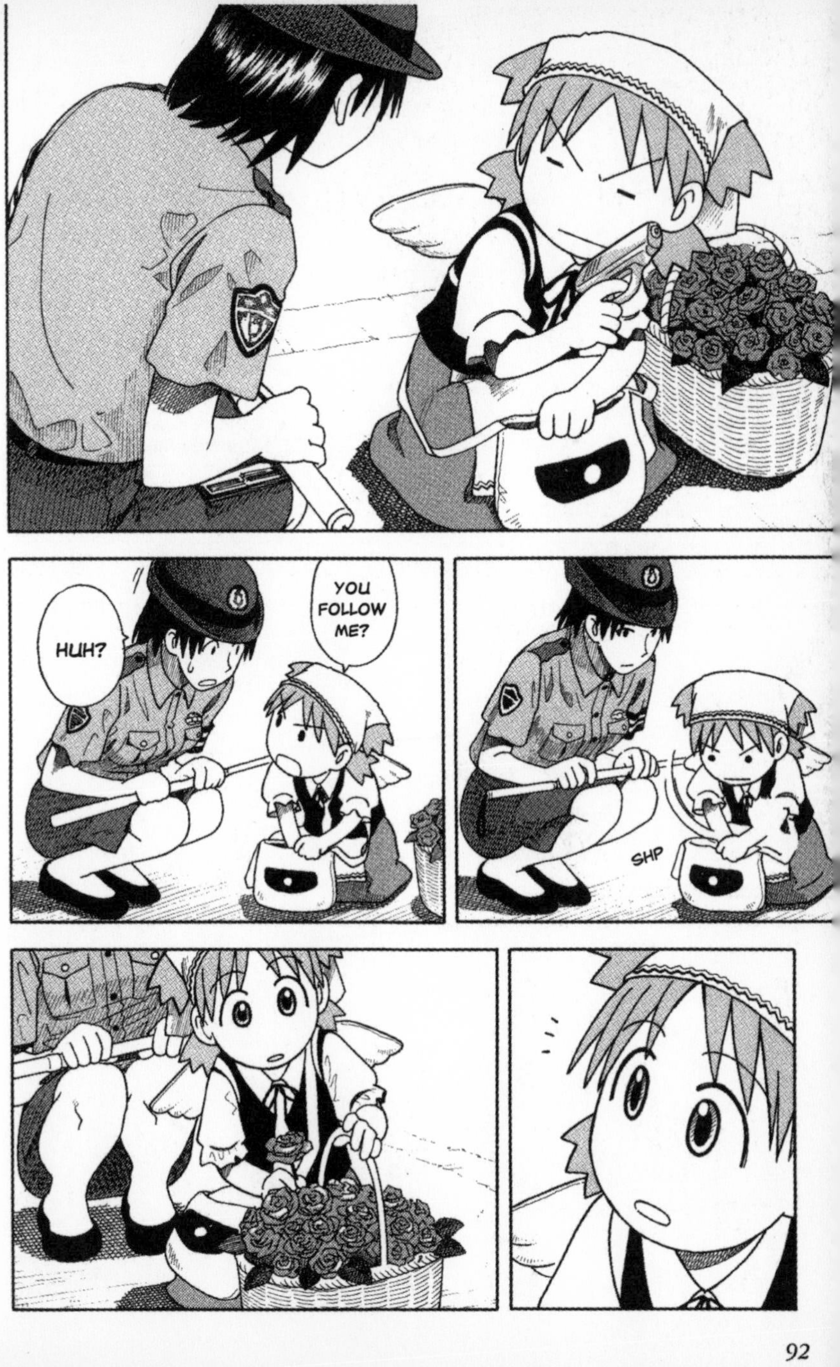
SHP
YOU FOLLOW ME?
HUH?

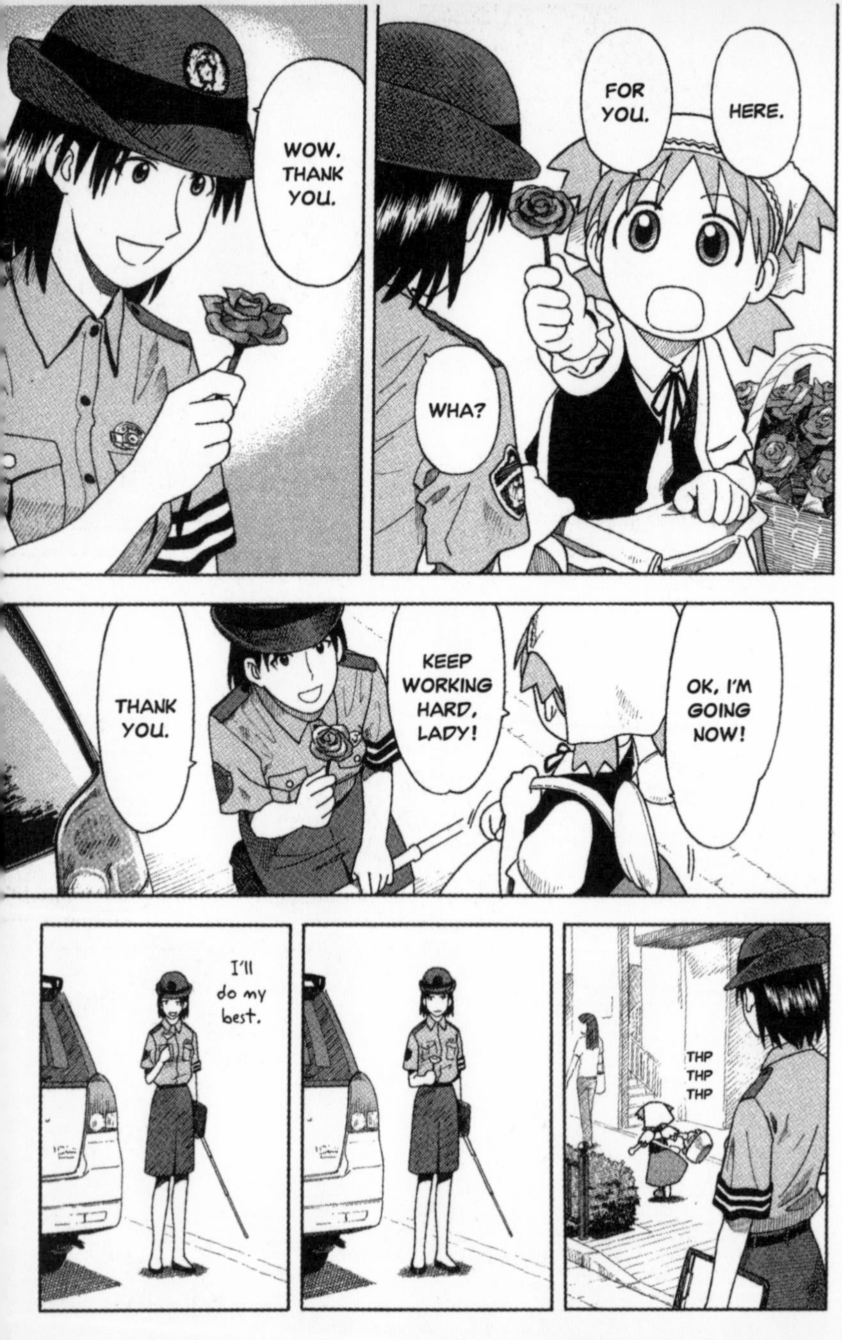
HERE.
FOR YOU.
WHA?
WOW. THANK YOU.
OK, I'M GOING NOW!
KEEP WORKING HARD, LADY!
THANK YOU.
THP THP THP
I'll do my best.

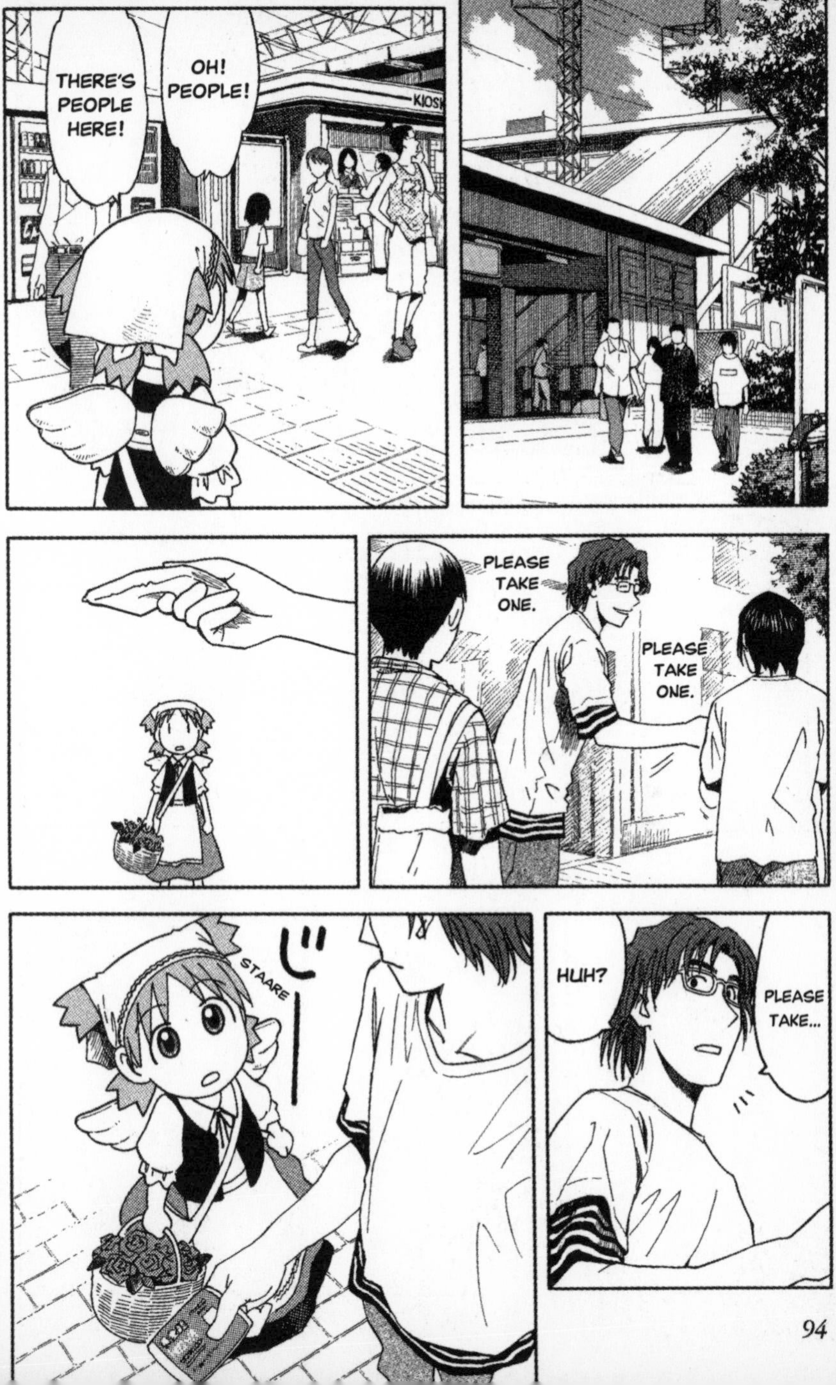
OH! PEOPLE!
THERE'S PEOPLE HERE!
PLEASE TAKE ONE.
PLEASE TAKE ONE.
PLEASE TAKE...
HUH?
じー
STAARE

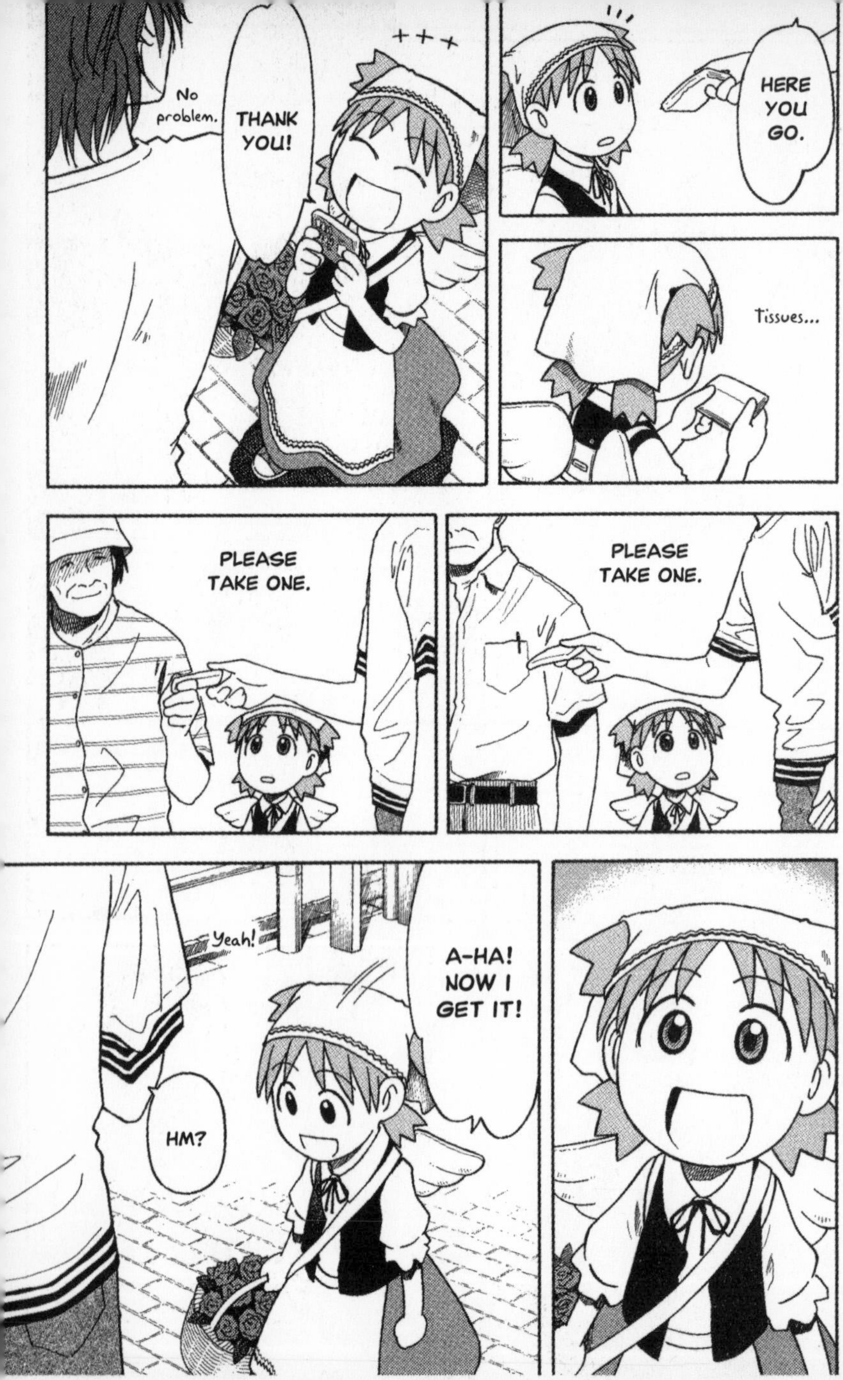
HERE YOU GO.
Tissues...
THANK YOU!
No problem.
PLEASE TAKE ONE.
PLEASE TAKE ONE.
A-HA! NOW I GET IT!
Yeah!
HM?

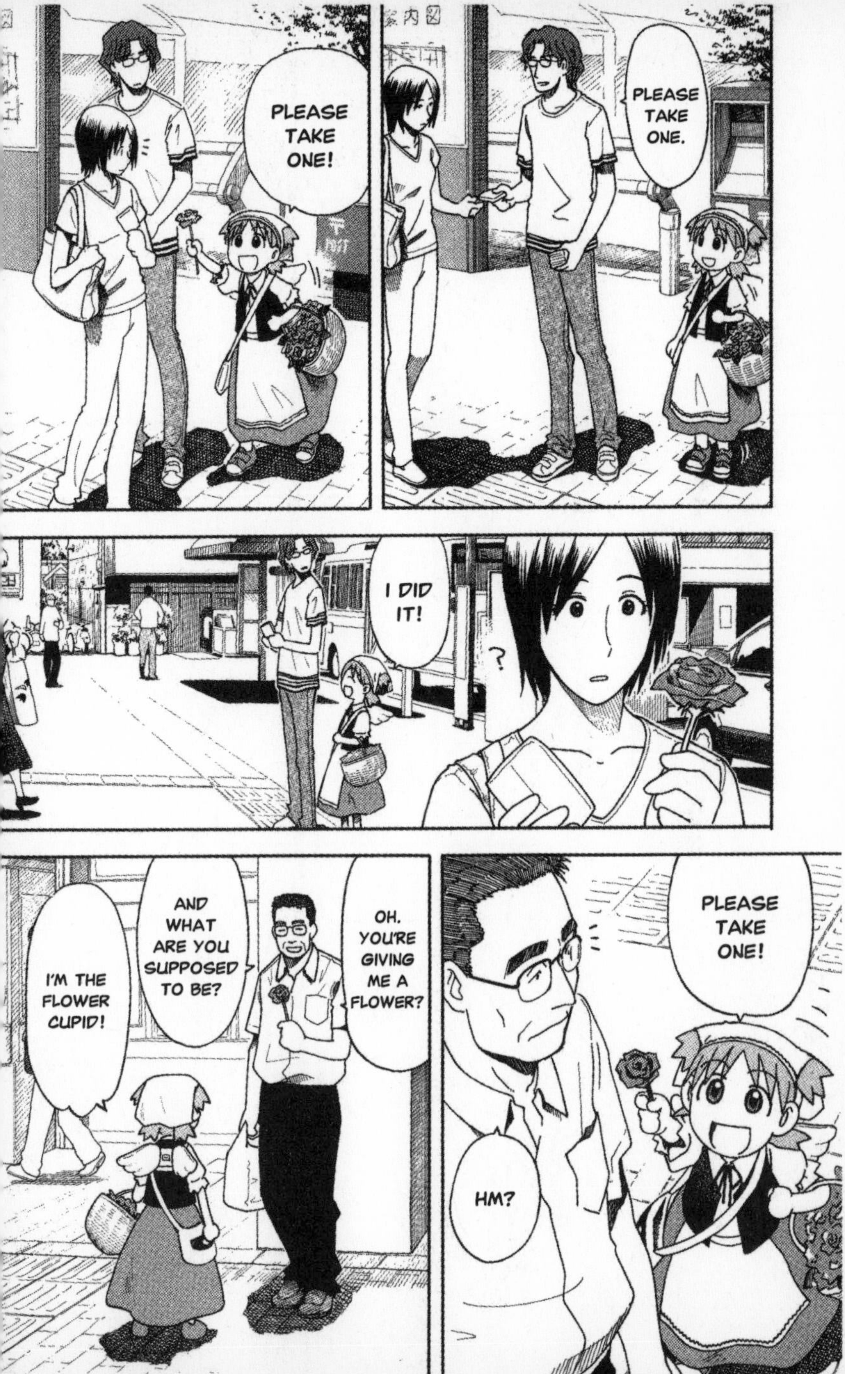
案内図
PLEASE TAKE ONE.
PLEASE TAKE ONE!
I DID IT!
?
PLEASE TAKE ONE!
HM?
OH. YOU'RE GIVING ME A FLOWER?
AND WHAT ARE YOU SUPPOSED TO BE?
I'M THE FLOWER CUPID!

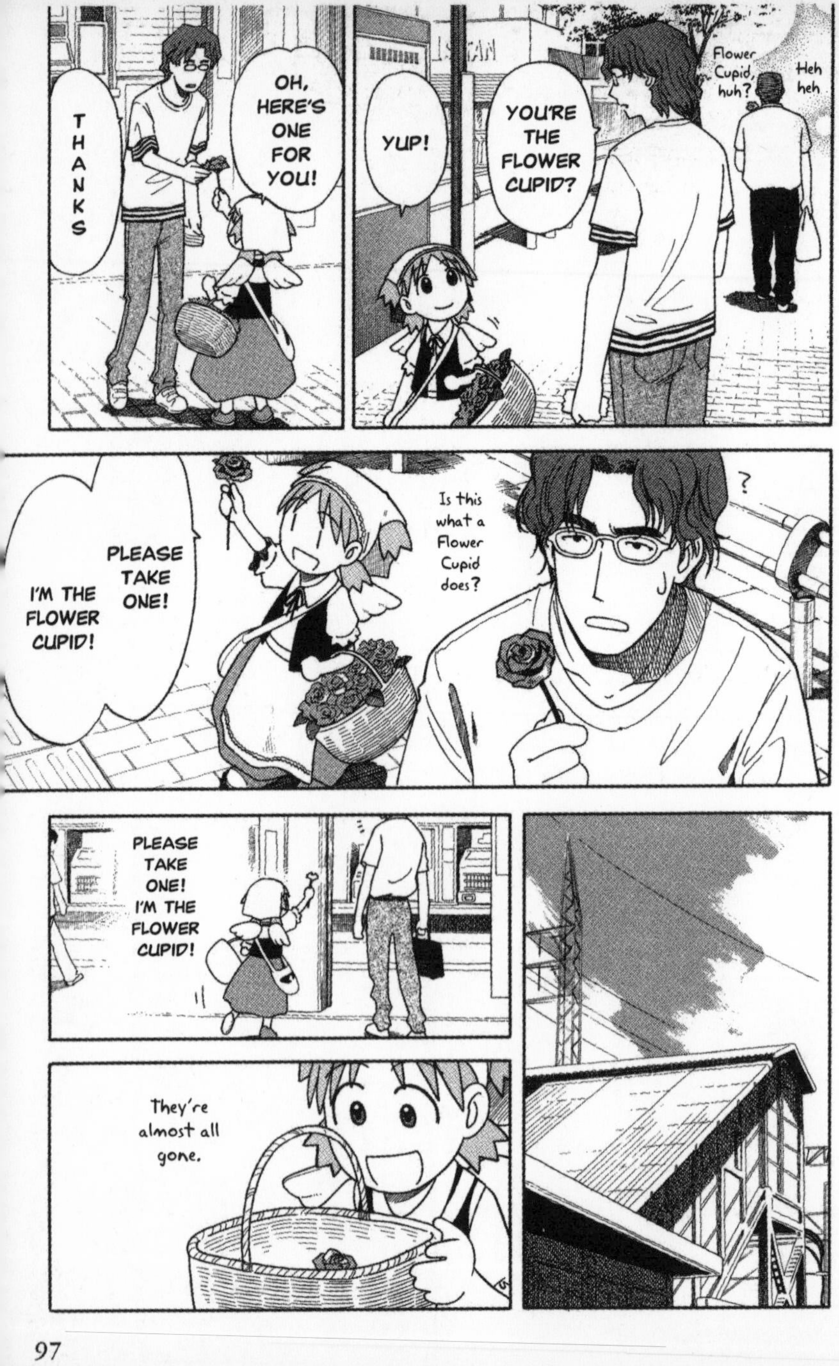
Heh heh
Flower Cupid, huh?
YOU'RE THE FLOWER CUPID?
YUP!
OH, HERE'S ONE FOR YOU!
THANKS
?
Is this what a Flower Cupid does?
PLEASE TAKE ONE!
I'M THE FLOWER CUPID!
PLEASE TAKE ONE! I'M THE FLOWER CUPID!
They're almost all gone.

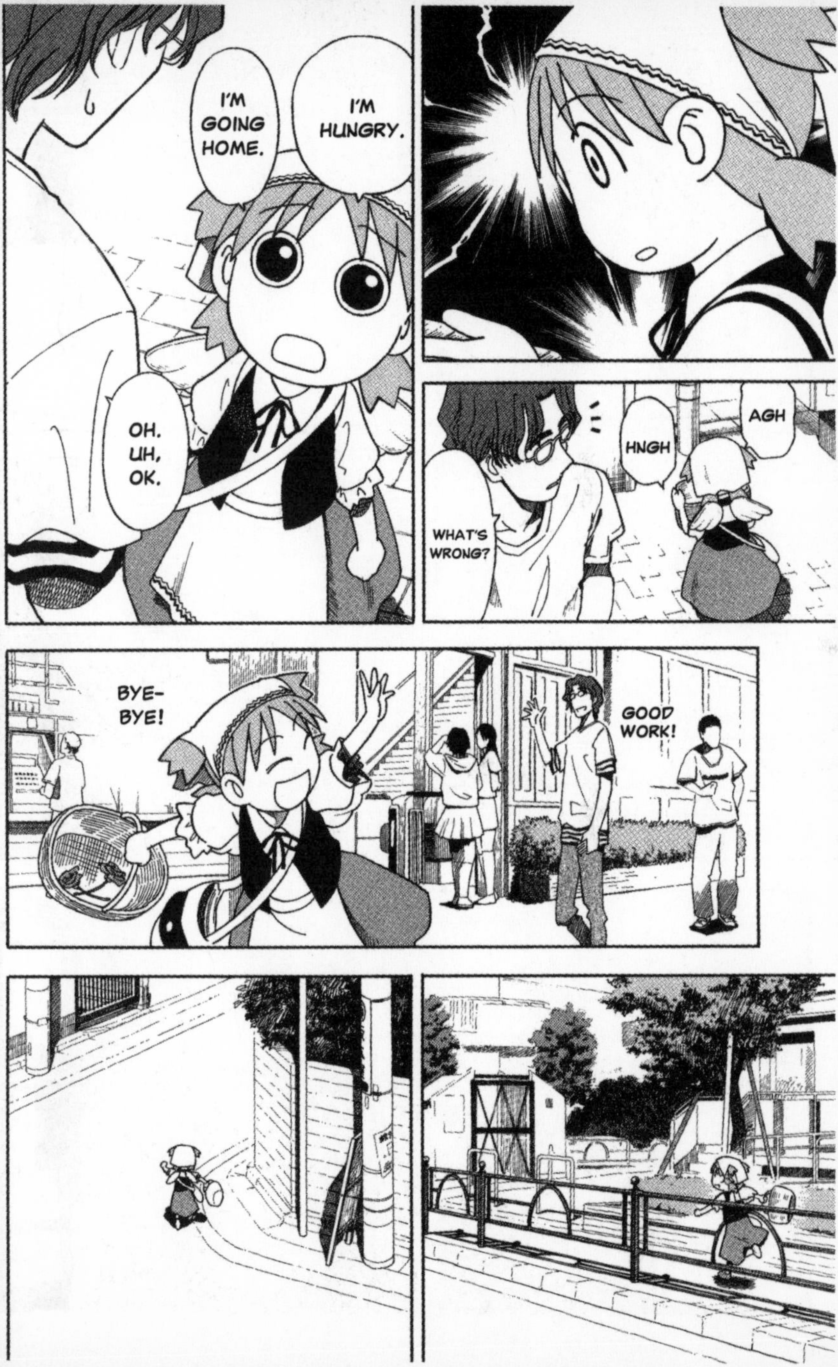
AGH
HNGH
WHAT'S WRONG?
I'M HUNGRY.
I'M GOING HOME.
OH. UH, OK.
GOOD WORK!
BYE-BYE!

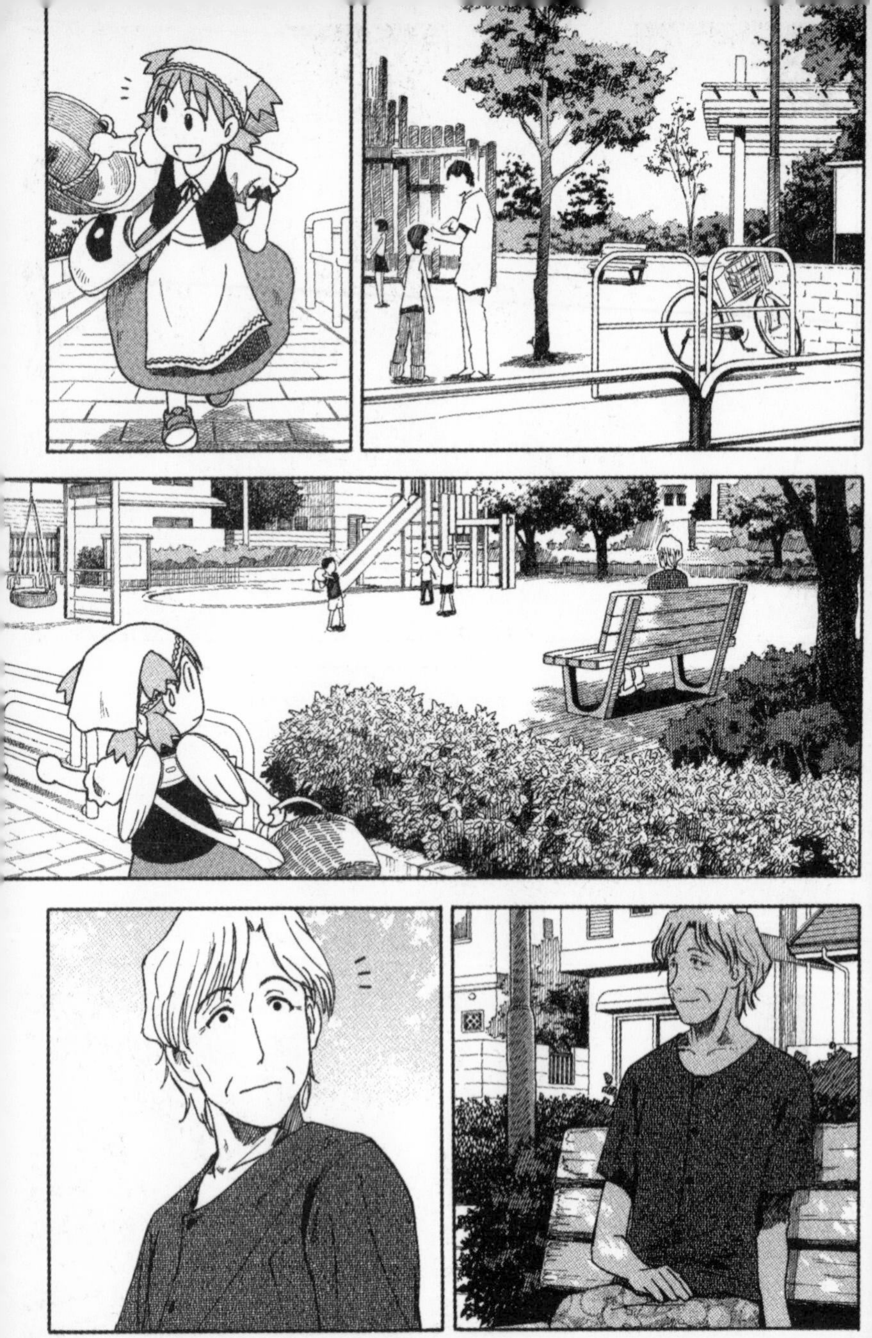

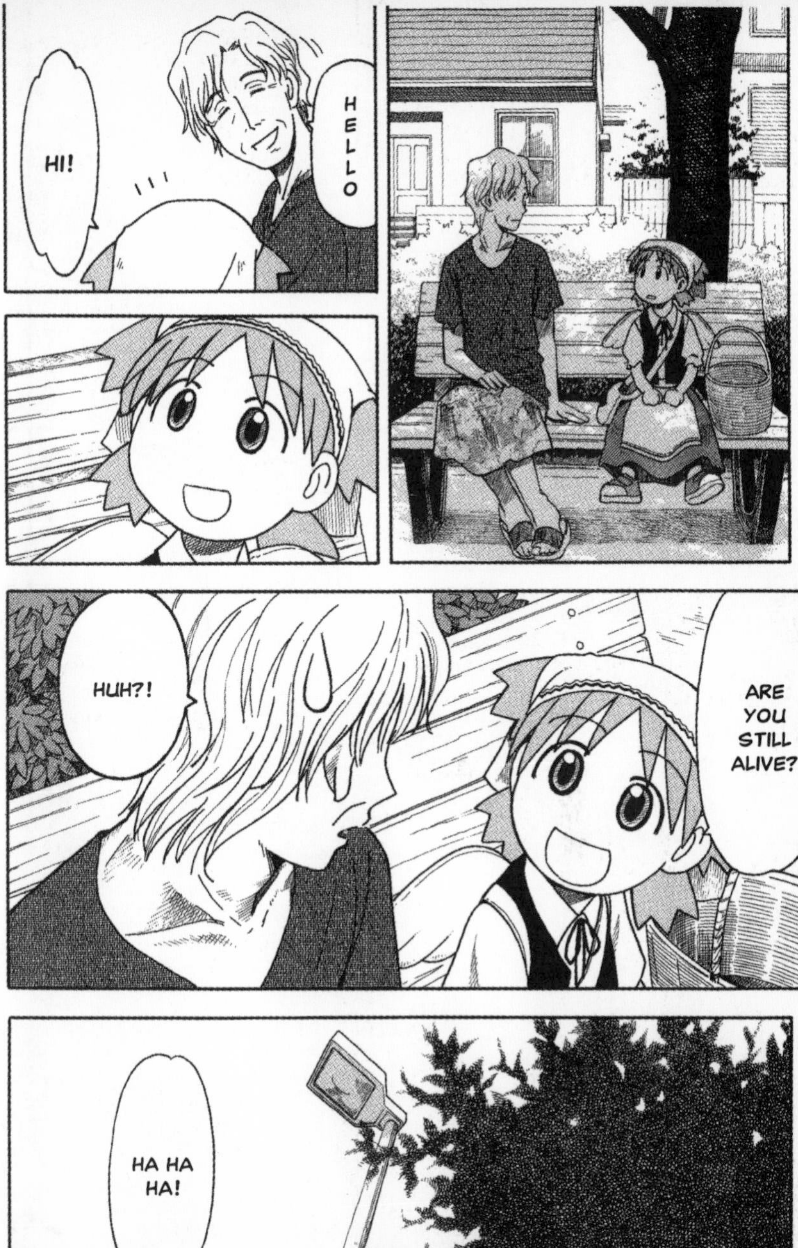
HELLO
HI!
ARE YOU STILL ALIVE?
HUH?!
HA HA HA!

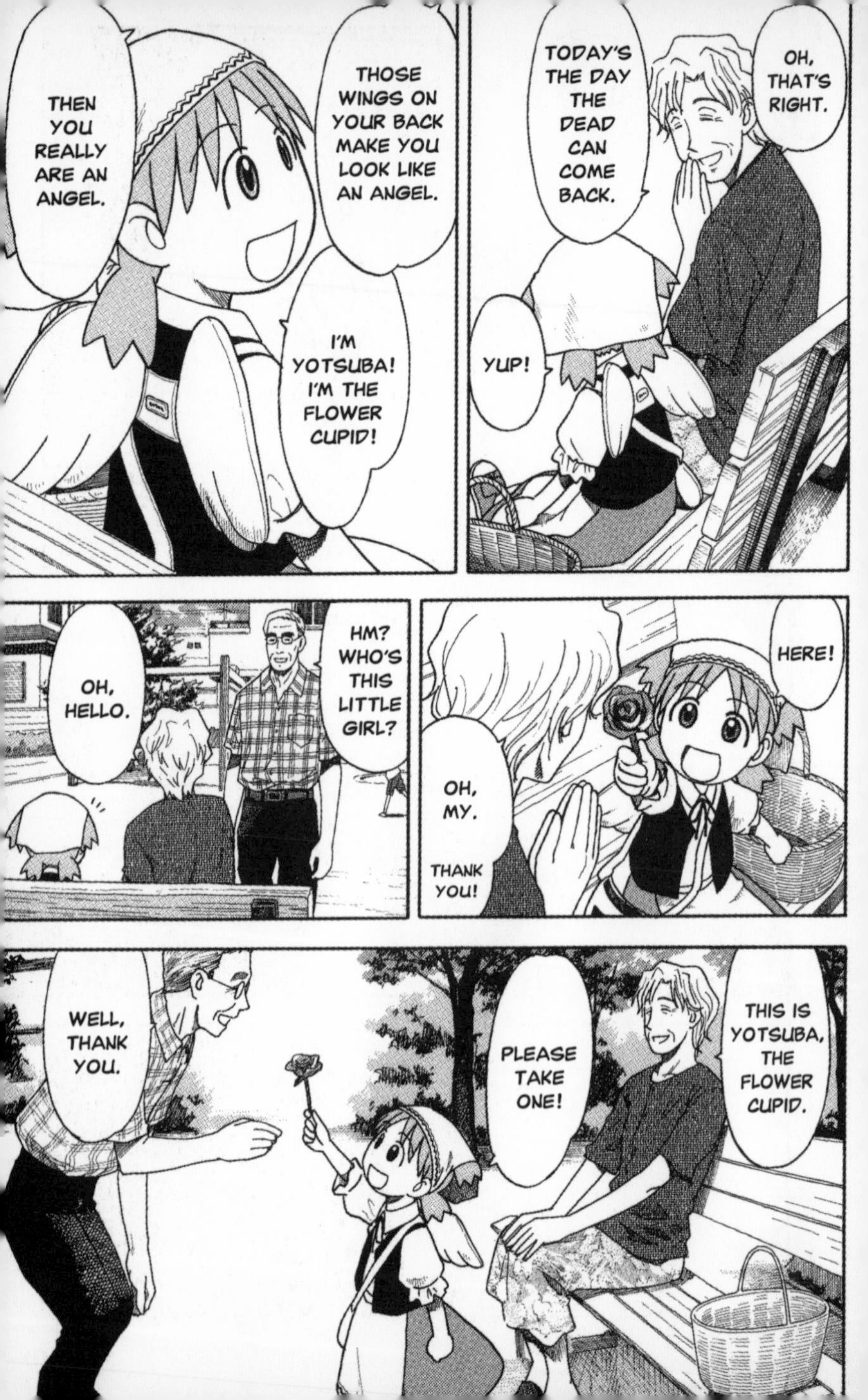
OH, THAT'S RIGHT.
TODAY'S THE DAY THE DEAD CAN COME BACK.
YUP!
THOSE WINGS ON YOUR BACK MAKE YOU LOOK LIKE AN ANGEL.
I'M YOTSUBA! I'M THE FLOWER CUPID!
THEN YOU REALLY ARE AN ANGEL.
HERE!
OH, MY.
THANK YOU!
HM? WHO'S THIS LITTLE GIRL?
OH, HELLO.
THIS IS YOTSUBA, THE FLOWER CUPID.
PLEASE TAKE ONE!
WELL, THANK YOU.

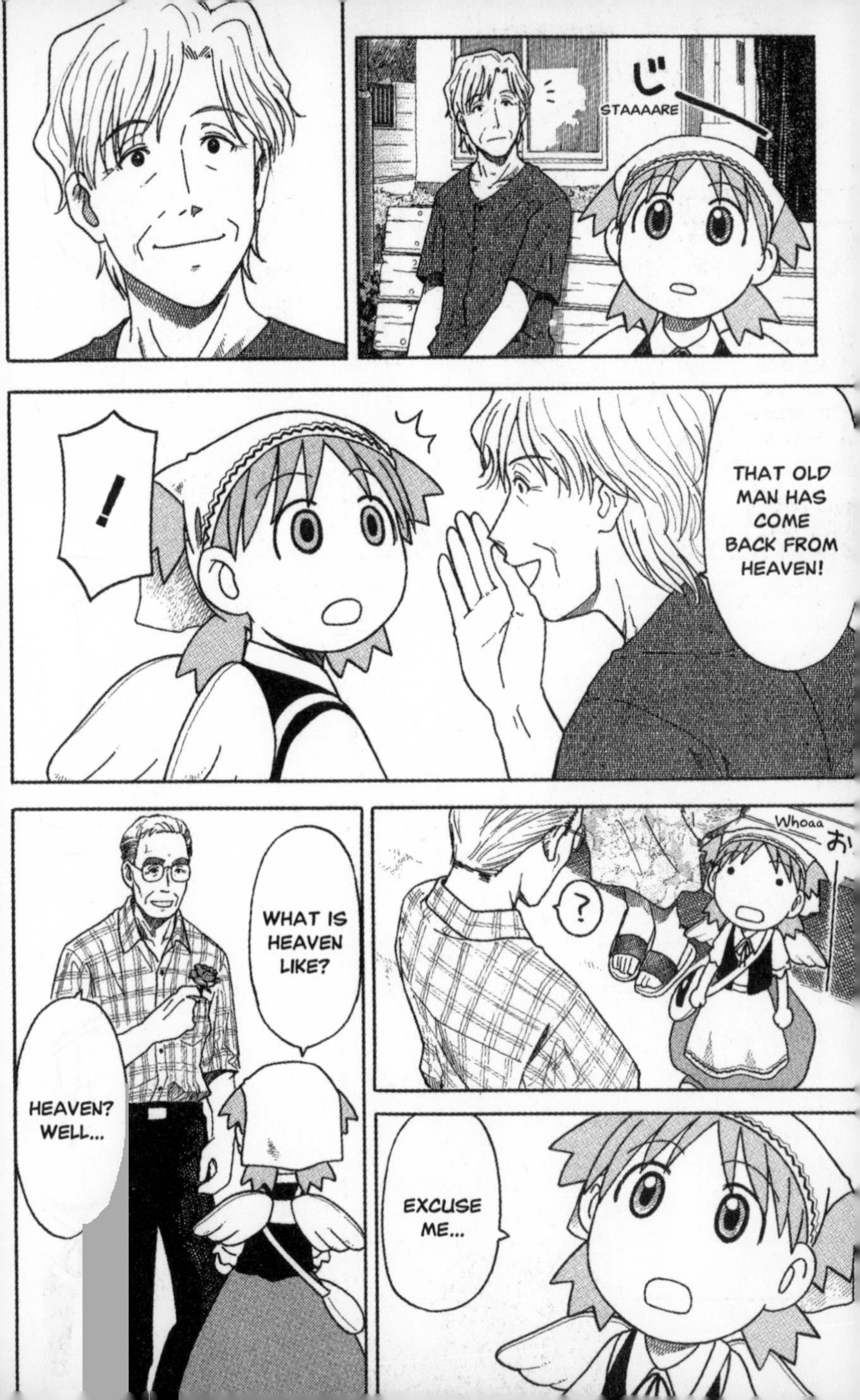
じ
STAAAARE
THAT OLD MAN HAS COME BACK FROM HEAVEN!
!
Whoaa
お
?
EXCUSE ME...
WHAT IS HEAVEN LIKE?
HEAVEN? WELL...

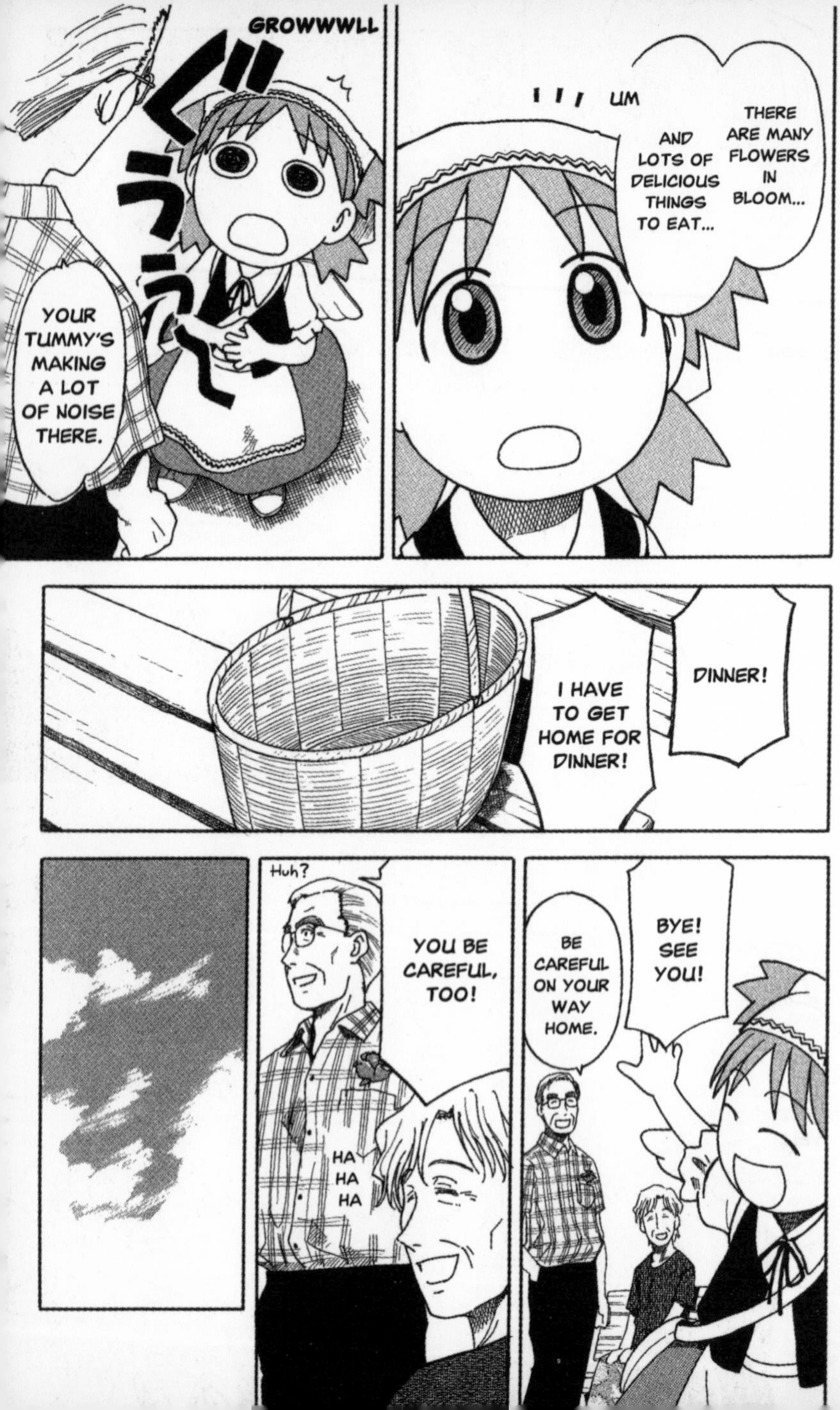
THERE ARE MANY FLOWERS IN BLOOM...
AND LOTS OF DELICIOUS THINGS TO EAT...
UM
GROWWWLL
YOUR TUMMY'S MAKING A LOT OF NOISE THERE.
DINNER!
I HAVE TO GET HOME FOR DINNER!
BYE! SEE YOU!
BE CAREFUL ON YOUR WAY HOME.
YOU BE CAREFUL, TOO!
Huh?
HA HA HA

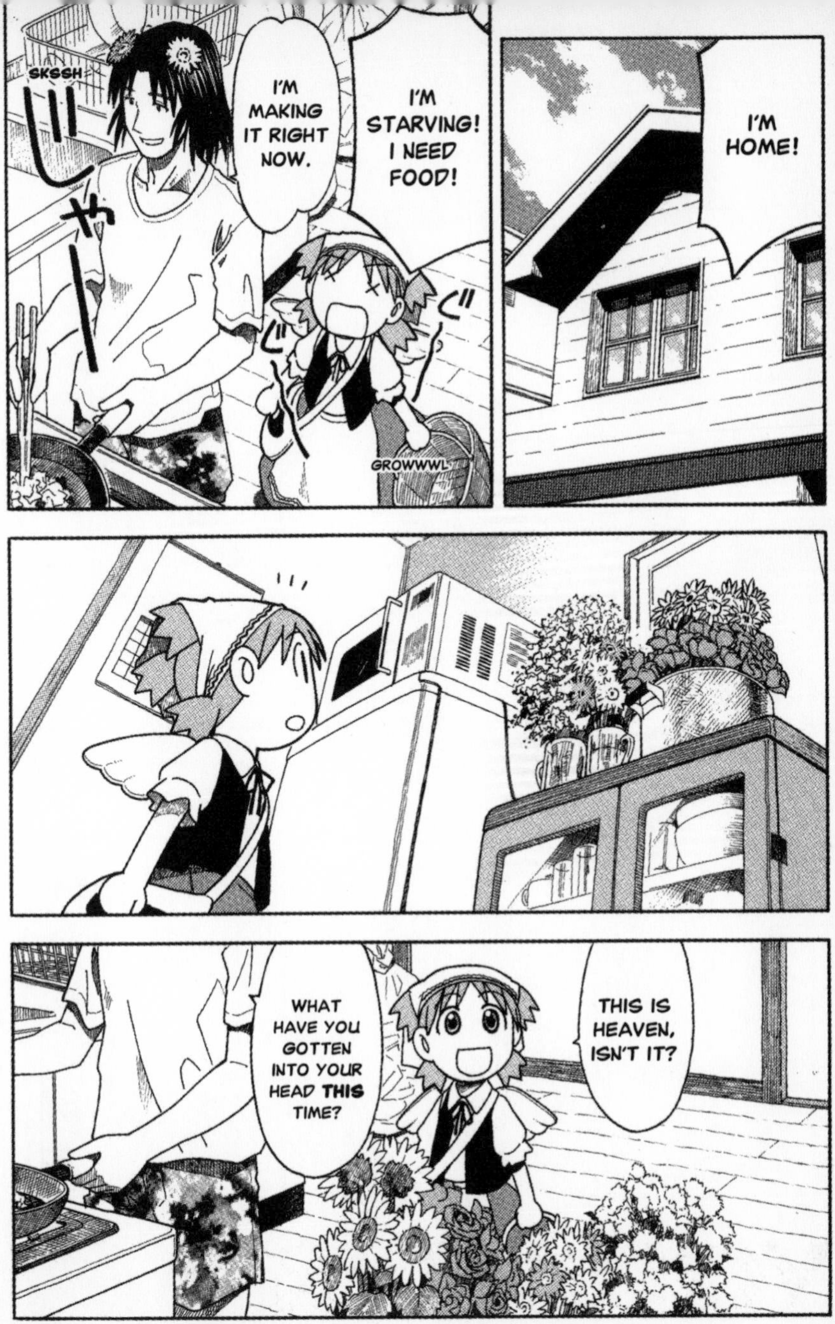
I'M HOME!
I'M STARVING! I NEED FOOD!
I'M MAKING IT RIGHT NOW.
SKSSH
GROWWWL
THIS IS HEAVEN, ISN'T IT?
WHAT HAVE YOU GOTTEN INTO YOUR HEAD **THIS** TIME?

YOTSUBA&!

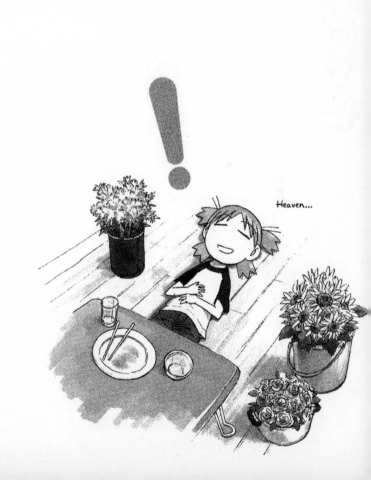

Heaven...

YOTSUBA & THE ELEPHANT

CHAPTER 19

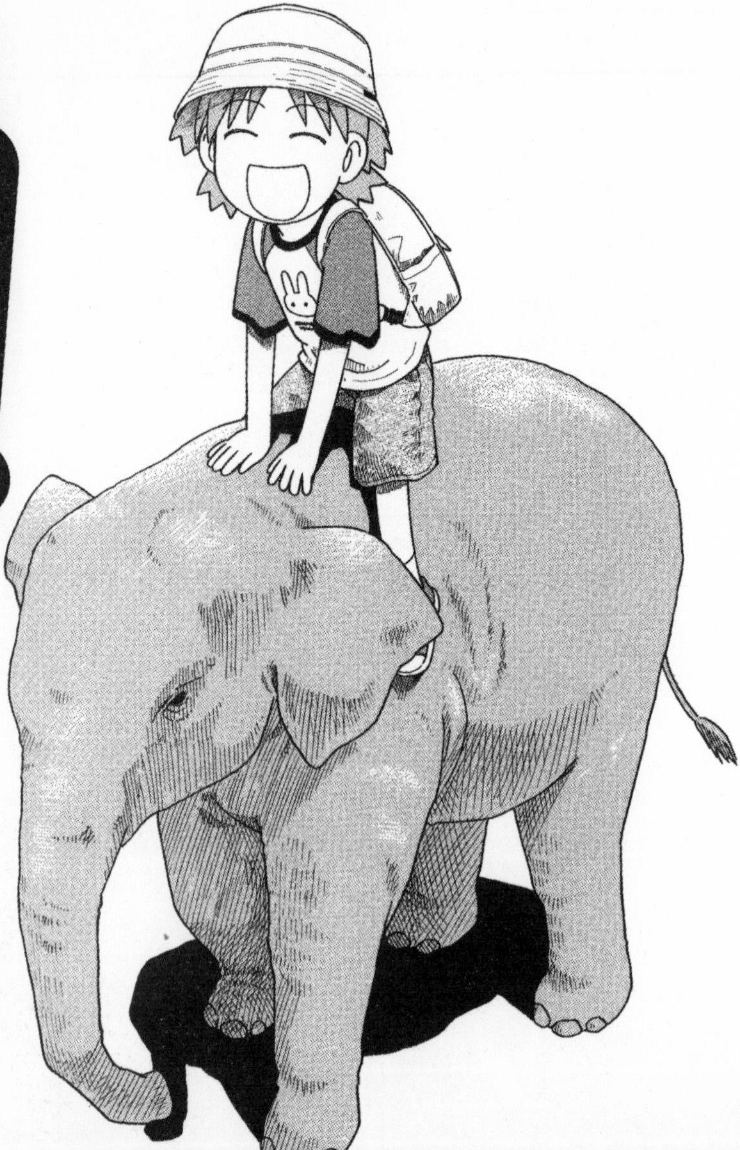

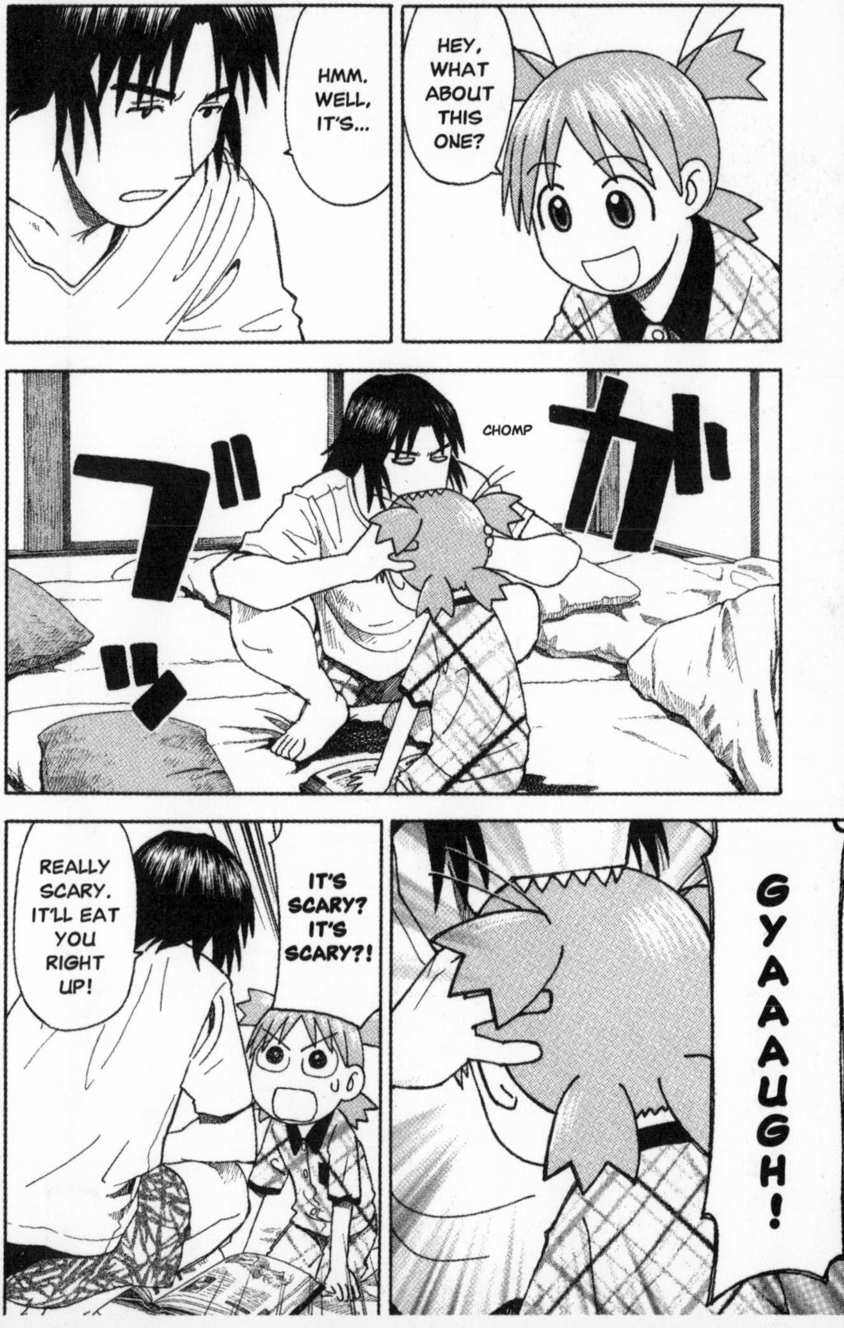
HEY, WHAT ABOUT THIS ONE?
HMM. WELL, IT'S...
ガブッ
CHOMP
GYAAAUGH!
IT'S SCARY? IT'S SCARY?!
REALLY SCARY. IT'LL EAT YOU RIGHT UP!

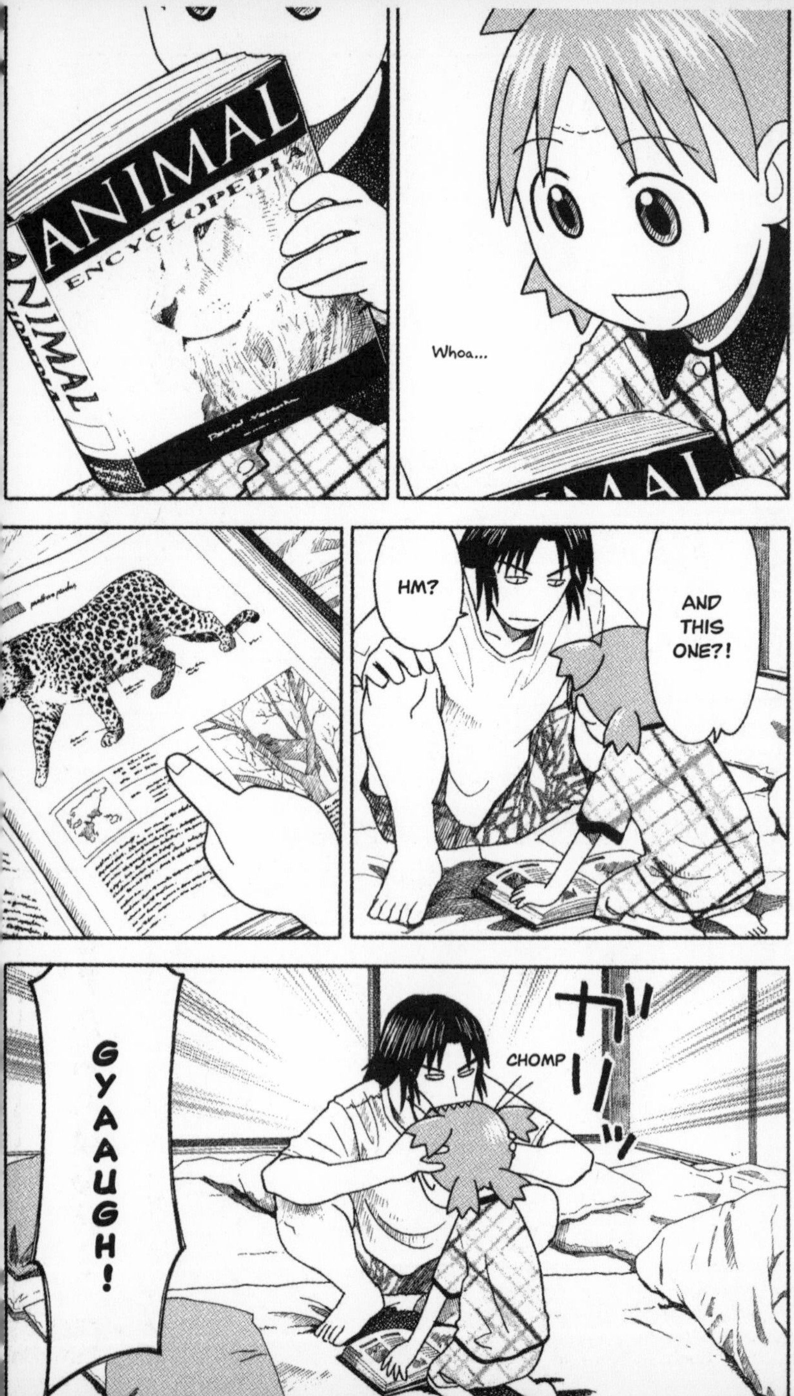
Whoa...
ANIMAL
ENCYCLOPEDIA
AND THIS ONE?!
HM?
ガリッ
CHOMP
GYAAUGH!

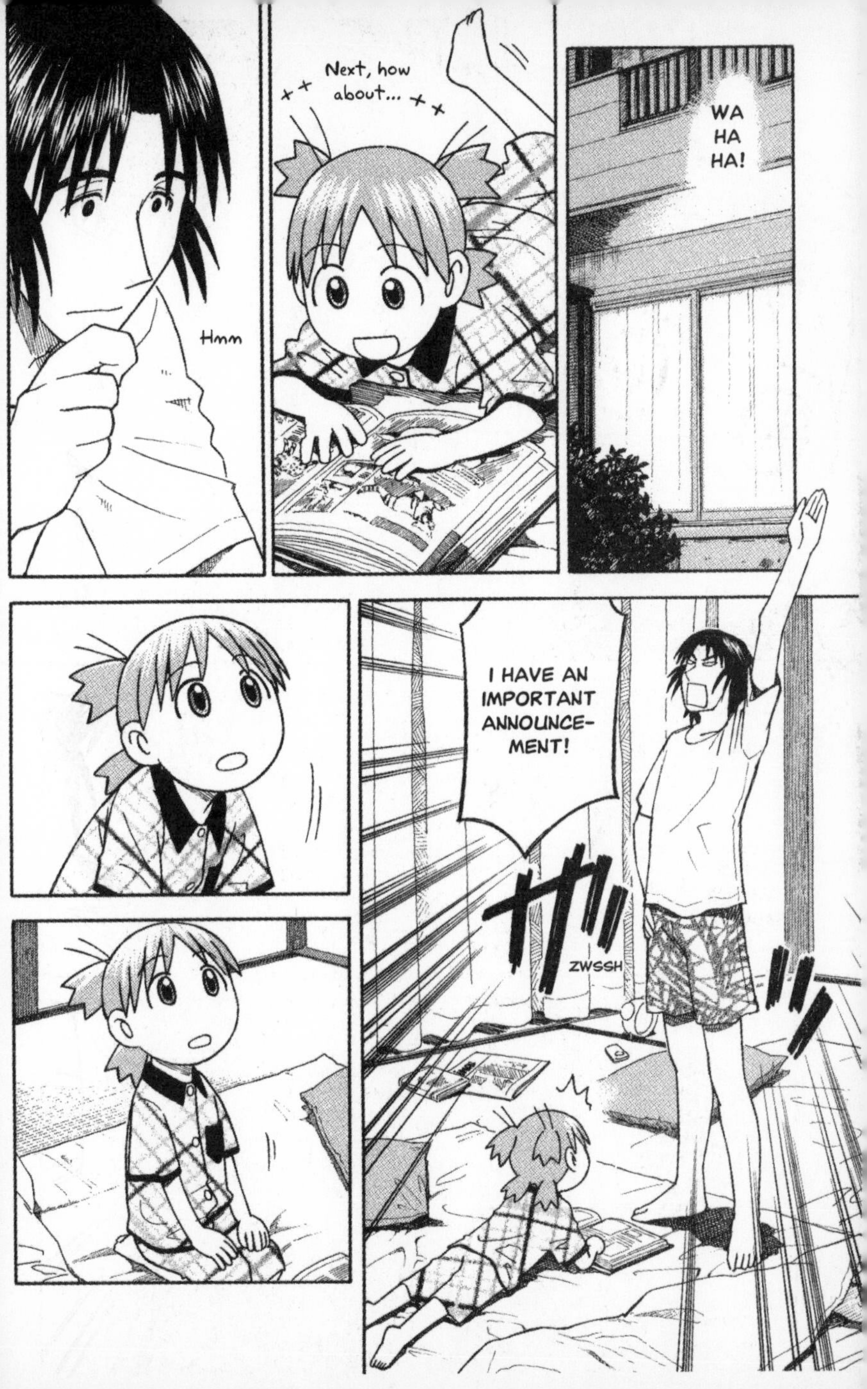
WA HA HA!
Next, how about...
Hmm
I HAVE AN IMPORTANT ANNOUNCEMENT!
ZWSSH

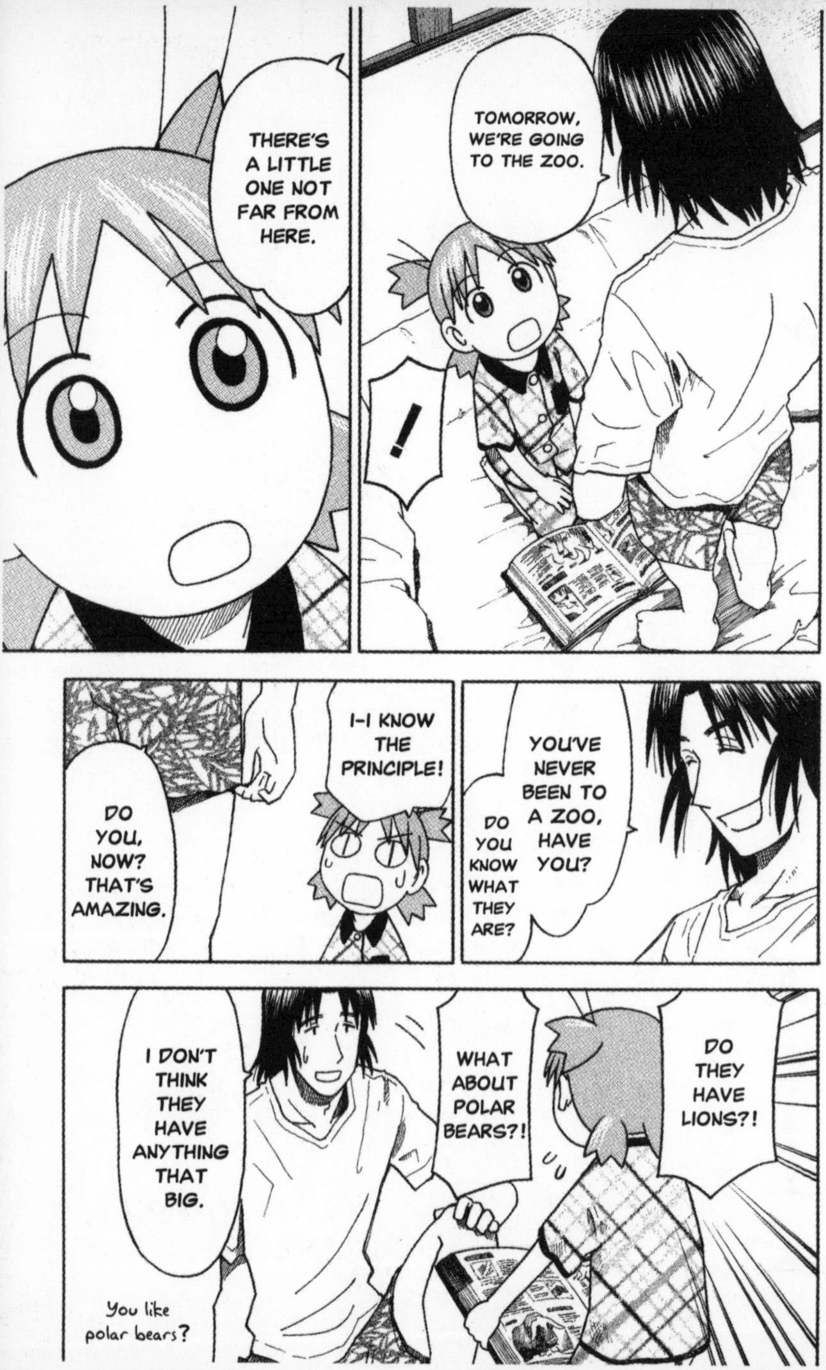
TOMORROW, WE'RE GOING TO THE ZOO.
!
THERE'S A LITTLE ONE NOT FAR FROM HERE.
YOU'VE NEVER BEEN TO A ZOO, HAVE YOU?
DO YOU KNOW WHAT THEY ARE?
I-I KNOW THE PRINCIPLE!
DO YOU, NOW? THAT'S AMAZING.
DO THEY HAVE LIONS?!
WHAT ABOUT POLAR BEARS?!
I DON'T THINK THEY HAVE ANYTHING THAT BIG.
You like polar bears?

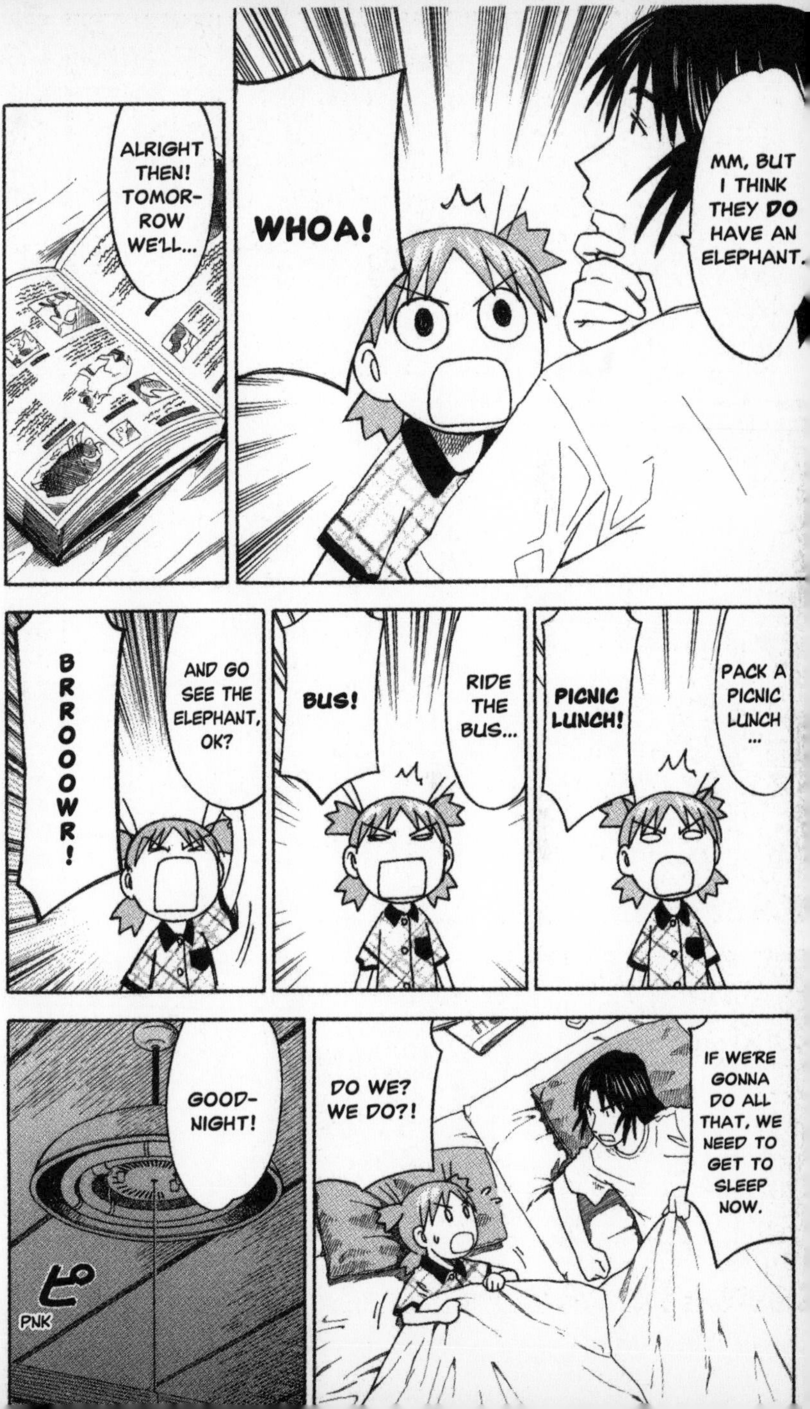
MM, BUT I THINK THEY DO HAVE AN ELEPHANT.
WHOA!
ALRIGHT THEN! TOMOR-ROW WE'LL...
PACK A PICNIC LUNCH ...
PICNIC LUNCH!
RIDE THE BUS...
BUS!
AND GO SEE THE ELEPHANT, OK?
BRROOOOWR!
IF WE'RE GONNA DO ALL THAT, WE NEED TO GET TO SLEEP NOW.
DO WE? WE DO?!
GOOD-NIGHT!
ピ
PNK

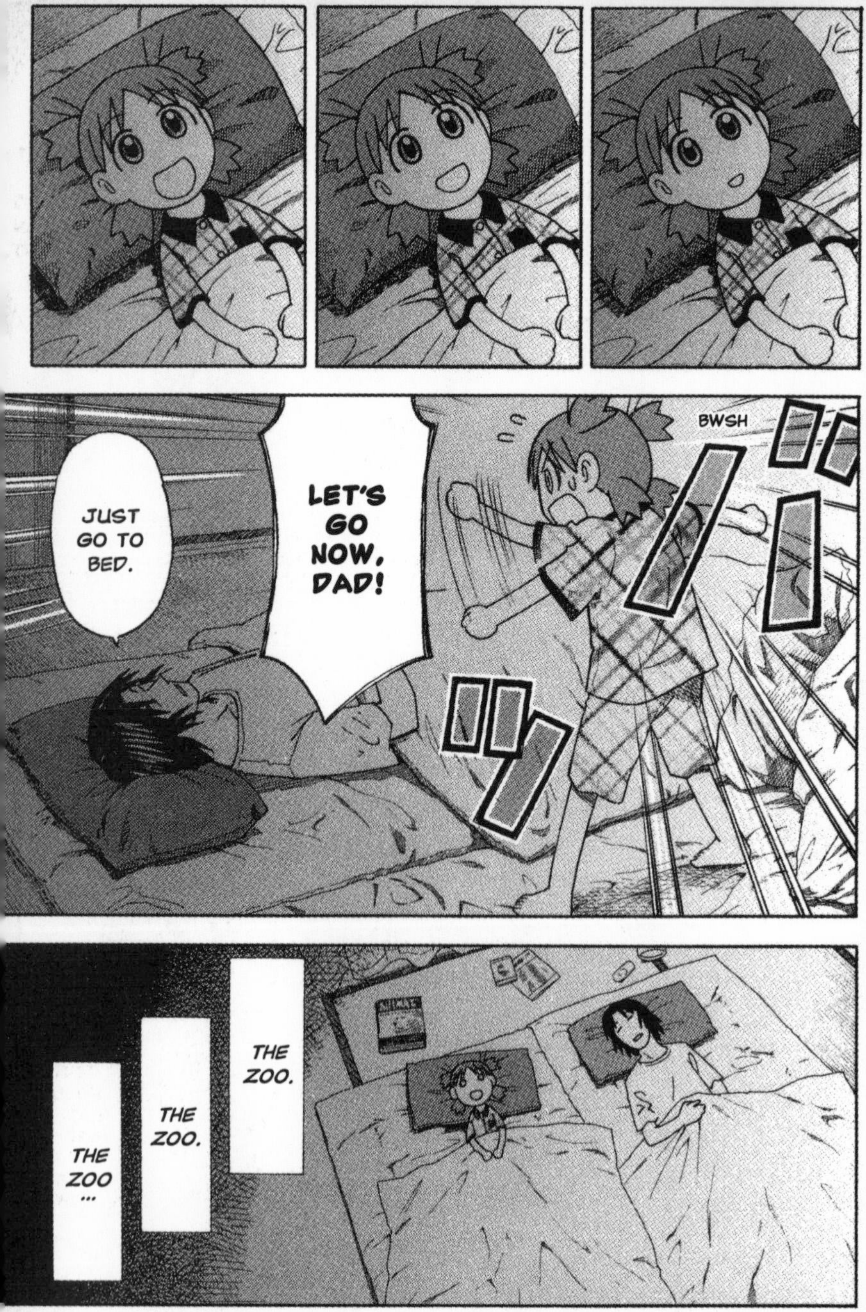
BWSH
LET'S GO NOW, DAD!
JUST GO TO BED.
THE ZOO.
THE ZOO.
THE ZOO ...

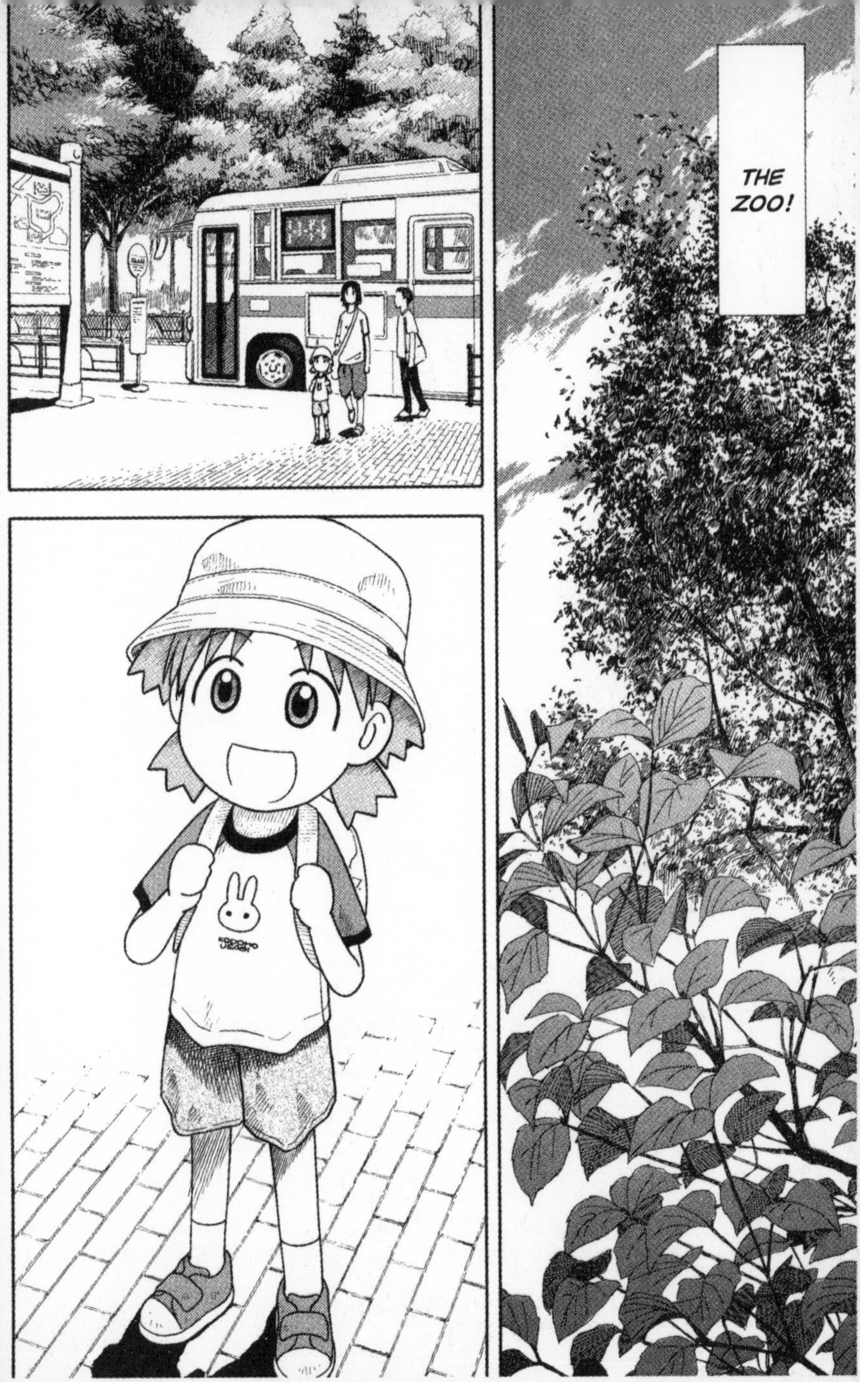
THE ZOO!

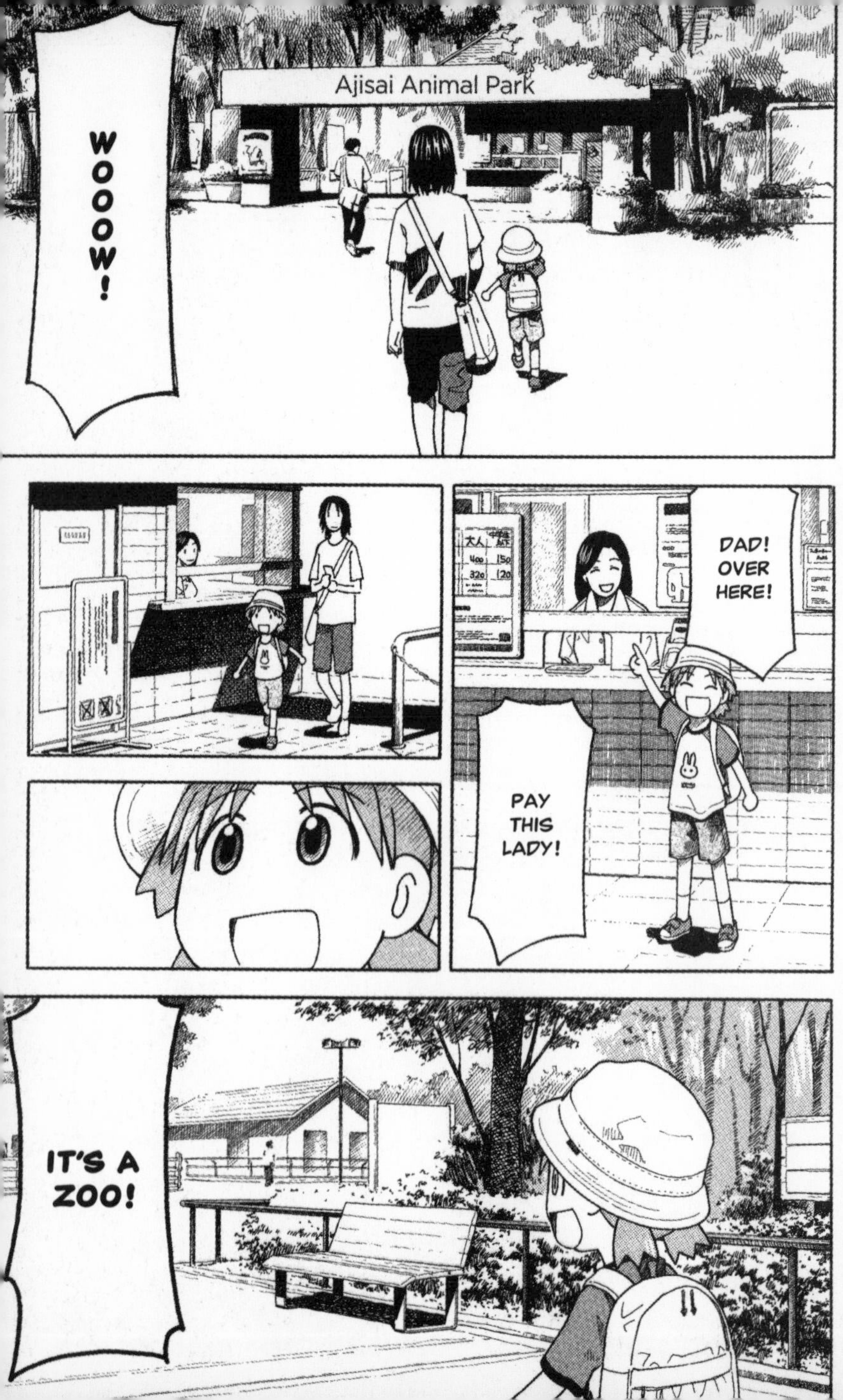
Ajisai Animal Park
WOOOOW!
DAD! OVER HERE!
PAY THIS LADY!
IT'S A ZOO!

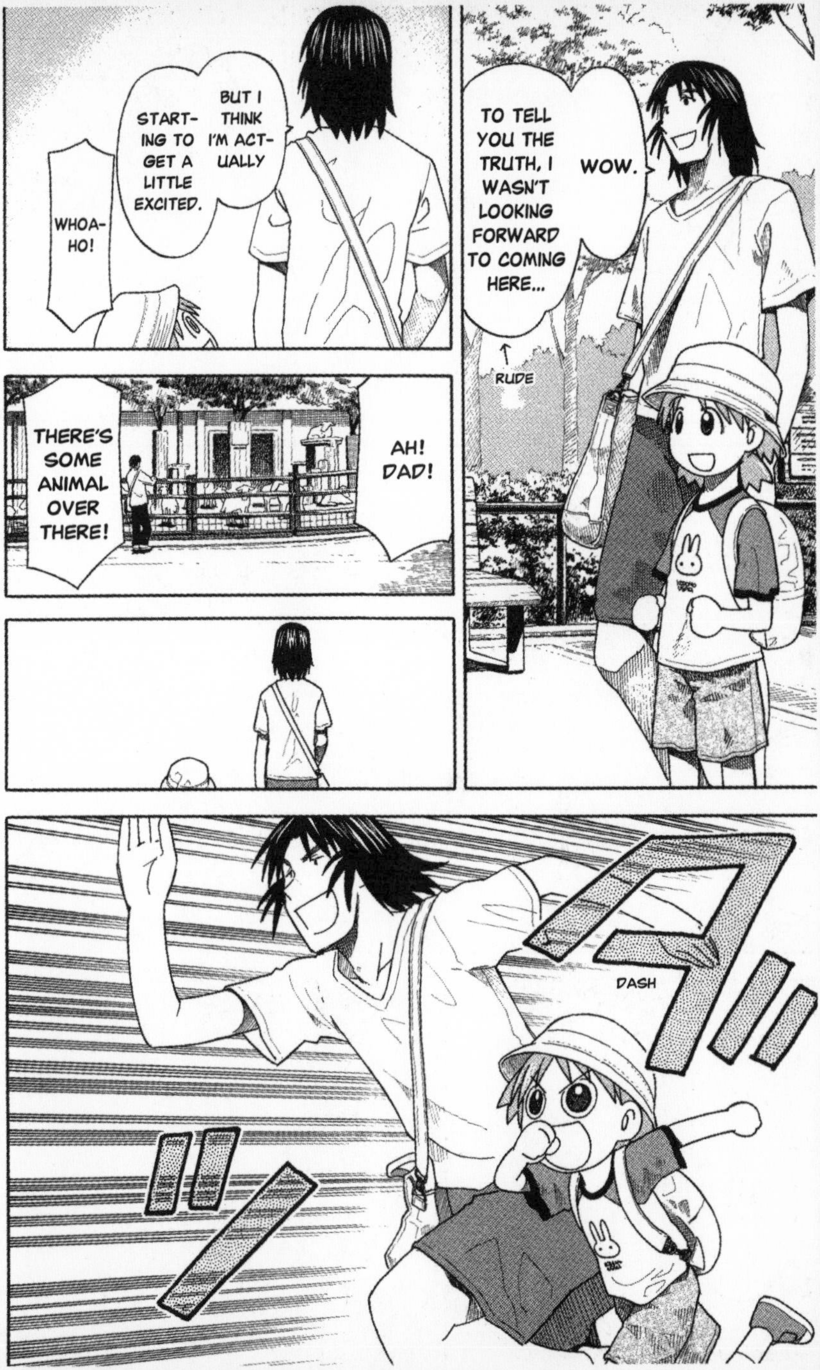
WOW.
TO TELL YOU THE TRUTH, I WASN'T LOOKING FORWARD TO COMING HERE...
RUDE
BUT I THINK I'M ACTUALLY STARTING TO GET A LITTLE EXCITED.
WHOA-HO!
AH! DAD!
THERE'S SOME ANIMAL OVER THERE!
DASH

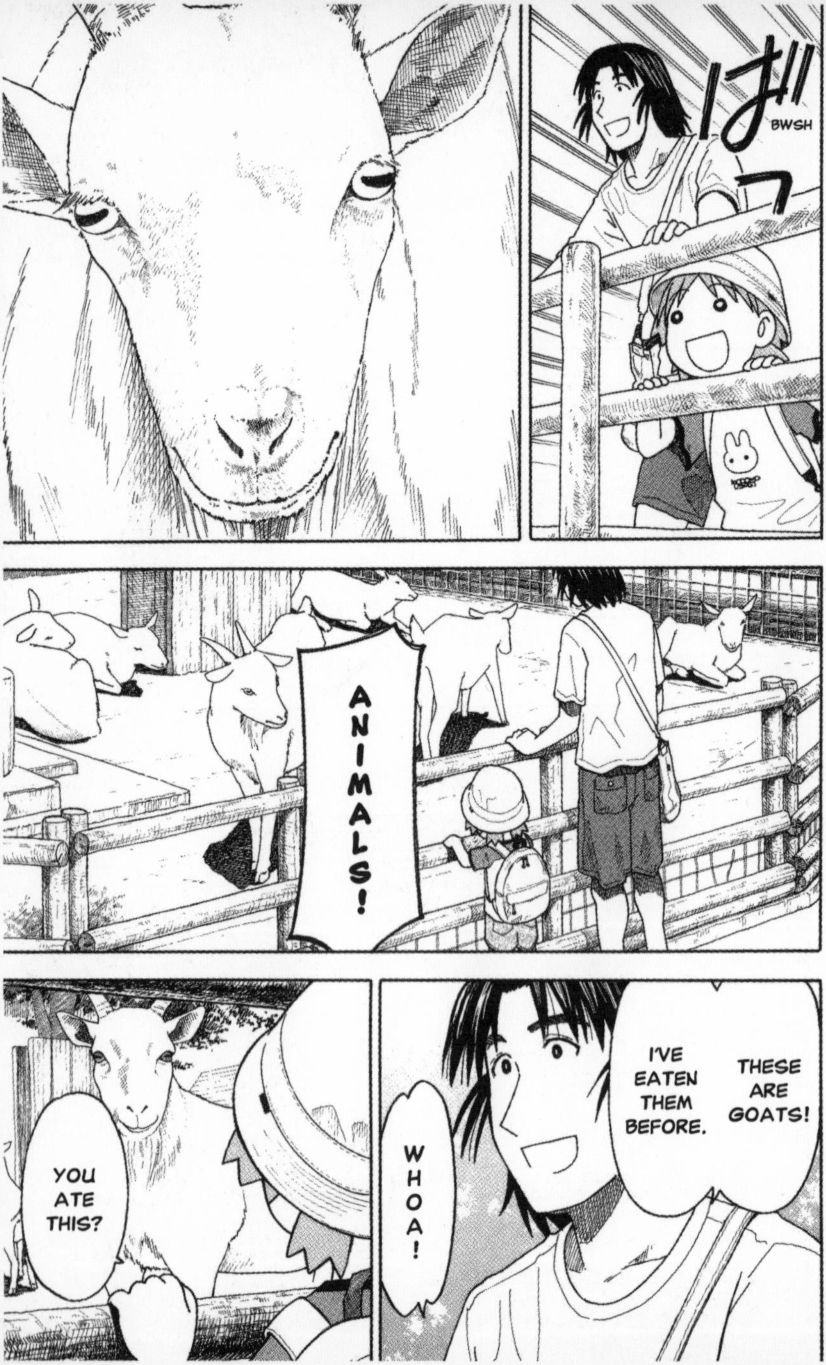
ばっ
BWSH
ANIMALS!
THESE ARE GOATS!
I'VE EATEN THEM BEFORE.
WHOA!
YOU ATE THIS?

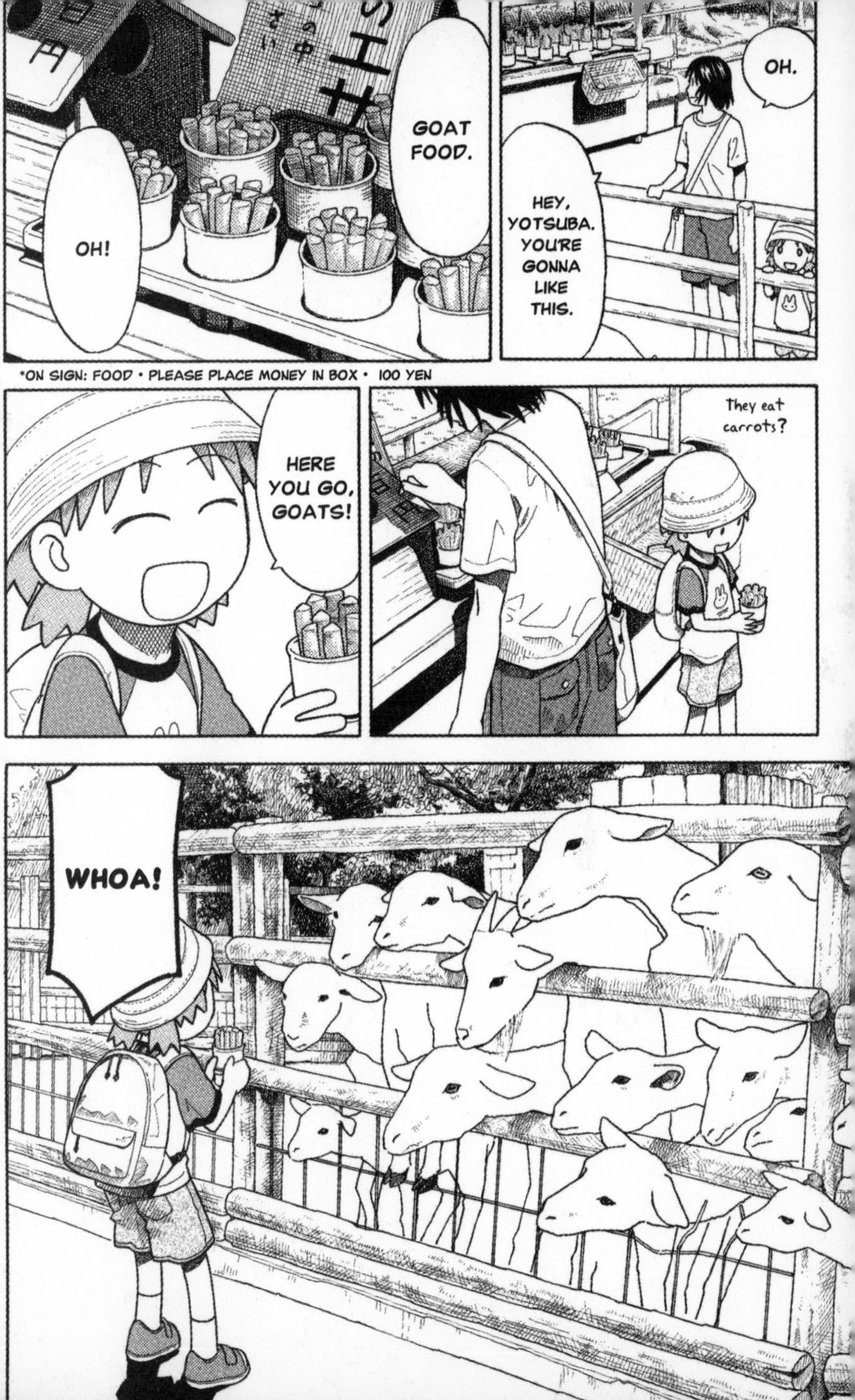
OH.
HEY, YOTSUBA. YOU'RE GONNA LIKE THIS.
GOAT FOOD.
OH!
*ON SIGN: FOOD • PLEASE PLACE MONEY IN BOX • 100 YEN
They eat carrots?
HERE YOU GO, GOATS!
WHOA!

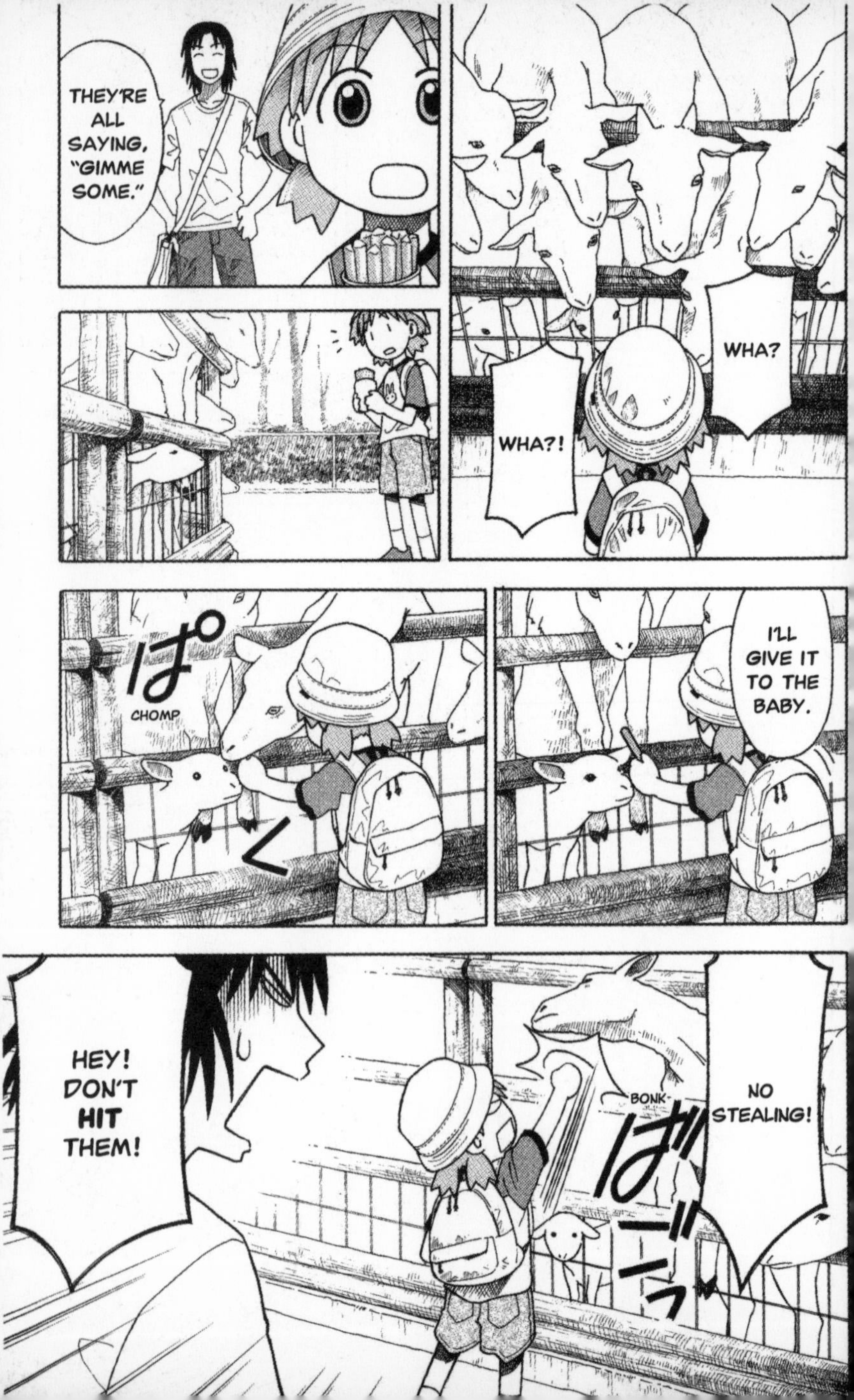
WHA?
WHA?!
THEY'RE ALL SAYING, "GIMME SOME."
I'LL GIVE IT TO THE BABY.
ぱく
CHOMP
NO STEALING!
BONK
ばごーっ
HEY! DON'T **HIT** THEM!

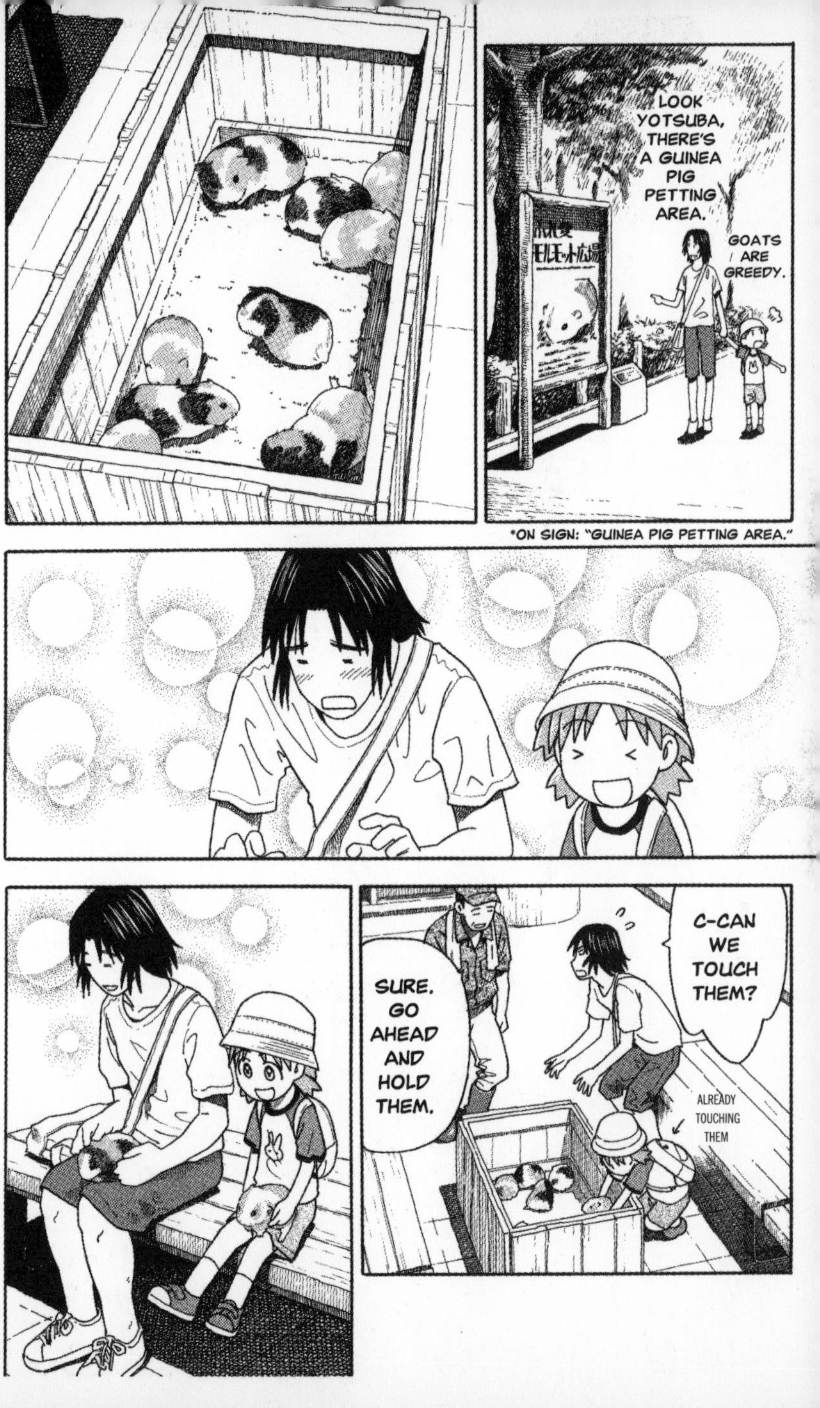
LOOK YOTSUBA, THERE'S A GUINEA PIG PETTING AREA.
GOATS ARE GREEDY.
C-CAN WE TOUCH THEM?
SURE. GO AHEAD AND HOLD THEM.
ALREADY TOUCHING THEM
*ON SIGN: "GUINEA PIG PETTING AREA."

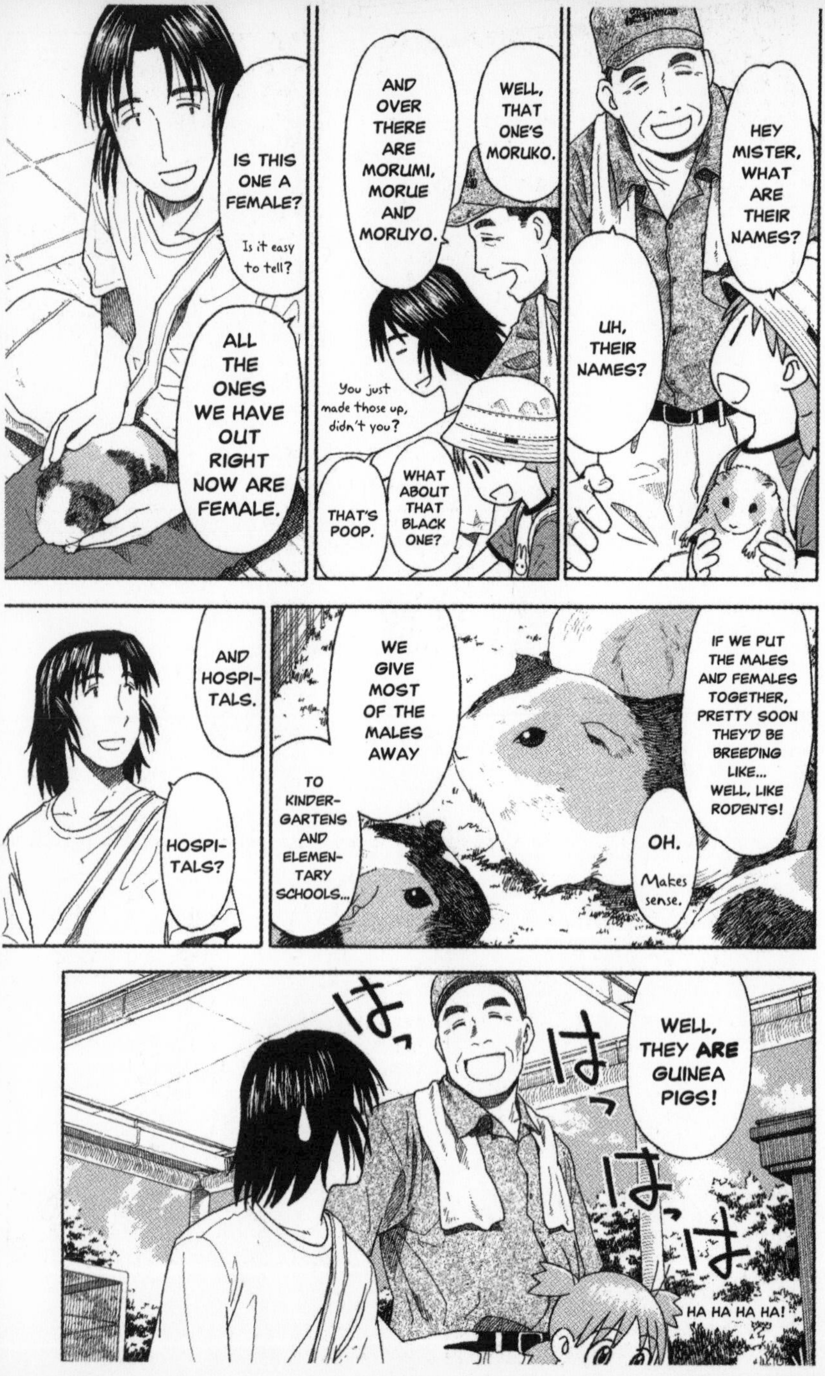
HEY MISTER, WHAT ARE THEIR NAMES?
UH, THEIR NAMES?
WELL, THAT ONE'S MORUKO.
AND OVER THERE ARE MORUMI, MORUE AND MORUYO.
You just made those up, didn't you?
WHAT ABOUT THAT BLACK ONE?
THAT'S POOP.
IS THIS ONE A FEMALE?
Is it easy to tell?
ALL THE ONES WE HAVE OUT RIGHT NOW ARE FEMALE.
IF WE PUT THE MALES AND FEMALES TOGETHER, PRETTY SOON THEY'D BE BREEDING LIKE... WELL, LIKE RODENTS!
OH.
Makes sense.
WE GIVE MOST OF THE MALES AWAY
TO KINDER-GARTENS AND ELEMEN-TARY SCHOOLS...
AND HOSPI-TALS.
HOSPI-TALS?
WELL, THEY **ARE** GUINEA PIGS!
はっ
はっ
はっ
は
HA HA HA HA!

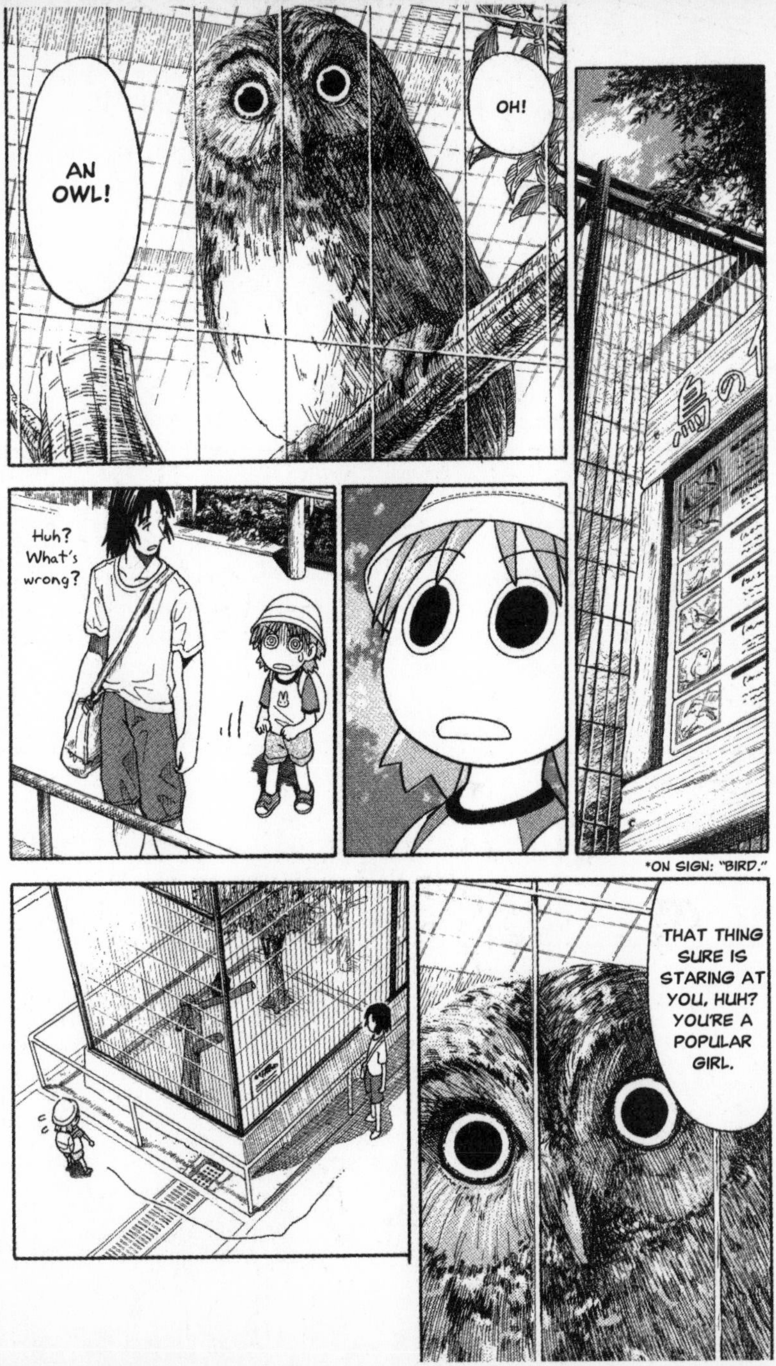
OH!
AN OWL!
Huh? What's wrong?
*ON SIGN: "BIRD."
THAT THING SURE IS STARING AT YOU, HUH? YOU'RE A POPULAR GIRL.

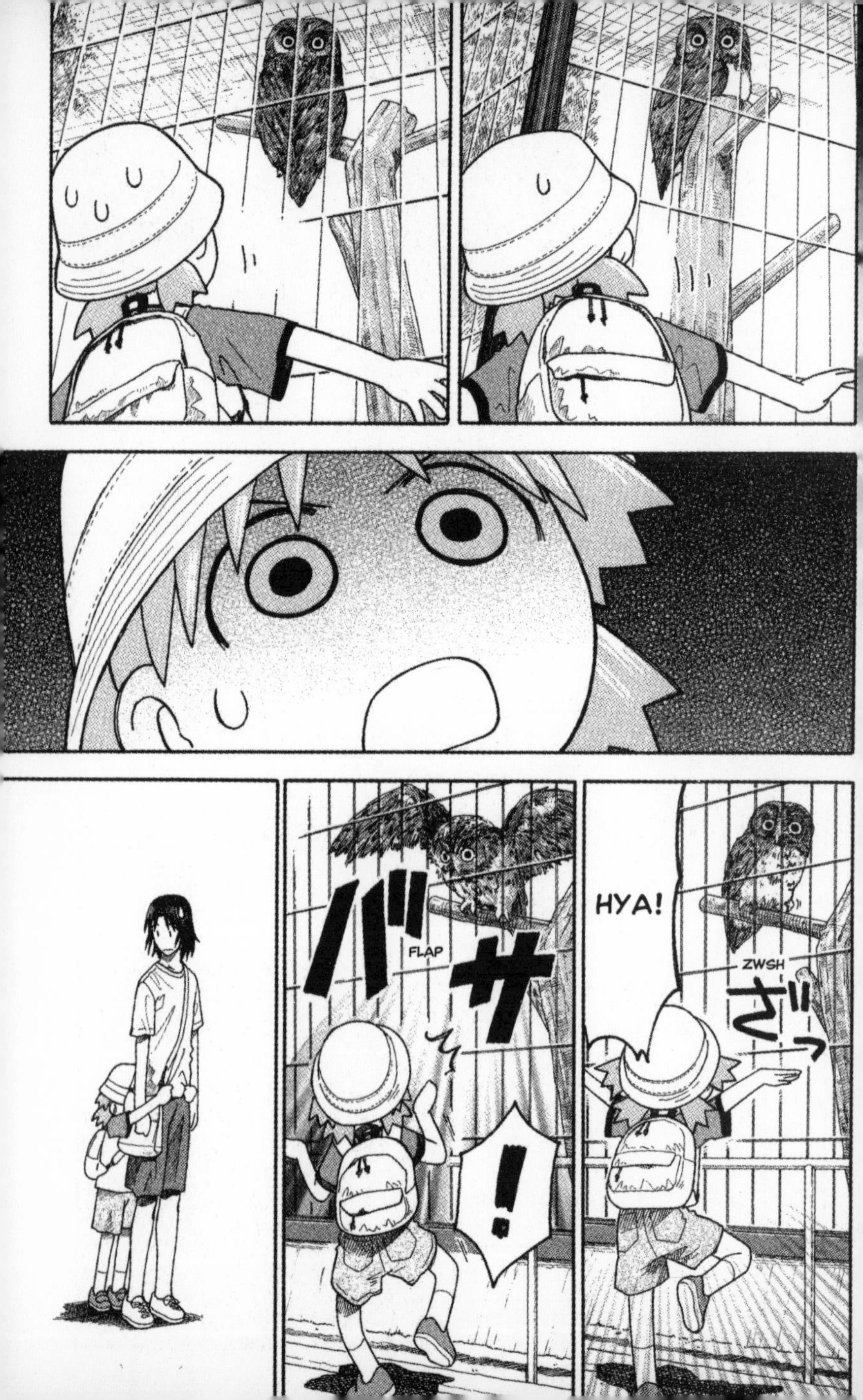
HYA!
ZWSH
ざっ
バサ
FLAP
!

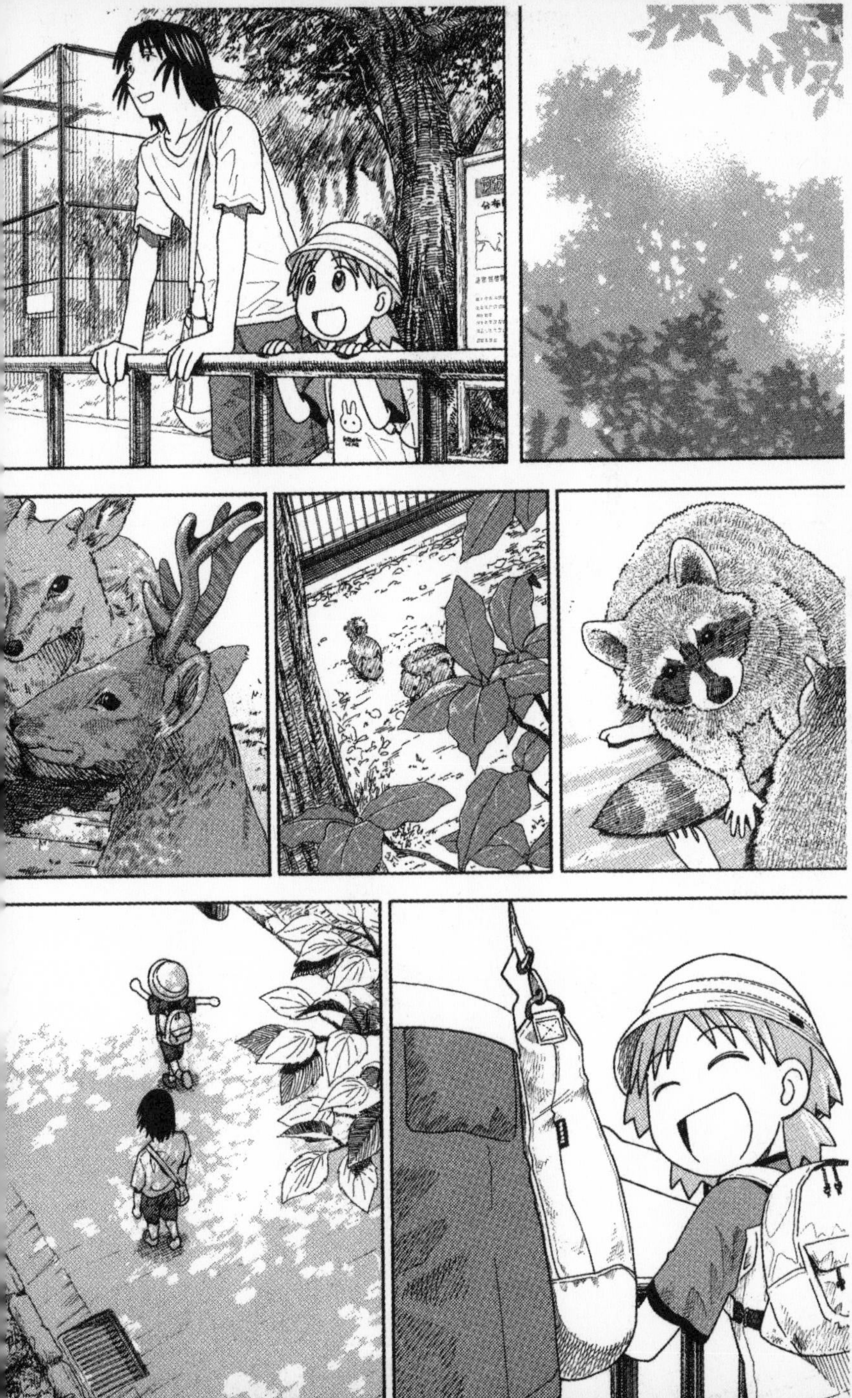

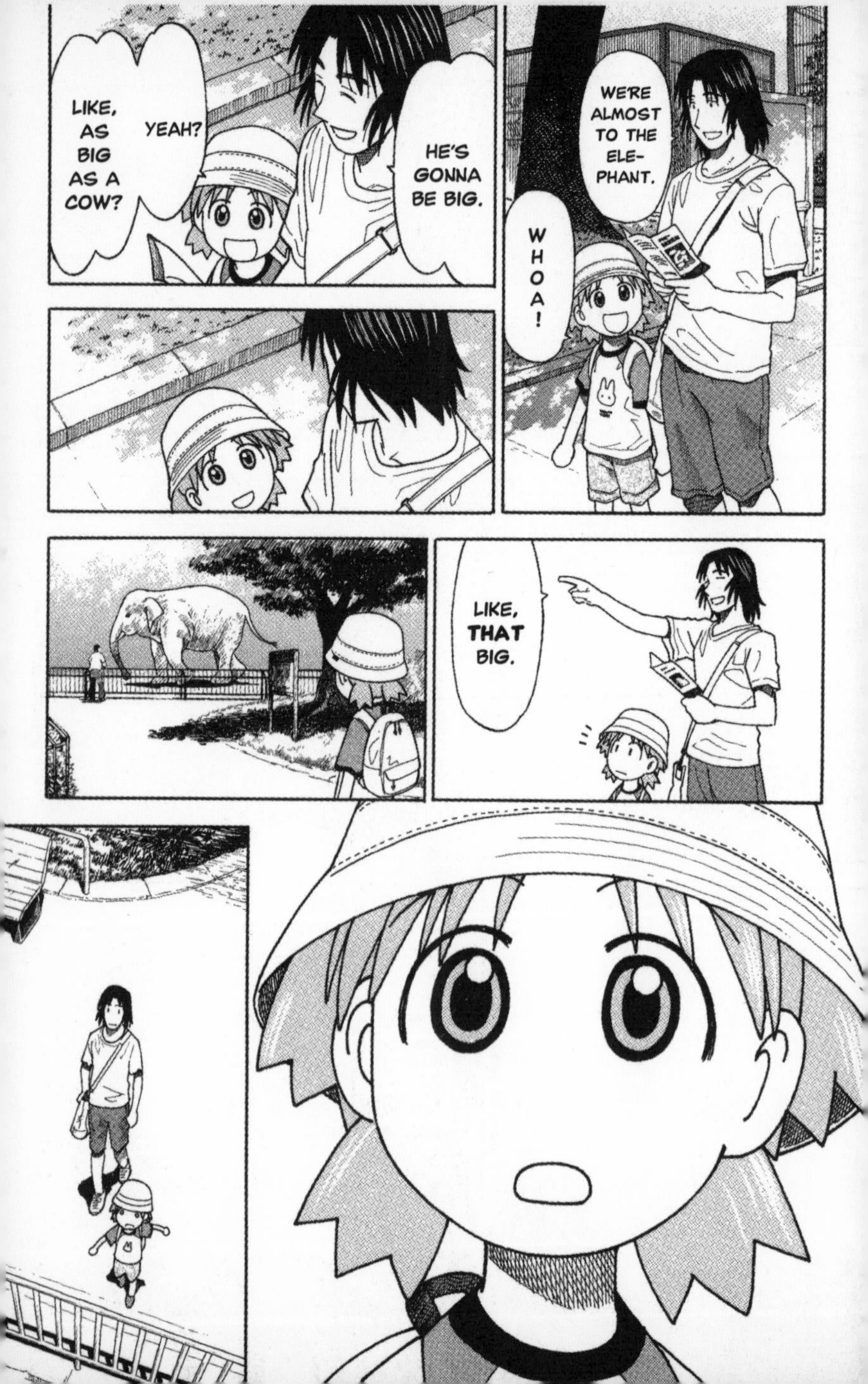
WE'RE ALMOST TO THE ELE-PHANT.
WHOA!
HE'S GONNA BE BIG.
YEAH?
LIKE, AS BIG AS A COW?
LIKE, **THAT** BIG.

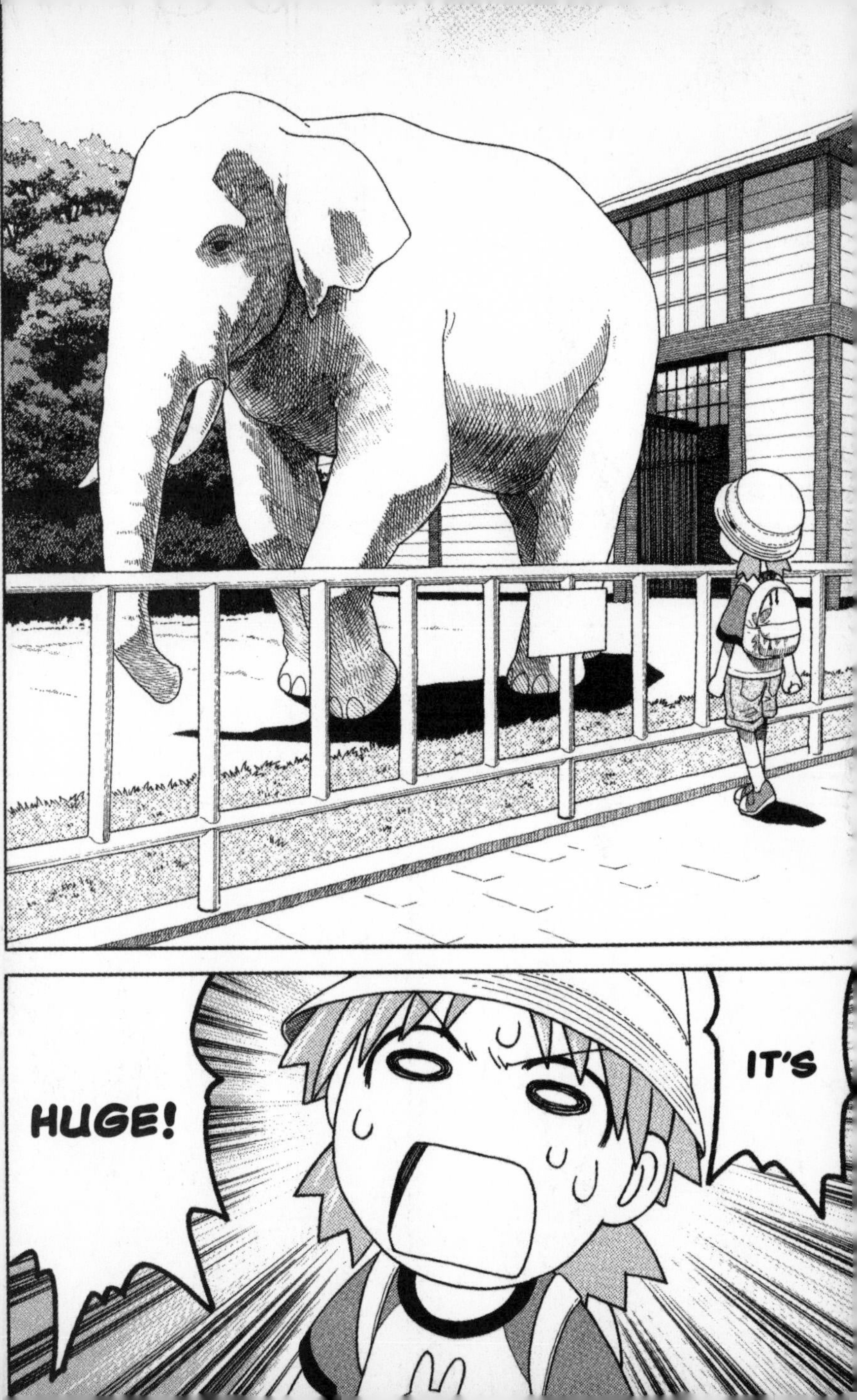
IT'S
HUGE!

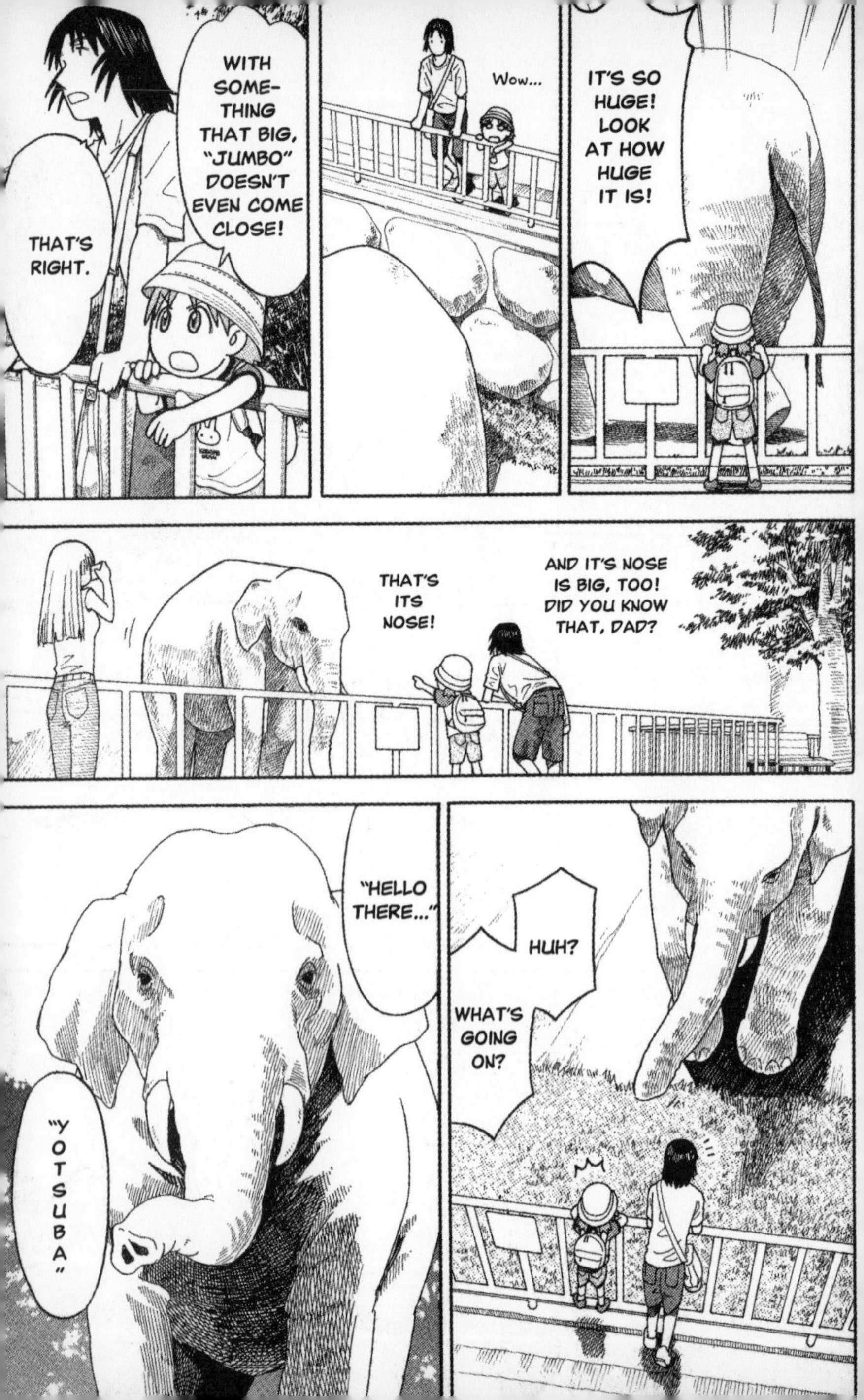
IT'S SO HUGE! LOOK AT HOW HUGE IT IS!
Wow...
WITH SOME-THING THAT BIG, "JUMBO" DOESN'T EVEN COME CLOSE!
THAT'S RIGHT.
AND IT'S NOSE IS BIG, TOO! DID YOU KNOW THAT, DAD?
THAT'S ITS NOSE!
HUH?
WHAT'S GOING ON?
"HELLO THERE..."
"YOTSUBA"

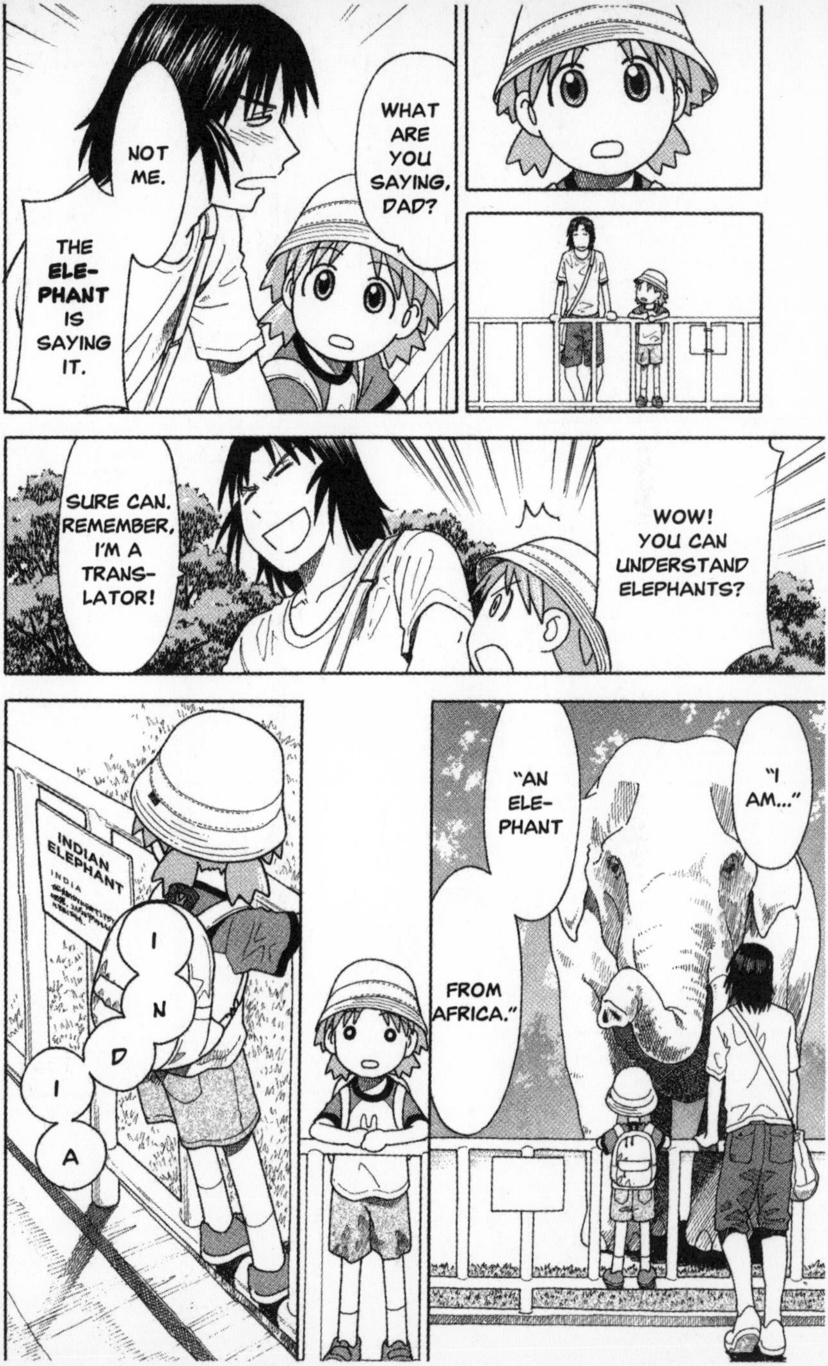
WHAT ARE YOU SAYING, DAD?
NOT ME.
THE ELEPHANT IS SAYING IT.
WOW! YOU CAN UNDERSTAND ELEPHANTS?
SURE CAN. REMEMBER, I'M A TRANSLATOR!
"I AM..."
"AN ELEPHANT
FROM AFRICA."
INDIAN ELEPHANT
INDIA
INDIA

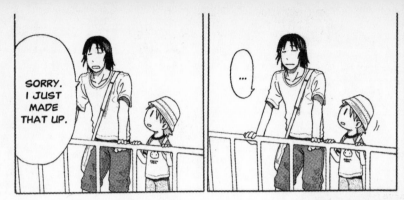

SORRY.
I JUST
MADE
THAT UP.

...

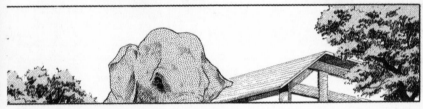

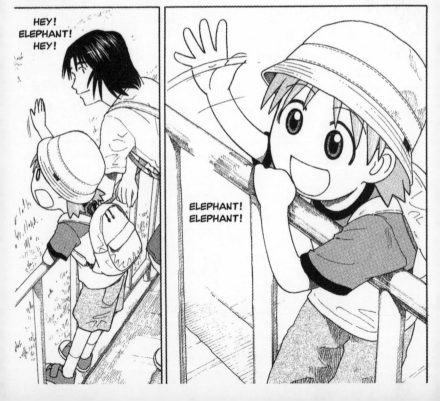

HEY!
ELEPHANT!
HEY!

ELEPHANT!
ELEPHANT!

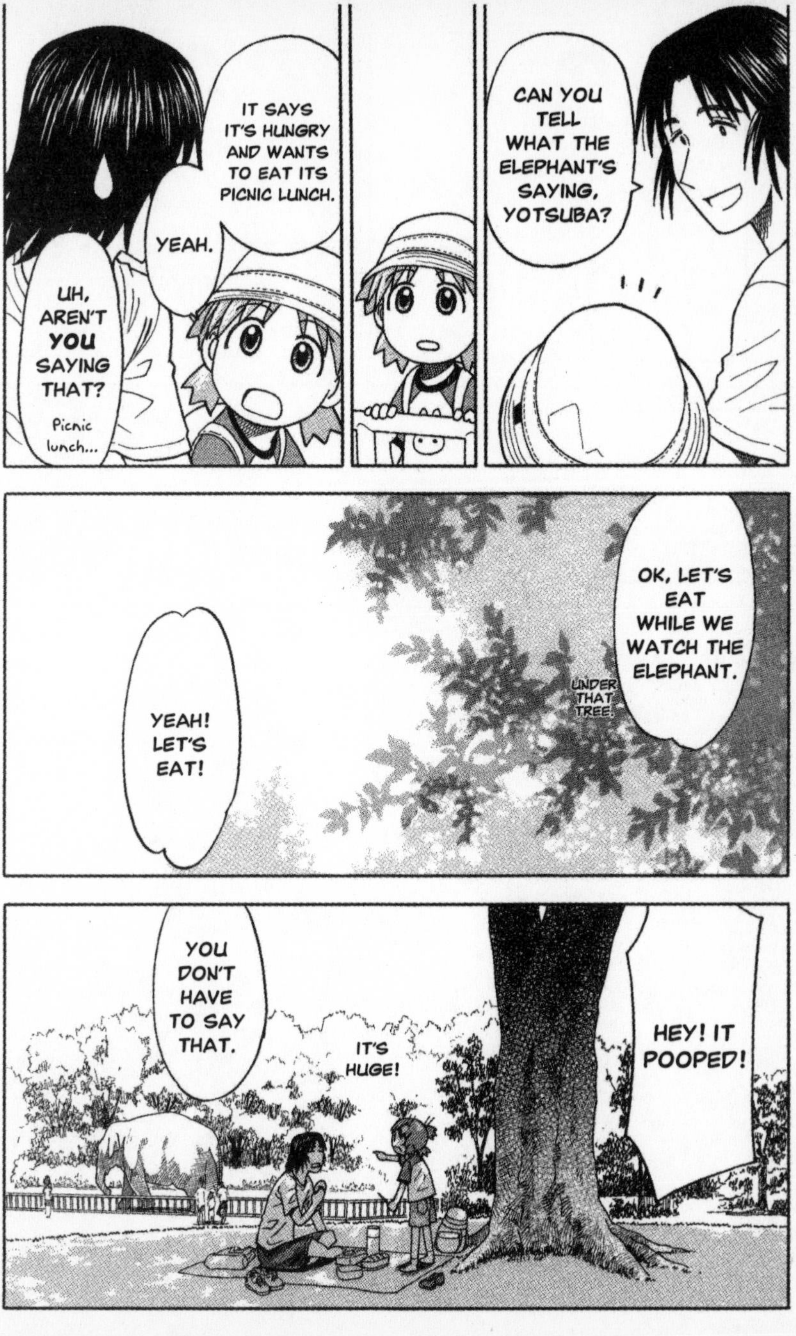
CAN YOU TELL WHAT THE ELEPHANT'S SAYING, YOTSUBA?
IT SAYS IT'S HUNGRY AND WANTS TO EAT ITS PICNIC LUNCH.
YEAH.
UH, AREN'T **YOU** SAYING THAT?
Picnic lunch...
OK, LET'S EAT WHILE WE WATCH THE ELEPHANT.
UNDER THAT TREE.
YEAH! LET'S EAT!
HEY! IT POOPED!
IT'S HUGE!
YOU DON'T HAVE TO SAY THAT.

YOTSUBA&!

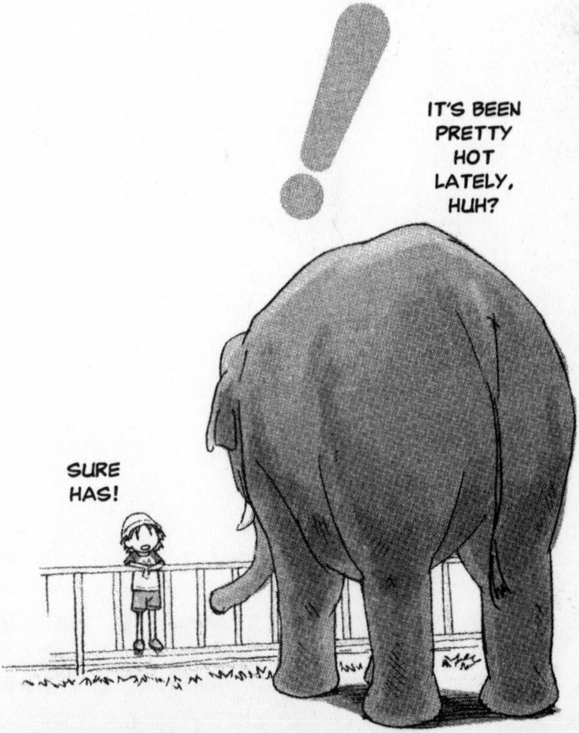
IT'S BEEN PRETTY HOT LATELY, HUH?
SURE HAS!

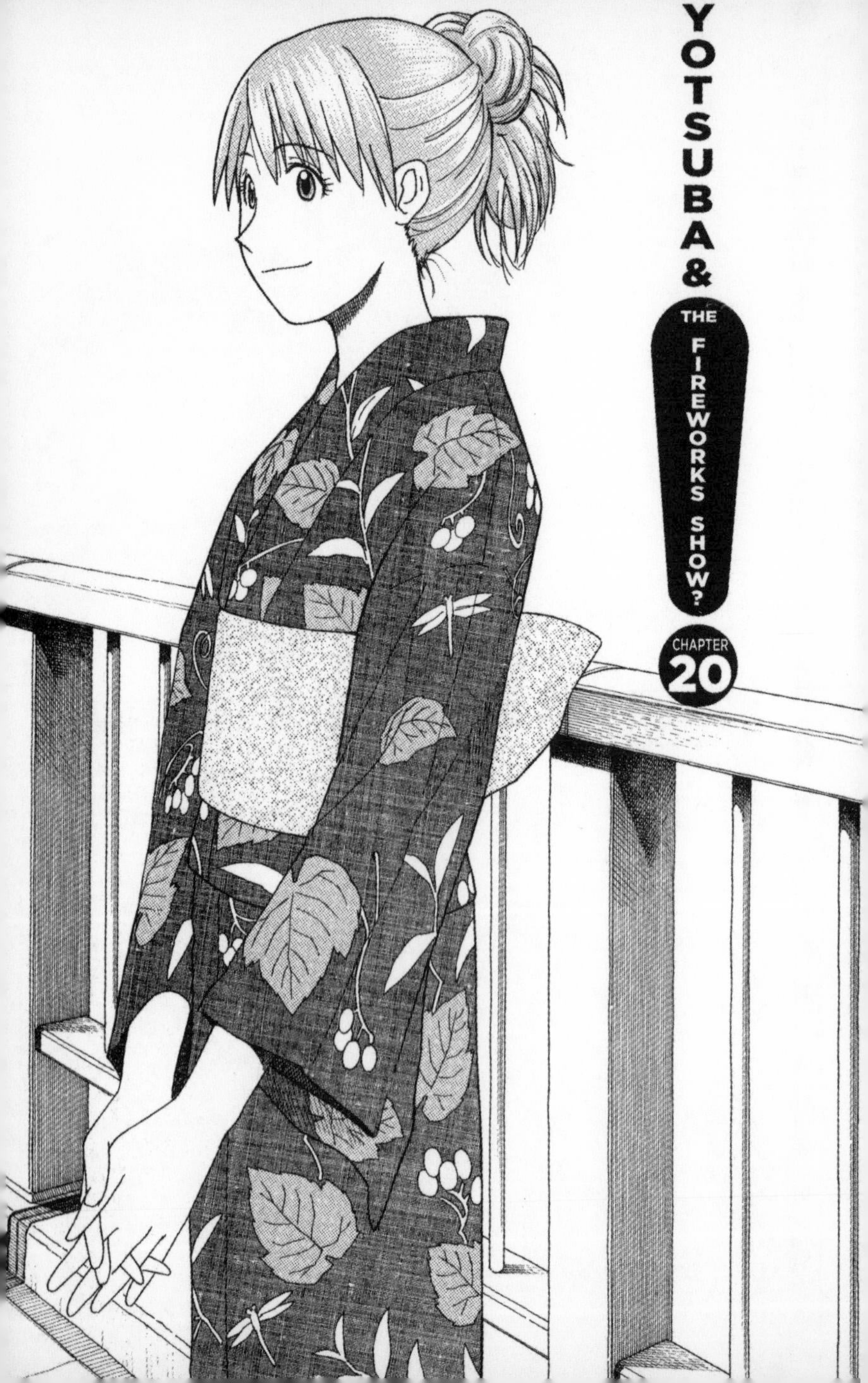
YOTSUBA&
THE FIREWORKS SHOW?
CHAPTER 20

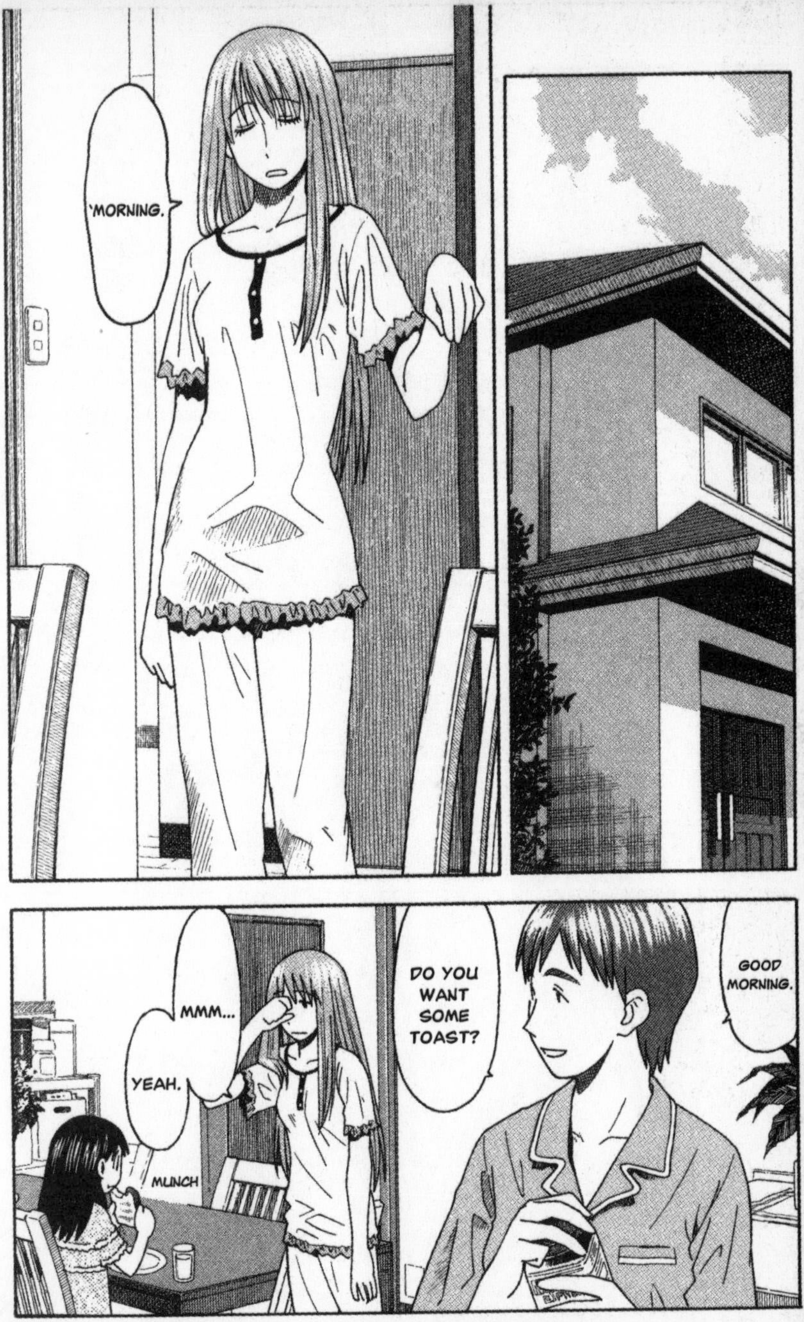
'MORNING.
GOOD MORNING.
DO YOU WANT SOME TOAST?
MMM...
YEAH.
MUNCH

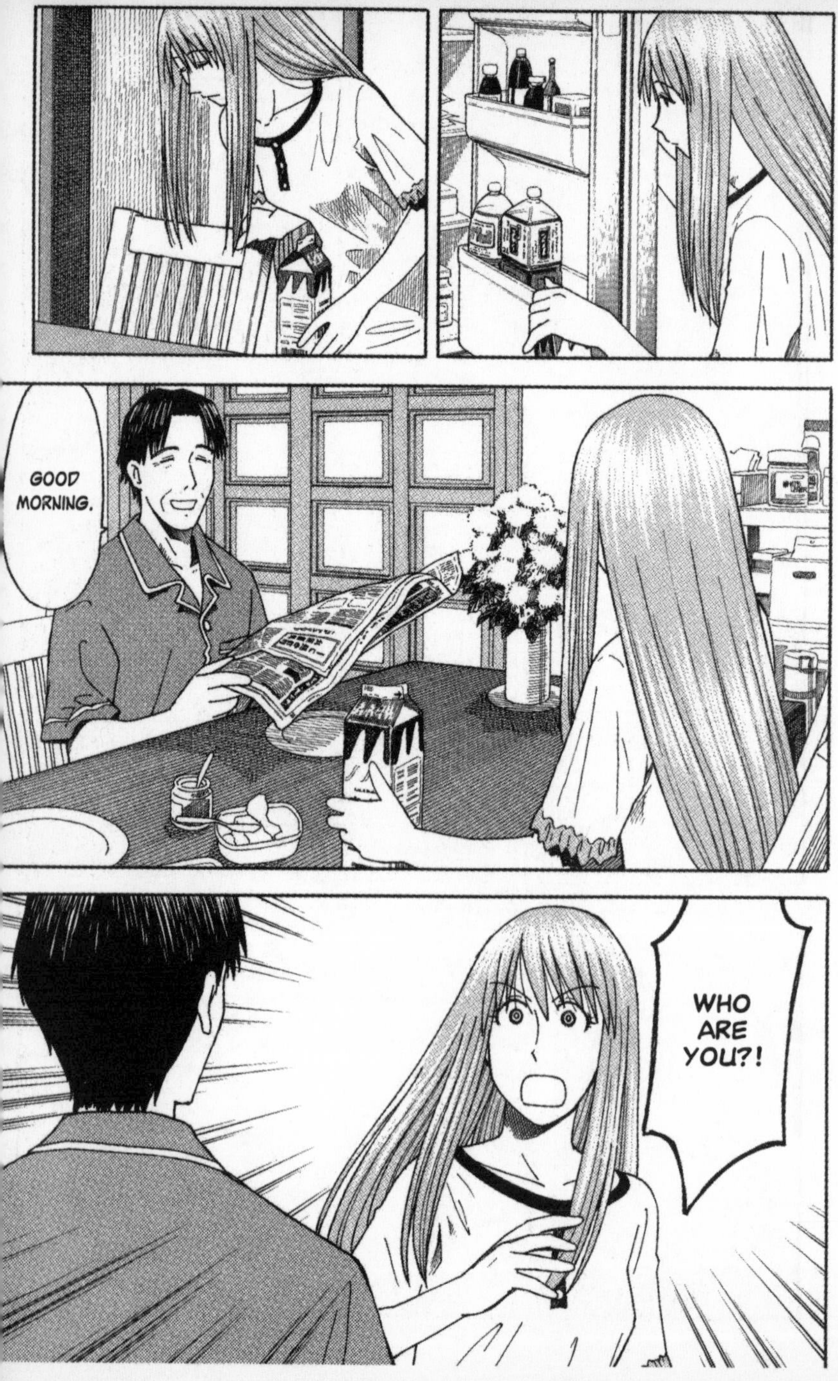
GOOD MORNING.
WHO ARE YOU?!

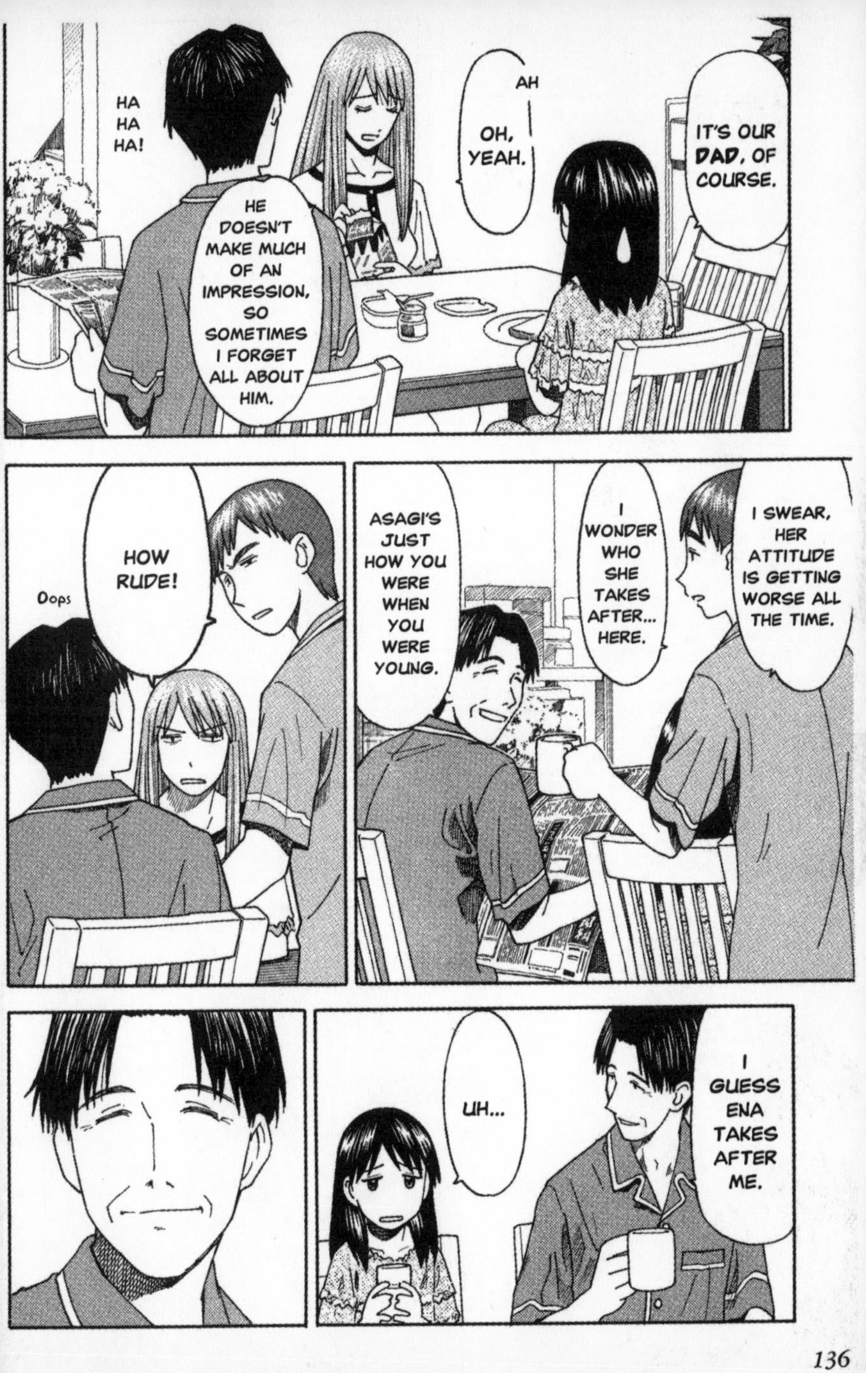
AH
IT'S OUR **DAD**, OF COURSE.
OH, YEAH.
HE DOESN'T MAKE MUCH OF AN IMPRESSION, SO SOMETIMES I FORGET ALL ABOUT HIM.
HA HA HA!
I SWEAR, HER ATTITUDE IS GETTING WORSE ALL THE TIME.
I WONDER WHO SHE TAKES AFTER... HERE.
ASAGI'S JUST HOW YOU WERE WHEN YOU WERE YOUNG.
HOW RUDE!
Oops
I GUESS ENA TAKES AFTER ME.
UH...

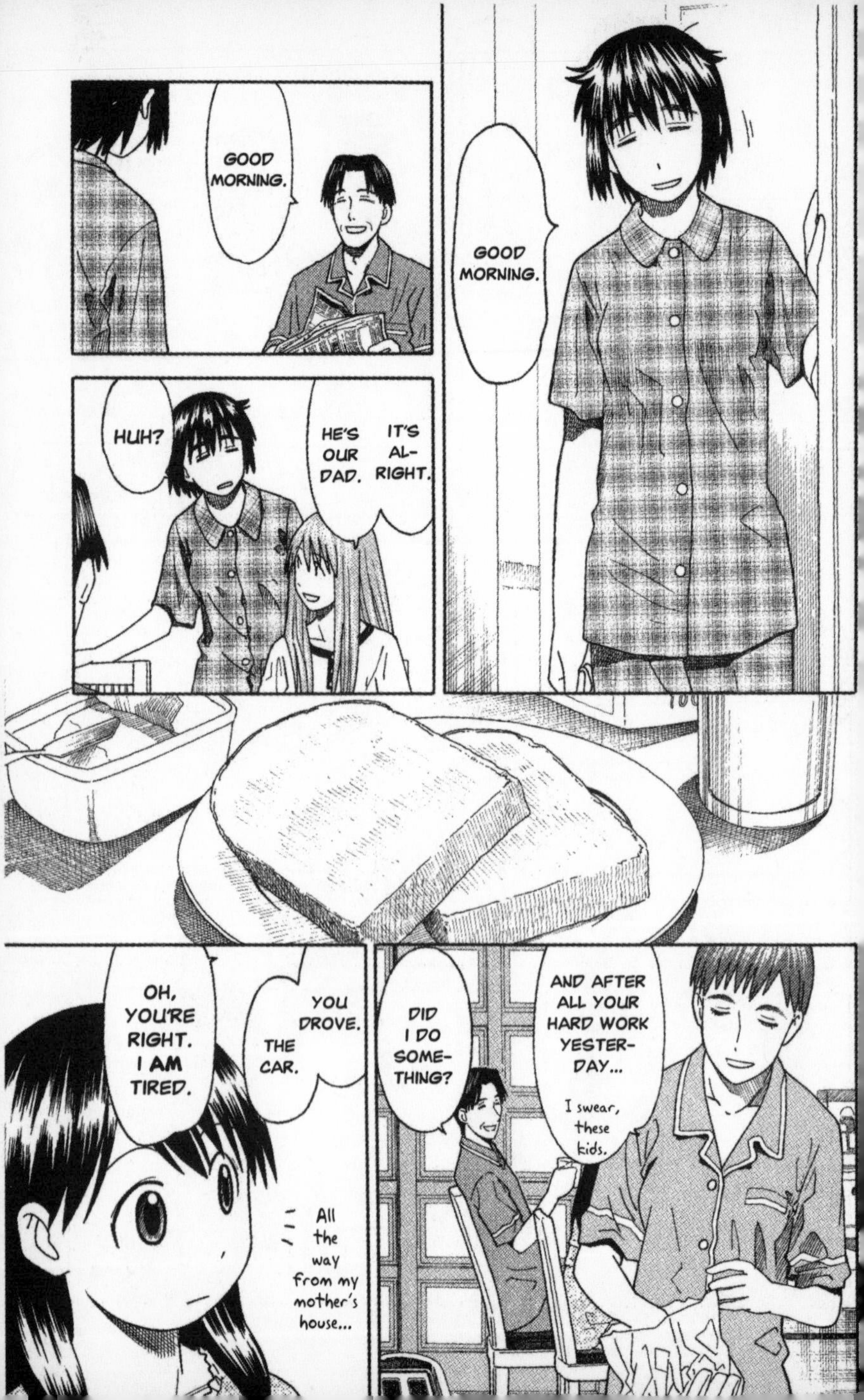
GOOD MORNING.
GOOD MORNING.
IT'S AL-RIGHT. HE'S OUR DAD.
HUH?
AND AFTER ALL YOUR HARD WORK YESTER-DAY...
I swear, these kids.
DID I DO SOME-THING?
YOU DROVE. THE CAR.
OH, YOU'RE RIGHT. I AM TIRED.
All the way from my mother's house...

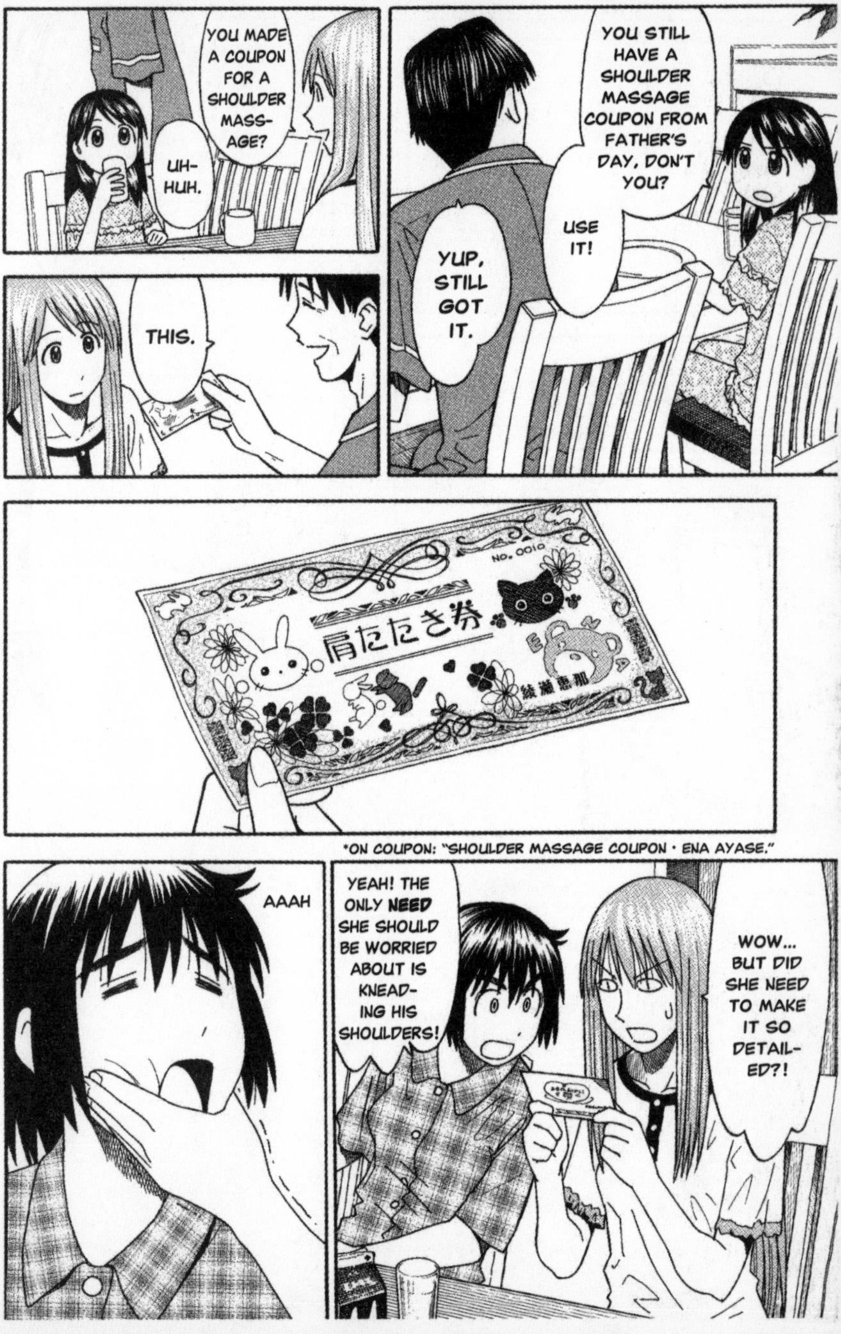
YOU STILL HAVE A SHOULDER MASSAGE COUPON FROM FATHER'S DAY, DON'T YOU?
USE IT!
YUP, STILL GOT IT.
YOU MADE A COUPON FOR A SHOULDER MASS-AGE?
UH-HUH.
THIS.
NO. 0010
肩たたき券
ENA
綾瀬恵那
WOW... BUT DID SHE NEED TO MAKE IT SO DETAIL-ED?!
YEAH! THE ONLY **NEED** SHE SHOULD BE WORRIED ABOUT IS KNEAD-ING HIS SHOULDERS!
AAAH
*ON COUPON: "SHOULDER MASSAGE COUPON • ENA AYASE."

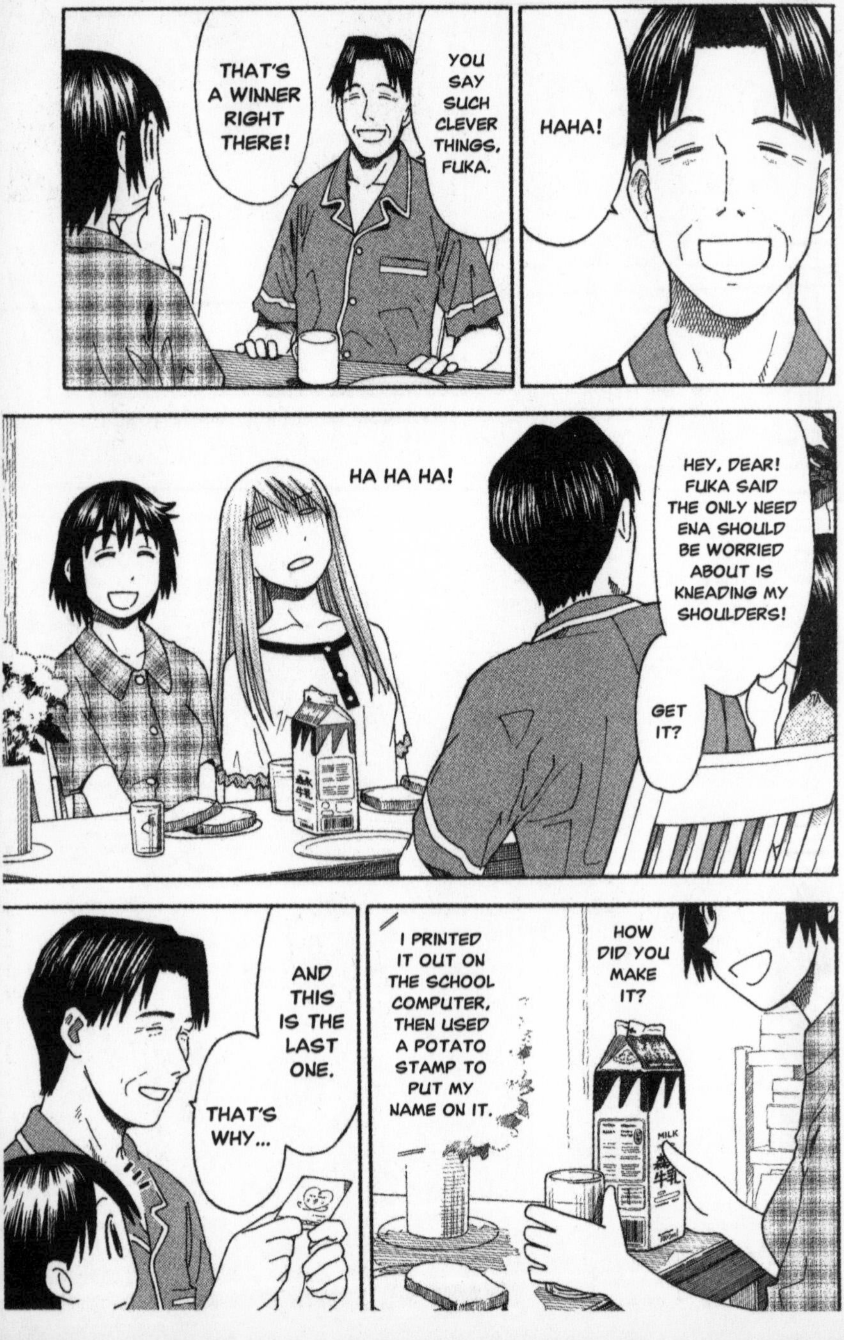
HAHA!
YOU SAY SUCH CLEVER THINGS, FUKA.
THAT'S A WINNER RIGHT THERE!
HEY, DEAR! FUKA SAID THE ONLY NEED ENA SHOULD BE WORRIED ABOUT IS KNEADING MY SHOULDERS!
GET IT?
HA HA HA!
HOW DID YOU MAKE IT?
MILK
I PRINTED IT OUT ON THE SCHOOL COMPUTER, THEN USED A POTATO STAMP TO PUT MY NAME ON IT.
AND THIS IS THE LAST ONE.
THAT'S WHY...

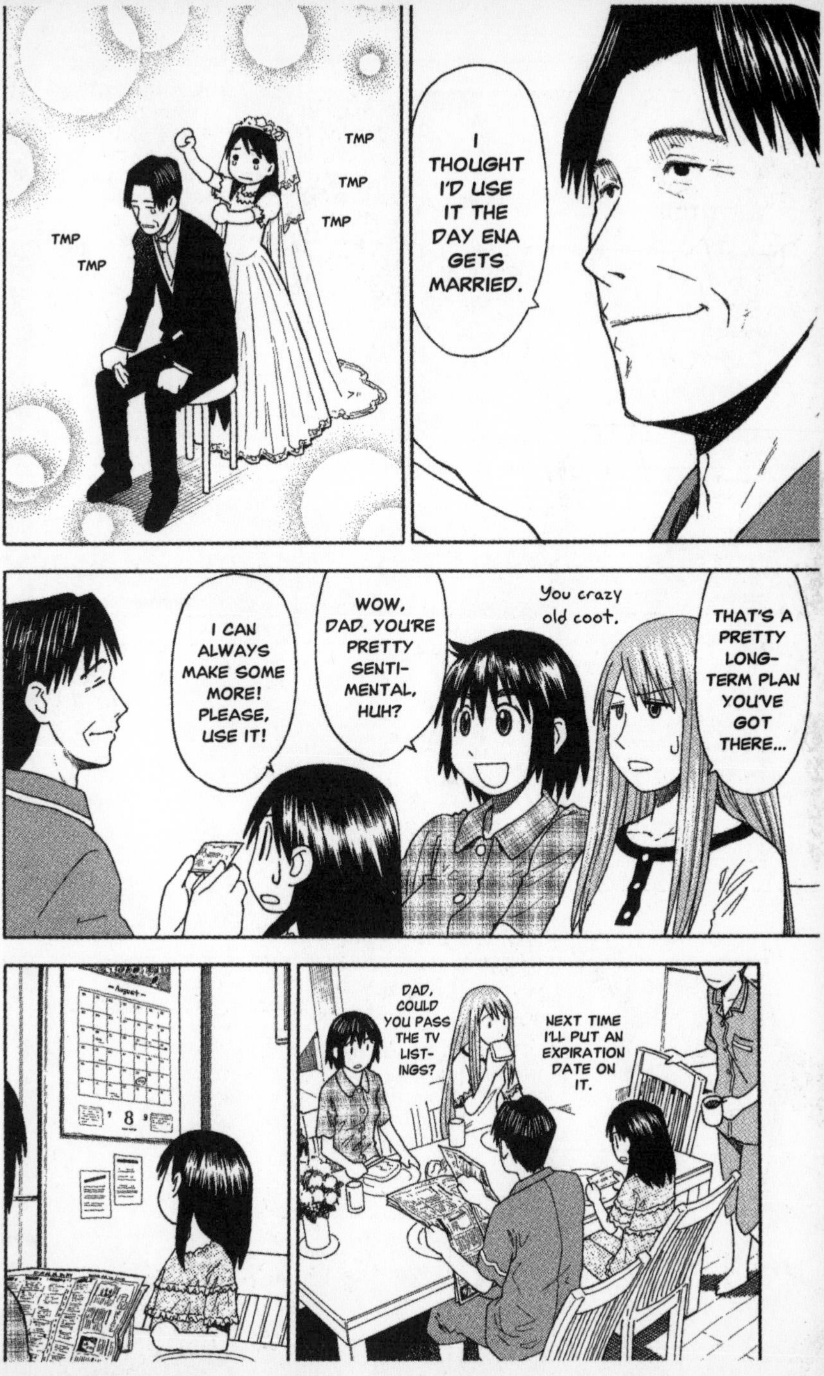
I THOUGHT I'D USE IT THE DAY ENA GETS MARRIED.
TMP
TMP
TMP
TMP
TMP
THAT'S A PRETTY LONG-TERM PLAN YOU'VE GOT THERE...
You crazy old coot.
WOW, DAD. YOU'RE PRETTY SENTIMENTAL, HUH?
I CAN ALWAYS MAKE SOME MORE! PLEASE, USE IT!
NEXT TIME I'LL PUT AN EXPIRATION DATE ON IT.
DAD, COULD YOU PASS THE TV LISTINGS?
August

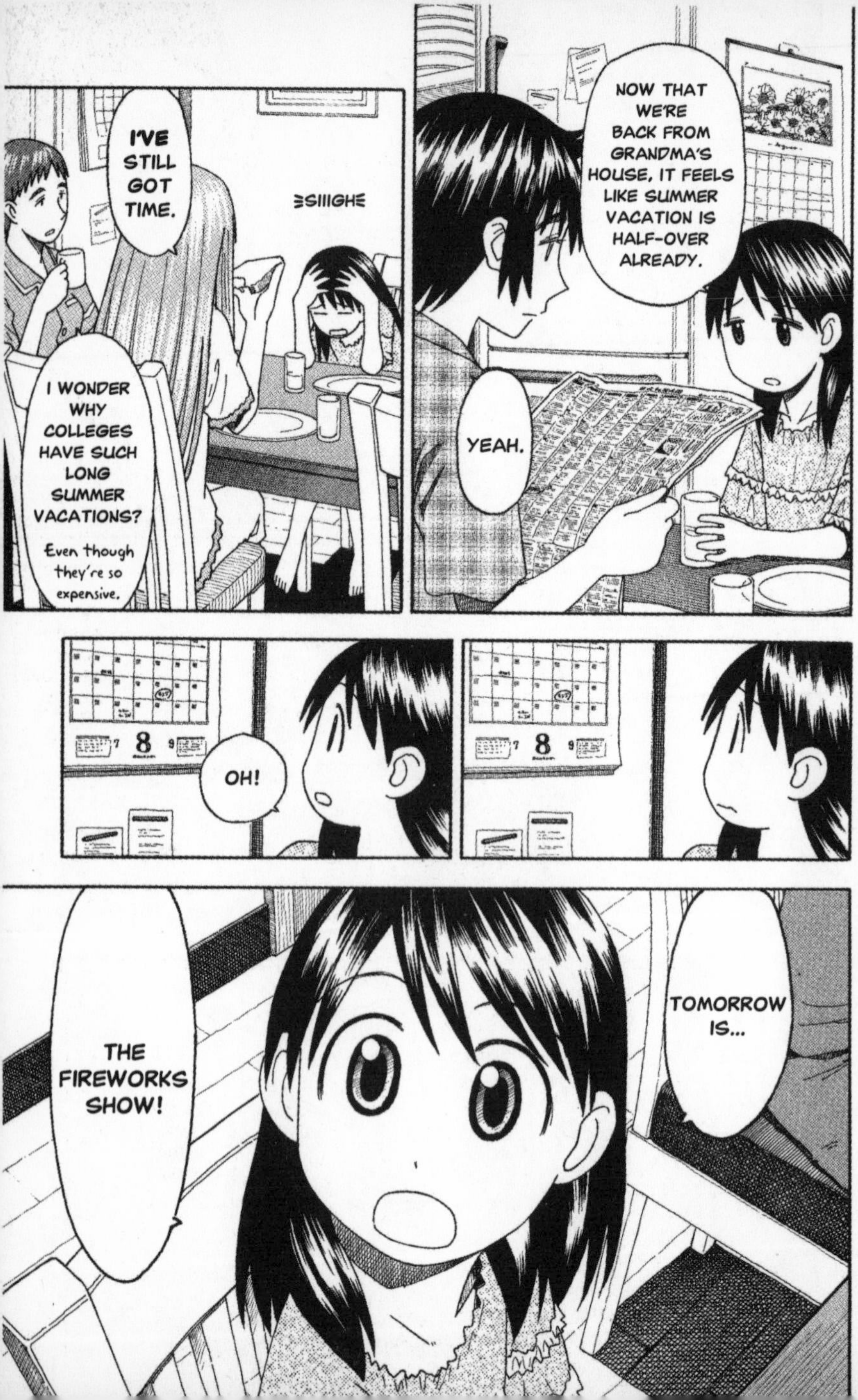
NOW THAT WE'RE BACK FROM GRANDMA'S HOUSE, IT FEELS LIKE SUMMER VACATION IS HALF-OVER ALREADY.
YEAH.
I'VE STILL GOT TIME.
≡SIIIGH≡
I WONDER WHY COLLEGES HAVE SUCH LONG SUMMER VACATIONS?
Even though they're so expensive.
OH!
TOMORROW IS...
THE FIREWORKS SHOW!

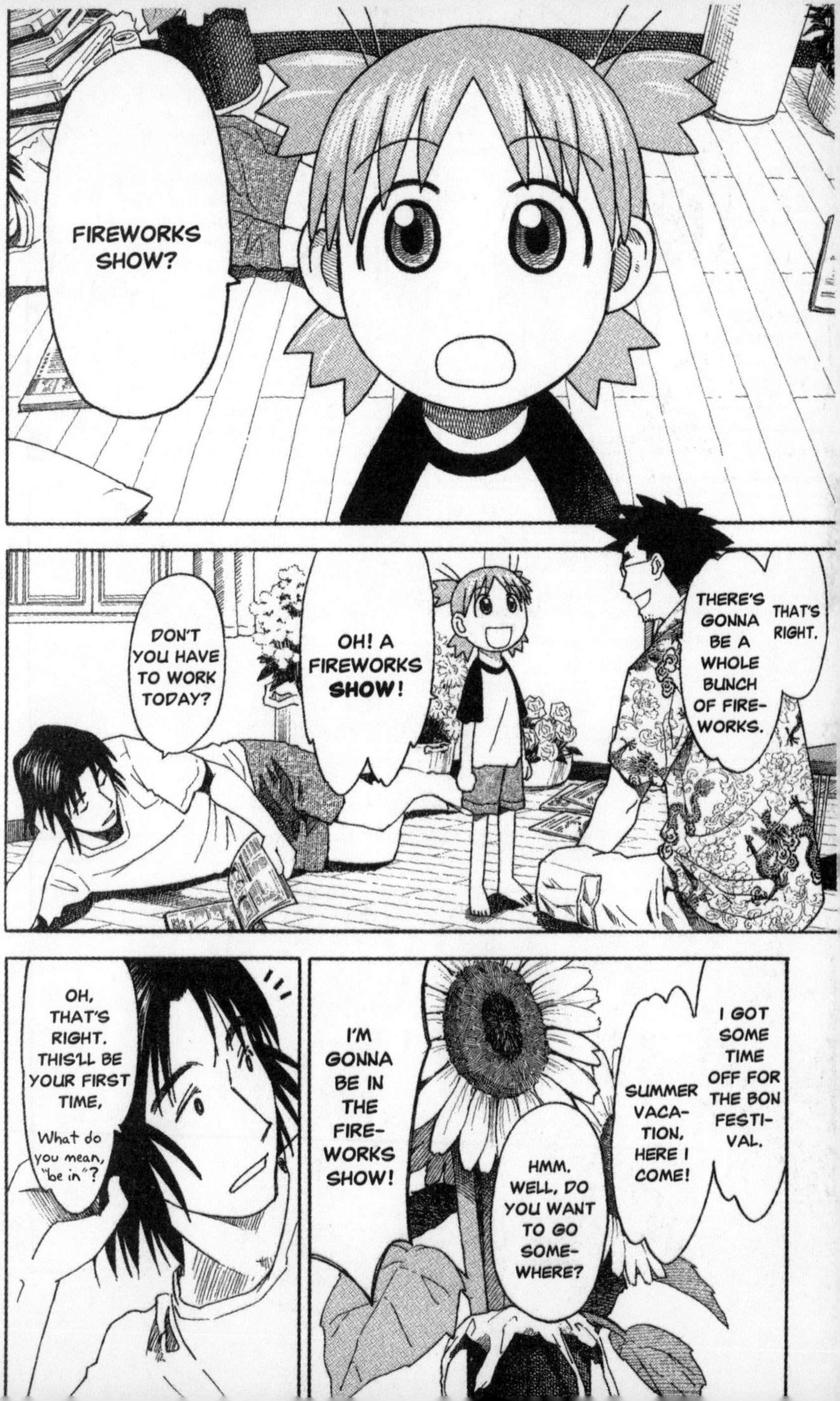
FIREWORKS SHOW?
THAT'S RIGHT.
THERE'S GONNA BE A WHOLE BUNCH OF FIRE-WORKS.
OH! A FIREWORKS SHOW!
DON'T YOU HAVE TO WORK TODAY?
I GOT SOME TIME OFF FOR THE BON FESTI-VAL.
SUMMER VACA-TION, HERE I COME!
HMM. WELL, DO YOU WANT TO GO SOME-WHERE?
I'M GONNA BE IN THE FIRE-WORKS SHOW!
OH, THAT'S RIGHT. THIS'LL BE YOUR FIRST TIME,
What do you mean, "be in"?

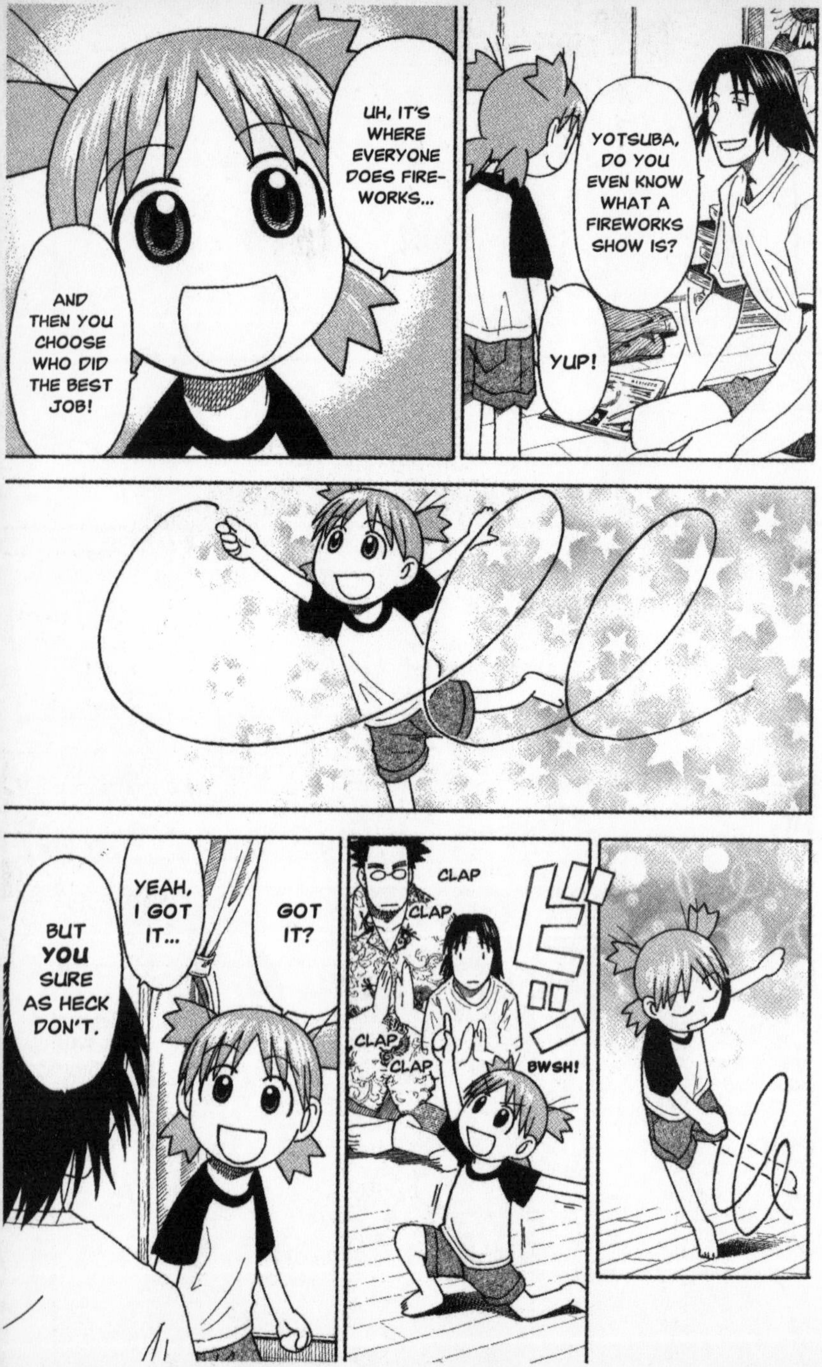
YOTSUBA, DO YOU EVEN KNOW WHAT A FIREWORKS SHOW IS?
YUP!
UH, IT'S WHERE EVERYONE DOES FIRE-WORKS...
AND THEN YOU CHOOSE WHO DID THE BEST JOB!
CLAP
CLAP
CLAP
CLAP
BWSH!
GOT IT?
YEAH, I GOT IT...
BUT **YOU** SURE AS HECK DON'T.

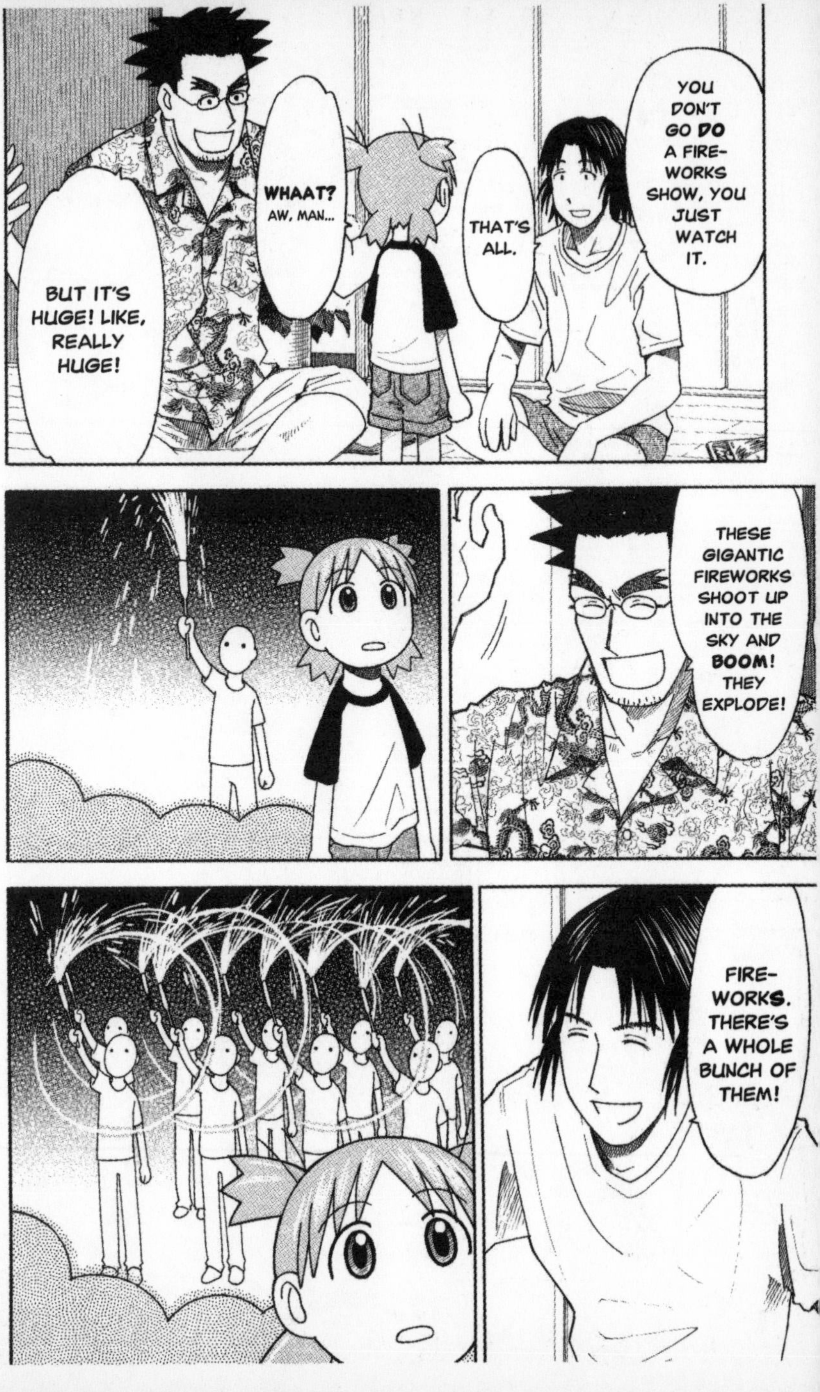
YOU DON'T GO DO A FIREWORKS SHOW, YOU JUST WATCH IT.
THAT'S ALL.
WHAAT? AW, MAN...
BUT IT'S HUGE! LIKE, REALLY HUGE!
THESE GIGANTIC FIREWORKS SHOOT UP INTO THE SKY AND BOOM! THEY EXPLODE!
FIREWORKS. THERE'S A WHOLE BUNCH OF THEM!

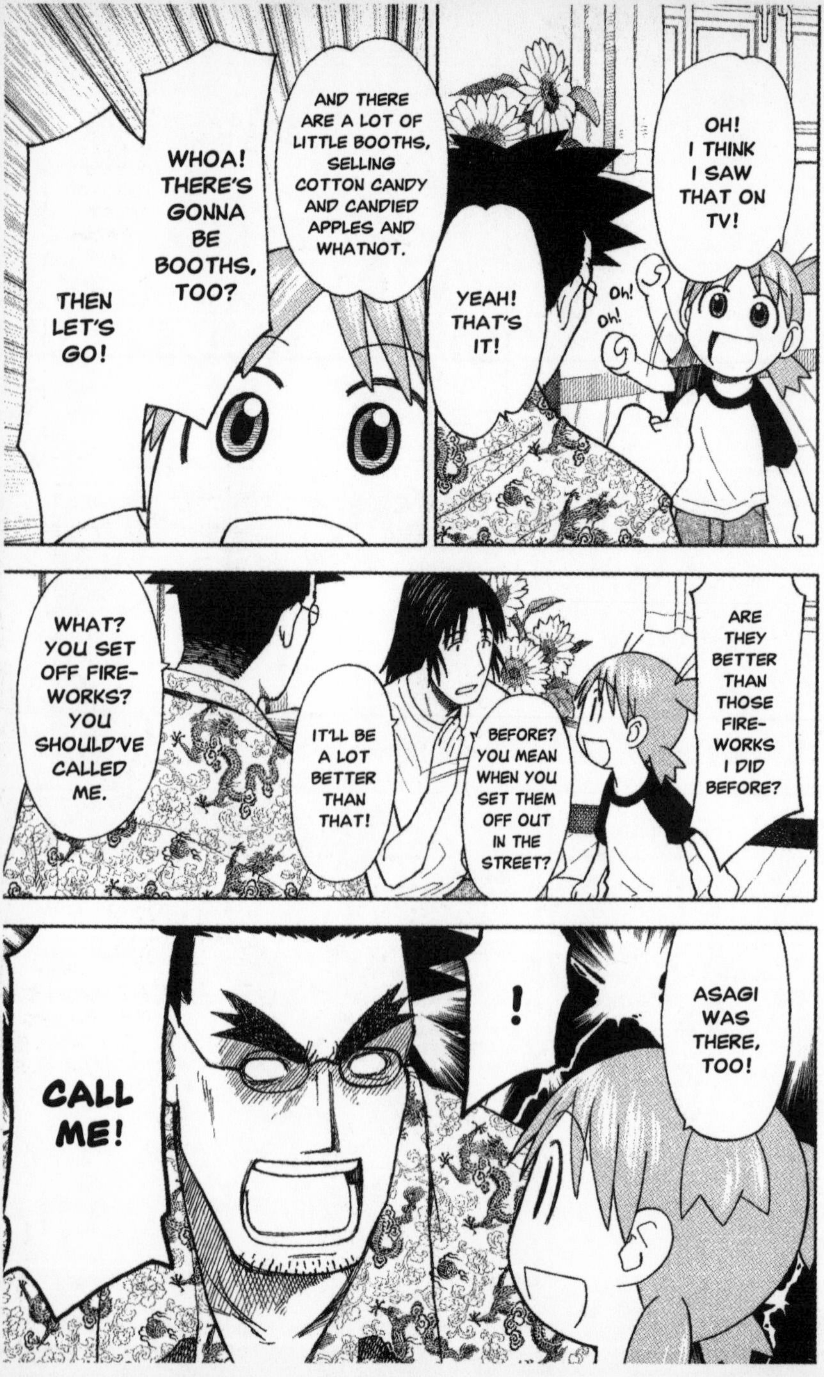
OH! I THINK I SAW THAT ON TV!
Oh! Oh!
YEAH! THAT'S IT!
AND THERE ARE A LOT OF LITTLE BOOTHS, SELLING COTTON CANDY AND CANDIED APPLES AND WHATNOT.
WHOA! THERE'S GONNA BE BOOTHS, TOO?
THEN LET'S GO!
ARE THEY BETTER THAN THOSE FIRE-WORKS I DID BEFORE?
BEFORE? YOU MEAN WHEN YOU SET THEM OFF OUT IN THE STREET?
IT'LL BE A LOT BETTER THAN THAT!
WHAT? YOU SET OFF FIRE-WORKS? YOU SHOULD'VE CALLED ME.
ASAGI WAS THERE, TOO!
!
CALL ME!

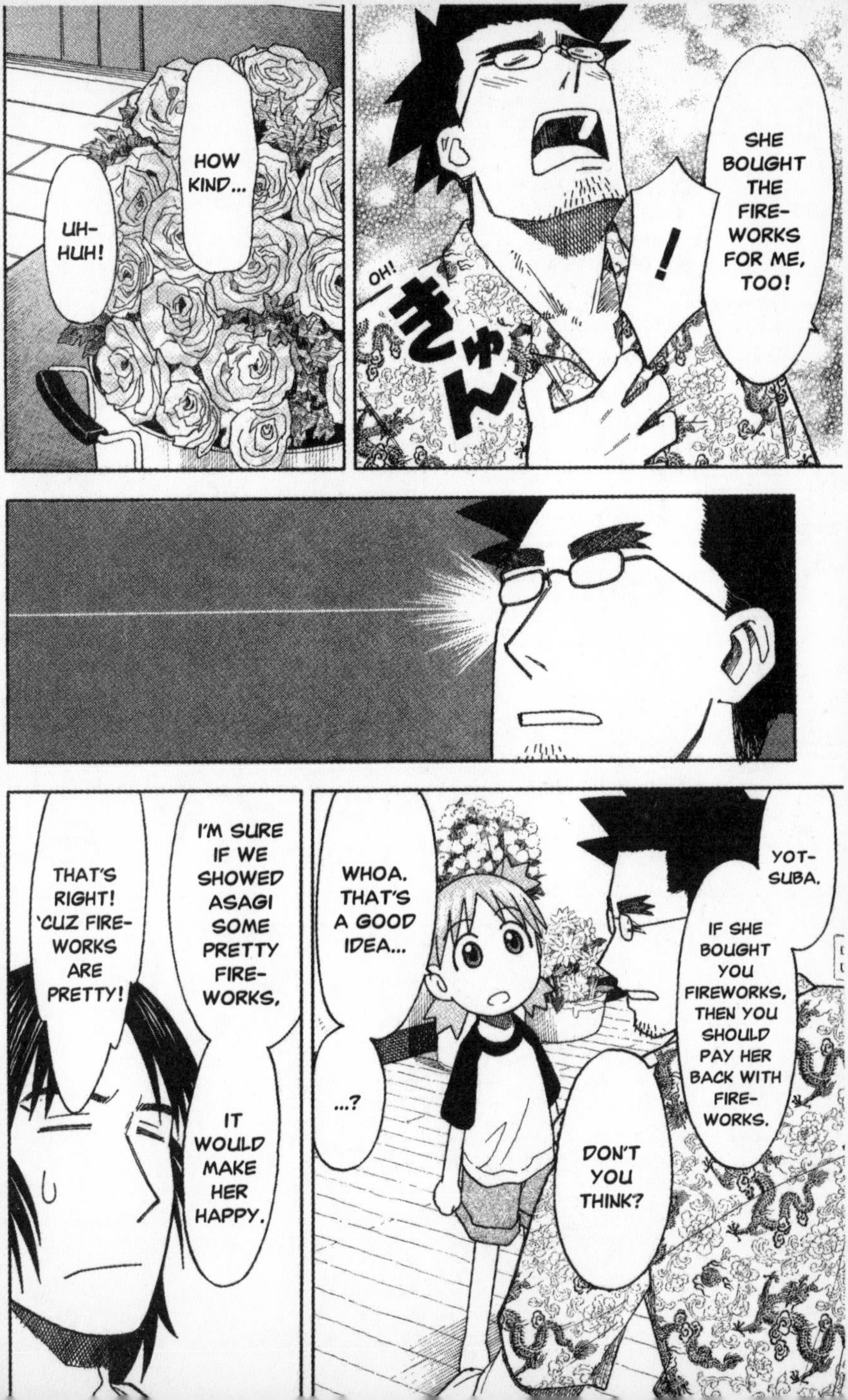
SHE BOUGHT THE FIRE-WORKS FOR ME, TOO!
!
OH!
きゅん
HOW KIND...
UH-HUH!
YOT-SUBA.
IF SHE BOUGHT YOU FIREWORKS, THEN YOU SHOULD PAY HER BACK WITH FIRE-WORKS.
DON'T YOU THINK?
WHOA. THAT'S A GOOD IDEA...
...?
I'M SURE IF WE SHOWED ASAGI SOME PRETTY FIRE-WORKS,
IT WOULD MAKE HER HAPPY.
THAT'S RIGHT! 'CUZ FIRE-WORKS ARE PRETTY!

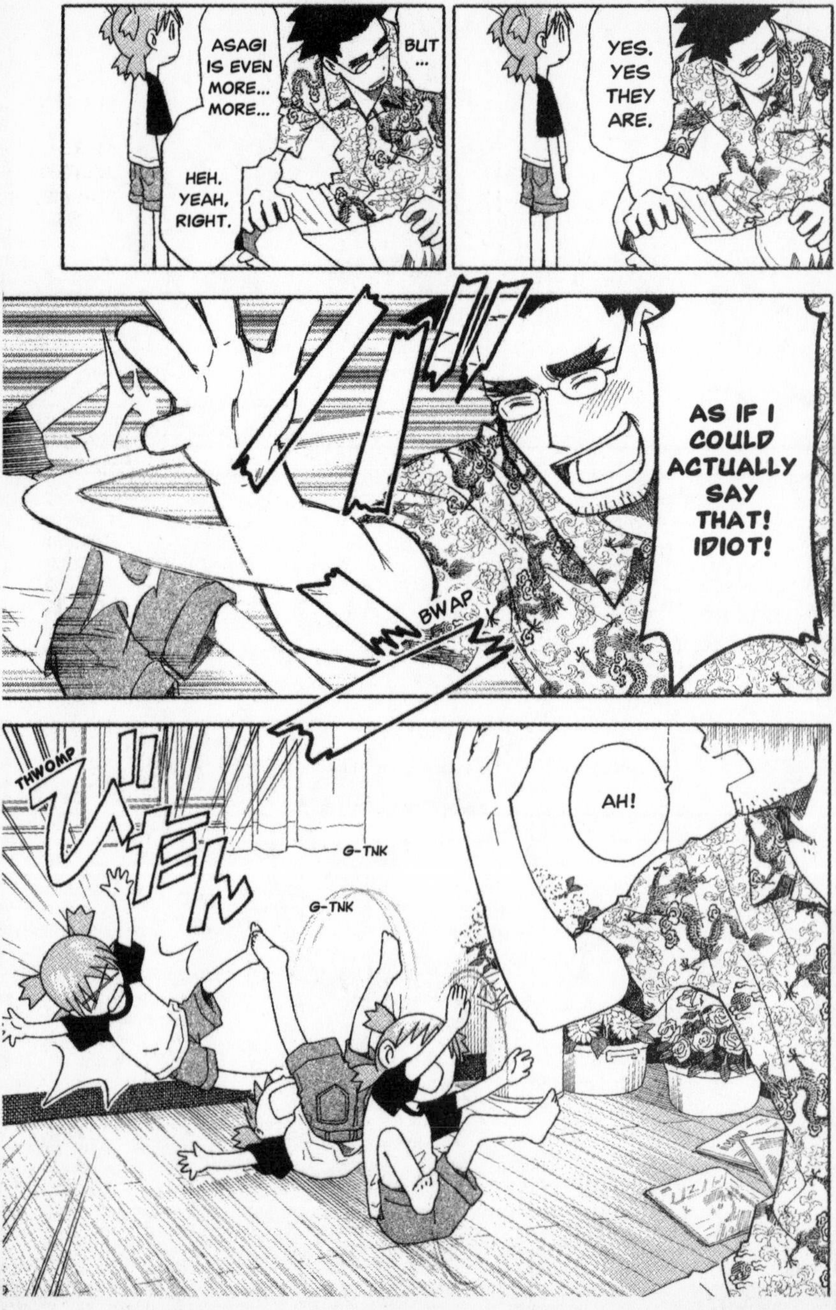
YES. YES THEY ARE.
BUT ...
ASAGI IS EVEN MORE... MORE...
HEH. YEAH, RIGHT.
AS IF I COULD ACTUALLY SAY THAT! IDIOT!
BWAP
AH!
THWOMP
びたん
G-TNK
G-TNK

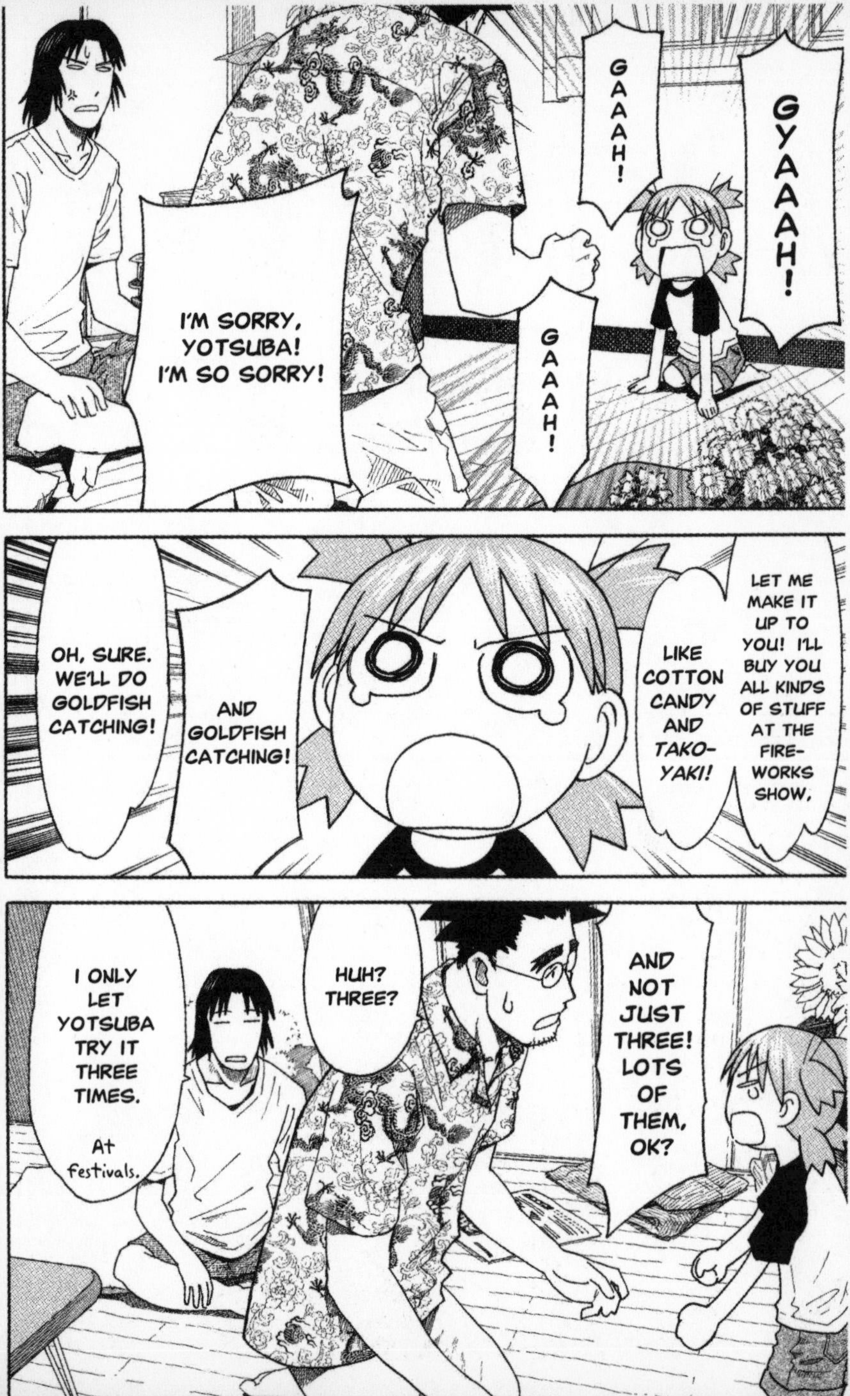
GYAAAAH!
GAAAH!
GAAAH!
I'M SORRY, YOTSUBA! I'M SO SORRY!
LET ME MAKE IT UP TO YOU! I'LL BUY YOU ALL KINDS OF STUFF AT THE FIRE-WORKS SHOW,
LIKE COTTON CANDY AND *TAKO-YAKI*!
AND GOLDFISH CATCHING!
OH, SURE. WE'LL DO GOLDFISH CATCHING!
AND NOT JUST THREE! LOTS OF THEM, OK?
HUH? THREE?
I ONLY LET YOTSUBA TRY IT THREE TIMES.
At festivals.

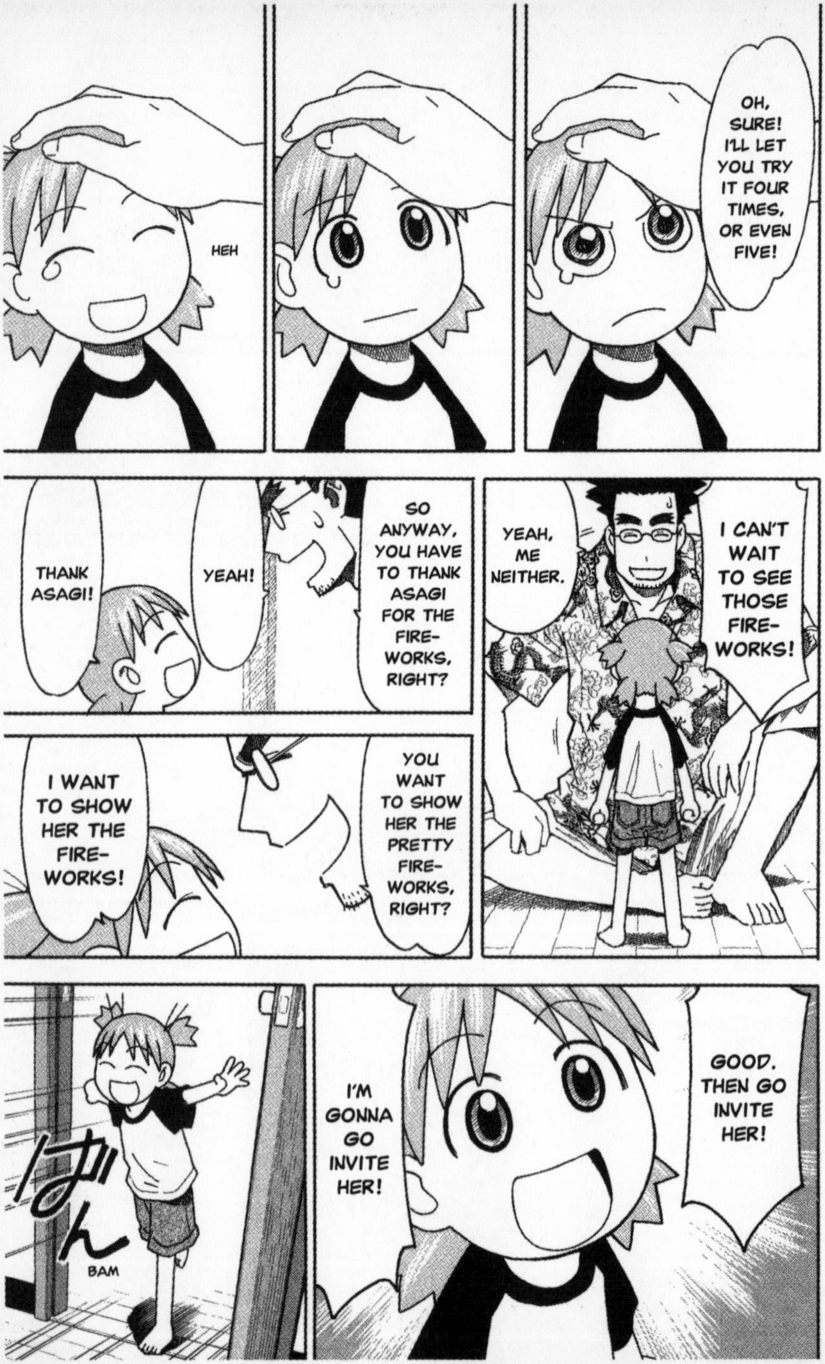

OH, SURE! I'LL LET YOU TRY IT FOUR TIMES, OR EVEN FIVE!
HEH
I CAN'T WAIT TO SEE THOSE FIRE-WORKS!
YEAH, ME NEITHER.
SO ANYWAY, YOU HAVE TO THANK ASAGI FOR THE FIRE-WORKS, RIGHT?
YEAH!
THANK ASAGI!
YOU WANT TO SHOW HER THE PRETTY FIRE-WORKS, RIGHT?
I WANT TO SHOW HER THE FIRE-WORKS!
GOOD. THEN GO INVITE HER!
I'M GONNA GO INVITE HER!
ばん
BAM

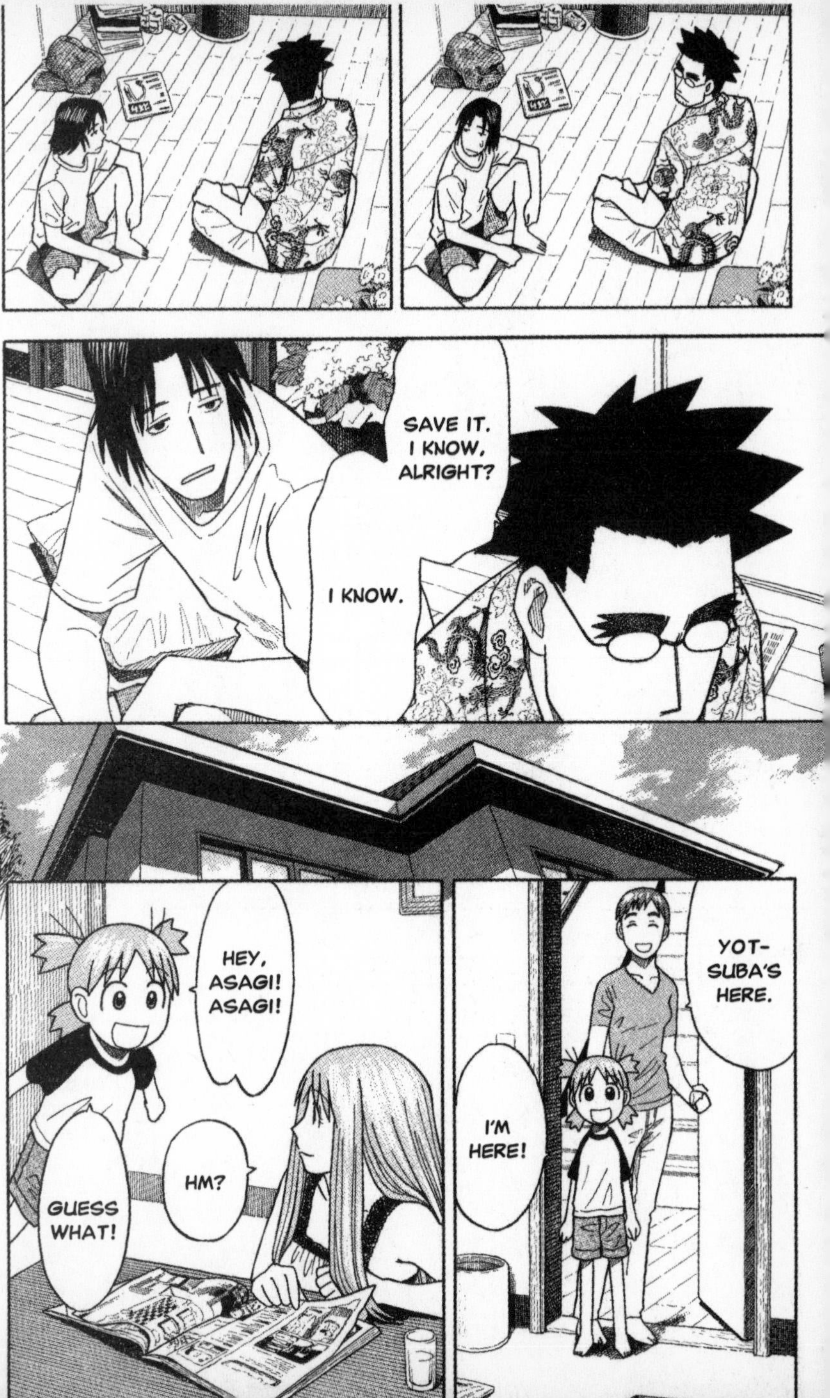
SAVE IT. I KNOW, ALRIGHT?
I KNOW.
YOT-SUBA'S HERE.
I'M HERE!
HEY, ASAGI! ASAGI!
HM?
GUESS WHAT!

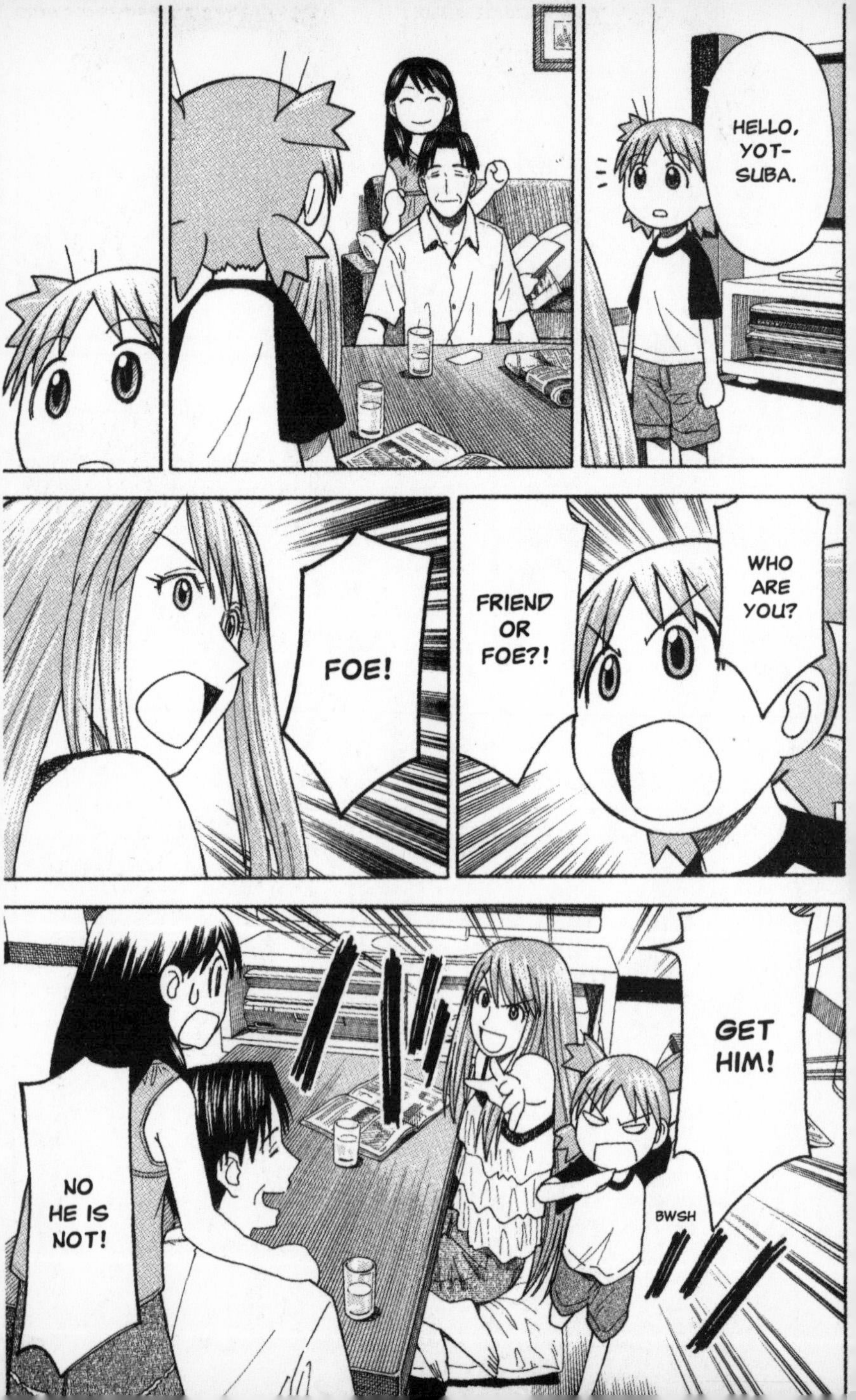
HELLO, YOT-SUBA.
WHO ARE YOU?
FRIEND OR FOE?!
FOE!
GET HIM!
BWSH
NO HE IS NOT!

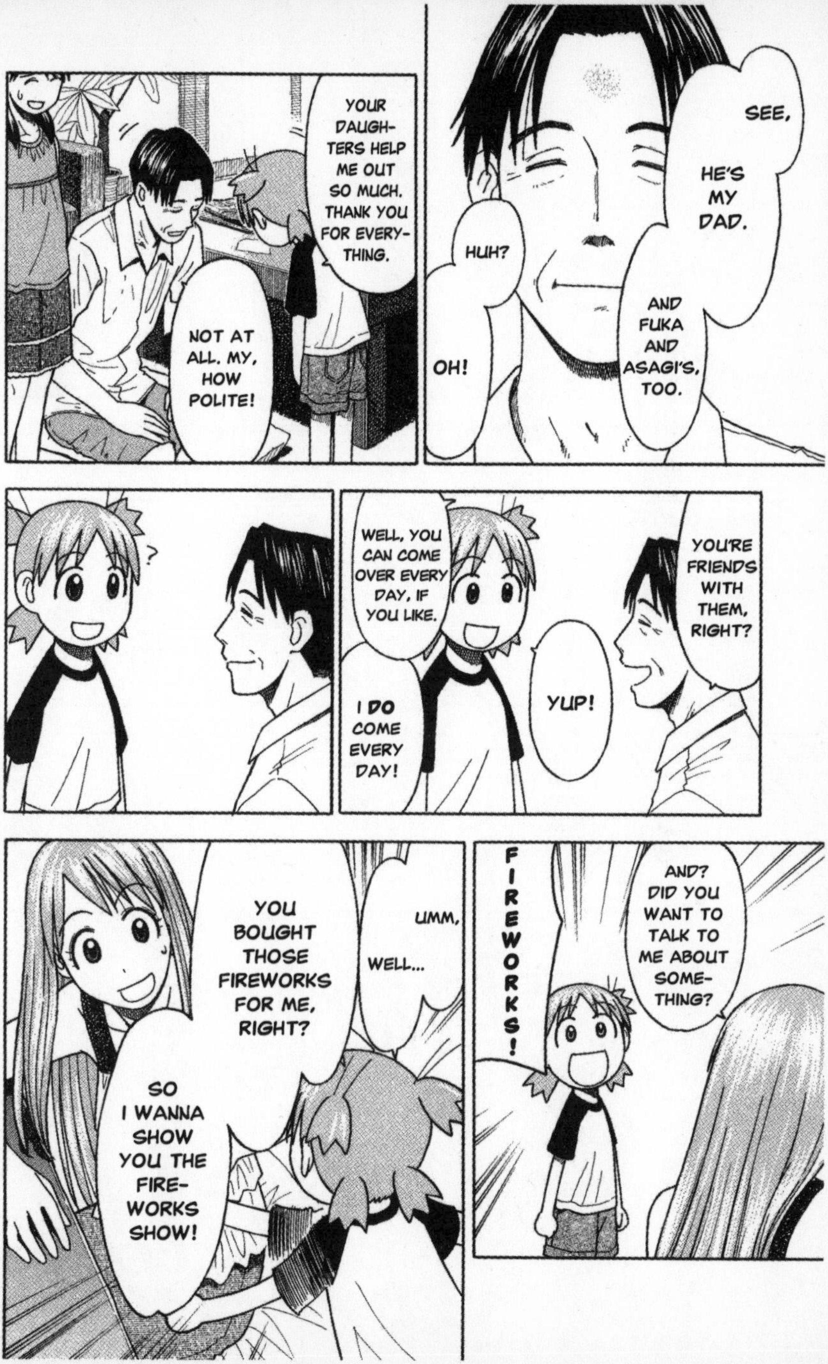
SEE, HE'S MY DAD.
HUH?
AND FUKA AND ASAGI'S, TOO.
OH!
YOUR DAUGHTERS HELP ME OUT SO MUCH. THANK YOU FOR EVERYTHING.
NOT AT ALL. MY, HOW POLITE!
YOU'RE FRIENDS WITH THEM, RIGHT?
YUP!
WELL, YOU CAN COME OVER EVERY DAY, IF YOU LIKE.
I **DO** COME EVERY DAY!
?
AND? DID YOU WANT TO TALK TO ME ABOUT SOMETHING?
FIREWORKS!
UMM, WELL...
YOU BOUGHT THOSE FIREWORKS FOR ME, RIGHT?
SO I WANNA SHOW YOU THE FIREWORKS SHOW!

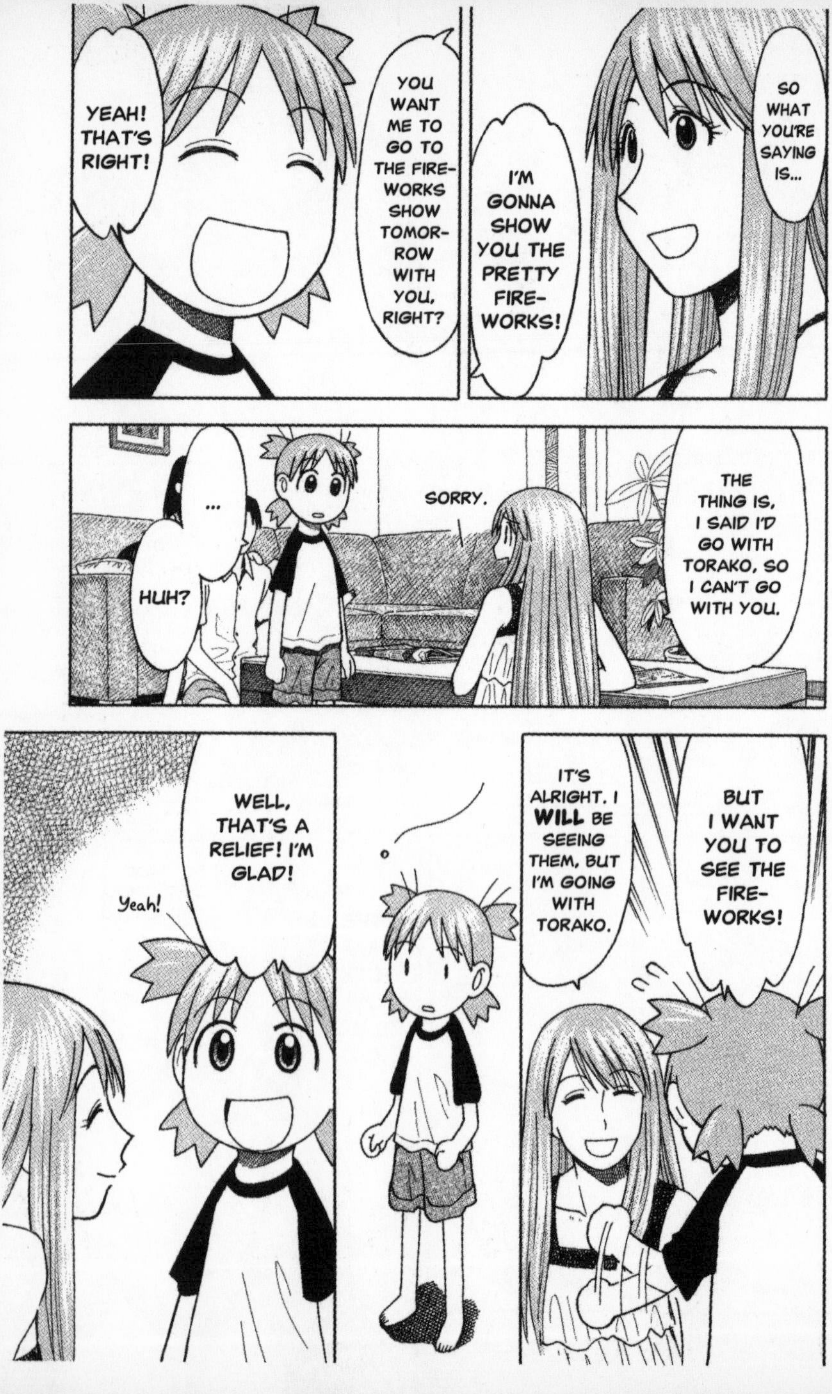
SO WHAT YOU'RE SAYING IS...
I'M GONNA SHOW YOU THE PRETTY FIRE-WORKS!
YOU WANT ME TO GO TO THE FIRE-WORKS SHOW TOMOR-ROW WITH YOU, RIGHT?
YEAH! THAT'S RIGHT!
THE THING IS, I SAID I'D GO WITH TORAKO, SO I CAN'T GO WITH YOU.
SORRY.
...
HUH?
BUT I WANT YOU TO SEE THE FIRE-WORKS!
IT'S ALRIGHT. I **WILL** BE SEEING THEM, BUT I'M GOING WITH TORAKO.
WELL, THAT'S A RELIEF! I'M GLAD!
Yeah!

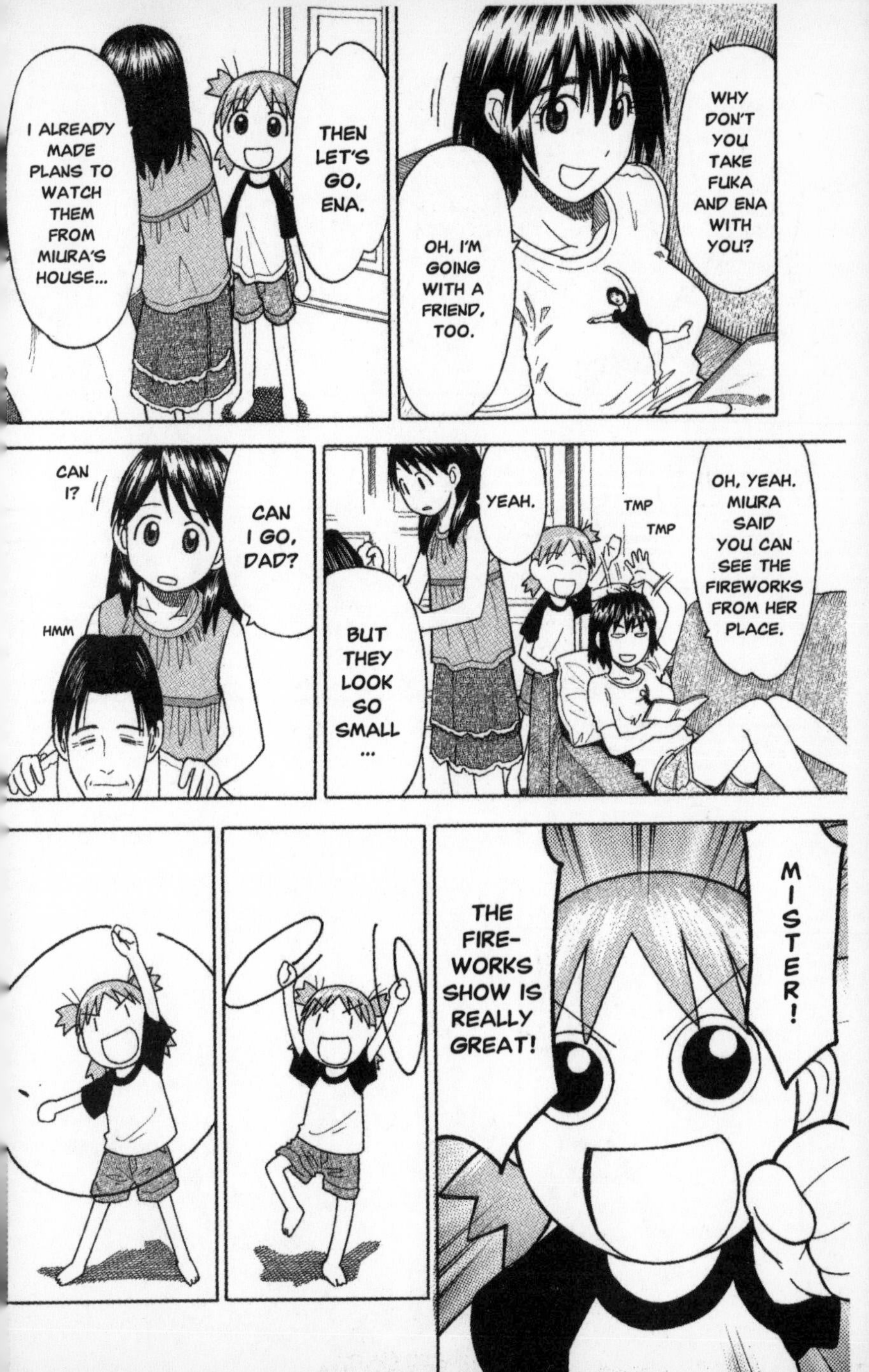
WHY DON'T YOU TAKE FUKA AND ENA WITH YOU?
OH, I'M GOING WITH A FRIEND, TOO.
THEN LET'S GO, ENA.
I ALREADY MADE PLANS TO WATCH THEM FROM MIURA'S HOUSE...
OH, YEAH. MIURA SAID YOU CAN SEE THE FIREWORKS FROM HER PLACE.
TMP
TMP
YEAH.
BUT THEY LOOK SO SMALL ...
CAN I GO, DAD?
CAN I?
HMM
MISTER!
THE FIRE-WORKS SHOW IS REALLY GREAT!

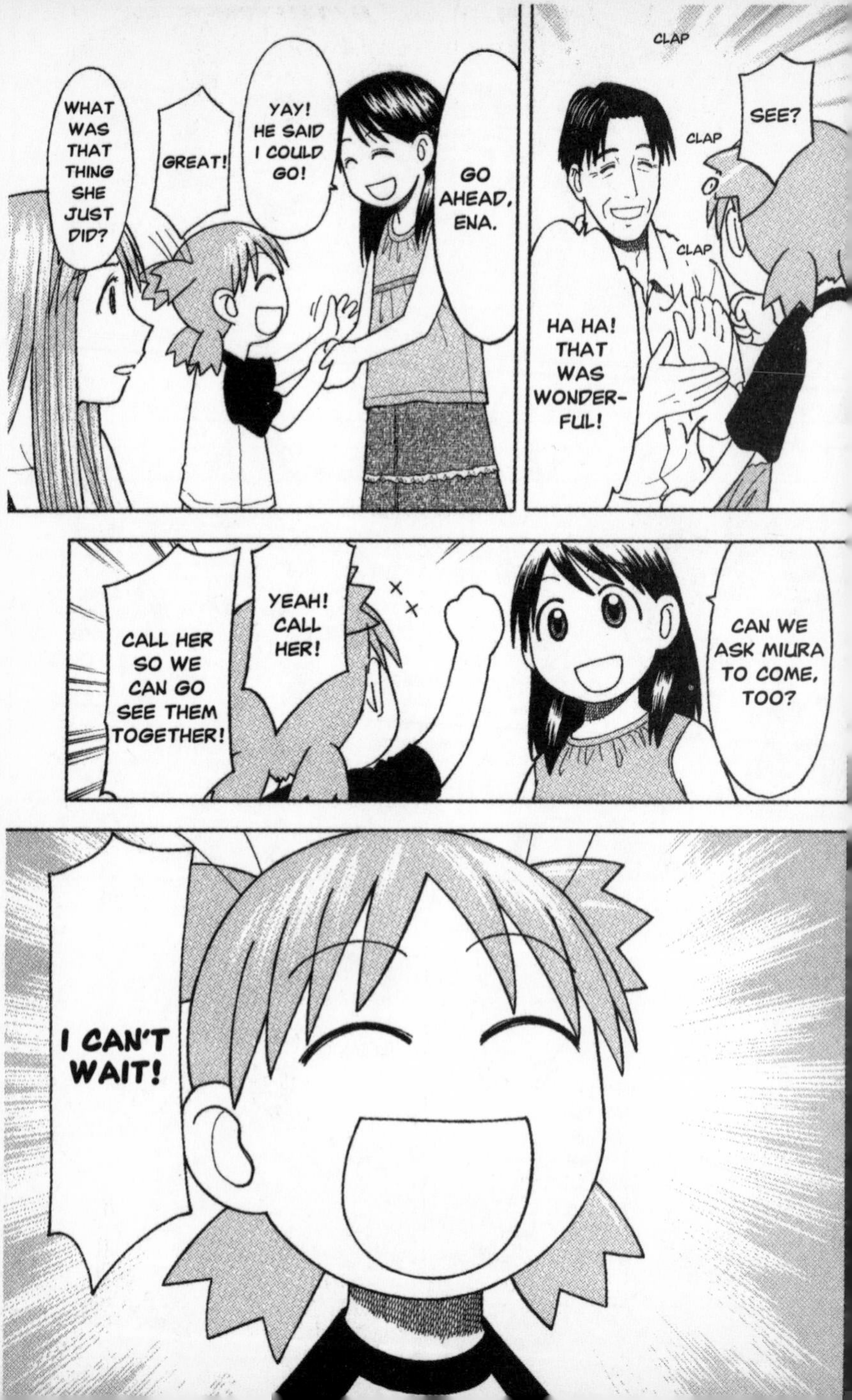
CLAP
SEE?
CLAP
CLAP
HA HA! THAT WAS WONDER-FUL!
GO AHEAD, ENA.
YAY! HE SAID I COULD GO!
GREAT!
WHAT WAS THAT THING SHE JUST DID?
CAN WE ASK MIURA TO COME, TOO?
YEAH! CALL HER!
CALL HER SO WE CAN GO SEE THEM TOGETHER!
I CAN'T WAIT!

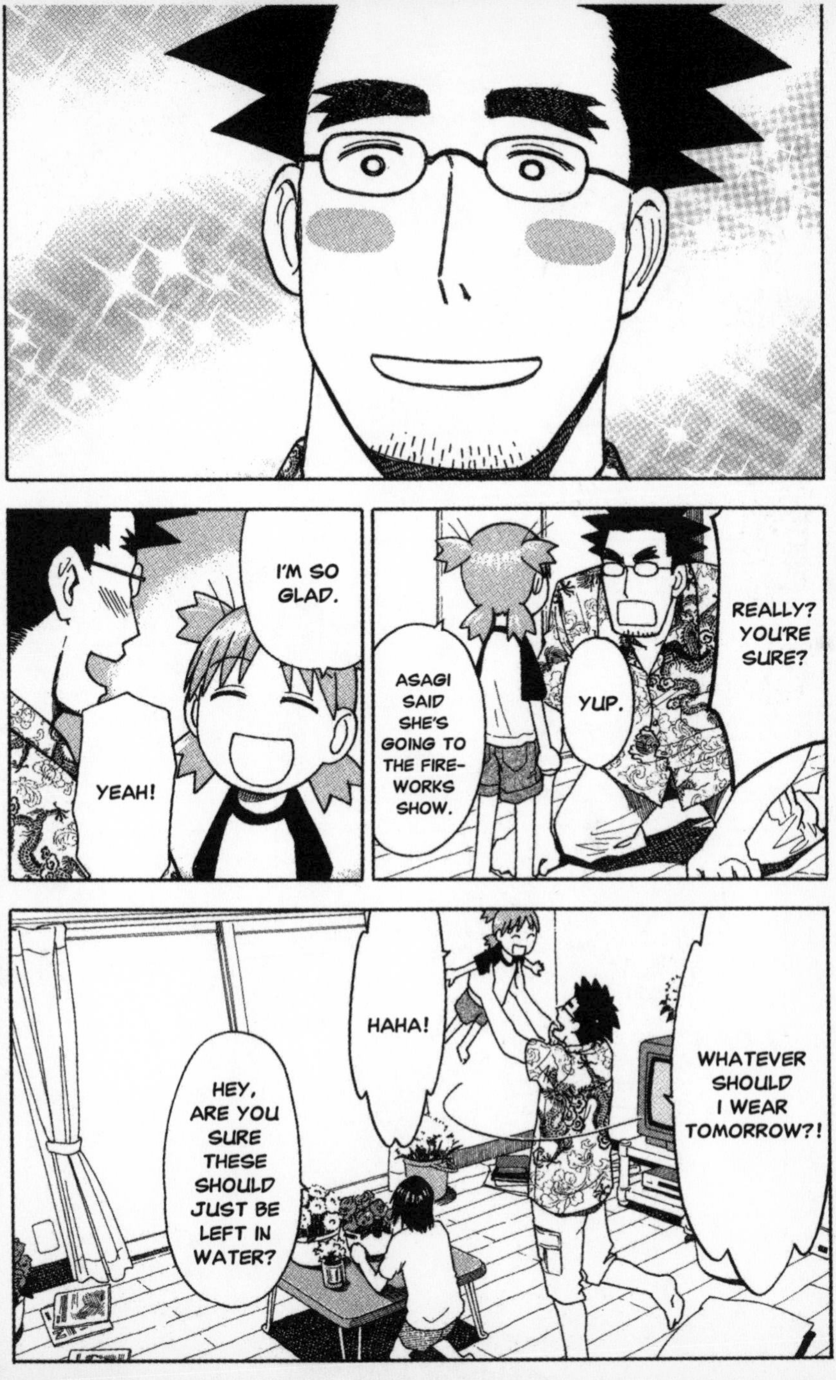
REALLY? YOU'RE SURE?
YUP.
ASAGI SAID SHE'S GOING TO THE FIRE-WORKS SHOW.
I'M SO GLAD.
YEAH!
WHATEVER SHOULD I WEAR TOMORROW?!
HAHA!
HEY, ARE YOU SURE THESE SHOULD JUST BE LEFT IN WATER?

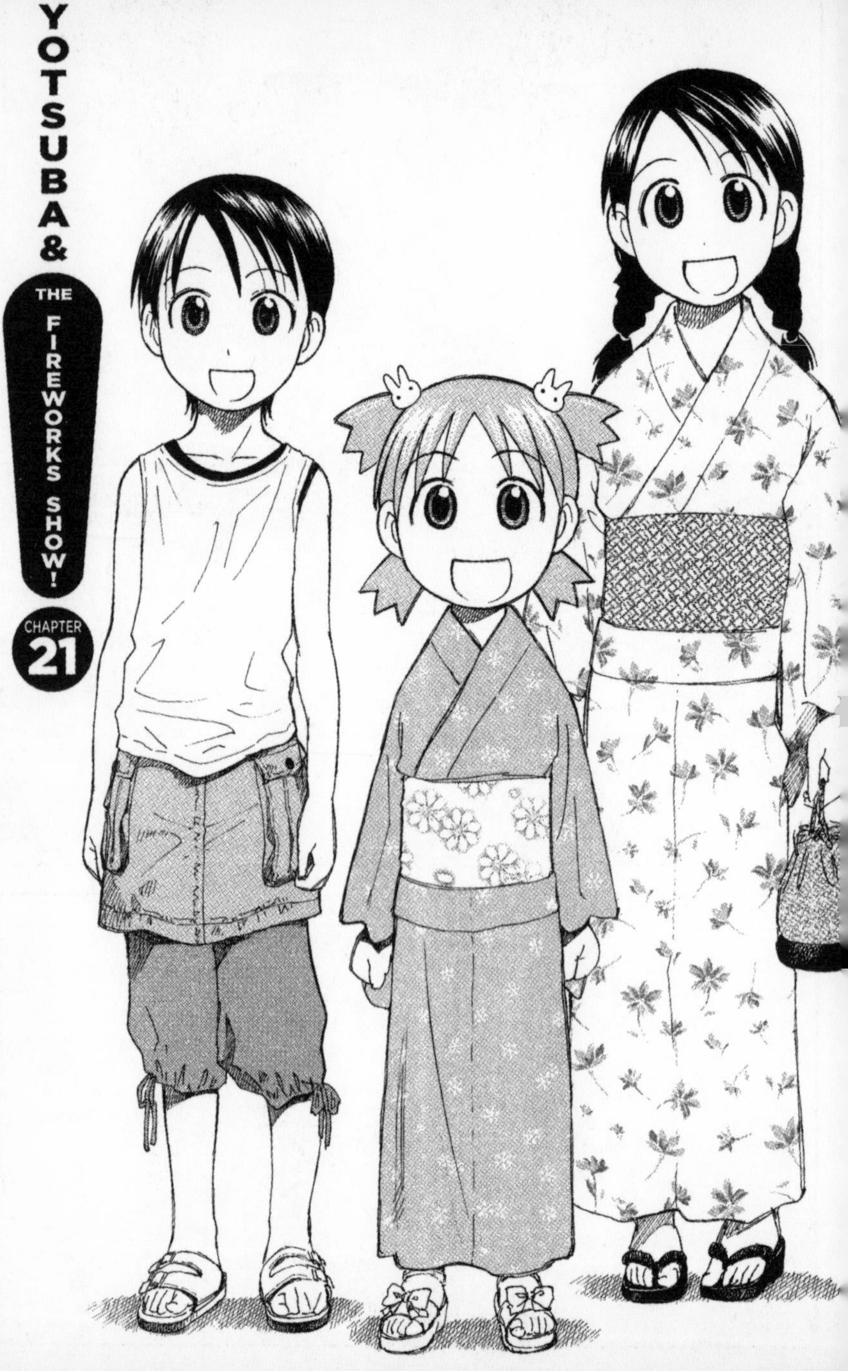
YOTSUBA & THE FIREWORKS SHOW!
CHAPTER 21

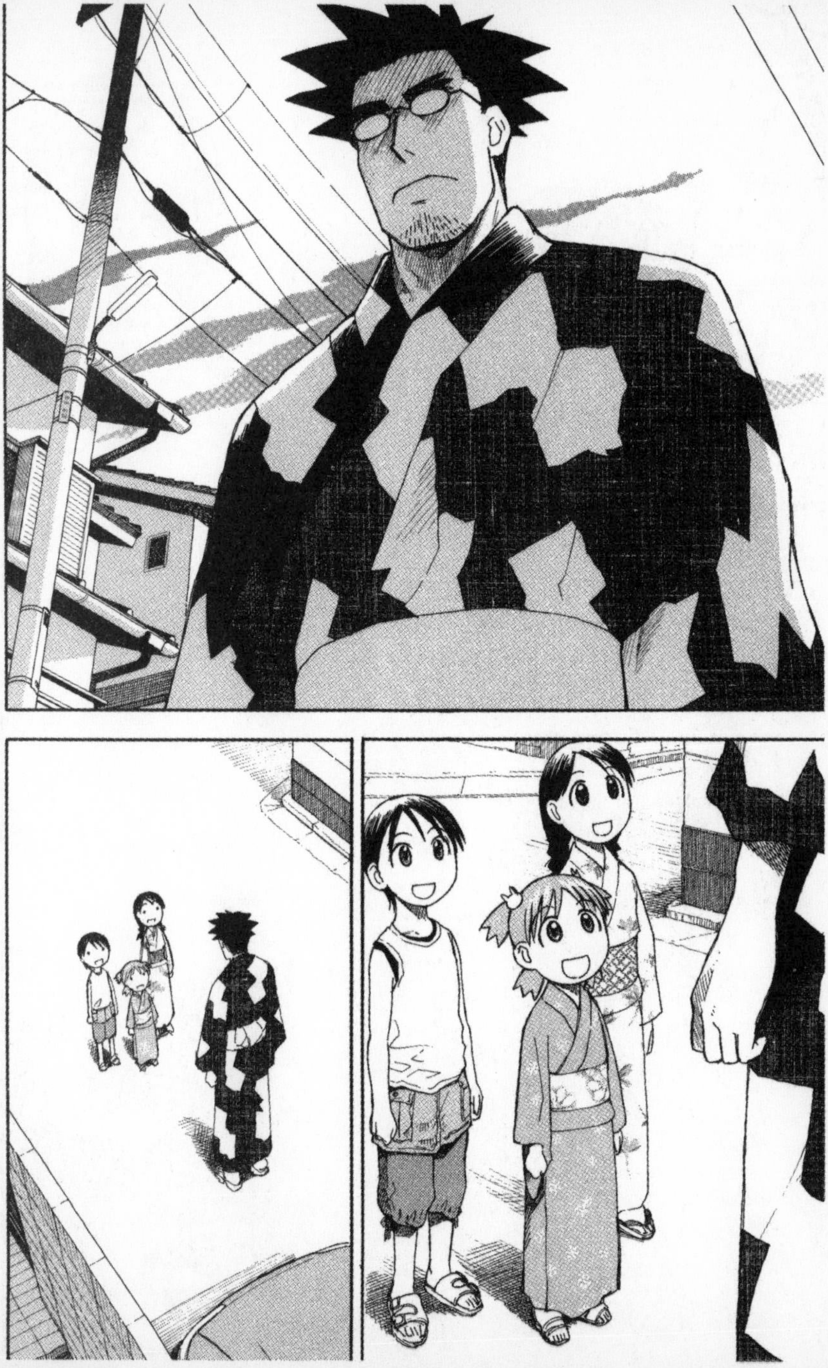

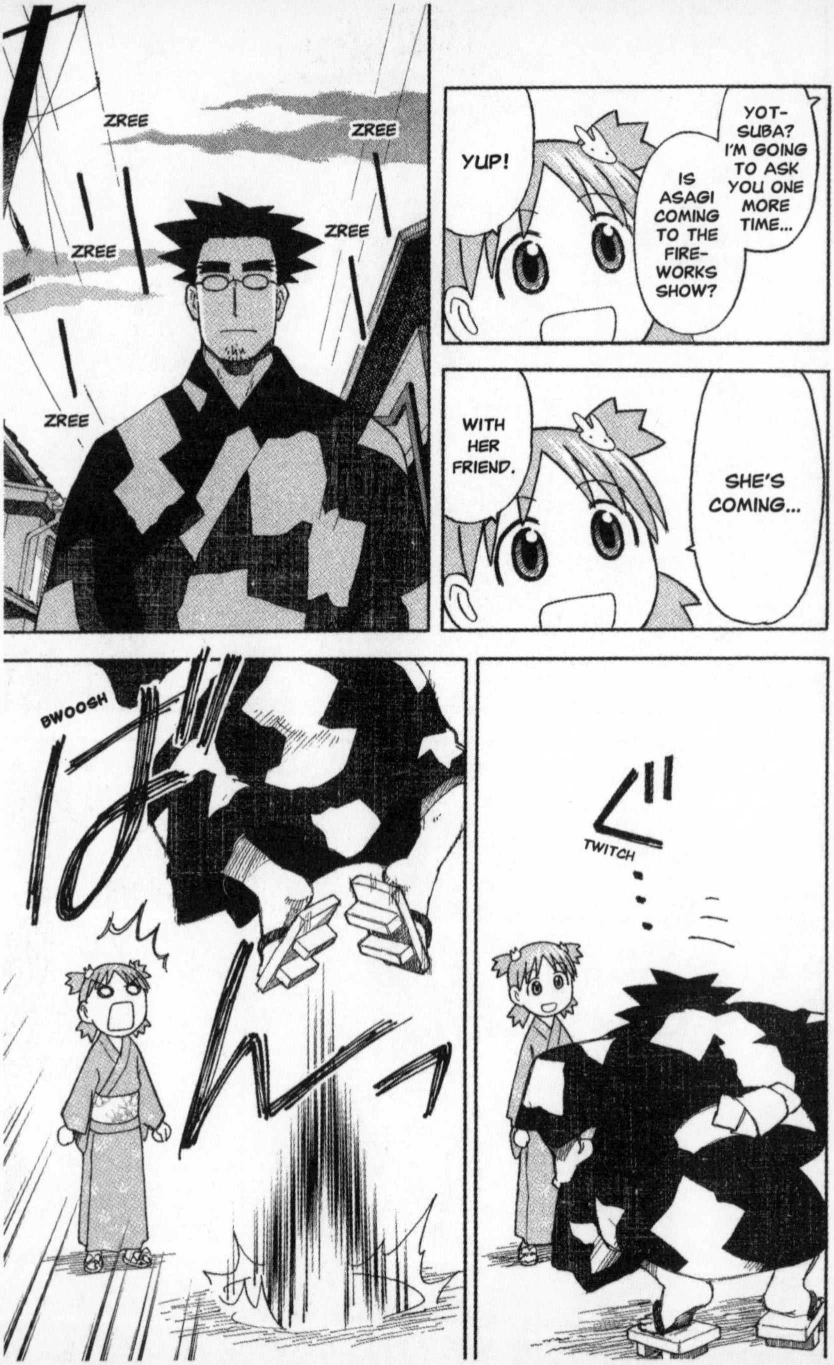
YOT-SUBA? I'M GOING TO ASK YOU ONE MORE TIME...
IS ASAGI COMING TO THE FIRE-WORKS SHOW?
YUP!
SHE'S COMING...
WITH HER FRIEND.
ZREE
ZREE
ZREE
ZREE
ZREE
TWITCH
BWOOSH

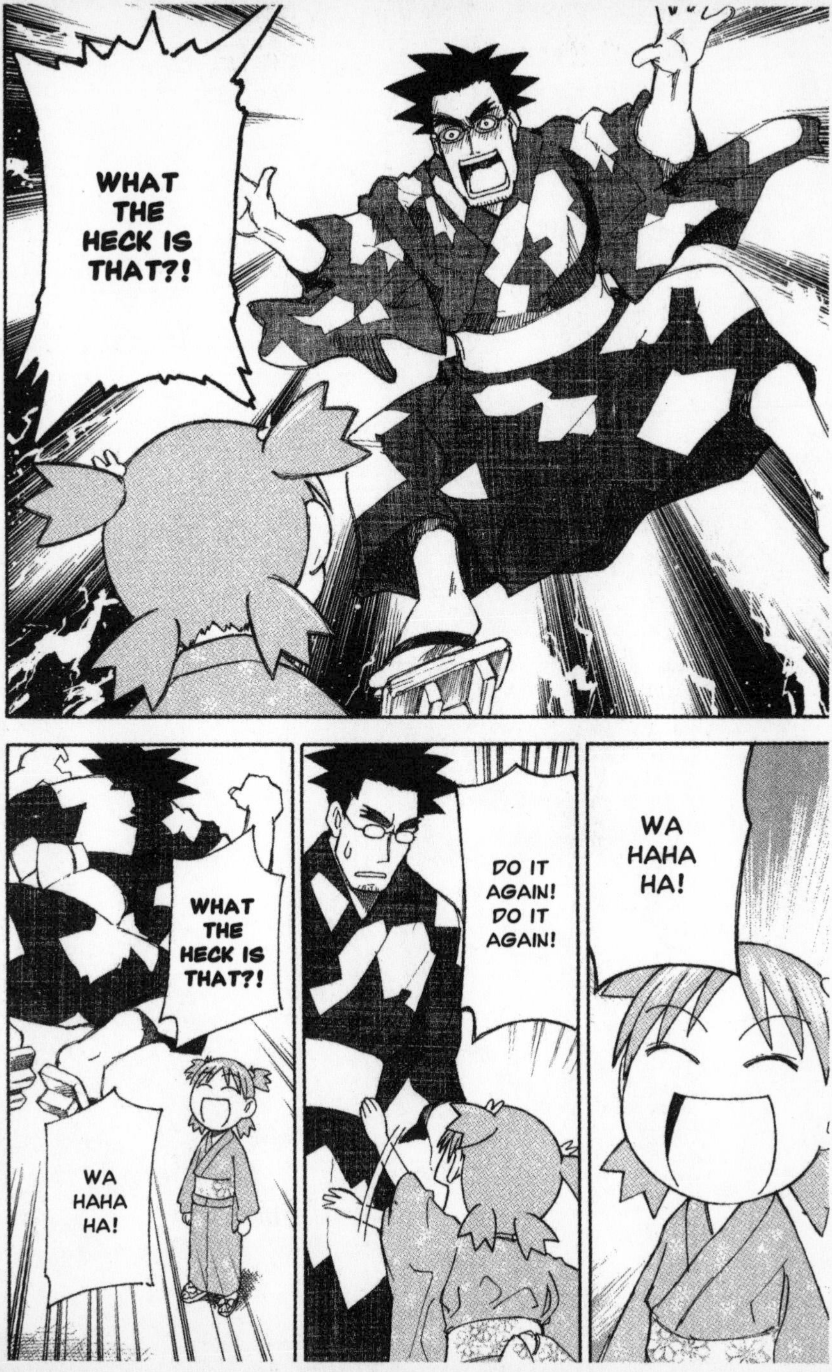
WHAT THE HECK IS THAT?!
WA HAHA HA!
DO IT AGAIN! DO IT AGAIN!
WHAT THE HECK IS THAT?!
WA HAHA HA!

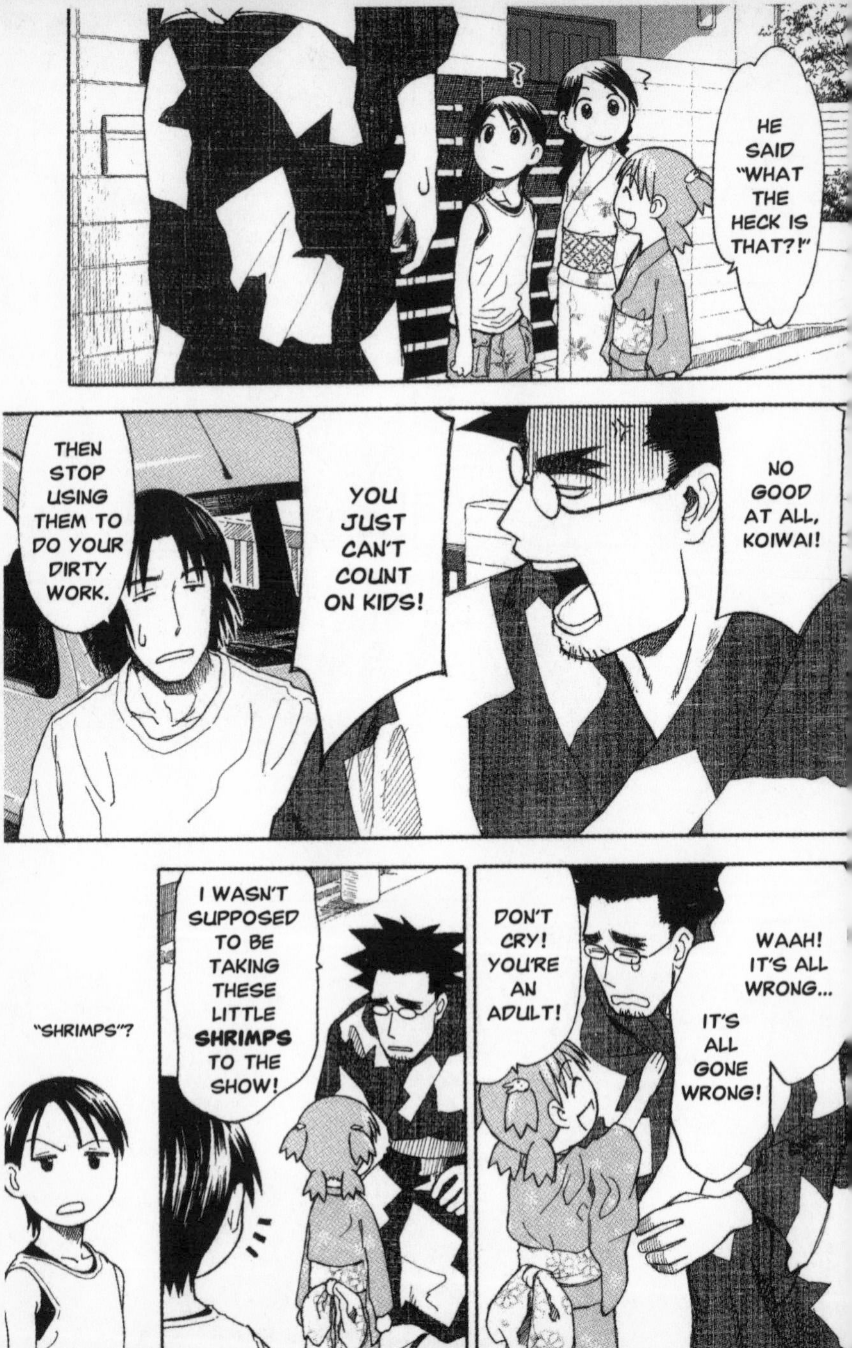
HE SAID "WHAT THE HECK IS THAT?!"
NO GOOD AT ALL, KOIWAI!
YOU JUST CAN'T COUNT ON KIDS!
THEN STOP USING THEM TO DO YOUR DIRTY WORK.
WAAH! IT'S ALL WRONG...
IT'S ALL GONE WRONG!
DON'T CRY! YOU'RE AN ADULT!
I WASN'T SUPPOSED TO BE TAKING THESE LITTLE **SHRIMPS** TO THE SHOW!
"SHRIMPS"?

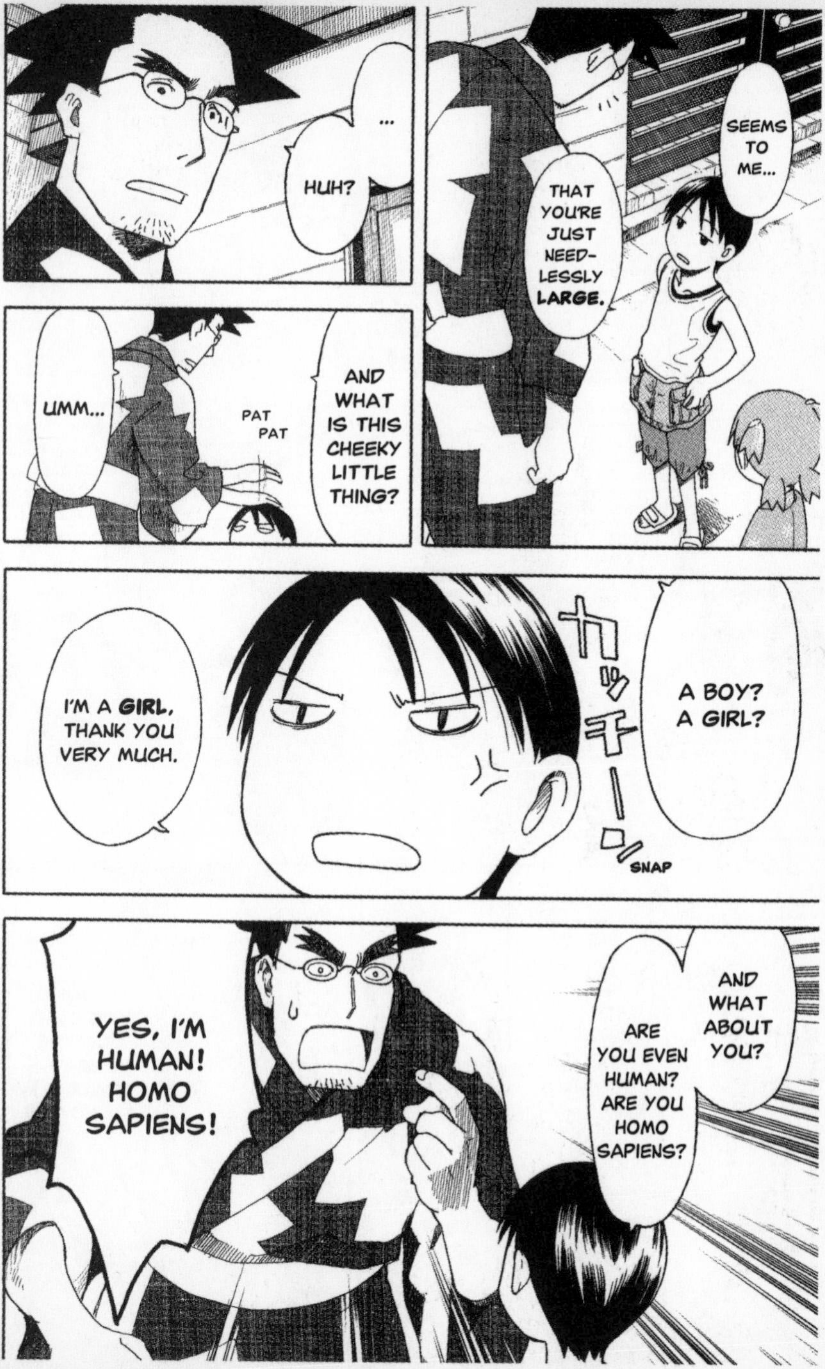
SEEMS TO ME...
THAT YOU'RE JUST NEEDLESSLY **LARGE.**
...
HUH?
AND WHAT IS THIS CHEEKY LITTLE THING?
PAT PAT
UMM...
A BOY? A GIRL?
SNAP
I'M A **GIRL**, THANK YOU VERY MUCH.
AND WHAT ABOUT YOU?
ARE YOU EVEN HUMAN? ARE YOU HOMO SAPIENS?
YES, I'M HUMAN! HOMO SAPIENS!

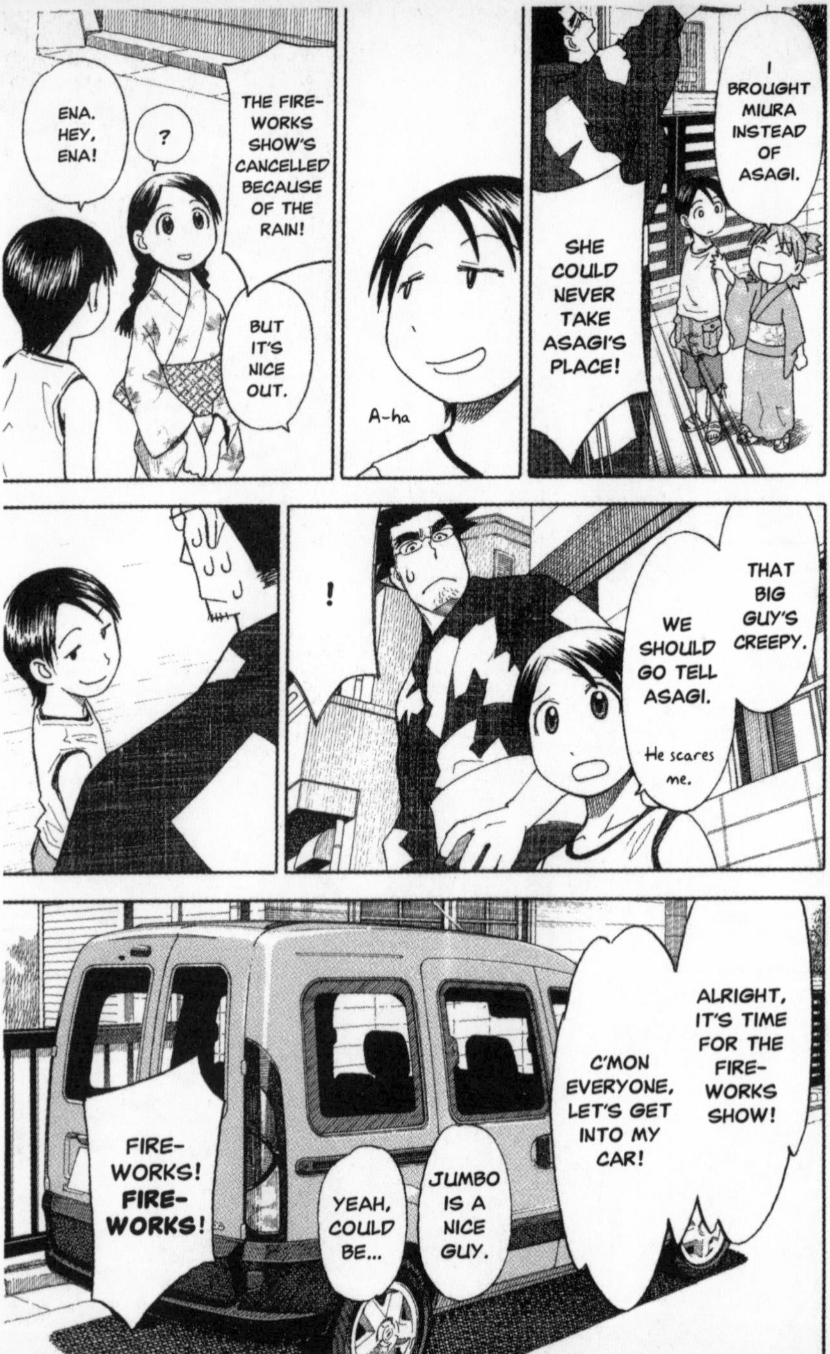
I BROUGHT MIURA INSTEAD OF ASAGI.
SHE COULD NEVER TAKE ASAGI'S PLACE!
A-ha
THE FIRE-WORKS SHOW'S CANCELLED BECAUSE OF THE RAIN!
BUT IT'S NICE OUT.
?
ENA. HEY, ENA!
THAT BIG GUY'S CREEPY.
WE SHOULD GO TELL ASAGI.
He scares me.
!
ALRIGHT, IT'S TIME FOR THE FIRE-WORKS SHOW!
C'MON EVERYONE, LET'S GET INTO MY CAR!
JUMBO IS A NICE GUY.
YEAH, COULD BE...
FIRE-WORKS! **FIRE-WORKS!**

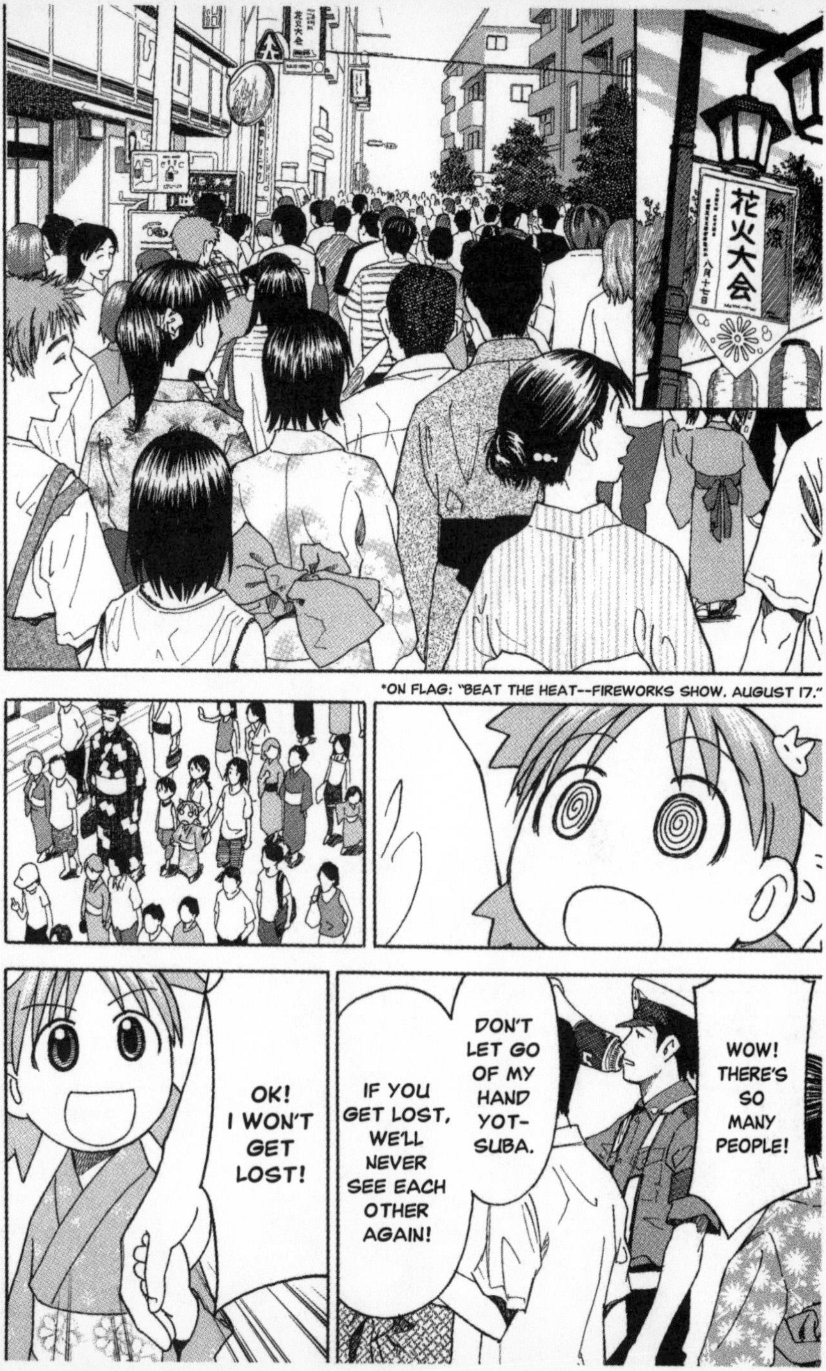
納涼
花火大会
八月十七日
*ON FLAG: "BEAT THE HEAT--FIREWORKS SHOW. AUGUST 17."
WOW! THERE'S SO MANY PEOPLE!
DON'T LET GO OF MY HAND YOT-SUBA.
IF YOU GET LOST, WE'LL NEVER SEE EACH OTHER AGAIN!
OK! I WON'T GET LOST!

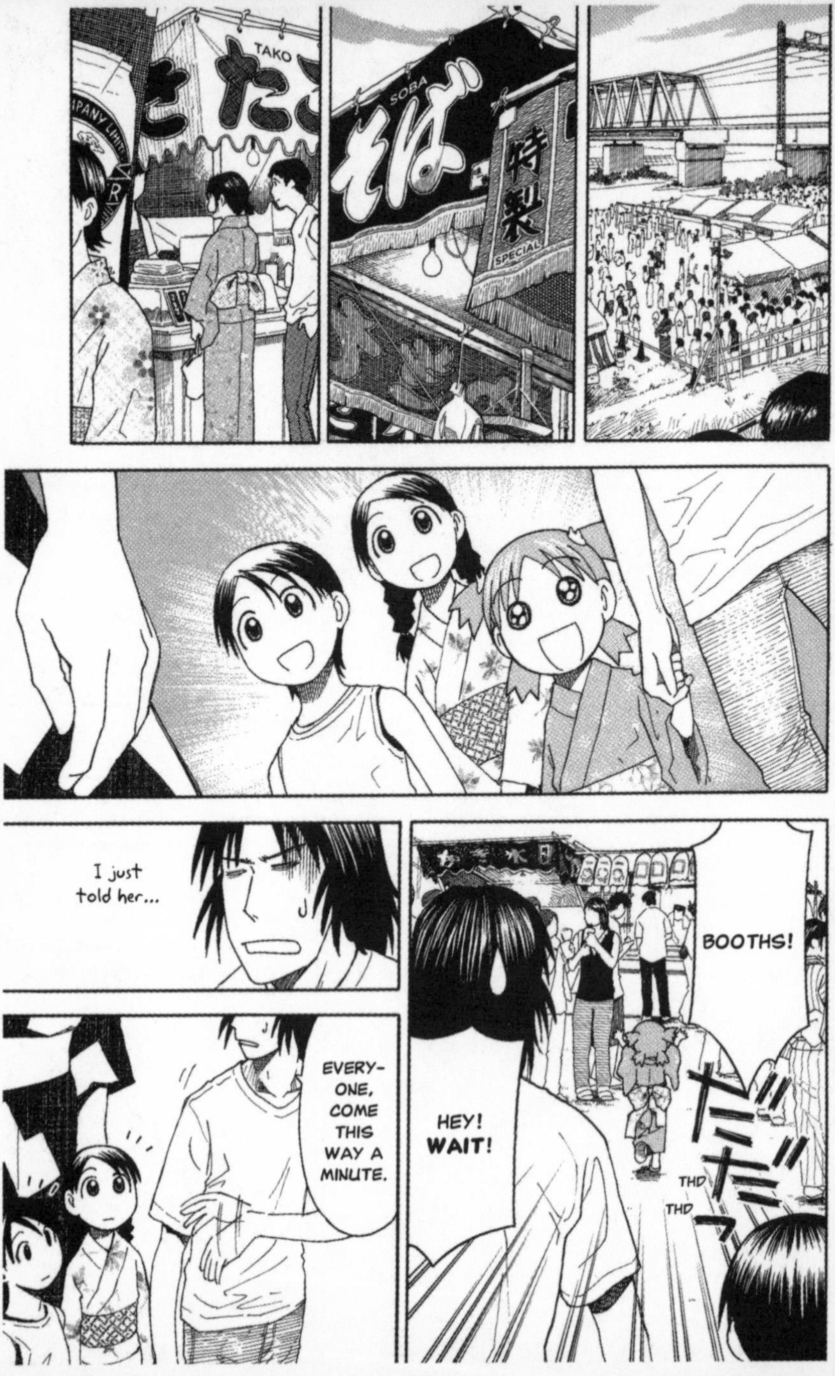
SOBA
SPECIAL
TAKO
BOOTHS!
HEY! WAIT!
THD
THD
I just told her...
EVERY-ONE, COME THIS WAY A MINUTE.

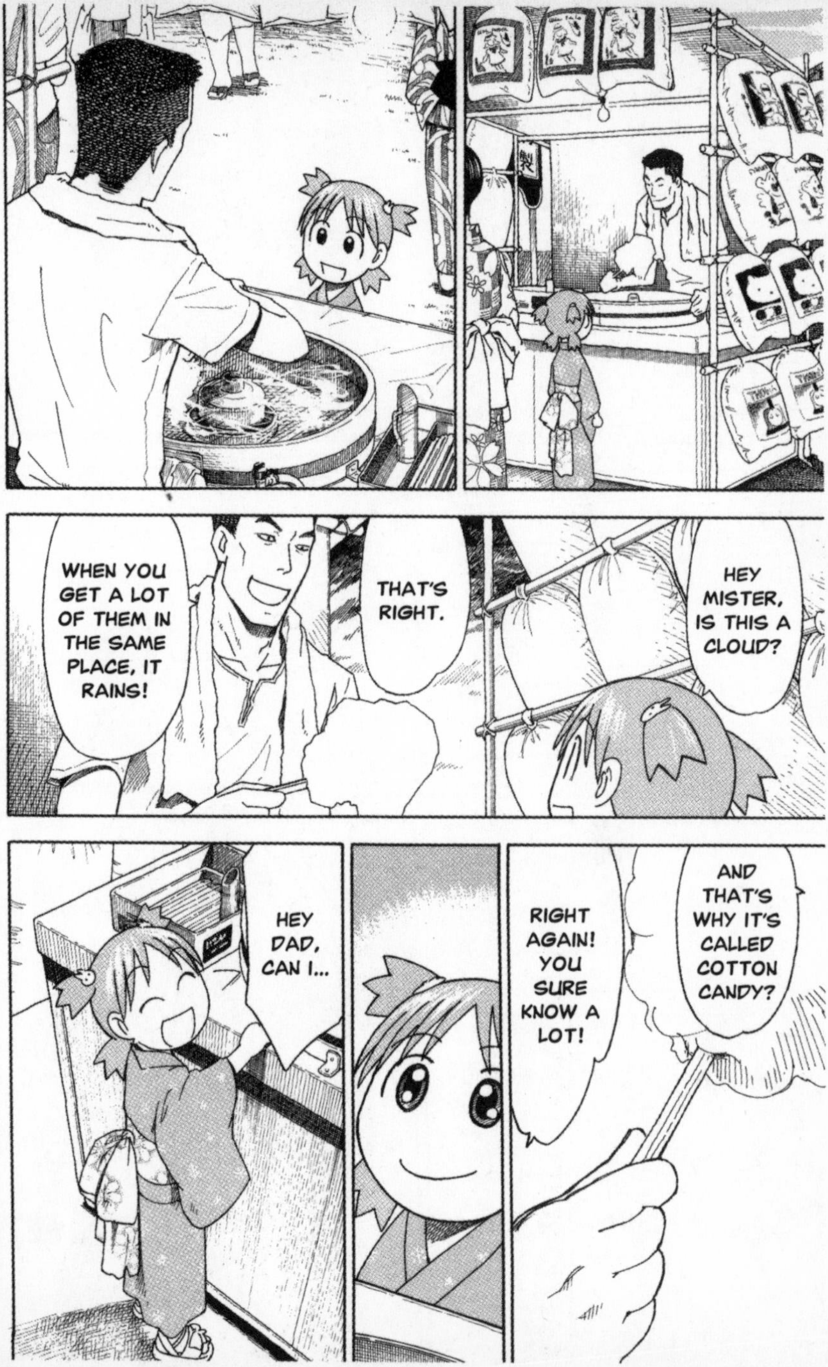
HEY MISTER, IS THIS A CLOUD?
THAT'S RIGHT.
WHEN YOU GET A LOT OF THEM IN THE SAME PLACE, IT RAINS!
AND THAT'S WHY IT'S CALLED COTTON CANDY?
RIGHT AGAIN! YOU SURE KNOW A LOT!
HEY DAD, CAN I...

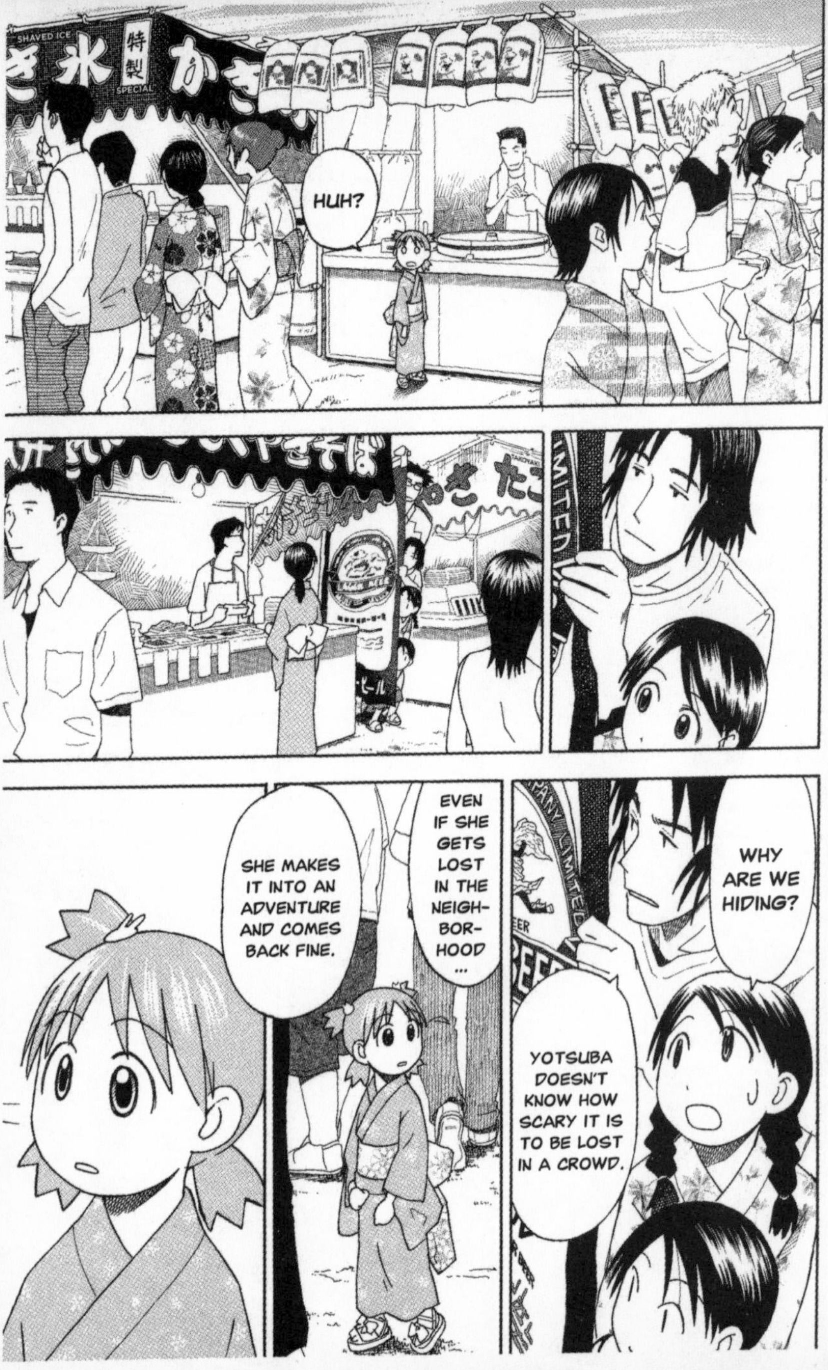
SHAVED ICE
特製
SPECIAL
HUH?
WHY ARE WE HIDING?
YOTSUBA DOESN'T KNOW HOW SCARY IT IS TO BE LOST IN A CROWD.
EVEN IF SHE GETS LOST IN THE NEIGH-BOR-HOOD ...
SHE MAKES IT INTO AN ADVENTURE AND COMES BACK FINE.

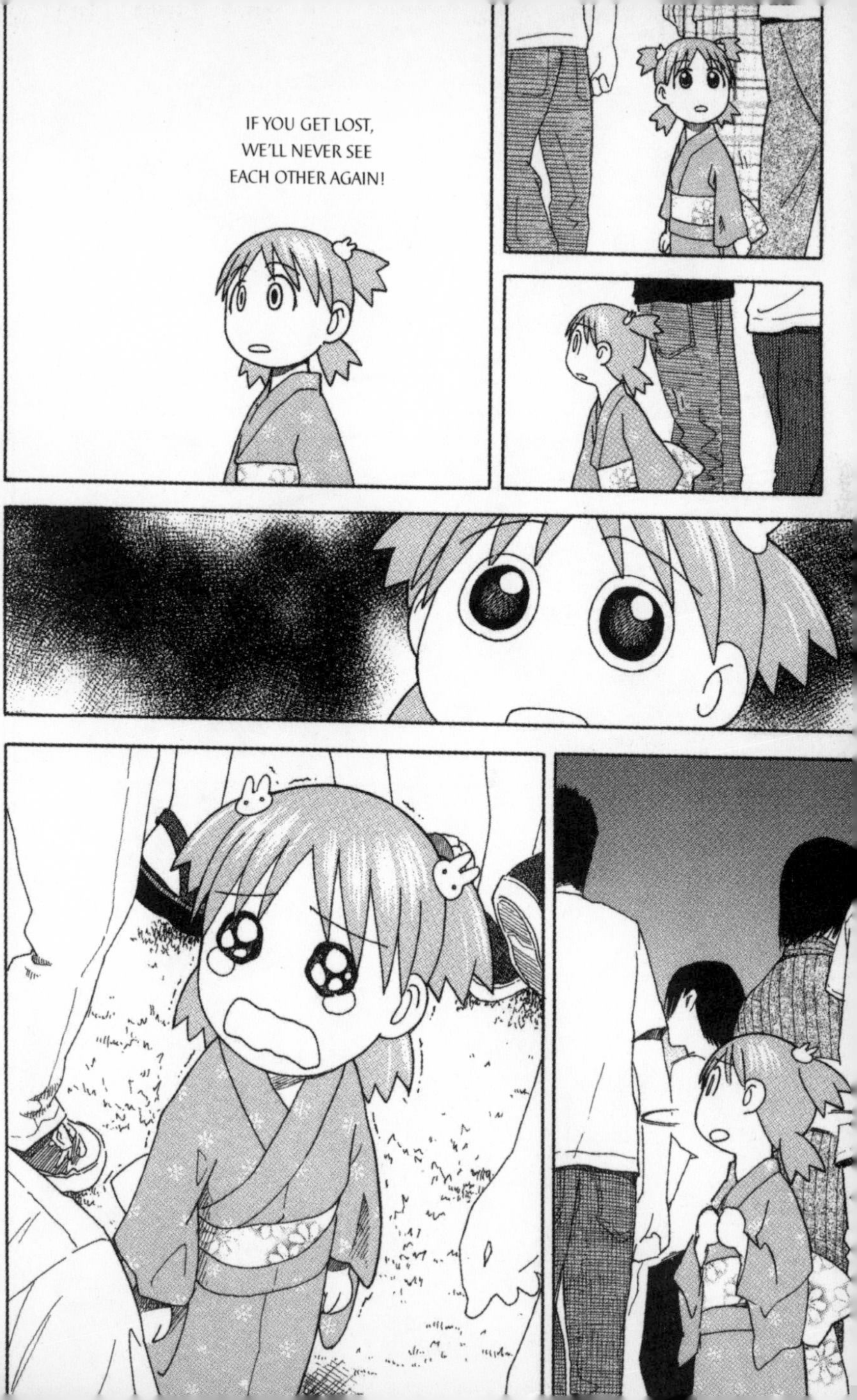
IF YOU GET LOST, WE'LL NEVER SEE EACH OTHER AGAIN!

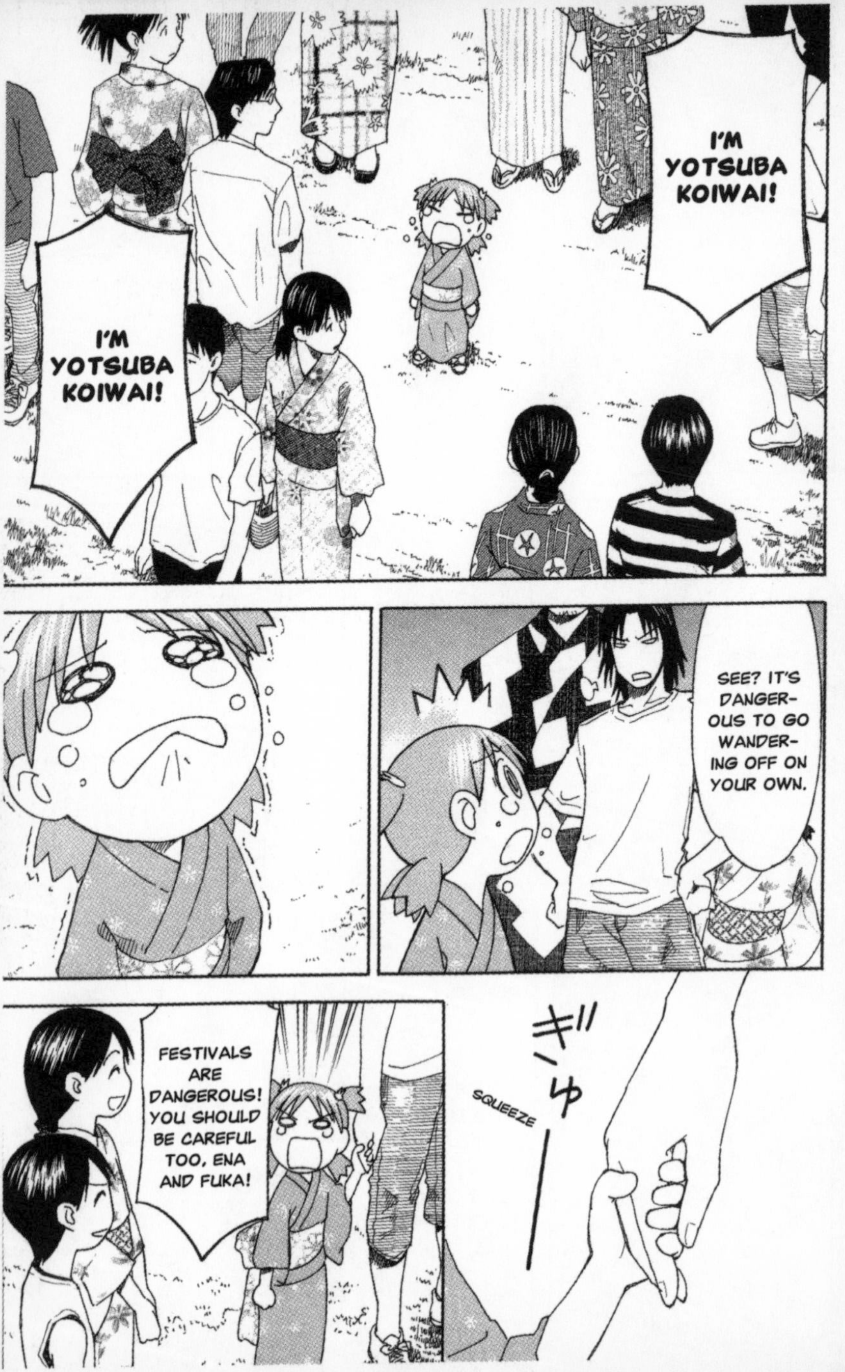
I'M YOTSUBA KOIWAI!
I'M YOTSUBA KOIWAI!
SEE? IT'S DANGER-OUS TO GO WANDER-ING OFF ON YOUR OWN.
ぎゅー
SQUEEZE
FESTIVALS ARE DANGEROUS! YOU SHOULD BE CAREFUL TOO, ENA AND FUKA!

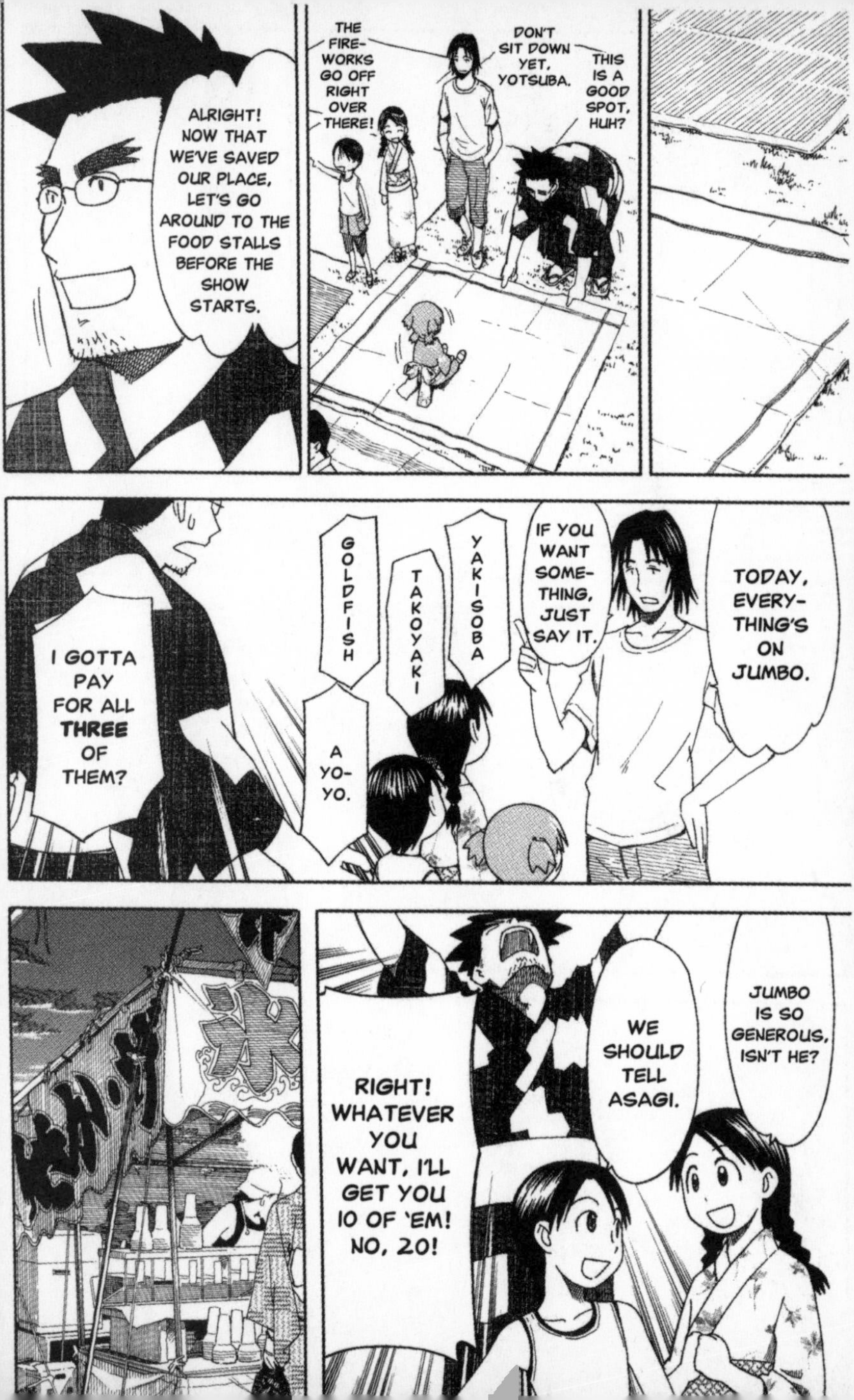
THIS IS A GOOD SPOT, HUH?
DON'T SIT DOWN YET, YOTSUBA.
THE FIRE-WORKS GO OFF RIGHT OVER THERE!
ALRIGHT! NOW THAT WE'VE SAVED OUR PLACE, LET'S GO AROUND TO THE FOOD STALLS BEFORE THE SHOW STARTS.
TODAY, EVERY-THING'S ON JUMBO.
IF YOU WANT SOME-THING, JUST SAY IT.
YAKISOBA
TAKOYAKI
GOLDFISH
A YO-YO.
I GOTTA PAY FOR ALL **THREE** OF THEM?
JUMBO IS SO GENEROUS, ISN'T HE?
WE SHOULD TELL ASAGI.
RIGHT! WHATEVER YOU WANT, I'LL GET YOU 10 OF 'EM! NO, 20!

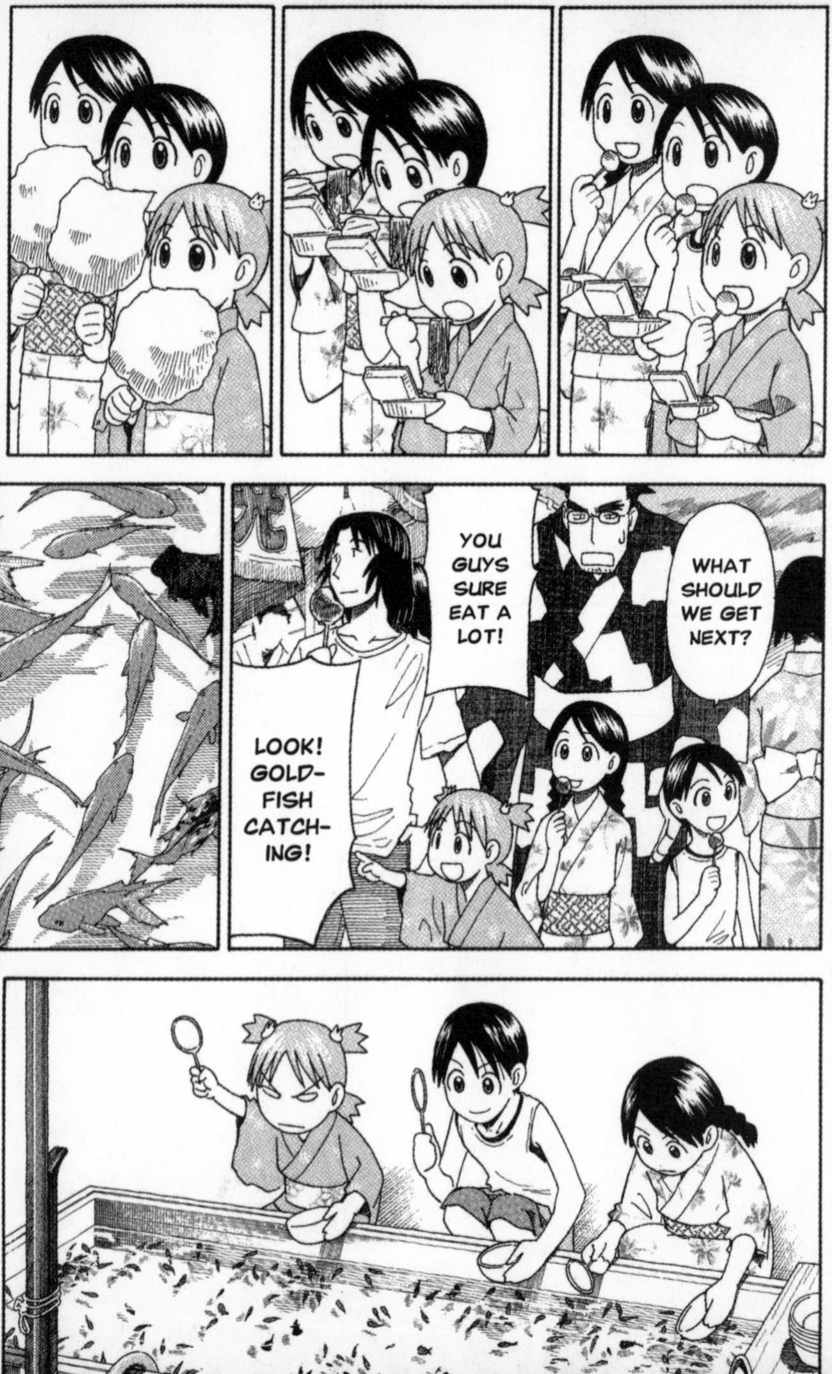
WHAT SHOULD WE GET NEXT?
YOU GUYS SURE EAT A LOT!
LOOK! GOLD-FISH CATCH-ING!

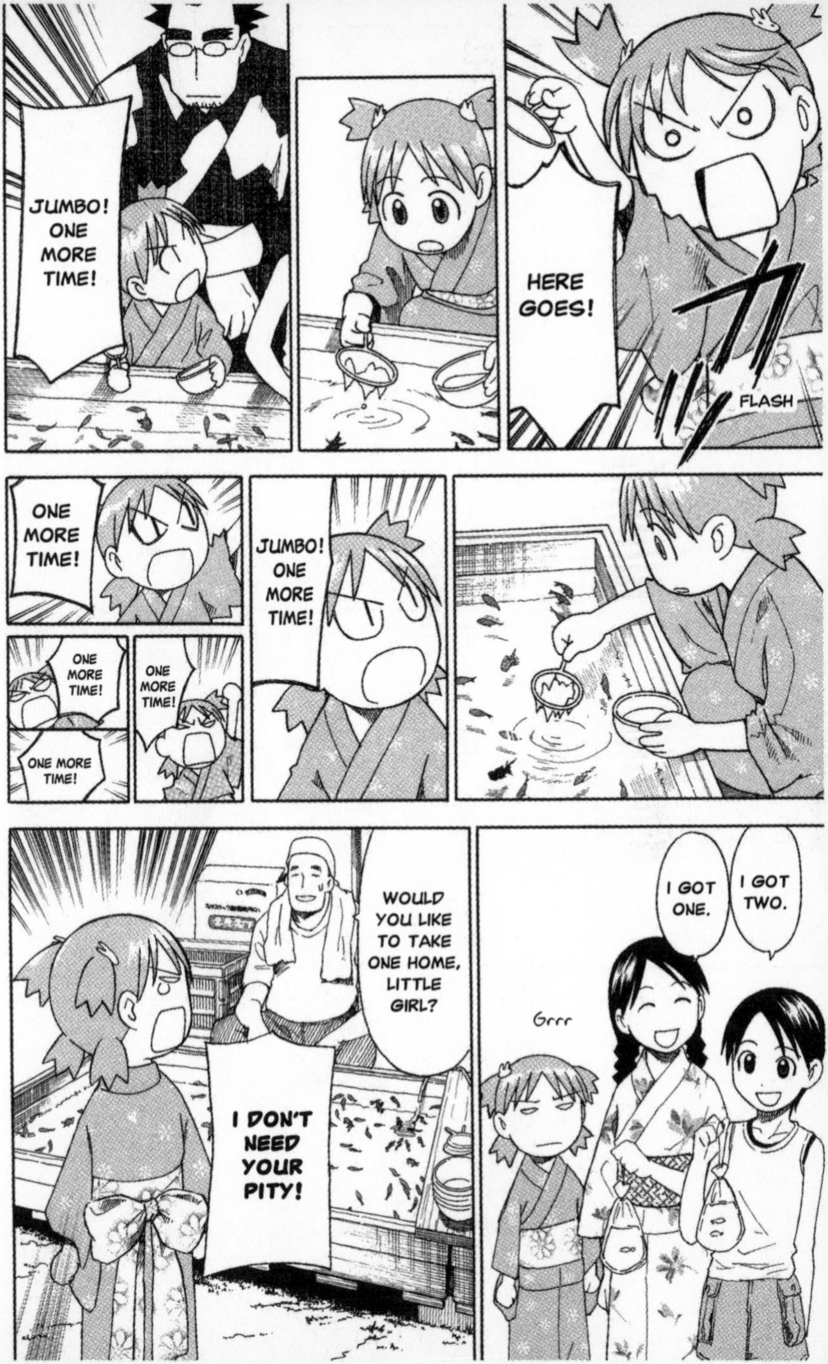
HERE GOES!
FLASH
JUMBO! ONE MORE TIME!
JUMBO! ONE MORE TIME!
ONE MORE TIME!
ONE MORE TIME!
ONE MORE TIME!
ONE MORE TIME!
I GOT TWO.
I GOT ONE.
Grrr
WOULD YOU LIKE TO TAKE ONE HOME, LITTLE GIRL?
I DON'T NEED YOUR PITY!

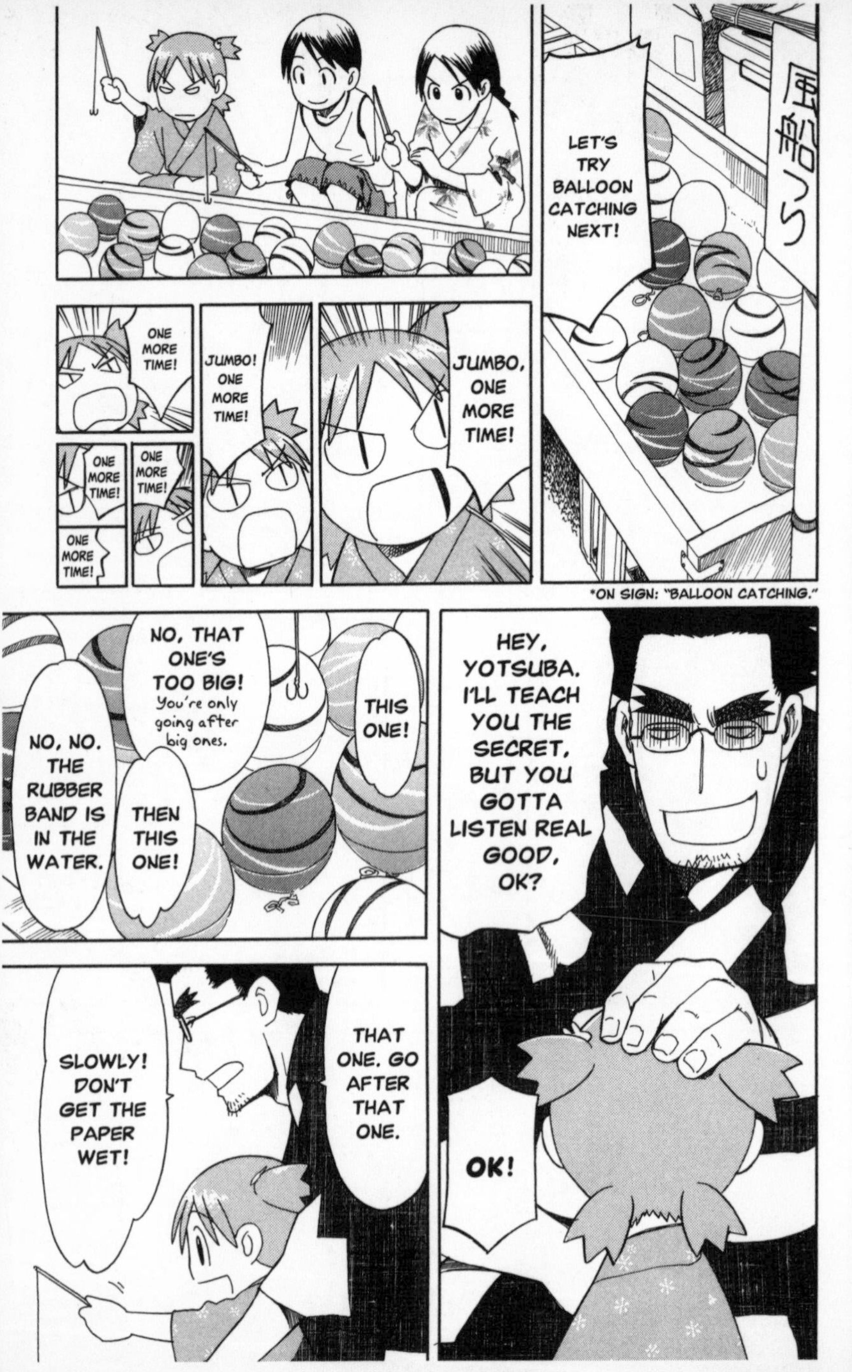
風船つり
LET'S TRY BALLOON CATCHING NEXT!
JUMBO, ONE MORE TIME!
JUMBO! ONE MORE TIME!
ONE MORE TIME!
ONE MORE TIME!
ONE MORE TIME!
ONE MORE TIME!
HEY, YOTSUBA. I'LL TEACH YOU THE SECRET, BUT YOU GOTTA LISTEN REAL GOOD, OK?
OK!
THIS ONE!
NO, THAT ONE'S TOO BIG! You're only going after big ones.
THEN THIS ONE!
NO, NO. THE RUBBER BAND IS IN THE WATER.
THAT ONE. GO AFTER THAT ONE.
SLOWLY! DON'T GET THE PAPER WET!
*ON SIGN: "BALLOON CATCHING."

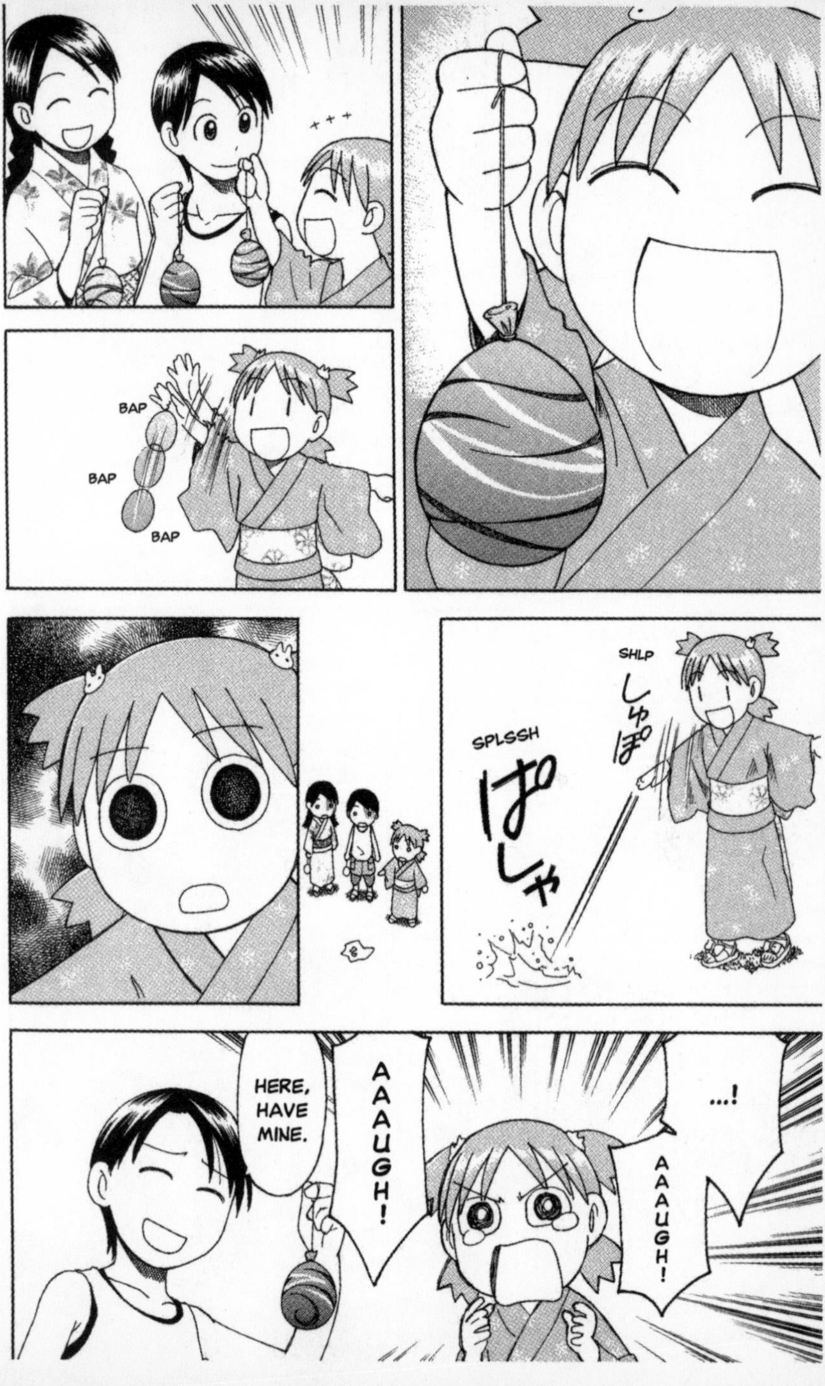
BAP
BAP
BAP
SHLP
しゅぽ
SPLSSH
ぱしゃ
...!
AAAAUGH!
AAAAUGH!
HERE, HAVE MINE.

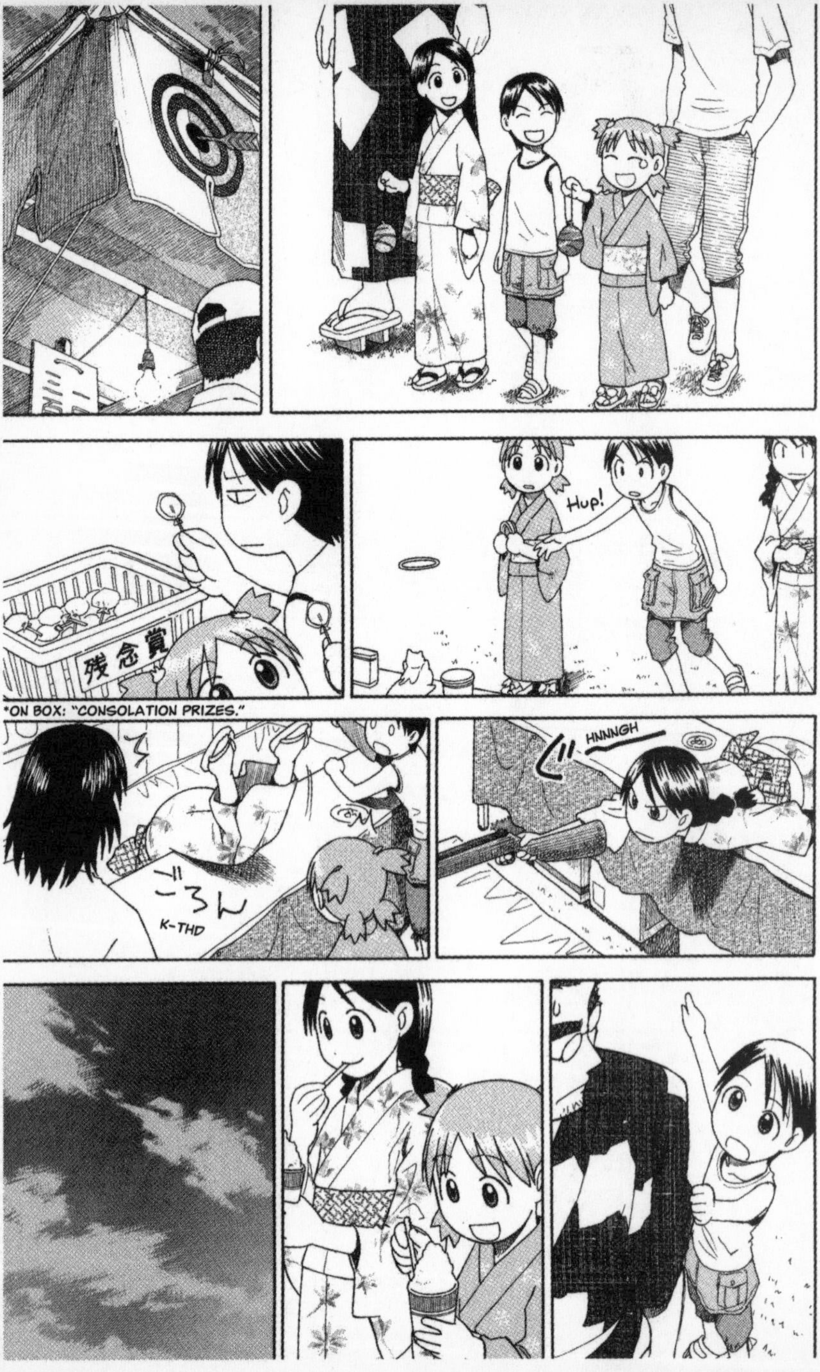
Hup!
残念賞
*ON BOX: "CONSOLATION PRIZES."
ぐ
HNNNGH
ごろん
K-THD

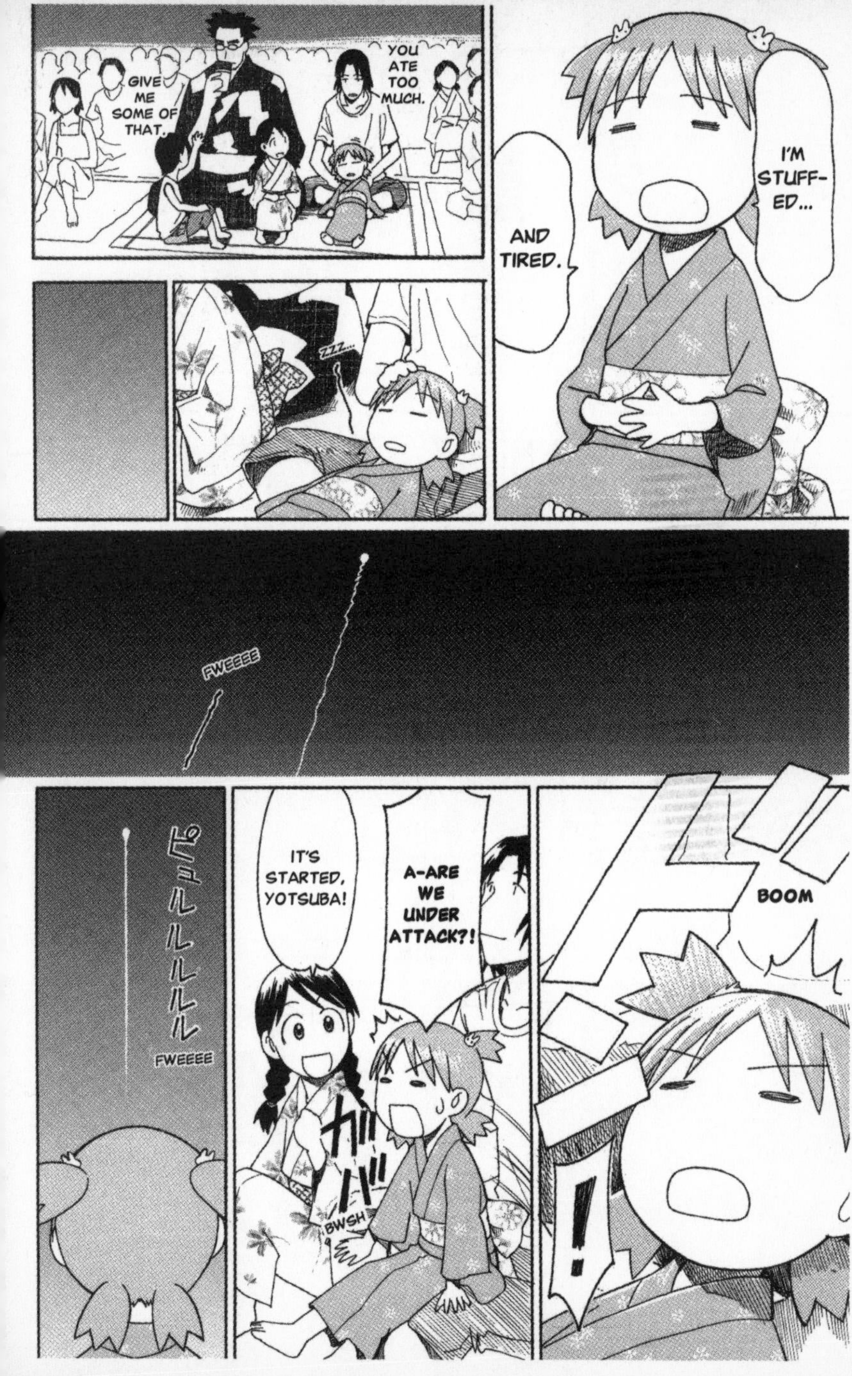
I'M STUFFED...
AND TIRED.
YOU ATE TOO MUCH.
GIVE ME SOME OF THAT.
ZZZ...
FWEEEE
BOOM
A-ARE WE UNDER ATTACK?!
IT'S STARTED, YOTSUBA!
ガバ
BWSH
ピュルルルル
FWEEEE

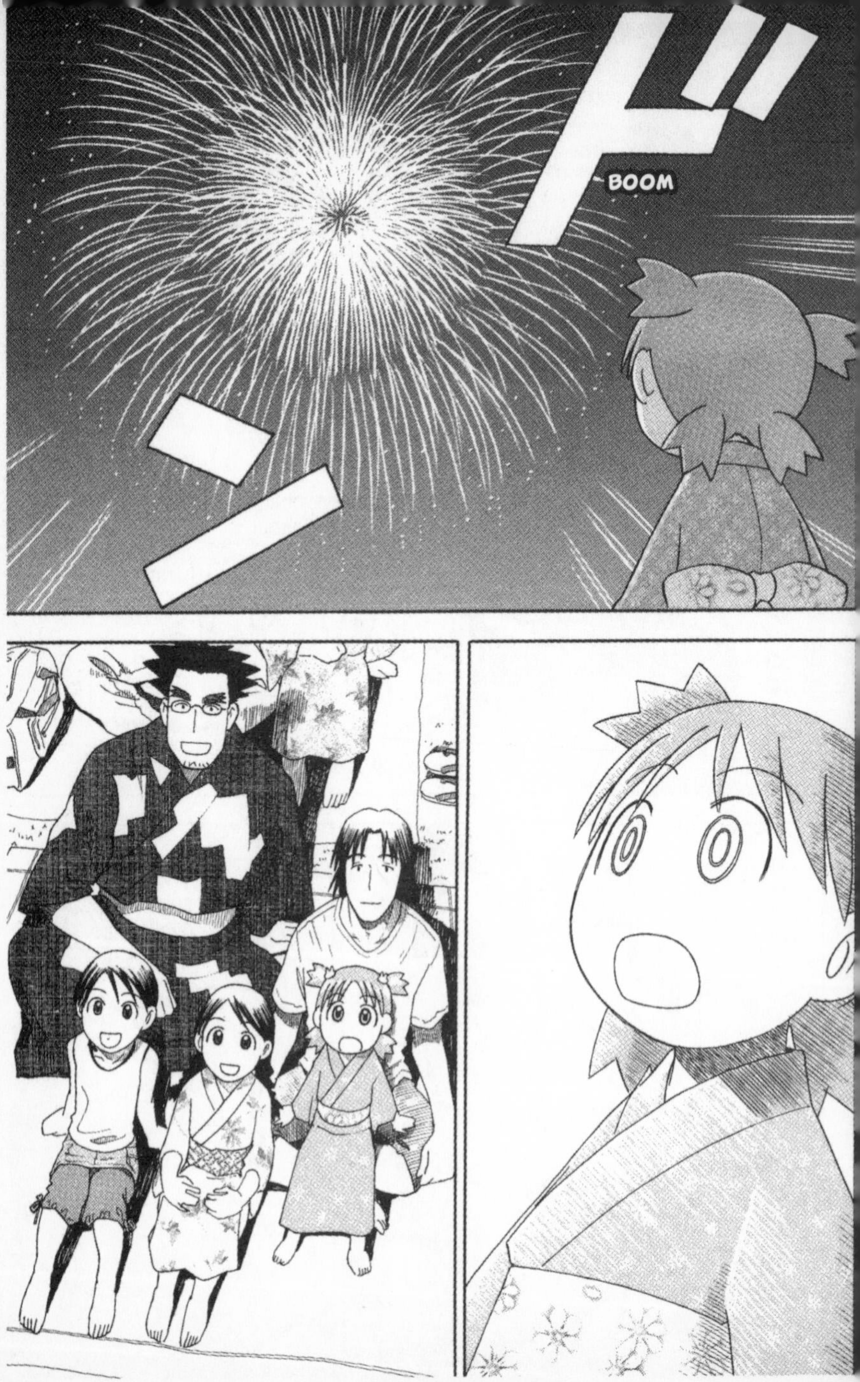
ドン
BOOM

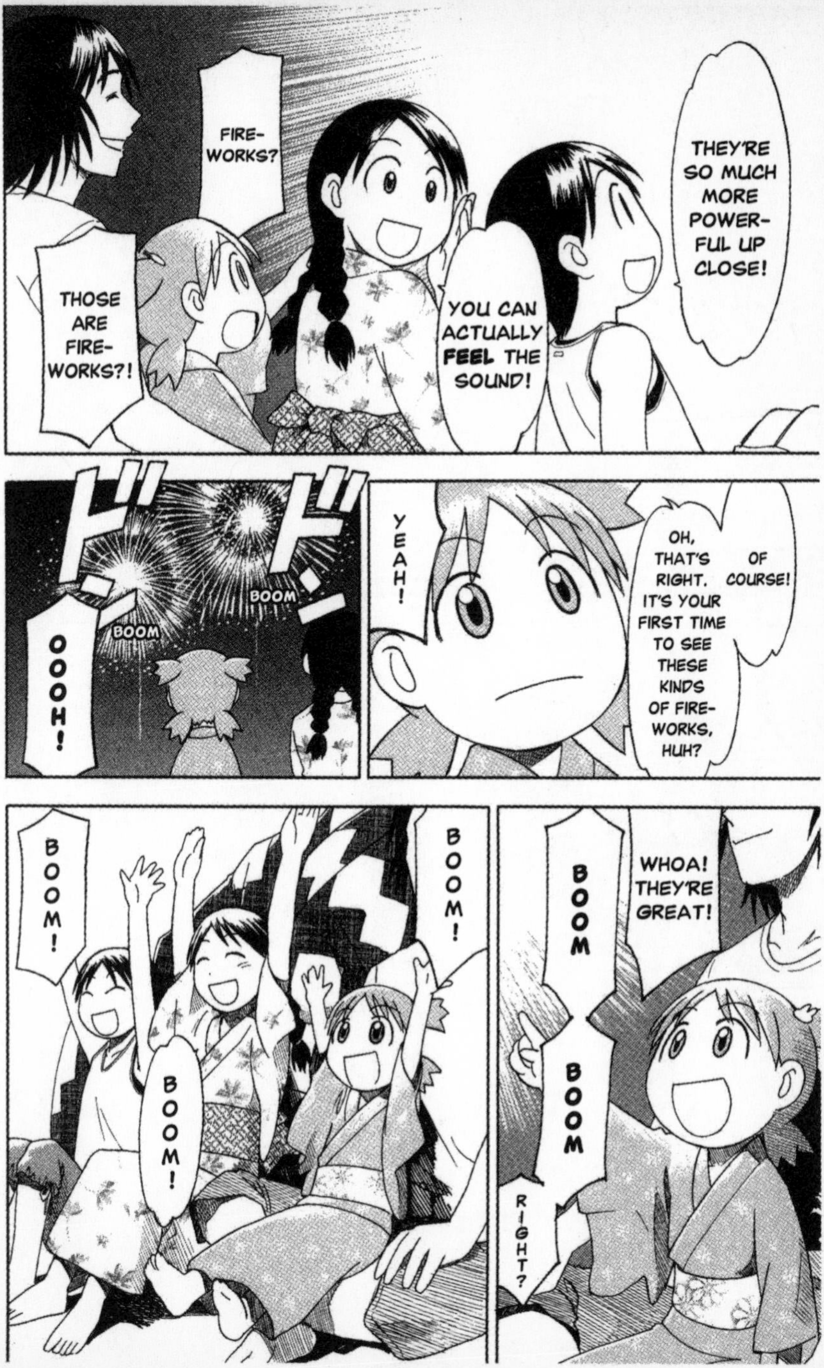
THEY'RE SO MUCH MORE POWER-FUL UP CLOSE!
YOU CAN ACTUALLY **FEEL** THE SOUND!
FIRE-WORKS?
THOSE ARE FIRE-WORKS?!
OF COURSE!
OH, THAT'S RIGHT. IT'S YOUR FIRST TIME TO SEE THESE KINDS OF FIRE-WORKS, HUH?
YEAH!
BOOM
BOOM
OOOOH!
WHOA! THEY'RE GREAT!
BOOM
BOOM
RIGHT?
BOOOM!
BOOOM!
BOOOM!

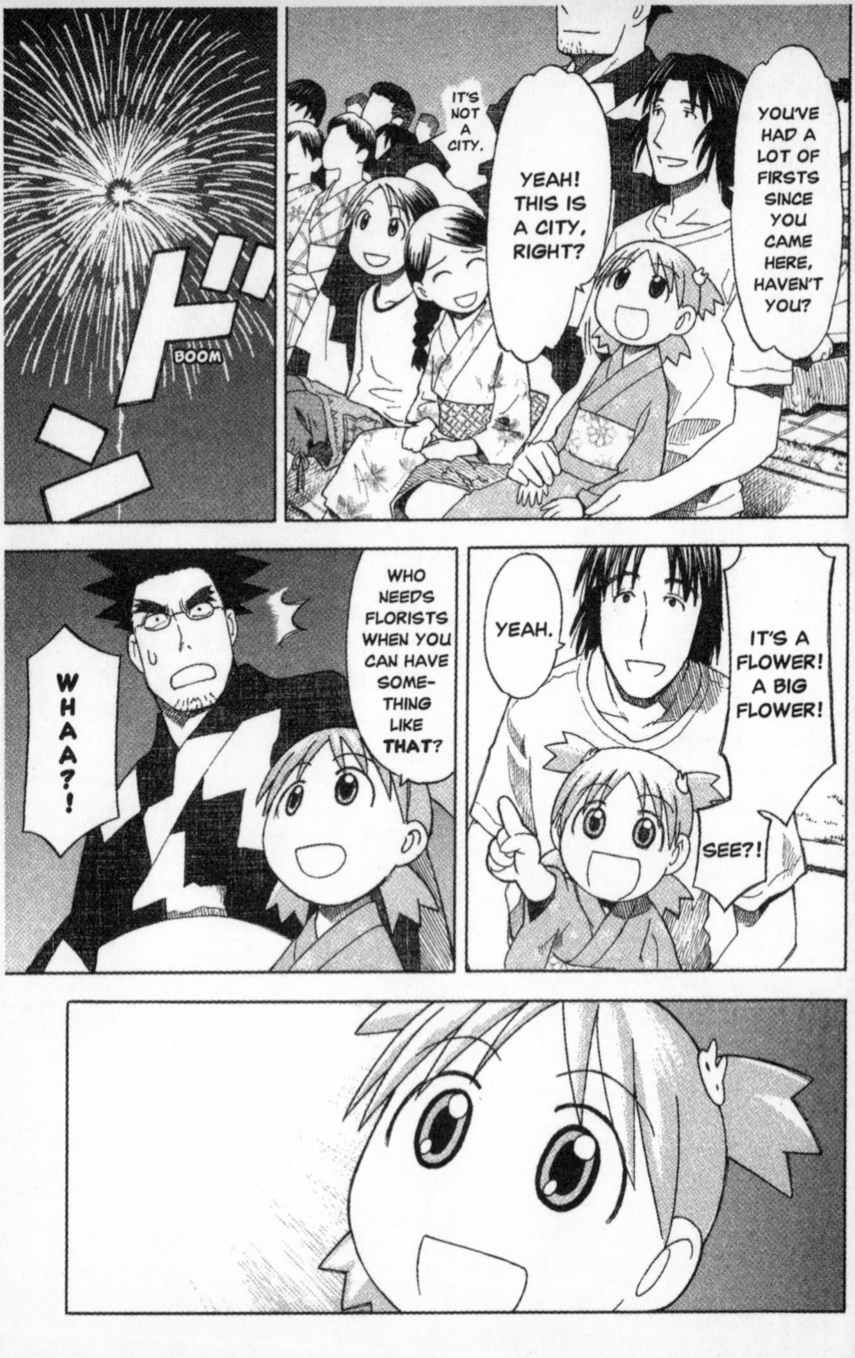
YOU'VE HAD A LOT OF FIRSTS SINCE YOU CAME HERE, HAVEN'T YOU?
YEAH! THIS IS A CITY, RIGHT?
IT'S NOT A CITY.
BOOM
IT'S A FLOWER! A BIG FLOWER!
YEAH.
SEE?!
WHO NEEDS FLORISTS WHEN YOU CAN HAVE SOME-THING LIKE **THAT**?
WHAAA?!

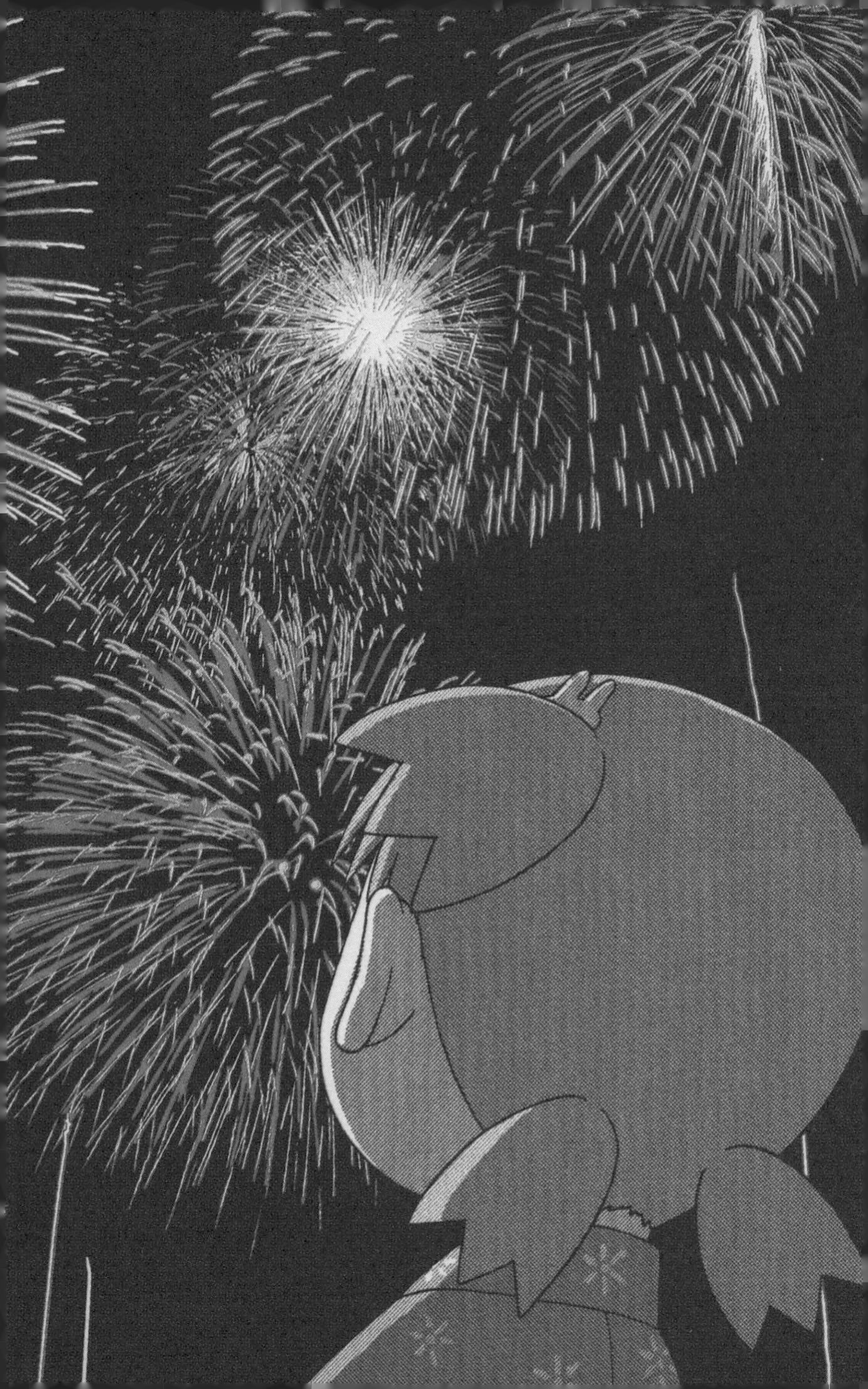

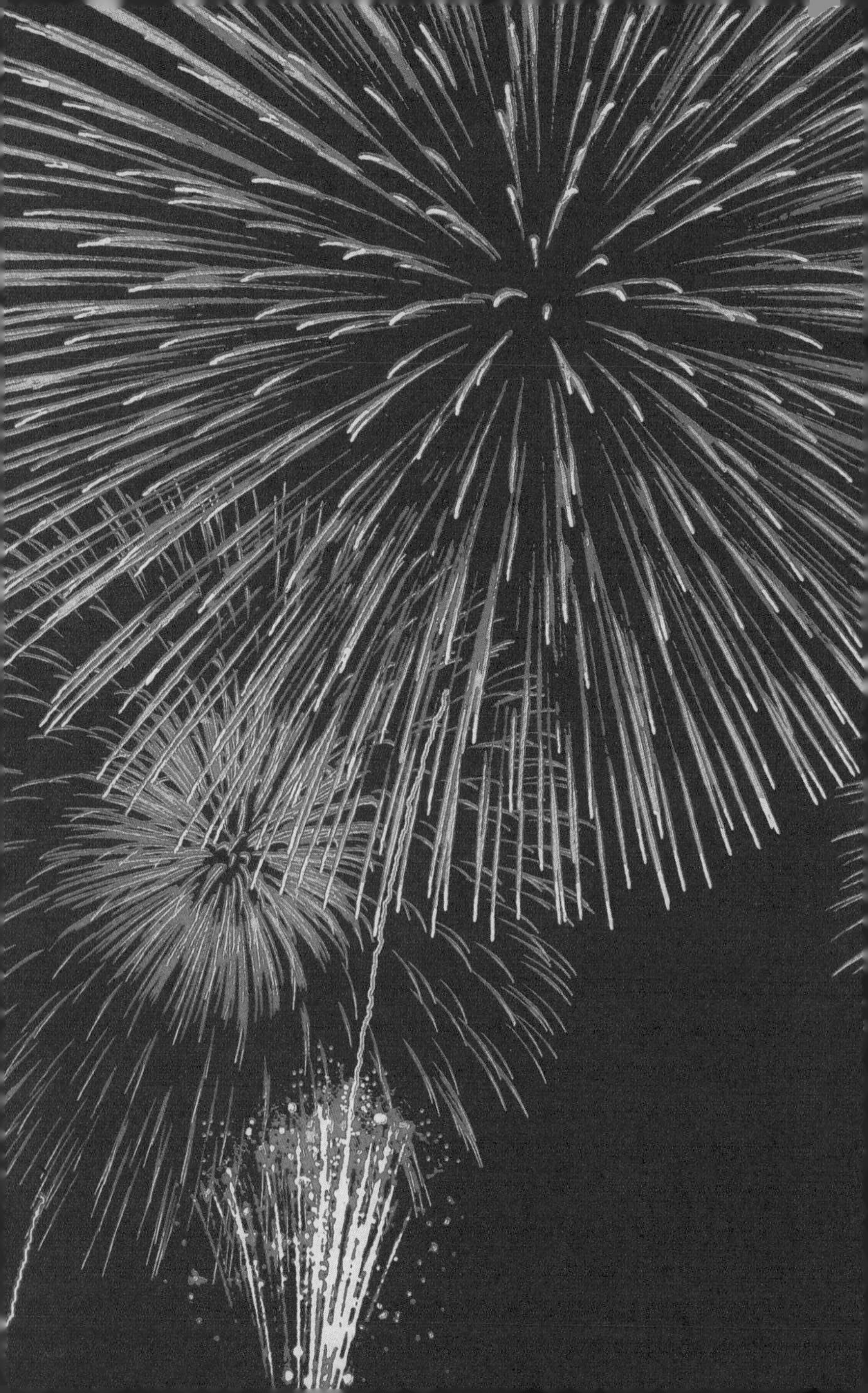

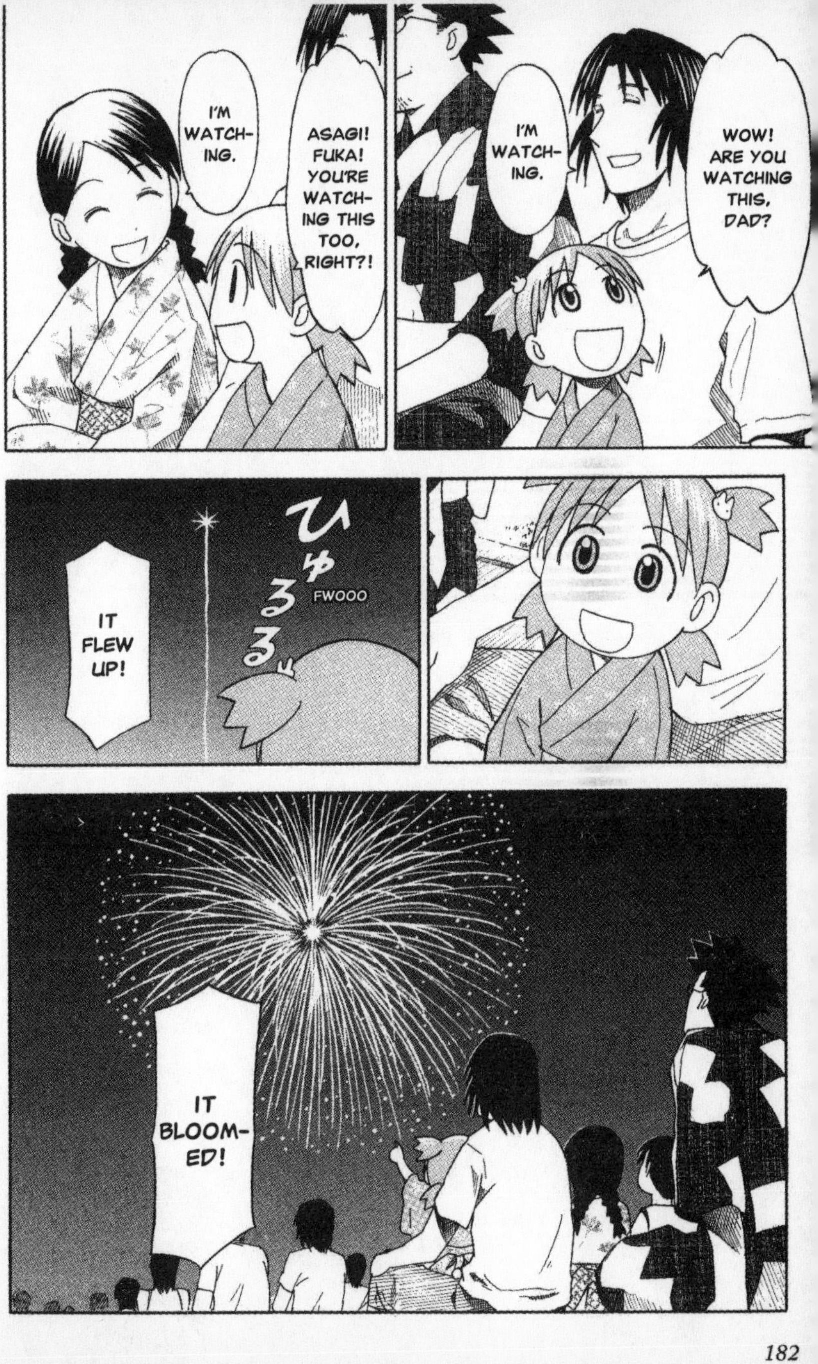
WOW! ARE YOU WATCHING THIS, DAD?
I'M WATCHING.
ASAGI! FUKA! YOU'RE WATCHING THIS TOO, RIGHT?!
I'M WATCHING.
ひゅるる
FWOOO
IT FLEW UP!
IT BLOOMED!

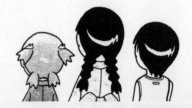

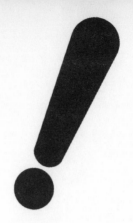

TO BE CONTINUED...

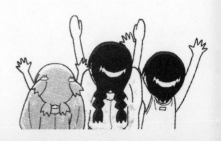

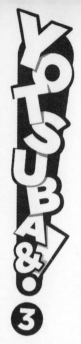

© KIYOHIKO AZUMA/YOTUBA SUTAZIO/MEDIAWORKS
First published in 2004 by Media Works Inc., Tokyo, Japan.
English translation rights arranged with Media Works Inc.

Editor **JAVIER LOPEZ**
Translator **AMY FORSYTH**
Graphic Artists **NATALIA REYNOLDS & MARK MEZA**

Editorial Director **GARY STEINMAN**
Creative Director **JASON BABLER**
Print Production Manager **BRIDGETT JANOTA**
Sales and Marketing **CHRIS OARR**

International Coordinators **MIYUKI KAMIYA & TORU IWAKAMI**

President, CEO & Publisher **JOHN LEDFORD**

Email: editor@adv-manga.com
www.adv-manga.com
www.advfilms.com

For sales and distribution inquiries please call 1.800.282.7202

ADV MANGA™ is a division of A.D. Vision, Inc.
5750 Bintliff Drive, Suite 210, Houston, Texas 77036
English text © 2005 published by A.D. Vision, Inc. under exclusive license.
ADV MANGA is a trademark of A.D. Vision, Inc.

ISBN: 1-4139-0329-0
First printing, October 2005
10 9 8 7 6 5 4 3 2 1
Printed in Canada

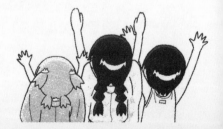

THE **HIT MANGA** FROM
NEWTYPE USA!

ANGEL/DUST

A SHY SOPHOMORE GETS CAUGHT UP
IN THE STRUGGLE BETWEEN **GOOD AND EVIL**

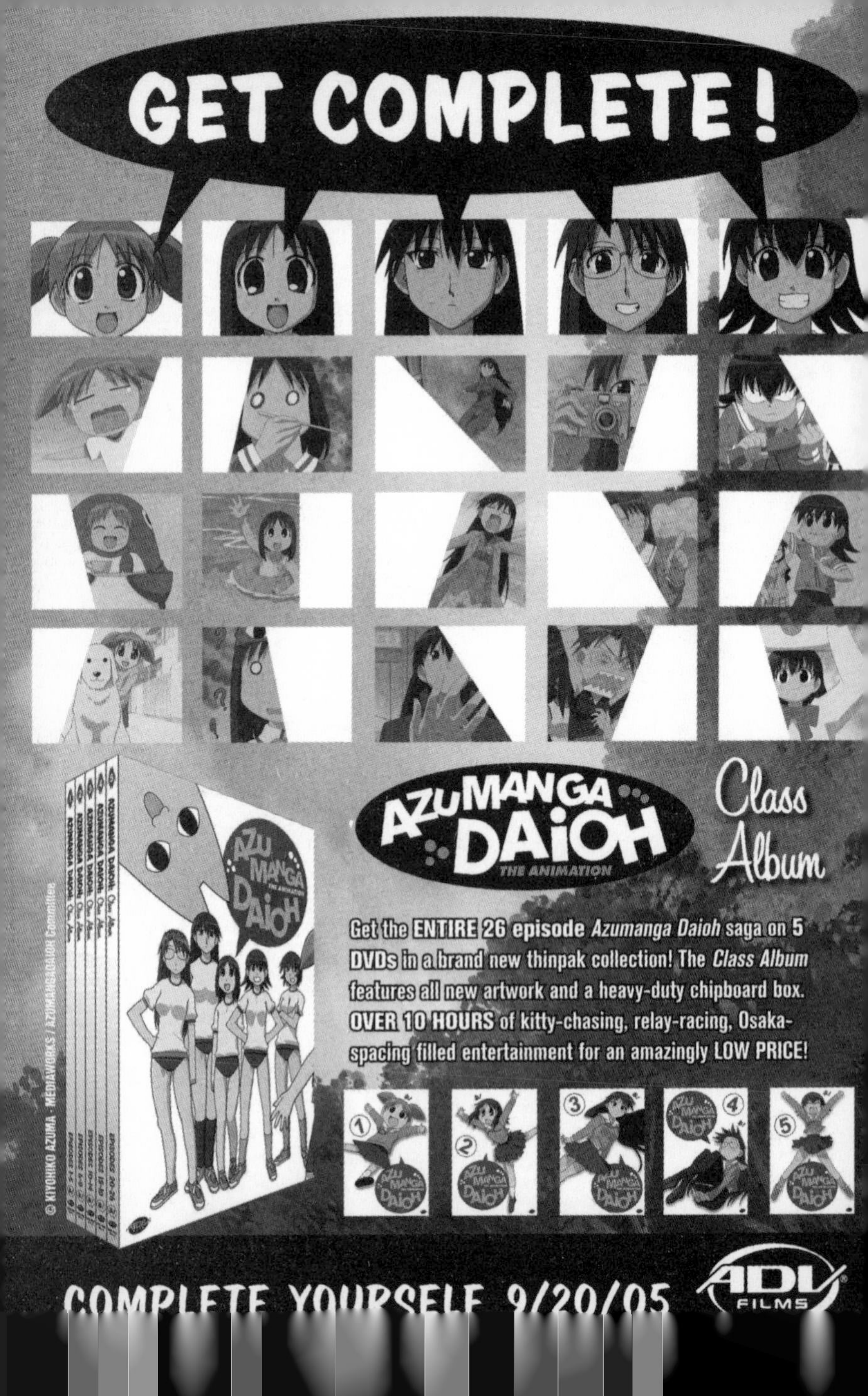
GET COMPLETE !
AZUMANGA DAIOH THE ANIMATION
Class Album
Get the ENTIRE 26 episode Azumanga Daioh saga on 5 DVDs in a brand new thinpak collection! The Class Album features all new artwork and a heavy-duty chipboard box. OVER 10 HOURS of kitty-chasing, relay-racing, Osaka-spacing filled entertainment for an amazingly LOW PRICE!
© KIYOHIKO AZUMA · MEDIAWORKS / AZUMANGADAIOH Committee
COMPLETE YOURSELF 9/20/05

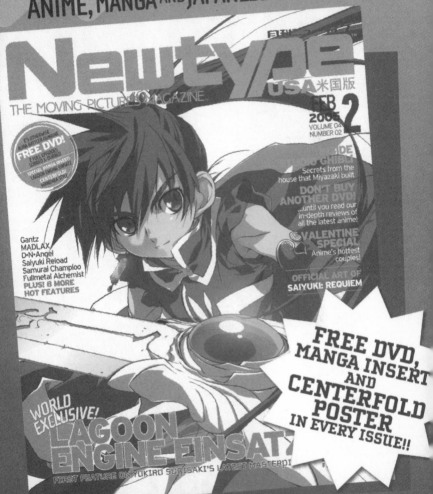

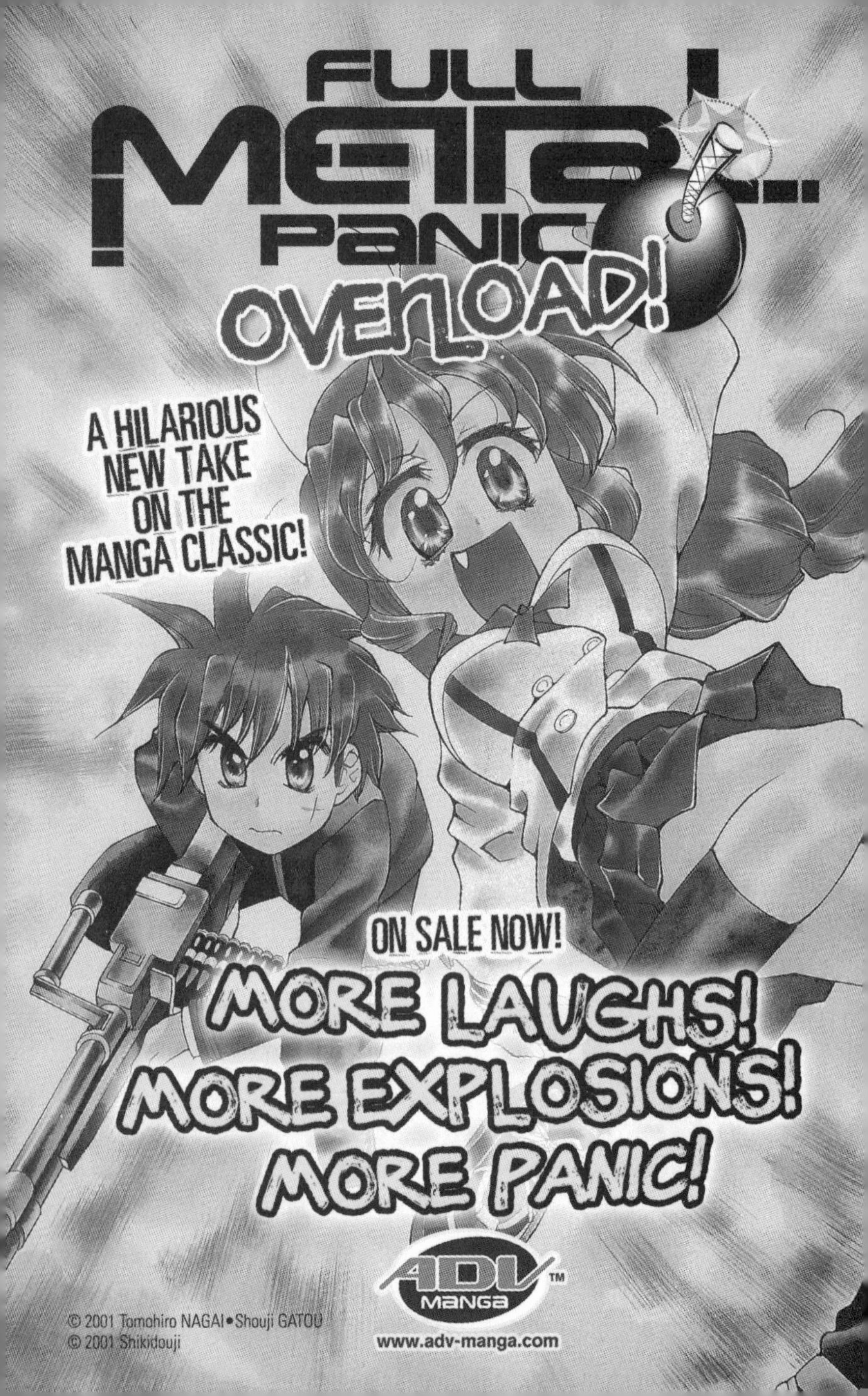
FULL METAL PANIC
OVERLOAD!
A HILARIOUS NEW TAKE ON THE MANGA CLASSIC!
ON SALE NOW!
MORE LAUGHS!
MORE EXPLOSIONS!
MORE PANIC!
ADV MANGA ™
© 2001 Tomohiro NAGAI • Shouji GATOU
© 2001 Shikidouji
www.adv-manga.com

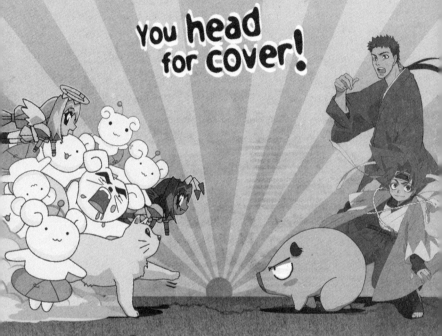
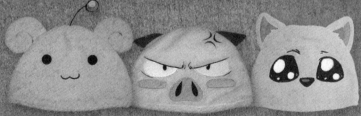

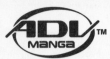 **MANGA SURVEY**

PLEASE MAIL THE COMPLETED FORM TO: EDITOR – ADV MANGA
%o A.D. Vision, Inc. 5750 Bintliff Drive, Suite 210, Houston, Texas 77036

Name:_____

Address:_____

City, State, Zip:_____

_____

E-Mail:_____

Male ☐   Female ☐   Age:_____

☐ **CHECK HERE IF YOU WOULD LIKE TO RECEIVE OTHER INFORMATION OR FUTURE OFFERS FROM ADV.**

All information provided will be used for internal purposes only. We promise not to sell or otherwise divulge your information.

1. Annual Household Income (*Check only one*)
- ☐ Under $25,000
- ☐ $25,000 to $50,000
- ☐ $50,000 to $75,000
- ☐ Over $75,000

2. How do you hear about new Manga releases? (*Check all that apply*)
- ☐ Browsing in Store
- ☐ Internet Reviews
- ☐ Anime News Websites
- ☐ Direct Email Campaigns
- ☐ Magazine Ad
- ☐ Online Advertising
- ☐ Conventions
- ☐ TV Advertising
- ☐ Online forums (message boards and chat rooms)
- ☐ Carrier pigeon
- ☐ Other:_____

3. Which magazines do you read? (*Check all that apply*)
- ☐ Wizard
- ☐ SPIN
- ☐ Animerica
- ☐ Rolling Stone
- ☐ Maxim
- ☐ DC Comics
- ☐ URB
- ☐ Polygon
- ☐ Official PlayStation Magazine
- ☐ Entertainment Weekly
- ☐ YRB
- ☐ EGM
- ☐ Newtype USA
- ☐ SciFi
- ☐ Starlog
- ☐ Wired
- ☐ Vice
- ☐ BPM
- ☐ I hate reading
- ☐ Other:_____

4. Have you visited the ADV Manga website?

- ☐ Yes
- ☐ No

5. Have you made any manga purchases online from the ADV website?

- ☐ Yes
- ☐ No

6. If you have visited the ADV Manga website, how would you rate your online experience?

- ☐ Excellent
- ☐ Good
- ☐ Average
- ☐ Poor

7. What genre of manga do you prefer?
(*Check all that apply*)

- ☐ adventure
- ☐ romance
- ☐ detective
- ☐ action
- ☐ horror
- ☐ sci-fi/fantasy
- ☐ sports
- ☐ comedy

8. How many manga titles have you purchased in the last 6 months?

- ☐ none
- ☐ 1-4
- ☐ 5-10
- ☐ 11+

9. Where do you make your manga purchases? (*Check all that apply*)

- ☐ comic store
- ☐ bookstore
- ☐ newsstand
- ☐ online
- ☐ other:________________
- ☐ department store
- ☐ grocery store
- ☐ video store
- ☐ video game store

10. Which bookstores do you usually make your manga purchases at?
(*Check all that apply*)

- ☐ Barnes & Noble
- ☐ Walden Books
- ☐ Suncoast
- ☐ Best Buy
- ☐ Amazon.com
- ☐ Borders
- ☐ Books-A-Million
- ☐ Toys "Я" Us
- ☐ Other bookstore: ____________________

11. What's your favorite anime/manga website? (*Check all that apply*)

- ☐ adv-manga.com
- ☐ advfilms.com
- ☐ rightstuf.com
- ☐ animenewsservice.com
- ☐ animenewsnetwork.com
- ☐ Other:________________
- ☐ animeondvd.com
- ☐ anipike.com
- ☐ animeonline.net
- ☐ planetanime.com
- ☐ animenation.com

All information provided will be used for internal purposes only. We promise not to sell or otherwise divulge your information.